The Excavations at Ancient Halieis

Volume 1

The Excavations at Ancient Halieis

Conducted by the University of Pennsylvania and Indiana University
Porto Kheli, Greece

– Volume 1 –

Halieis Publication Committee
Michael H. Jameson
Marian H. McAllister
Wolf W. Rudolph
James A. Dengate

Coordinating Editor, Christina F. Dengate

The Fortifications and Adjacent Structures

Marian H. McAllister

with contributions by

Michael H. Jameson, James A. Dengate, and Frederick A. Cooper

Indiana University Press

Bloomington & Indianapolis

The publication of this book has been supported
by the E. A. Schrader Fund,
Indiana University Foundation.

This book is a publication of

Indiana University Press
601 North Morton Street
Bloomington, IN 47404-3797 USA

http://iupress.indiana.edu

Telephone orders   800-842-6796
Fax orders   812-855-7931
Orders by e-mail   iuporder@indiana.edu

The paper used in this publication meets the minimum requirements of American National Standard for Information Sciences—Permanence of Paper for Printed Library Materials, ANSI Z39.48-1984.

Manufactured in the United States of America

Library of Congress Cataloging-in-Publication Data

Excavations at ancient Halieis.
v.   cm.
Includes bibliographical references and indexes.
Contents: v. 1. The fortifications and adjacent structures / Marian
H. McAllister ; with contributions by Michael H. Jameson, James A.
Dengate, and Frederick A. Cooper — v. 2. The houses : the organi-
zation and use of domestic space / Bradley A. Ault.
ISBN 0-253-34710-6 (cloth : v. 1 : alk. paper) — ISBN 0-253-34709-2
(cloth : v. 2 : alk. paper)
1. Halieis (Extinct city)—Buildings, structures, etc. 2. Excavations
(Archaeology)—Greece—Portokhélion. 3. Portokhélion (Greece)
—Antiquities.   I. McAllister, Marian Holland.
DF261.H25E93 2005
623'.19388—dc22

2005018886

1 2 3 4 5 10 09 08 07 06 05

Designed and set by Anne & Christopher Chippindale,
Cambridge, England

To the memory of my parents,
Leicester Bodine Holland and Louise Adams Holland,
who introduced me to the study of ancient worlds

Contents

Illustrations follow page 178

Illustrations

Plates

Editor's Note

The first volume in the series The Excavations at Ancient Halieis was to have been a description of the acropolis and the nearby "Industrial Terrace," the first areas to be extensively excavated at the ancient city. It was to include a history of the ancient city and a history of the excavations. Michael Jameson was preparing these chapters, as well as chapters on the acropolis sanctuary, the Industrial Terrace, and the inscriptions and graffiti of these areas, at the time of his death in August 2004.

This made necessary a change in the order of the Halieis publications. It was decided to publish Marian H. McAllister's study of the Halieis fortifications as volume one and Bradley A. Ault's study of the Halieis houses as volume two. The acropolis and Industrial Terrace will be published as volume three and will include Jameson's chapters. Other volumes (including the Sanctuary of Apollo and the finds from the lower town) will follow in due course. We have included here a select bibliography (Appendix A) that was originally planned for the acropolis volume to complement Jameson's introduction to the excavation. But it seems appropriate now to publish it with this first volume of the final publication. This bibliography is not exhaustive but is intended to introduce readers to the scholarly discussion on Halieis that has developed over several decades.

Although I cannot attempt to present the history of the excavations nor give comprehensive acknowledgments to all those who helped further the Halieis project, I believe that Michael Jameson would have thought a brief history of the Halieis project and summary of acknowledgments to be appropriate here.

Archaeological excavation at the site of Halieis, at modern Porto Kheli in the Argolid of Greece, began in 1962 for the University of Pennsylvania, under the leadership of Michael H. Jameson, and with the cooperation of the American School of Classical Studies, Athens, and the Greek Archaeological Service. In 1967 Indiana University joined the project. The Pennsylvania team had excavated the acropolis and the second terrace below the acropolis to the east (named the "Industrial Terrace"), as well as making two tests in the lower town. The team continued exploration of the submerged remains both off the town site and on the northeast side of Porto Kheli Bay. It was agreed that the Indiana team would be responsible for the excavation of the town site and that the Pennsylvania team would be responsible for the acropolis, the Industrial Terrace, and the underwater remains. Marian McAllister, who had been a member of the excavations as architect in the early years, made an independent study of the city's fortifications. Excavation by the Pennsylvania team ceased after 1974 (Jameson moved to Stanford University in 1976) and by the Indiana team a few years later, except for some salvage work requested by the Greek authorities. Subsequently the Halieis Publication Committee was formed to ensure the scholarly publication of the site.

During the many years of excavation and study of the finds, the Halieis project has benefited from the guidance and assistance provided by the Ephorate of Antiquities for the Argolis and Korinthia, which has generously provided space in its storerooms for the excavation finds. The Halieis excavations were conducted under the aegis of the American School of Classical Studies at Athens. We are grateful to the School, its directors, and its staff who, among their many duties, included oversight of this project.

The excavation of Halieis, the study of its many and varied finds, and the final publication would not have been possible without the generosity of those who supported this exploration of an ancient Greek city. The following organizations helped to fund the excavations at Halieis as well as the study of the artifacts: the Ford Foundation (Archaeological Traineeships), the National Endowment for the Humanities, the National Geographic Society, the American Philosophical Society, the American Council of Learned Societies, the Schrader Fund of the Indiana University Foundation, the University of Pennsylvania, and the Triopian Foundation for Archaeological Research.

We are grateful to Indiana University Press and especially to Robert Sloan, Jane Quinet, and Emmy Ezzell, who, with unfailing patience, have guided us through the complications of publishing. Compositors Anne Chippindale and Christopher Chippindale have taken our rudimentary files and turned them into professional pages. To Bradley D. Cook and the staff at the Indiana University Archives, all of us who are working on Halieis material now and all future researchers owe thanks. Because of their diligence, the Halieis records have found a secure, well-organized home.

In addition, I would like to thank Karen Donne Vitelli who, more than any other person, has made the publication of Halieis possible. While serving as head of the Classical Archaeology Program at Indiana University, she undertook the responsibility of securing the preservation of the Halieis records in the Indiana University Archives. She worked to acquire funding for the publication of the series. And she gave encouragement when it was most needed to those of us involved in the Halieis series.

Finally, I want to express the gratitude of all those who worked with Michael Hamilton Jameson as part of the Halieis project. In the midst of his many other responsibilities, Mike devoted much time and energy to this undertaking, fostered the careers of young archaeologists who began their work at Halieis, and was always generous in sharing with other researchers the scholarly riches offered by this remarkable site. We miss his intelligence, his steadfast support, his presence. We hope that this volume and those to come will be a worthy tribute to him.

Christina Dengate
Coordinating Editor
for the Halieis Publication Committee
January 2005

Preface

Excavations at Porto Kheli to investigate the remains of the town of Ancient Halieis were conducted in the 1960's and 1970's under the aegis of the University of Pennsylvania and Indiana University. This volume is the first of the initial pair of volumes publishing the results. My chapters on the fortifications have been a long time in preparation, beginning in 1970 when Michael H. Jameson, originator of the project, asked me to change the subject of my dissertation. I had already been on the site as field architect, and the topic was an obvious one. It required no excavation to see the line of the walls around the town, even those under a meter or more of water along the shore. Depending chiefly on Charles K. Williams's 1962 survey, excavations made then and over the next ten years, and my own survey especially of the West Wall and Southwest Gate, the dissertation was submitted to Bryn Mawr College in September 1972. Since then, however, much information has been added, partly from excavations after that date but also from repeated examination, especially in the course of Frederick A. Cooper's survey of the site.

Many people have contributed to these results. There were those who, with fortitude and surprising good nature, balanced on boulders or plunged into thorn bushes to hold a stadia rod or the "dumb end" of the measuring tape. I apologize to those whom I am unable to mention by name, but I thank Robert Soffian in 1965, who stood among thistles higher than his head, volunteers among the visiting students from the Germantown Friends School (Philadelphia) in 1967, Nikos Staikopoulos and David Blackwell in 1970, and Larry Holderly in 1972. Julian and Eunice Whittlesey, with unfailing enthusiasm, supplied aerial photographs especially of the underwater remains but also of dry-land locations that I selected. Above all, I am indebted to the two chief surveyors: Thomas D. Boyd, with whom I surveyed the West Wall, recorded much of the excavated area and worked closely with Cooper on the general survey. Fred Cooper taught me almost everything I know about surveying and was a constant source of acute observations. The general survey that he engineered and supervised and the town plan that Tom Boyd has reconstructed are basic to this study.

Encouragement has come from many. Wolf W. Rudolph supported my work on the walls while I was nominally recording his excavations. Dr. Robert Giegengack answered my many questions on rocks and soil. Bradley A. Ault read the dissertation and has contributed suggestions and parallels. Frederick E. Winter read a draft of this volume; his comments inspired a new approach to old material. James A. Dengate has conscientiously read many drafts, suggested references, and, from his long acquaintance with the excavations, provided information from old notebooks or his own knowledge. Christina Dengate has been a steady source of information from the excavation catalogues, cheerfully taking on research in the archives on trips to Bloomington. Bradley D. Cook, in charge of the Halieis material at Indiana University Archives, provided much assistance. While the Dengates have made our joint visits there pleasant and fruitful, they have also saved us even more long drives. From first to last, Mike Jameson gave thoughtful consideration to my theories and interpretations, providing historical and literary information as well as his underwater findings, acute comments on my drafts, and always incentive to persevere.

I am grateful to The American Philosophical Society for a grant in 1973 in aid of photography for the study and publication of the fortifications. To James H. Ottaway Jr. I owe thanks for a travel grant used in part to visit other Greek fortification sites in 1998.

Finally, with pleasure and gratitude I acknowledge the support of my family. My mother put aside her own scholarly work to look after my children, at home or at Halieis. My sons accepted the excavations as part of our life. And my husband, Louis, though not himself an archaeologist, has driven with me to visit the archives, tramped the Greek countryside at the hottest season to photograph comparanda, and contributed his architectural and engineering experience to the consideration of technical problems ancient and modern.

Following the report here on the fortifications are three other contributions. James A. Dengate has presented his study of the evidence for a mint in the building here called the Northeast Command Post. For the convenience of readers, he has included the coins from all Halieis findspots, although the acropolis and Industrial Terrace will be published in a later volume.

Michael H. Jameson reports on the submerged remains of the town, supplying the evidence for an important section of the fortifications. Finally, Frederick A. Cooper recounts the history of the general survey. Although the survey is germane to all the Halieis reports, none is more likely than the study of the fortifications to take full advantage of the results.

The unexpected postponement of the acropolis volume after this one was already in press has meant that some data wanted for comparison is not yet available. As a practical solution some material has been added to chapter 6 that might otherwise have appeared earlier in this text, so that the basis for discussion may be more complete.

September 2004

The Excavations at Ancient Halieis

Volume 1

Introduction

Across the narrow harbor entrance from the modern town of Porto Kheli the walls of a Classical town still stand, now scarcely more than knee high. They enclose a site that spreads across the southern shore of the ample harbor and climbs the steeper slopes behind, where the walls converge on the acropolis.[1] The identification of this place as ancient Halieis is discussed in Jameson n.d., chapter 1, together with literary references and the record of nineteenth- and earlier twentieth-century visitors.

The line, or trace, of the fortifications can be followed throughout its circuit (Fig. 19), with significant gaps only at the far northwestern angle, the middle of the Southwest Wall, and the northern part of the Middle Wall. Although most of the remains along the shore are now submerged, they lie at a depth of less than three meters and can in large part be made out in aerial photographs. These images, however, have their limitations: while the low walls on land may be obscured by thick tangles of acacia and holly oak, allowed to flourish as field boundaries where the plow is precluded, the walls in the water are sometimes hidden by silt and sea growths.

The fact that the walls, together with a number of towers, can be discerned in many places without excavating, or even clearing, makes them a natural subject for this series of studies on ancient Halieis. A systematic investigation reveals a complex history of building and rebuilding over more than three centuries, with a number of special features, intriguing problems, and inevitably new questions as well as answers to old ones. The modern surveys, excavations, and underwater explorations, especially those performed by the University of Pennsylvania and Indiana University under the auspices of the American School of Classical Studies at Athens, are detailed in Jameson n.d., chapter 1.

The study of Greek warfare in the 5th and 4th centuries, and especially siegecraft, has been ably furthered by the work of Lawrence and Garlan, and more recently Rusch, while Winter, followed by Lawrence, has covered the elements of the fortifications used by the walled cities of that time. Since much more evidence is available for the succeeding Hellenistic period, the bibliography based on it is correspondingly more extensive. By the late 4th century, however, the people of Halieis were reduced to patching old construction and were not expending the considerable resources needed to keep up with new developments in military architecture.

The ability of this country town to defend against attack or withstand a siege was no doubt more important in the eyes of the inhabitants than in the political history of the rest of Greece. The powerful, however, like Sparta, Athens, Argos, and the Theban hegemony, found the site, and particularly its harbor, important in maintaining or recovering a dominant position. The primary aim in this volume is to record the Halieis fortifications, or rather what remains of them. To make the most of the material some interpretation is inevitable, and numerous suggestions have been made where there can be no certainty. In order to understand not only what the inhabitants of Halieis built but why they chose to build as they did, I have drawn heavily on both the details and

---

[1] The crown of the acropolis at a little over 50 meters elevation is the highest point. Inside the circuit of walls (ca. 1,900 m), the total area is about 18.2 hectares; some 10.2 hectares, the lower, more gentle slopes, show remains of buildings. This does not include the acropolis, Industrial Terrace, or widely scattered blocks evident in almost all parts except the most steep.

the conclusions put forth by Winter and Lawrence, and to some extent by McNicoll and Milner, although the focus on Near Eastern sites in their volume cautions against close comparisons. In all cases it is important to remember that Halieis was not a major player; even at its greatest extent it was much smaller than the principal cities in area, population, and wealth. The design of these fortifications was naturally influenced by current alliances and what was happening elsewhere in Greece, but its execution was dependent on local conditions and resources: terrain, materials, and man power.

The terrain is determined by the conglomerate stone that forms the peninsula of the Halias.[2] The rounded hills reach no great height (Fig. 17). The underlying beds are generally horizontal, forming low "scarps" a meter or two in height along the contour lines. Between these drops, accumulated rubble and thin soil form terraces, sloping fairly steeply in the upper part, but on the town site spreading out into nearly level fields toward the shore. In the upper parts, bedrock is so close to the surface that it sometimes appears as ledges subdividing the terraces.

This account of the fortifications begins with the materials and methods that were used in construction not only of the fortifications but houses and other buildings in the town. Next, the trace, or route, of the circuit wall and the interior Middle Wall is presented to provide a framework on which to hang the description of the various elements and to explain their topographical relationship. The acropolis is the only area where systematic excavation of the wall has revealed a sequence of building periods together with material to date them; the results are presented in Williams n.d. The most conspicuous elements in the rest of the circuit, the towers and gates, are so interconnected that they are discussed together. They are followed by the curtain, the wall and its walkway that constituted the chief defense. At some sites with large circuits, the curtain runs for kilometers punctuated by a repetition of towers, but here the curtain presents such variety that it is considered in sections, often from tower to tower. Closely associated with the curtain are the means of access to the walkway (generally stairs), the drains that pierced it, and the service streets or open areas that allowed the defenders to move quickly along the base of the wall. Special constructions like the Chambered Curtain and the two command posts are most easily described following the curtain. Finally, there are a few other structures closely associated with the walls but not necessarily military in nature. The last chapter reviews the evidence and the problems it raises, in order to determine the sequence of the various elements and the rationale for the design of the fortifications. A chronology that is coordinated with that developed for the acropolis is the final step.

Dates given below, unless otherwise specified, are before the present era. The chronology developed for the fortifications is secondhand, that is, it is tied to those proposed for the acropolis and the Lower Town (Phases 1 through 7 and Levels D through A, for which see Williams n.d. and Ault 2005, 1), both of which are based on excavation stratigraphy. The way in which these associations are made is influenced by the historical sources, which are discussed in Jameson n.d., chapter 1.

The reader should be aware of three devices that are used to make the descriptions as clear as possible. First, the discussion in each section uses the same sequence, following the trace from the northwestern corner of the circuit at Tower **1** counterclockwise to Tower **18** and ending with the Middle Wall. Second, to locate easily points along the circuit that have no close association with a feature such as a tower, an arbitrary running line has been drawn on a diagrammatic map (Fig. 19), following the trace closely but not exactly, and places of special interest have been identified by measurements along this line. These are not field measurements, which would be difficult for the visitor to identify on the site, but serve only as reference points. Third, to describe the two lines of masonry of the double-wall base used throughout the fortifications, the word "wythe" has been borrowed from 20th-century architectural practice, where it is used for each of the two parallel lines of brick or block in hollow-wall construction. Thus most stretches of curtain are composed of an inner and an outer wythe, each of which has an inner and an outer face; frequently only one wythe is preserved.

Aside from the acropolis, only a few excavation trenches, primarily on the southeast side, actually involved the fortifications, but the

---

[2] In geological terms, "young marls," soft and easily eroded in contrast to the hard limestone of the southern Argolid; Jameson et al. 1994, 17.

walls were a principal concern for those working offshore. The account of this part of the underwater work is given by Michael Jameson below (chapter 7).

In the course of the excavations, successive directors and their field architects instituted four different systems for laying out and recording the trenches. The first was based on visible surface remains, the trenches being sunk specifically to investigate them. A few base points were established according to an earlier Greek survey, in order to locate the excavated areas on a general site plan. Each area was assigned a letter designating its trench supervisor, and the trenches were identified descriptively, for example, as "main" or "northwest." Finds were located in relation to the building being cleared. Second, Charles K. Williams II divided the site into 5-meter grid squares. This grid was used to locate trenches on the acropolis (Fig. 21) and, in 1965, was extended to the Industrial Terrace (Jameson n.d., chapters 1, 3, and Williams n.d.).

In 1969 a permanent marker with the coordinates N[orth] 6597.22/E[ast]16058.83 was constructed on the acropolis for a geodetic survey made by the Greek army. As a result, in 1970 it was possible to establish a grid for the site based on that survey; orientation was based on triangulation with two other markers visible on similarly elevated sites (see below, Appendix C). The site was divided into 100-meter squares identified by numbers proceeding from south to north and by letters (using the complete English alphabet) from west to east. The trenches were laid out in rectangles parallel to the lines of the grid; they were numbered in sequence, following the letter and number of the grid square, and identified for the record by the coordinates of the southwest corner. The trenches in the East Tower Area (technically J5) were laid out approximately at right angles to the southeast face of the tower and lettered in sequence.

In 1972 the current system of 5-meter-square trenches was established, a 1-meter balk being left initially on the north and east sides. The trenches were identified by the coordinates of the northeast corner, generally shortened to the final three digits of each. For the record, the grid coordinates of the East Tower Area trenches from 1970 were calculated but were never used because they ran to many decimal places.

The names given to the various sections of the fortifications are topographic for the most part; the West Wall actually wraps around the southwest quarter and turns east before ending at Tower **5**. The acropolis is clearly defined, and the name of the Industrial Terrace, now firmly entrenched in previous reports, has been explained in Jameson n.d., chapter 3. The tower numbers originally assigned in my dissertation were revised in Boyd and Rudolph 1978. The revisions have been retained to avoid confusion, although for the purposes of this volume **18A** has been added.

Throughout this volume there are references to specific excavation trenches, their supervisors, and the field notebooks in which their findings were recorded (see Appendix B). The greater part of the data, however, comes from architectural and survey notebooks: NB 22 (Walls), Charles K. Williams II (1962–66); the notebook that with the working plan recorded the 1972 survey, Cooper and McAllister; and my own field books for 1968 (No. 1), 1970 (No. 2 [515]), 1970 & 1972 (No. 3 [516]), 1974, and 1976 & 1980. In NB 741 I copied excerpts from NB 22 and NB 503 (Sea, 1967) and made a few notes for 1971. Much of this material was translated into graphic form by Thomas Boyd or me as the regular architectural record of each season's work. There were also many sketches and detail drawings made in studying the fortifications. Cooper's survey plan dated 1972/ 1974 was the basis for several restored site plans produced by Boyd, one of which was published as Boyd and Rudolph 1978, pl. 87. Dr. Boyd tells me (per lit.) that he went over the ground again, especially those areas involved in his study of the street layout, and in some cases refined the orientation of blocks or scraps of wall but he thinks not their location.

The plans of the submerged walls were based on sketches made by divers and swimmers but relied heavily on the aerial photography of Julian and Eunice Whittlesey as well as the Sea notebooks. It cannot be stated too strongly that accuracy under these conditions is difficult to achieve. The photographs, while revealing much detail, vary from shot to shot depending on what the divers were able to clear and what the currents had buried or reburied in silt. The photographs show no scale and were made into drawings in proportion to the actual measurements. The first drawings of the western part of the town were made in this fashion, but the measurements were later checked by Cooper and Boyd. They were able to add house walls, west of the Northwest Command Post in water of wading depth, that did not show in the photographs.

The excavation of a small area in the eastern part of the town (adjacent to Street 5) was conducted by the Greek Archaeological Service (Ephoreia of Classical and Prehistoric Antiquities at Nauplion) in 1979 but has not been published (see Ault 2005, 21, n. 34). A plan of their discoveries was generously provided to bring the site plan up to that date.

The site plan (Fig. 18) used in this volume is drawn from a number of sources. The contour lines, the line of the fortifications with the adjacent structures, and the 20th-century buildings and roads are taken from a print at 1:1000 of Cooper's inked version of his survey, dated 1972/1974 (see below, 14–15). The surface remains are taken principally from Boyd's plan at 1:1000 of the Classical town with his proposed street layout; it is undated, but is based on his survey plan at 1:500, which is dated 1970–1975. Where the two surveys differ, Boyd's has generally been followed, but some remains not shown there have been added from Cooper's. The excavated areas have been taken from the field drawings made at 1:50 and my field notes. For the submerged sections from the Northwest Command Post to the Late Roman/Early Byzantine bath I have restudied the plans and notes made by the divers as well as the aerial photographs. The resulting drawing represents the site to the best of my ability; I believe that it should serve to illustrate the volumes in this series. Nevertheless I would caution those who would use it to develop reconstructed plans of the town or locate future excavation trenches. First, while the contours probably have changed little since Classical times, the lines shown are 20th century and in short stretches may be affected by terrace walls, which are not shown. Second, any area as yet unexcavated should be resurveyed to verify details of the position and especially the orientation of the surface remains before arguing from them too closely. Since I was unable to verify them myself in the field, it is entirely possible that, in working from so many sources, despite my best efforts I may have erred in my choice in a particular case.

The facts concerning the fortifications, as I see them, are presented here with the expectation that such a study will help to fill out the picture of the town as a whole, in its historical setting, and assist in the investigations of similar contemporary communities. The account includes considerable detail, even though these data may not be used in further discussion here, in the expectation that they may give rise to other studies at Halieis or serve as comparanda for work at other sites. In addition, because some of the details recorded here may be lost to modern construction and erosion, it seems better to provide as much information as possible now. Interpretation has for the most part been postponed to the final chapter, the exceptions being discussions of discrete elements (the Chambered Curtain, the two command posts, and the shrine) where other publications are cited.

CHAPTER ONE

Materials and Methods of Construction

The fortifications of the Archaic and Classical periods in mainland Greece that are visible today and increasingly known through surveys and a few excavations fall into three general categories. The simplest form is an earth embankment crowned with a palisade of branches; it could be constructed quickly and at little cost. Chiefly effective against small raiding parties of pirates or marauding wild animals, its use after the Archaic period was probably limited to temporary camps. Understandably, remains are rare, to be found only in excavations where later construction of more permanent forms has not entirely removed the earthworks, but literary references to their use should encourage archaeologists to watch for their traces.

Where available funds, labor, and material permitted, stone construction not only produced the most imposing defenses but required little upkeep, once the original expense had been met. Walls of this type, dating for the most part from the end of the 5th century or later (Winter 1971, 77), even now present an appearance of wealth and power.

The third form employs stone only to provide a weather-proof base for a mud-brick superstructure.[1] It was recommended for its resilience against battering rams and stone-throwing catapults (see below, 6, note 9) as well as its economy of labor and material where

suitable clay was locally available. While there are indications of earthworks at Halieis, it is to this third type that the principal remains belong.

Materials

Earth

The earthwork of which traces were found south of Tower **10** (below, 18–19) was made of red soil similar to that used to make mud brick at Halieis in the Classical period. Trench A, a test trench dug nearby in the bottomland east of the town site, produced virtually nothing but sterile red earth,[2] an indication that this material would have been available in abundance near the location of the earthwork.[3]

Cobbles and Pebbles

Water-rounded fist-size stones were used as a base for the earthworks near Tower **10** (see above). A good source was always at hand on the shingle beach along the shore. The earth mass near the Northeast Command Post (below, 19) lay on a thin layer of pebbles described in the reports for trenches inside and outside the southwest wall of the building.[4] The rubble used for fill in the curtains and towers would have been gleaned from the fieldstones available everywhere on the ground, augmented with trimmings left by the masons.

---

[1] Lawrence 1979, 213. Note, however, that Lawrence warned that the "assemblage of undressed stones" no more than a meter in height now representing some "rustic or temporary fortresses" was more probably topped by some sort of palisade than by mud brick (Lawrence 1979, 207). Winter (1971, 69) named three categories: (1) mud brick on a stone socle; (2) stone for the curtain and towers to the level of the walkway, with mud brick and timber above; and (3) all stone. The walls at Halieis belong to the first of these, since the evidence indicates that "the main structural mass" (1971, 70) was of mud brick.

[2] Trench A (3.00 x 30.00 m), 60 meters due east of Tower **10** and

running almost exactly north-south.

[3] For other possible locations of earthworks, see the discussion of the Archaic defenses (below, 17–19).

[4] NB 135/375(1972), 36–37, in a deep cut inside the Northeast Command Post; NB 130/375(1976), 34, in front of the Northeast Command Post. On the acropolis, a line of cobbles formed a rudimentary socle for a facing of mud bricks added on the inside of the Phase 3 wall; it ran westward from the western offset of the Phase 2 construction for 8.25 m (see Fig. 21; Williams n.d.). Pebbles and small cobbles were also used as the underlayment for plaster floors in some of the houses.

Mud Brick

The mud brick used at Halieis has a very characteristic appearance, even when the bricks themselves are broken up: it is liberally filled with flecks and nodules of lime that have permeated the clay to fill the voids left by decomposed vegetable matter, such as straw mixed in to increase tensile strength. The clay commonly found in levels of the Archaic and later periods is red; dark, almost black disintegrated brick, however, was found on the Industrial Terrace as well as on the acropolis, where several colors were recorded (Williams n.d.).[5] The brick used in Phase 6 for Tower **6** was laid in buff "mortar." It sometimes appears to be in alternating courses of dark and light red with some buff, but since it was to be covered with plaster, there can have been no aesthetic intent. Williams (NB 22, 113) termed the variations "haphazard." Very likely, it was a matter of calling on different suppliers to keep the work moving ahead. The source of the red clay could be any of the bottomland where the iron leached from the rocks at higher levels has colored the soil.[6] Sources for the other clays have not been identified. Bricks that could be measured were found on the acropolis (Williams n.d.) and at the Northeast Command Post (52, note 30). Some mud brick alternating with layers of lime could be seen in the south scarp of Trench 990/350 at the Southeast Gate.[7]

Mud brick, generally on a stone wall-base or at least a socle, was a very common material for Greek fortification walls.[8] Its use seems to have depended as much on the relative availability of suitable clay and stone as on a need for speed or economy of construction. In fact, its homogeneous and more resilient nature provided advantages over masonry in resisting rams and the more advanced types of artillery.[9] It was chosen even for the Hellenistic walls at Sparta and Demetrias as an acceptable alternative to the fully developed ashlar masonry already in use at Messene and elsewhere.[10] The walls at Mantinea were always mud brick. While the only mud brick preserved in situ at Halieis was that found on the acropolis, in Trench 990/350, and at the Northeast Command Post, its use throughout the fortifications can be assumed, even though most of the arguments are negative (see below, 13).

Terracotta

Fragments of tiles of standard Lakonian type (broad, shallow pan tiles and semicircular cover tiles) are plentiful in the trenches excavated around the houses. These tiles are of red fabric, frequently washed with red or black paint, and are surely local in manufacture.[11] Where they have been excavated in locations adjacent to the defense walls, they could have come from either fortifications or houses, and indeed, the same type of tile could have been used for both. Only excavations outside the circuit could establish an association with the city walls.[12] Tiles were commonly used, as they are today, to protect the tops of parapets and courtyard walls as well as on roofs (see below, 13).

Tiles of Corinthian type are also found, the variation in scale and detail indicating that more than one roof system is represented.[13] Examples found along the circuit wall, unfortunately all fragmentary, are notably heavy and well made; a

---

[5] In Trench I5-1, an 8 m cut 1.5 m wide across the line of the curtain between the Southeast and East gates, the excavator recorded darker soil in the center of the trench: "It demonstrates some kind of archaic preserve here, but the sample is very small (NB 105, 39–40)." Only one sherd (unspecified) was found. It is tempting to identify this sample as early mud brick, but the value of the evidence is debatable.

[6] See the description of Trench A above, 5.

[7] NB 990/350, summary, p. 38.

[8] Orlandos 1955, 66–67. For examples of mud-brick walls dating from the Geometric period to the Hellenistic, see Winter 1971, 71 with note 4.

[9] In the 19th century, Rochas d'Aiglun wrote that a sufficiently thick rampart of earth was the only practical obstacle to cannon fire (1881, 7). This property of mud brick was recognized in antiquity by Pausanias (8.8.8–9) and, more authoritatively, by Apollodoros of Damascus, writing at the beginning of the 2nd century of our era (*Poliorketika*, MS fol. 34 recto, as edited by Wescher 1867, 157–58). The use of the ram dates from some time in the 5th century; it was certainly used at Plataiai at the beginning of the Peloponnesian War (Thucydides 2.76.4).

[10] Sparta: Wace 1905/1906, 284–88. Winter (1971, 73, note 12)

gave speed and economy as the reason for its use in the late reinforcements at Demetrias (Stählin et al. 1934, pls. 7–10).

[11] The dimensions of Lakonian cover and pan tiles found in the drain beside the mess building on the acropolis and probably used on its roof can be recovered from HC 120 (cover: L. 0.95, W. 0.18, Th. 0.012 m) and HC 121 (pan: pres. L. 0.39, W. 0.51, Th. 017 m). See Dengate n.d., chapter 8.

[12] In accordance with the specifications of the excavation permits, nearly all the trenches were laid out inside the line of the ancient wall. The only trenches to cross the wall were Trench H4-5 at the upper end of the Chambered Curtain, those revealing the Southeast Gate and the adjacent shrine, Trench I5-1 (between the East and Southeast Gates), and a few trenches near Tower **10** (East Tower Area). (Trench A, outside the archaeological zone in Field 29 east of the East Tower, was dug in 1968 at the request of the landowner.)

[13] The designation "Corinthian" that appears in some of the notebooks means Corinthian in shape (broad, flat pans and angular, "peaked" covers) and of pale buff clay. It is in some entries clearly distinguished from the "tower tiles," which may appear in the same trench (see below, e.g., 7, note 16: Trench I5-1).

large piece of a pan tile in this category was set in the floor of a room on the Industrial Terrace.[14] Like that of other Corinthian examples the form of these heavy tiles is crisp and angular; it has a beveled rim on the sides of the pan, somewhat less pronounced at the upper end. The underside of the lower end of the tile is molded with a broad rabbet that curves upward at the sides and an angular lip projecting downward as a drip over the tile in the row below. At each side at the inner edge is a lug beveled toward the center of the tile that forms the contact point with the upper edge of the tile below (Pl. 17b).[15]

The fabric of these tiles is pale greenish buff ranging to salmon at the core, with much coarse, red or black temper. When well preserved, the profiles are sharp and the surface is covered with a fine, pale green slip. The clay, if not the actual tiles, may have been brought from some little distance, an expense that might well have been necessary to produce such large tiles and justifiable for "public works." Cover-tile fragments are very rare, but a large fragment was found outside the Southeast Gate beside Tower **9** (NB 990/360, 29).

Fragments of these heavy tiles have appeared as surface finds outside the West Wall, the Industrial Terrace Wall, and the Southeast Gate, and east of the excavated section of the Middle Wall. They have been found in the excavations of the Southeast Wall. A few pieces were excavated at the Middle Wall, one of them under a block of the defense wall. Examples were found in the East Tower Area (Trench M, 1970, below, note 16), giving rise to the term "tower tile" found in some notebooks, and just west of the Northeast Command Post (Trench 135/370, 1972). The finest examples of the clay slip were on surface finds, noted outside the circuit at the Industrial Terrace and at the center bastion of the Northeast Wall.[16]

If the rabbeted pan tiles were sometimes used at the eaves of later structures, as Kelly suggests (note 15 above), they may also have been similarly employed on the fortification parapets, where a single row of tiles would have sufficed. The merlon cap stones on Tower **6** indicate that that parapet was little more than 40 centimeters in thickness (Williams n.d.). Some of the tower tiles

---

[14] Jameson 1969, 322, fig. 4, center of Eastern Unit, Room A; rest. W. 0.60 m. (See now Jameson n.d., chapter 3.) Others similarly used were found in excavating this area, which is immediately adjacent to the circuit wall. A large pan tile of a different type, found in the destruction debris of Tower **6**, is 0.675 m long; of greenish fabric, it tapers in thickness from 0.052 m (top) to 0.031 m (bottom) and in width from 0.592 m (top) to 0.570 m (bottom), where there is a slight lip (NB 16, 140–41; NB 22, 113). For other examples, see below, note 16.

[15] A complete tile of this type (HC 629), found in the Verdelis excavations of the necropolis in 1958, was published by Nancy J. Kelly (Cooper 1989, pl. 57), who will be publishing the Halieis tiles. The dimensions are recorded: L. 0.688 m, W. 0.582 m, H. 0.08–0.063 m. Large-scale tiles found at the necropolis were used to line and roof a cist of the Classical period (Dengate 1976, 275). Dr. Kelly tells me (per lit. 6/19/03) that she "saw tiles of this type come out of the dry land excavations. Some had red color on them; some had the color in the groove or rabbet and extending back several centimeters from the groove on to the body of the tile. I wondered at the time whether they had been re-used on houses along the eaves and painted red for decoration, or if the red was some substance that made the tiles less porous and would have been put on the surfaces that might be wet by wind driven rain." I am much indebted to Dr. Kelly for guiding me in my discussion of these tiles; any errors in my conclusions are not her responsibility.

[16] The thickness of several of these fragments is recorded as 0.33 m but, unfortunately, no complete length is preserved. It is probable that throughout the notebooks cited here, unless tiles are specified as "Corinthian" or "tower type," they are "Lakonian." Not all the excavators were consistent in their identification of type or shape, but Thomas Hitzl, supervisor of Trench M and the trenches in H4 and I5 listed below, kept an eye out for tower tiles at my request. *Trench H4-1 (across Tower **8** and road west of it)*: "Many rooftile

fragments including one of so-called tower tile type" (NB 112, 3). ". . . debris stratum, extending westward from point some 2.00 m. W of E scarp; . . . solidly packed with numerous Corinthian-style roof-tile fragments (approximately 6 boxes in 1/4 hour)" (NB 112, 8). "E end: similar debris ["high percentage of poor quality BG"] including 2 fragments of so-called 'tower tiles'. . ." (NB 112, 9). *Trench H4-2 (across inner wall of Tower **8**)*: Masses of roof tiles [no mention of "tower tiles"] (NB 112). *Trench H4-5 (across outer line of curtain)*: Heavy fall of tiles to south outside city wall (S of WB-4): "fragments of so-called 'tower-tile' type predominate"; other Corinthian tiles . . . (NB 112, 30). Few finds north of city wall, primarily at N end of trench. 20 tile frags. (both Corinthian and tower-tile types; NB 112, 31). Five joining frags. of "tower-tile" from S of WB-4; 2 faces preserved, 0.48 x 0.52 m as preserved (NB 112, 32–33). *Trench H4-7 (across house and road west of curtain)*: Heavy tile fall; no "tower-tiles" (NB 105, 30). *Trench I5-1 (across double curtain wall)*: Tile fall (Corinthian and "tower tiles," NB 105, 23). *Trench J5-2 (inside East Gate)*: Many tile fragments reported [no mention of "tower tiles"] (NB 103). *Trench B (East Tower, S corner)*: Layer of fallen tiles [type unspecified] at level of top of foundation course (0.61 m below datum, top of first conglomerate course), sloping down to east (NB 511, 23). Large pan tiles, glazed underneath (HC 264)–(ibid., 25). *Trench E (East Tower, NE side)*: [No mention of tiles.] *Trench K (East Tower, SE side)*: "Many roof tiles in first basket" [these appear in a photograph to be of Lakonian type (NB 101)]. *Trench M (across double curtain wall)*: One fragment of "tower tile" was the only find in the fourth pass outside the wall (NB 105, 11). A few fragments in the western extension of Trench M (eighth pass) included those of "tower type" (ibid., 16). *Trench O (across double curtain wall)*: A layer of Corinthian pan tiles was reported at the east side of the trench [outside the wall?], fewer to the west; whether these were "tower tiles" is uncertain (NB 104, 4). *Trench U (across double curtain wall)*: No "tower tiles" reported (NB 107).

may be assigned to the parapet of the circuit wall and associated military structures; other large-scale tiles of Corinthian type found throughout the town may have been used on public buildings, somewhat lighter ones on domestic structures.[17]

Stone

The red soil of the region colors everything buried in it to a greater or lesser degree depending on the nature of the material. This is particularly striking in the case of the more absorbent types of stone, especially the matrix of the conglomerate and sandstone described below. When first unearthed the great round towers on the acropolis and at the Southeast Gate were the red-gold color characteristic of the whole excavation area. Blocks that had been partly exposed, however, like some of those in the acropolis square tower, showed the change to a darker gray, similar to the color of local conglomerate outcroppings. This color is now apparent on blocks that have been exposed and weathering over the last 30 years or more, in part owing to the surface erosion of the matrix but also to the leaching of the added iron oxide. The local limestone is too hard to be affected. The poros soon powders to white. Plaster or stucco and shelly limestone were probably a pale gray originally. The creamy yellow color that seems natural in the latter has weathered to blue-gray in the coping blocks laid out on the acropolis; the material, which hardens over time, appears less absorbent than the conglomerate matrix.

A study of the various architectural fragments inventoried under HS might be rewarding. It should be accompanied by further investigation of the types and sources of stone and the dates at which they were used.

Conglomerate. The underlying rock of the region is conglomerate, a coarse material with occasional streaks of hard, blue limestone. The aggregate is all water worn, mostly limestone, varying from coarse grit, which gives the effect of sandstone, through all sizes of pebbles. The commonest variety contains stones ranging from a few millimeters to ten centimeters in diameter, in a coarse, white, lime-and-sand matrix that becomes

very friable when weathered. In its natural form it has the appearance of modern structural concrete. Exposure of excavated blocks soon produces deep pitting as the surface matrix weathers away, but the material is basically very strong in compression. When a piece of the conglomerate remains in one position for a long time, particularly on soil, a smooth lime coating may build up on the under surface, covering the lumpy aggregate like a hard, thin coat of plaster. In the same way, a natural cementing process may disguise the joints of long-weathered blocks. Despite the obvious difficulty of working stone when the aggregate is much harder than the matrix, conglomerate was the material used for all the major masonry projects at Halieis. The traces of walls shown everywhere on the site on the survey map characteristically consist of conglomerate blocks 0.30–0.40 m in width and 1.20–1.40 m in length; the height may be 0.25–0.30 m for a stretcher, twice that or more for an orthostate.

The stone tends to split horizontally along thick bedding planes. Where it is exposed in scarps and along the outer shoreline, there is a deceptive suggestion of quarry cuts. Signs of ancient quarrying on the site itself are difficult to identify, but undoubtedly the material near at hand was used in the early stages of the development of the town. The rock face along the modern road in the western part of the site appears channeled like the inside face of some of the defense-wall blocks. There was certainly quarrying at locations along the hillside southeast of the site, beyond the sanctuary of Demeter (Fig. 17). Conglomerate, which would have been the obvious material at Halieis, was not generally used at Athens before the 4th century, when it began to replace poros in foundations. Above ground it was not popular there even for fortification and retaining walls; one of the earliest examples is the Phaleric wall, followed at the beginning of the 4th century by the grave monument of Dexileos.[18]

Poros (Conglomerate). Occasionally beds of a much softer material from the same formation as the conglomerate were quarried for use in foundation courses at or below grade.[19] These blocks often

---

[17] Corinthian tiles found in the *kopron* of House D vary in size and section (Ault 1999, 552–53, figs. 7, 8 and Ault 2005, 46, where he refers to an unpublished paper written for Indiana University by Louis Jerkich, "Some Corinthian Tiles Excavated at Halieis in 1974"). Representative of the type in domestic use, they may have been from both Houses D and E, salvaged from various

sources (Ault, per lit., August 2001).
[18] Scranton 1938, 525–26. See Thompson 1937, 45; Wycherley 1978, 272.
[19] For convenience, it is here called poros from its resemblance to the Attic stone. It is almost pure matrix with little or no aggregate, easy to work but not weather resistant.

appear as plinths laid horizontally to form a socle for conglomerate orthostates. The poros commonly found in Attica, where it was economical because of its local origin in Peiraieus and its ease of fabrication, was widely used for foundations in the later part of the 5th century; the softer grades were restricted to inner and subsoil locations or coated with plaster.[20] At Corinth, a brown poros was used extensively above ground in less vulnerable parts of the Hellenistic fortifications, since it was more easily quarried and trimmed than the alternative, Acrocorinth limestone.[21]

Probably among the earliest examples of poros foundation plinths at Halieis are those in the Phase 5 square tower and the mess building on the acropolis (see Williams n.d.), now dated about 400. Such plinths were set barely above ground level, projecting slightly from the orthostates above; indeed, considering how rapidly the material erodes when exposed, in antiquity they were probably covered by the dust of adjacent roadways, not to mention seasonal grass and weeds. Whether the initiation of this type of construction was due to the discovery of a convenient source for the material or to outside influence is a matter only for speculation; very likely both reasons were involved. Phase 6 saw the same detail used in the acropolis barracks.

Elsewhere on the site poros plinths were used for Tower **10**; full foundation blocks of poros were employed at the south corner in an exceptional situation.[22] The wedge-shaped blocks that back the wall-base orthostates of Tower **9** are of poros. A course of poros underlies the wedge-shaped blocks in Tower **14**, as well as the conglomerate Projection and its spur, on the opposite side of the Harbor Gate, and poros edges the mole between Towers **13** and **14**. In these locations, the poros courses may have been at ancient sea level. Substantial buildings in the town, both domestic, such as House 7 and House A, and public, like the Northeast Command Post, had poros plinths, as did at least one section of the Middle Wall.

Perhaps the only poros blocks used above grade are those that barred the Southeast Gate; the material may have been chosen because it was easily cut and relatively light to move. The great blocks were probably stuccoed over to resemble the more substantial construction of Tower **9** and the adjacent curtain. A similar explanation is offered below for the poros blocks in the curtain on the Industrial Terrace.

Limestone. This hard blue-gray material is often found on examination to contain some pebbles, in fact to be partly conglomerate. Its use is generally confined to small blocks in repairs or as fillers, or in walls of mixed materials, for the most part late alterations. Large blocks of limestone are not common, but some well-cut hammer-dressed blocks have been noted, for example, on the Industrial Terrace and in the Middle Wall.[23] These scattered instances suggest reuse, but with the exception of the temple of Apollo no structure entirely of limestone has been identified at Halieis. Since the line between limestone and conglomerate as quarried seems to be blurred, perhaps there was a limited source near the town site, drawn upon when expediency was more important than appearance. Any major source presumably lies somewhere to the north but probably no more than a few kilometers away; the limestone is common in the general areas of Koilada and Hermioni.

Sandstone (Conglomerate). The fine-grained conglomerate resembling sandstone is easily split along its bedding planes. Set with the planes vertical, it has little resistance to weathering. It was used occasionally for heavy floor slabs in houses of the Greek period.[24] It seems never to have been chosen for original construction in the fortifications except as drain cover slabs or, in its coarsest form, drain walls; in the latter position the vulnerable edges were covered. A single slab was used at the corner of the mess building on the

---

[20] E.g., the Hephaisteion, Erechtheion, Stoa of Zeus, and new work on the Propylaia. See Thompson 1937, note 3; Wycherley 1978, 271–72.

[21] See Winter 1991, 115 with figs. 8, 9. I have no information on the comparative durability of poros used at Corinth and at Halieis, but since at Corinth it has survived in reasonably good condition, I must assume that the Corinthian poros is a much more substantial material, available for uses where the Halieis masons had to rely on conglomerate.

[22] An example of its use described as "above ground level" was noted in Trench 165/210 where it was employed for the foundations of interior crosswalls (NB 165/210 & 165/215, 37, Final Analysis), but the tops of these blocks were probably not much above the finished floor.

[23] An early use is noted by J. A. Dengate (per lit. 8/12/02) at the southwest corner of the earlier mess building on the acropolis (see Williams n.d.).

[24] The house partially excavated in Trenches 165/210 and 165/215 in 1974 had three very large sandstone floor slabs (Unit 21) overlaid by cement, probably a base for storage containers. It was dated "first third of the fourth century" (see above, note 22).

acropolis, over the otherwise-open street drain (Williams n.d.). The doorsill (Fig. 14), column shaft, and bases of the Northeast Command Post were of sandstone, probably because it could be brought to a fairly smooth finish but was more durable than poros, especially for exterior use, but the column shaft at least was presumably stuccoed. Toward the end of the Classical occupation, blocks of sandstone conglomerate were often set vertically in house walls, where they have eroded badly on the lines of the bedding planes. Because the size of the pebbles is very small, the material is relatively easy to cut, probably even more so when freshly quarried. No doubt for this reason and because of the ease of splitting out layers in the quarry, it was the favorite cover-slab material for the Late Roman/Early Byzantine graves.[25] No specific quarry site has been identified.

Shelly Limestone. For fine work, the masons of Halieis used a pale buff or gray limestone, entirely permeated with the impressions of cockle shells of various types and sizes; in most cases the shells themselves have dissolved away. The source of this distinctive material has not yet been identified.[26] Accustomed to the recalcitrant conglomerate, the masons were able to cut fine moldings on the light but surprisingly strong stone. Although probably, like travertine, easy to cut when freshly quarried, this material could not be polished; it always shows the marks of a fine-toothed chisel. Since the surface even when "finished" is full of holes, it could not have been used in exterior locations without a coating of stucco.

While its principal known use is in the coping blocks found on the acropolis (see Williams n.d.), fragments of this material can be found in many parts of the site, often built into rubble walls.[27] Decorative elements such as a Doric capital found in the Northeast Command Post and an Ionic one unearthed nearby were presumably stuccoed even for interior use.[28] A number of molded pieces coated with varying amounts of plaster have been inventoried; some may be anta caps or from door jambs. There were rectilinear fragments among the buildings on the Industrial Terrace and in the terrace wall along the modern road near the Southeast Gate; one piece was found there beside the northeast socket block. Several slabs excavated in the vicinity of Tower **10** had been reused as cover slabs for Late Roman/Early Byzantine graves.[29] It is not clear in these cases whether the first use of the blocks was even in the vicinity, since they were easily transported.

Marble. Very little marble has been found at Halieis and none in connection with the fortifications. Although an Ionic base in marble was found near the East Gate (below, 27), shelly limestone was used for the capitals at the Northeast Command Post. Small worked fragments of marble were found northwest of that building, presumably decorative elements from one of the houses in that area (Trench T, NB 1.1, 141), imported as finished items.

Methods

The style of the masonry generally used in the curtain walls and square towers may be termed trapezoidal (made of blocks with horizontal top and bottom joints but not necessarily vertical ones at the ends) or simply ashlar.[30] In most cases, there

---

[25] Rudolph 1979, 298, pl. 80, a. In the photograph, the nearer two slabs are shelly limestone, the rest sandstone conglomerate.
[26] Limestone containing shells of this type, which is quite different from the oolitic limestone at Olympia, has been reported at the Fountain of Theagenes, Megara, but (in a letter to C. Dengate) F. A. Cooper wrote that it does not seem to be the same as that found at Halieis. He says that it is common in the East Peloponnese, even in the Mani. The material, despite its light weight, unlike marble is hardly worth transporting any great distance, and yet it was common at Halieis. Its source should be somewhere in the southern Argolid, probably south of Mt. Dhidhimo, on one of the nearby islands, or near the coast across the Argolic Gulf at Prasiai. For another suggestion, see below, note 29.
[27] A pair of shelly limestone slabs, perhaps rejects from the construction of Tower **6**, topped the open drain just south of the Mess on the acropolis.
[28] HS 6 and HS 381 (below, 68, 69).
[29] See above, note 25. Three monolithic sarcophagi of shelly limestone, each topped by two slabs of the same material, were found in the necropolis, east of the town site (Dengate 1976, 275 with note 5). The author dated them to the Classical period and cites 14 similar ones at Eleusis (Mylonas 1975, 275–76), with the suggestion that they came from a common source. In that case, the workshop is likely to have been closer to Eleusis than to Halieis. Even a two-meter sarcophagus could be easily imported by sea, especially if it was already hollowed out.
[30] While it is risky to compare one or two courses of masonry to a wall a story or more in height, the general appearance of the Halieis stonework is similar to the well-known rounded tower at Messene. There, while the impression is of ashlar masonry, closer examination shows that in some places "vertical" joints may be sharply canted, and the horizontal joints are adjusted with steps to accommodate blocks of varying height. Adam (1982, 27) compared the Halieis stonework to that at Phigaleia, noting that trapezoidal blocks would be most economical of material. In the following chapters, the description of each component includes any special features of the stonework.

is only one course of masonry remaining. Where there is more than one, the masonry is coursed but with some irregularities: there are occasional filler and L-shaped blocks, as well as stackwork (fillers composed of small, flat stones set in horizontal layers [Pl. 5a]). These details do not seem to indicate date so much as a practical approach to assembly with little sophistication in appearance. Special treatment of the blocks, other than a greater amount of refinement in the finish above the socle level, seems to be confined to technical details such as occasional drafting on the face or corner to facilitate alignment in aligning upper courses (for example, Towers **3**, **6**, and **10**).

Most of the stonework was dressed only to a relatively smooth surface; the available materials did not permit polishing in any case. The faces of the blocks in Towers **6** and **9** (Pls. 5b, 8c) when newly excavated preserved a neatly hammer-dressed appearance for the most part; a rougher preliminary finish was found only at ground level. Margin bands are uncommon. Occasionally on the inner, hidden face of the fortification blocks a rougher finish is preserved: the inside face of one of the blocks of the inner wythe of the northeast curtain preserves broad diagonal "flutes" that may be the marks of quarrying, now smoothed by a naturally deposited coating of lime; similar vertical channels were left on the inner face of the block forming the return at the west outer corner of the Southeast Gate. The inner side of the west corner block of Tower **10** shows the marks left by a point.[31] The treatment here used for routine shaping of the block was adopted at other sites for the finished surface.[32]

There seems to have been no attempt at a deliberate aesthetic treatment such as rustication; the blocks retain their utilitarian construction surfaces. Drafted corners should be distinguished from drafted margins, although both originated in construction techniques and became popular as decorative treatments. Martin stressed the use of the drafted corner to emphasize angles (1965, 414, with note 3). Pouilloux assigned the stylistic use to the 4th century (1954, 50, note 1) to which

most of the published examples belong. To Martin's extensive list of examples may be added Plataiai and Apollonia (Epeiros) cited by Orlandos (1955, II, 259, with note 5), Kisseli (Aitolia; Lerat and Chamoux 1947–1948, 68), and the Masi tower and grave terrace of Lysimachides at Acharnai (Wrede 1933, 24, no. 58; 37, no. 103). Most of these instances are towers; the rest are fortification and retaining walls, where some angles may have blocks with drafted corners and others not. The blocks may be trapezoidal, ashlar, or even polygonal, but present a rough, rugged appearance, whether quarry faced, bossed, or rusticated in a more restrained and artificial manner. At Halieis, as at Plataiai (Aravantinos, Konecny, and Marchese 2003, 297, fig. 7, 298, fig. 8, 300, fig. 9, 301, fig. 10), the corner drafting (e.g., Tower **10**) seems to be functional, facilitating the alignment of two or more wall courses, and indicates less sophistication than the later use that was also decorative.

The actual construction of the fortifications varies according to the particular site conditions and should not necessarily be taken as indicative of the date or historical phase. Thus while the curtains are formed of conglomerate orthostates or stretchers set in a double line, in most places only one course high, these blocks may be set on earth, on or even into bedrock, or on a course of roughly worked stones or plinths of the same or a different material. The evidence for the under-pinning of the wall blocks is minimal. In most places along the West Wall, for instance, either the inner or outer wythe is missing. Only at Tower **2** was there any cleaning to determine the height of the blocks. It appears, however, that the inner wythe often rested on conglomerate plinths. The outer wythe was fitted to the bedrock, frequently with the aid of an intermittent leveling course of small stones in the form of a socle that projected as much as 0.35 m on the exterior face.[33] The practical reason for this distinction between the wythes may have been to fit the outer one as firmly as possible to the bedrock, even though the inner might require a plinth on fill to maintain a parallel course.

---

[31] Similar tool marks are conspicuous at Plataiai (Aravantinos, Konecny, and Marchese 2003), both vertically on 5th-century orthostates (292, fig. 3) and later horizontally as well (300, fig. 9; the illustration shows the parallel tool marks on the lowest blocks have been trimmed away around the edges of the face).

[32] Adam 1982, 31–32. Compare the walls at Mantinea (ibid., phot. 46, 47) and Aigosthena (phot. 50) and the 4th-century walls at

Eleusis (phot. 49; Winter 1971, 79, note 28 with fig. 58). In his discussion of stonework, Bessac (1986, 275, 276) said that blocks may retain an identifiable quarry face or may be split naturally from the quarry bed but that many were trimmed to size at the quarry to save weight in transport. The retained faces at Halieis noted above were in hidden positions.

[33] For a block cut with such a projecting "base" see below, 45, note 3.

This system may have been standard throughout the rockier part of the circuit. Plinths were used on the Industrial Terrace; at the Middle Wall, which runs across rather than along lines of exposed bedrock, they were of poros rather than conglomerate and were used for both wythes. In the upper part of the Southeast Wall (the Chambered Curtain) stretchers were set on poros blocks, at least at Tower **8** (see below, 64), or on packing over bedrock. In the lower part between the Southeast Gate and Tower **10**, where there was deep soil over the bedrock, the walls were founded on large unworked stones.

In order to maintain a roughly horizontal bed for the superposed courses of mud brick, the masonry on slopes was stepped, sometimes resulting in short stretches two courses in height. Where the evidence is preserved, the masonry base of the towers and bastions is higher but is composed of larger blocks rather than more courses. The space between the wythes of masonry was filled with rubble and earth. The Middle Wall (below, 54–56), on a steeper grade than elsewhere at Halieis, was subdivided by cross blocks into compartments that would have helped to consolidate the fill. Elsewhere in the circuit in a few places a single cross block has been noted but is so exceptional that the question of a passageway or other special construction immediately arises.[34]

It was necessary only to level the top of the masonry base course before continuing the wall construction in mud brick. In two places (at Towers **9** [Pl. 7b] and **10**) the top surface of conglomerate blocks has been tooled to a more finished surface. In both cases these blocks are at the end of the course, that is, at the corner or, in the case of Tower **9**, the last block of the curving wall. It seems likely that these surfaces served as datum points for a superposed course of masonry, much as the vertical dressing at the corner of Tower **10** would have provided the reference for the vertical alignment. One of the orthostates on the southeast side of the Northeast Command Post appears to have been dressed to receive a superimposed block (Fig. 27; below, 68). Other than these details and pry holes noted on the orthostates of a building in Trench 145/235, there is no specific evidence that cut stone was used at Halieis above a conglomerate base; in most cases

the upper walls would have been of rubble masonry or mud brick.

Cuttings. Since most of the fortification construction consisted of a single course of masonry, there was little occasion for cuttings; they were not often found in other structures. The only dowel cuttings recorded in a notebook are in the poros plinths of the Northeast Command Post; the large-scale (1:50) trench drawings show them toward the outside of two adjacent poros plinth blocks on the northwest side of that building. In the East Tower Area two dowel cuttings ca. 0.65 m apart are shown on a house-wall plinth in Trench R.

Pry holes are rare, occurring for the most part on poros socle blocks, for example, of the barracks by Tower **6** (Fig. 21; see Williams n.d.), the Northeast Command Post, and several blocks of House A nearby on Avenue B. The top of a coarse conglomerate block would never have been very smooth; pry holes, if not redundant, would be difficult to identify now on a weather-eroded surface. They were noted, however, on conglomerate orthostates of a house exposed beside a road surface in the central area of the town.[35] A pry cutting is shown on the second conglomerate block of the stair at Tower **10** (Fig. 26).

A few miscellaneous cuttings have been recorded in domestic structures, some undoubtedly for doorposts or fastenings. There are cuttings for the gate sockets in the pivot blocks at the Southeast Gate. The only known instance of a clamp is found in the projecting platform at the Harbor Gate (Fig. 10b).

Tower construction. Two principal types of construction are employed in the square towers, depending on whether the ground-floor level was filled solidly with earth and rubble or contained a chamber. The towers along the west side (**1–5**), as well as Towers **10** (Pls. 12b, c) and **19** and the predecessors of Towers **6** (Pl. 5a) and **9**, were of the first type, the fill contained at the base by a course of conglomerate orthostates. The ground floor of those along the Northwest Wall (**12, 13, 16,** and **18**) was hollow.[36] In Towers **12, 13,** and **16,** there appears to be a second, inner row of narrower orthostates.

---

[34] E.g., west of the acropolis (below, 47); Industrial Terrace (below, 43).

[35] In Trench 145/235.

[36] Tower **8** had a room at ground level but was probably not a true tower.

The three types of construction evident in the round towers depend both on the nature of the ground-floor space and on the subsoil conditions. Towers **6** and **7**, built on bedrock that must always have been at or close to the surface, required only a ring of massive orthostates, on a socle, to retain the fill. Tower **9** and probably Towers **11** and **14**, however, were built on compacted earth; their builders spread the masonry load by using a thicker line of masonry in the form of wedge-shaped headers. It is not apparent why a conglomerate socle was chosen for Towers **6**, **7**, and **9**, in contrast to one of poros for Tower **14**; the choice may have depended on the availability of material and skilled labor, the circumstances of location, or assignment to different building programs. The use of conglomerate blocks for the fill of Tower **14** may have been determined by the vulnerable position in the water. At Tower **15**, a double wall, consisting of inner and outer orthostate stretchers alternating with headers, provided greater strength for the walls of the hollow ground floor than would the simple backing orthostates used in Towers **12**, **13**, and **16**. It is not known what lies below this course, but trenches dug both on- and offshore along the modern shoreline produced no sign of bedrock, suggesting that Tower **15** may also have been constructed on a platform or at least a ring of wedge-shaped blocks.

It is assumed that the walls of the towers, as well as the curtains above the base course, were of mud brick, although inevitably the evidence is generally lacking. The following arguments are persuasive, however: The top line of the masonry where preserved is even and close to horizontal, if not actually so, stepping down in a regular fashion where required to follow the slope. The wall base is preserved intermittently for almost the whole circuit, but nowhere is there any excess masonry that might have come from higher courses. Clay is locally available and was used in

early fortification construction on the site. Tiles associated with the wall suggest the need for protecting the curtain from the weather, although they might have been used on open or roofed breastworks above masonry walls carried to the level of the walkway.[37] Perhaps most convincing, part of the brick of the acropolis round tower (Tower **6** [Pl. 5c]) is preserved (see Williams n.d.); it is unlikely that mud brick would have been used there if the curtains or other towers were of full-height stonework. If there is no accumulation of fallen mud brick, it is because most of the site has been denuded by natural erosion; the soil removed in excavating along the walls seems generally to be disintegrated mud brick. With the decline of the town at the end of the 4th century, demonstrated by the impoverished nature of the excavated house walls of that date, the curtains, which were never the vast constructions of Demetrias or Old Smyrna, would have soon begun to deteriorate from neglect.

The chief drawback to mud brick was, of course, the need for constant maintenance. In the long run, it could prove more costly than the initially more expensive stone. The mud brick that probably composed the major part of the Halieis curtains and towers would have been coated with a lime plaster to make it more weatherproof.[38] The tops of such walls were commonly protected by tiles.[39] Fragments of one type of Corinthian tile that may have been used on the walls are described above (6–8).

If the curtains were topped with tiles, the acropolis round tower (Tower **6**) at least was crenellated; the openings were carefully trimmed with blocks of shelly limestone (see Williams n.d.for a discussion of these coping blocks). Fragments of the same material have been found in other parts of the circuit near the walls or towers, but none can be so clearly associated with the fortifications.[40]

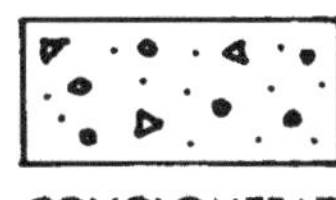

CONGLOMERATE

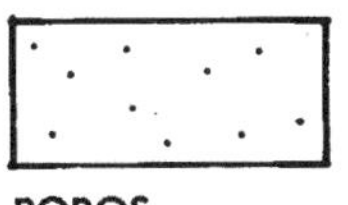

POROS

LIMESTONE

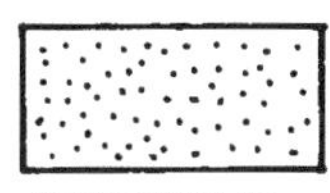

SANDSTONE

[37] For battlements and tower chambers of brick and wood, see Winter 1971, 73–77. Aeneas Tacticus (33.3) warned of the danger from fire to wooden towers and parapets.

[38] For the general practice of plastering mud-brick walls with clay or lime stucco, see Winter 1971, 132. For evidence of the practice on the acropolis (Tower **6**) at Halieis, see Williams n.d.

[39] Orlandos 1955, 81; Winter 1971, 132. Nicholls (1958/59, 112–13) proposed that, since there were no appropriate tiles found

at Old Smyrna, those battlements were protected with reeds or wood plastered with clay. Thucydides mentioned tiles dislodged from the top of the wall in a hurried attempt at nocturnal escape by some of the Plataian defenders (3.22.4). Examples of city-wall tiles of the Hellenistic period are recorded at Demetrias (Arvanitopoulos 1928, 19), Sparta (Wace 1906/1907, 13–15), and Tegea (Bérard 1892, 548).

[40] See above, 10, for specific instances.

– CHAPTER TWO –

The Trace

Ruinous as they are, the fortification walls are nevertheless the most conspicuous and comprehensible of the unexcavated ancient remains at Halieis. The trace as it appears today,[1] since it is very nearly complete, makes a convenient framework on which to locate the various elements (towers, gates, curtain, and so forth), which can then be described in detail. The significance of the different forms it takes and the dating of its successive phases can be postponed until what evidence we have has been set forth.

In the last two centuries the fortification walls have attracted the attention of visitors, some of whom left a record of what they saw. The first of these were the surveyors on H.M.S. Beacon, whose primary interest doubtless was the large sheltered harbor. They were, we may hope, more accurate in their soundings than in their indications of architecture on the British Admiralty chart (Pl. 1);[2] they must have recorded what they found there in the first part of the 19th century, although sometimes they seem to have misinterpreted it (see Towers **1** and **18A**). The site was too obscure and difficult of access by land to attract the attention of the general traveler, perhaps further discouraged by the fact that Pausanias (3.36.2) had not found the city, then deserted, worth visiting. In 1909, however, Alexandros Philadelpheus made notes recording his visit to the area, as did A. Frickenhaus and W. Müller about the same time; W. Wrede visited the site in 1926.[3] A serious attempt to record the fortification walls was first made in 1959 by Charles K. Williams II and Nicholas Verdelis, who undertook some clearing and cleaning, but already some sections had been destroyed.[4] A topographical plan of the site was made by Williams in 1962; it included a record of the visible fortification walls that has been confirmed by subsequent surveys of the trace.[5] A complete survey of the walls then preserved on land was undertaken in 1970, and corrections and amplifications were made in 1971.[6] Even in that short interval, a large section of the West Wall was seriously damaged and partly removed in the course of relocating the modern road to a villa at the northwest corner of the site. Further work in 1972, 1974, 1976, and 1977 recorded on the general

---

[1] The description of the trace and of the elements of the fortifications discussed in the following chapters is written in the present tense although the observations were made for the most part between 1965 and 1980; the rate at which the remains are disappearing is clearly accelerating with each decade.

[2] No. 1502, "Port Kheli," recording a survey made in 1838.

[3] With the exception of brief notices (Philadelpheus 1909, 182; Frickenhaus and Müller 1911, 38), these travelers' notes are unpublished. Alexander Philadelpheus's wife entrusted his notebook to Michael and Virginia Jameson in 1954 (Jameson 1969, 311). It is now in the Halieis archives at Indiana University; with it is an English translation made by Giannis Kazazis of any archaeological information. Philadelpheus's report (1909, 182–83) mentions extensive underwater remains of foundations. Walther Wrede provided the Jamesons with copies of the German notes on file at the Deutsche Archäologische Institut in Athens.

[4] It is said, for instance, that the public quay at Porto Kheli where the Customs House is indicated on the British Admiralty chart is built with blocks from the west end of the Northwest Wall. Indeed, before the quay was expanded in the early 1970s to accomodate the hydrofoil vessel from Athens, large conglomerate blocks could be seen in a course at the water line. The distance across from the site is not great, nor would it be difficult to move large blocks by water from a position in the shallows.

[5] Williams's notes, including some sketches of details, are to be found in NB 22.

[6] Following suggestions made by F. A. Cooper, the survey of the fortifications in 1970 was conducted by T. D. Boyd with the assistance of McAllister and David Blackwell. In 1971, McAllister, with the assistance of Nikolas Staikopoulos, made selected block-by-block surveys and other checks to clarify minor discrepancies and took some measurements of elevations. In 1972, Larry Holderly assisted Cooper and McAllister in the season's surveying, especially in taking elevations to establish the site contours.

topographical survey of the site additional sections as they were excavated or discovered.[7]

The submerged section of the Northeast Wall and the parts of the Northwest Wall that were also in shallow water were surveyed first by Frank J. Frost and David Owen in 1965.[8] Divers in 1967 and 1968 cleared some limited areas. At the same time, the trace of the Northwest Wall was outlined from aerial photographs.[9] The North Wall and the area just west of the Harbor Gate, including the Northwest Command Post, were given intensive study by the underwater excavators under Jameson's direction; adjacent stretches on either side were plotted to the extent that they could be measured by swimmers without any clearing (Jameson 1969, 325).

The towers were assigned numbers on the plan published in 1978 (note 7 above), beginning at the northwest angle and running counter-clockwise (Fig. 18). Those numbers are retained to avoid confusion; inevitably, further investigation may result in additions or deletions to the final list of towers.

The Classical Defenses (Fig. 19)

The wall trace is roughly 1,900 m long, enclosing an area measuring some 700 m between the eastern and western extremities and a maximum of 380 m from north to south, or about 18.2 hectares. Beginning at the northwest angle, which is no longer visible, the wall runs directly uphill and almost due south to a small knoll overlooking the entrance channel of the harbor.[10] From there it takes a meandering course along the ridge in a generally southern direction to a second high point, where it turns in a wide sweep to run eastward to the acropolis. This section, designated the West Wall, is entirely unexcavated. The short stretches that survive have generally made themselves useful as field boundaries. Where both wythes exist, they have retained enough of the ancient fill to support sturdy growths of holly oak, often making it difficult to follow the trace visually and allowing only intermittent measurements to locate the position of the blocks. The line appears to consist of relatively short straight sections, probably interrupted by the West Gate and punctuated at roughly even distances by square towers **1** to **4**. Very likely there was another tower (Tower **18A**) at the northwest end of the West Wall, where it met the Northwest Wall at the shore; the southwest section terminated against Tower **5** at the acropolis.

The line of the West Wall is usually just at the high point of the terrain.[11] Lawrence points out that the object of fortification design in the Classical period was "to deny the enemy all positions that might enable them to overlook the wall or even come level with the foot." The latter consideration was principally for defense against siege engines, at Halieis doubtless primarily battering rams. He also notes that the circuit laid out on this principle might be a relatively large enclosure "however small a fraction of the area would be occupied by buildings" (Lawrence 1979, 117), although the actual length of the circuit was of necessity limited by the manpower available

[7] The general topographic survey drawing of all natural features, as well as blocks and structures ancient and modern, begun by Cooper in 1972, forms the basis for the plan by Boyd that was published as Boyd and Rudolph 1978, pl. 87. (Note that the 20-meter contour line on the knoll at Tower **1** has been omitted; cf. Jameson 1969, 316, fig. 2.)

[8] The results of their work was published in a plan drawn by Richard S. Pratt and Helen Pratt, architects (Ervin 1967). For an account of the basic underwater survey of the submerged walls, see Jameson 1969, 325.

[9] Julian and Eunice Whittlesey produced an invaluable series of photographs taken with a camera suspended from a balloon (Jameson 1969, 332–33, pls. 86–91, a). Although seaweed patterns are sometimes misleading, the photographs provided a rapid method of preliminary surveying, often revealing information not apparent to swimmers at close range. The high altitude photographs are particularly useful in showing the positions of the various sections in relation to each other and to the present shoreline. The large number of overlapping exposures greatly reduced the potential problem of distortion at the edges of the view. Photographs repeated over the course of the project permitted comparison studies of parts that were cleared and then resilted by water currents, especially a problem at shallow depth. A uniform distortion of rectangles to parallelograms evident in the Frost-Owen survey sketches, which resulted from the impossibility of an overall view for the swimmer, was easily corrected from the photographs. Some additional work was done by Cooper and Boyd in 1975.

Photographs over the land areas were taken with a camera suspended from a balloon or from an airfoil. They were more helpful in recording the terrain than they were the walls, which are often obscured by vegetation overlying them or by the shadows of trees. Here also, however, the relationship of different parts of the site can be easily appreciated, as well as the outcroppings of bedrock with small "scarps" that mark the natural terracing of the slopes.

[10] The exact line of the wall at the far northwest is difficult to determine. The general area was surveyed in 1959, 1970, and 1972, and sections have been given more concentrated study, but it is not easy to reconcile the exact position of the few remaining traces as shown on the resulting plans.

[11] "A wall overlooking a slope usually keeps somewhat below the crest, to which it thus barred access" (Lawrence 1979, 117). The Halieis wallbuilders chose to use the broad flat top of the ridge rather than to move the line west another twenty or thirty meters to any appreciable outward slope.

for its defense, especially in small towns like Halieis. The topographical survey shows fragments of walls, most likely of houses, scattered over the valley on the west side of the city, which suggests that at least at some period most of the enceinte was occupied by structures however sparsely. Without excavation it is not possible to say whether they are contemporary with each other or with the fortifications, or even whether some walls may not represent reuse of blocks for terracing.

There are scanty remains that suggest that the acropolis once had its own enclosure. The segment that runs along the south side, coinciding with the city wall, is the only part to have been excavated. These fortifications are described and discussed in Williams n.d. The great round tower (Tower **6**) is at the highest point on the circuit. From there, the trace continues northeastward to the Industrial Terrace, the line bending inward to follow the ridge. At the angle, there is also a low rock scarp dividing the acropolis section of the wall from that of the Industrial Terrace below, which runs southeastward to Tower **7**. This round tower at the east end of the Terrace marks the junction with the Southeast Wall.

Halfway down the first terrace northeast of Tower **7** all surface remains disappear; the wall presumably continued down the slope to the top of the scarp some seven meters lower than the tower (at about the 25-meter contour). There is a steep drop of about four meters, then bedrock ledges descend abruptly another four meters to the top of the next sloping terrace. There is no sign of angle or jog, but when the wall appears again (at the 18-meter contour)[12] the direction has changed; the trace has swung in, running slightly more to the north. On this line the trace again continues straight, gradually converging with the low scarp that edges the valley to the southeast, and extending to the East Tower (Tower **10**) with only minor irregularities of line.

Some excavating was done in the upper stretch (Upper Southeast Wall) where the ground falls away more steeply. In the lower, more level part (Lower Southeast Wall), several trenches were sunk, especially near the East Tower. The connection between the two sections was not clear, however, until the discovery of the Southeast Gate and Tower **9** in 1972 helped to account for an offset in the trace. In the Upper Southeast Wall there may

have been a Tower **8** between Towers **7** and **9**.[13] Midway between Towers **9** and **10** in the Lower Southeast Wall is the East Gate.

From the East Tower the trace runs northwest in a virtually straight line to the Hermion Gate beside the Late Roman / Early Byzantine bath that overlies Tower **11**; there is very little change in level. There has been some excavation at the Northeast Command Post adjacent to the midpoint of this Northeast Wall; the northwestern part of it is under water. Three bastions make equal divisions of the stretch, which is conspicuous for its regularity.

The North Wall runs west from Tower **11** to Tower **14**, the two straight segments forming a slightly re-entrant angle; the two intervening towers are somewhat closer to each other than to those at either end. This section has been followed by divers and on the aerial photographs; it is the final trace for this part of the fortification. The remains of the Late Roman / Early Byzantine bath now hide the connection of this curtain to the square tower behind Tower **11** at the Hermion Gate. It is probable, however, that an earlier trace ran southwest from Tower **11** paralleling Street 8. On the aerial photographs a continuous line of blocks can be seen extending southwestward toward the shore with a number of scattered blocks to its southeast (see below, 53).

The final trace of the fortifications on the north side of the city makes a deep jog to the south at the Harbor Gate, which lies between Towers **14** and **15**. The Northwest Wall, which like the North Wall is entirely submerged, then continues irregularly northwestward past the Northwest Command Post; its course presumably reflects the ancient shore line. Towers **16**, **17**, and **18** are spaced somewhat unequally along it.

The main trace thus varies from the meandering line of the West Wall to the geometric regularity of the Northeast Wall. The former, in what may be termed a "natural" trace, follows the ridges but makes no apparent attempt at a design according to the theories of siegecraft. The latter, where neither shoreline nor rise of ground could have any influence, is clearly a "planned" trace but of the most basic sort. In general, the impression is that of a simple enclosure of space, determined largely by convenience. The Northwest Wall in general follows the current and presumably also the ancient shoreline, but the

---

[12] In Trench H4-5 at the upper end of the Chambered Curtain.
[13] The peculiarities of the Upper Southeast Wall (Chambered

Curtain), which seems to have consisted of rooms, and the question of whether Tower **8** rose above the walkway are discussed below.

projection of its towers was probably influenced by defensive sight lines. The motivation for the design of the North Wall is more difficult to analyze because the line of the ancient shore over this stretch is unknown. In its final form, this section must have been determined by the area it enclosed.

The Middle Wall runs northward from the acropolis; scattered blocks suggest that there may have been two different lines for the upper part of the course. The sections identified by Cooper and Boyd (the western trace) proceed directly from Tower **5** and run along the west side of the acropolis (Boyd and Rudolph 1978, pl. 87). With three irregular offsets to the east that each allowed an overview of the next downhill section, the wall connects with the principal offset at Tower **19**. This defense line for the acropolis would run at the bottom of its west scarp rather than the top. On the north side of the acropolis, where the abrupt drop is marked by conglomerate boulders, a block is oriented north–south in a position where it could only have been of use for a fortification wall. Proceeding northward down the slope, a pair of parallel walls appears to continue this (eastern) trace. Other blocks along this line would bring it to meet the Cooper-Boyd line at the offset shown on the survey at the 30-meter contour. The western line would include somewhat more ground in the circuit, which presumably enclosed the eastern part of the city, while the more eastern trace would run directly down the contours spreading to the north of the acropolis.

The trace of the Middle Wall below the modern road has not been identified, nor has any connection to the Northwest Wall. A straight run to the shore from Tower **19** would end at Tower **15**, where walls just east of the tower suggest a massive, unexplained construction. A terminus more to the west to include the Northwest Command Post would require a reverse offset, perhaps at a gate in the built-up area, or at least an outward bend to the northwest. A pair of parallel blocks shown on the level ground near the shore line on the survey lie to the west of the direct line and are probably too far apart to belong to the double-wall base; they are more likely to define a narrow street or alley. While a connection to the earlier trace of the North Wall is another possibility, there is no present evidence to support it. The likelihood of a continuation of the Middle Wall as far as the shore and various related problems are discussed in the final chapter.

The positions of four gates are known and have already been mentioned: the Southeast Gate, the East Gate, the Hermion Gate beside the Late Roman/Early Byzantine bath, and the Harbor Gate between Tower **14** and Tower **15**. In addition, there was a small gate by Tower **16** (Fig. 8) in the Northeast Wall and possibly a postern beside Tower **13** (Fig. 7) in the North Wall. Other gates may be restored on slim evidence backed by some probability, notably in the West Wall, Middle Wall, and on the Industrial Terrace. The actual position of the gates in the trace, in virtually every case where the remains can be identified, was clearly determined by the streets inside and the roads outside the town;[14] consequently this factor must be considered in evaluating the likelihood of any additional openings in the fortification walls. All these questions are treated in connection with the discussion of gates (see below, chapter 3).

The Archaic Defenses (Fig. 32)

The fortification walls now visible, whose course has been described above, belong to the Classical period. Excavations at several points, however, revealed traces of earlier defenses. On the acropolis the early mud-brick walls were thrown down in a comprehensive destruction at the beginning of the 6th century, whole sections of brick falling together. The first masonry walls were constructed on top of the rampart created from the resulting debris.[15] A scrap of evidence for pre-Classical fortifications may have been found in a small trench (Trench 910/150) opened in 1972 on the Industrial Terrace (Fig. 22). Beneath the foundations of the Classical wall blocks was a layer of light tan clay, covering dark mud brick like that on the acropolis. The earliest associated sherds were Geometric in date; others appeared to be 6th century or earlier, in line with the early 6th-century destruction of the acropolis.[16] The

---

[14] The postern beside Tower **13** is an exception, since the position of any streets in this area is unknown.

[15] Lawrence's reference (1979, 34) to "the base of a mudbrick wall with a hollow tower, destroyed before 600," revealed in excavations at Halieis, resulted from some misunderstanding. He referred later (380) to the Phase 5 tower, which he dated to the 5th century, but it was not hollow at ground level (see Williams n.d.).

[16] Geometric: HP 2283, from an open vessel, has cross-hatching and parallel vertical bands; HP 2284, a body fragment, has a solid triangle surrounded by cross-hatching; HP 2282, from the lowest level, is a rim fragment offset from the body of a large vessel. Sixth century or earlier: base of East Peloponnesian black-glazed bowl; fragments apparently with a horizontal handle, similar to Samos hydriai.

implication is that the acropolis defense line included this terrace, which would have more than doubled the area available for the support of a small garrison, although still far too little to serve as a refuge for the townsfolk.

There are other indications of early defenses. In the course of the 1970 season, several trenches (M, O, and U) were opened at right angles to the double line of the city wall just southwest of the East Tower (Tower **10**) (Fig. 26). In this stretch the curtain was clearly indicated by a few blocks of conglomerate that remained above the modern surface level.[17] The wall blocks still in situ were not removed, but soundings inside, outside, and between the two wythes made it possible to reconstruct a section at this part of the curtain. The blocks were not laid on bedrock but on an embankment of red-brown earth, which sloped down on either side at a gentle angle; at the base it was about nine meters wide.[18] In Trench U the bank was a meter high under the wall blocks and extended four meters to the outside. Originally, it probably extended an equal distance on the inside, but a low wall surrounding an Archaic well[19] cut through the bank at this point. The embankment rested on a layer of fist-sized stones that had been spread over sterile red earth.[20] Bedrock was not reached by the excavators in this area; a deceptively solid layer of broken conglomerate 0.20 m thick was found in deep soundings, but it covered still more earth, also sterile.[21] Sherds of Corinthian-style pottery, perhaps 6th century, were found in the top layer of the earth rampart, inside the line of the Classical wall.[22] Outside, with the exception of Late Roman / Early Byzantine graves,[23] finds were notably scarce.

The earth bank was identified as the remains of a rampart of the Archaic period, perhaps originally faced with stakes and crowned with brush and brambles; there may even have been a wooden tower on the site of Tower **10**.[24] The profile at that time would have been somewhat steeper, since the load it was expected to carry would not have been great. Years of disuse or the requirements of the much greater load of the Classical wall could account for the low ratio of height to width that now shows in the section.

No lumps of mud brick were identified in the East Tower trenches that crossed the rampart, but it might have been difficult to do so without the contrast in color. The earliest acropolis brick is described (Wiliams n.d.) as "red, light gray, yellow and pebbly dark to black" (Phase 1) and "white to tan and pebbly black" with "red clay mortar" (Phase 2). The sterile red earth of the East Tower rampart was taken to be the same as that excavated by the barrowload in Trench A, which ran across the level field a short distance to the east. It could have come from that handy source but been used in the form of a wall of bricks or pisé, only to dissolve in the rain when it was abandoned, perhaps even without being overthrown. The significant difference between the two sites, however, is in the layer of cobbles that extended the width of the earth mound in the East Tower Area, indicating that the original form was a deliberately constructed, wide-based rampart rather than a wall.

To the north of these trenches, more red earth containing Archaic sherds was found outside the southeast face of Tower **10**. Also in 1970, Trench I5-1 was opened southwest of the East Gate at a point where blocks of the Classical wall were exposed on the surface. The original intention was to examine that wall, but in consideration of the rampart at the East Tower, the trench was carried deeper to look for signs of an earlier defense. Although a small pocket of dark earth indicated

---

[17] See below for the description of the Classical curtain. Phillip Betancourt, who supervised Trench U, was particularly helpful in discussing his findings.

[18] Lawrence (1979, 162) commented that loose material heaped in a bank was probably not used except where timber was unavailable and that it would need to be "immensely thick at the base" if it were to be topped with a walkway or parapet.

[19] Trench P, SE, well, basket 21. The pottery included HP 1469, a chytra dated ca. 500; HP 1470, a plain-ware jug dated to the mid-6th century; HP 785, the rim of an early Archaic Argive(?) krater; HP 787 and HP 806, fragments of a hydria dated ca. 800–725; HP 807, a pyxis dated from the late 8th to the early 7th century (Rudolph 1991, 177–83); HP 880, a Late Geometric Argive skyphos-krater fragment; and HP 994, an Attic black-glazed cup fragment, ca. 525–500.

[20] Other fragments of early Archaic pottery were found in Trench

P adjacent to the well: e.g., HP 826, a fragment of an Argive or Lakonian fine-ware stand with a hatched meander, possibly 9th or 8th century.

[21] The stone layer appeared in Trenches R, T, P, and U at levels below that to which Trenches O and N were carried (approximately 0.83 masl) ca. 0.27 masl in Trench T.

[22] Pass 6: two painted Corinthian sherds, one incised (6th?), and HP 798, a neck fragment from a 7th-century krater.

[23] See Rudolph 1979, 294–324.

[24] Defenses of this sort were used for temporary military camps in the 5th century (Lawrence 1979, 160–61). Thucydides (4.90.1–3) describes the fort at Delion as protected by a bank of earth dug out of the surrounding ditch and retained with stakes; he also mentions stockades around camps in Sicily at Syracuse and Naxos, with wooden towers as required (6.64.3, 74.2). If there was a ditch at Halieis no trace has been recovered.

Archaic occupation, soil overlaid by sand and small pebbles sloped down gently to the northeast as well as the northwest, and no indication of a rampart or earlier wall was identified.[25]

Trench H4-5 (Fig. 12) was opened in 1970 to investigate the city wall farther up the hillside to the south, below the scarp (about the 25-meter contour) in the upper section of the Southeast Wall (NB 112, 30, 33). Although the outer wythe was found (see below, 49–50), on the inner side the rubble core seemed to be bounded by fine, yellowish brown, sterile sandy clay with no trace of overlying masonry, provoking speculation on the existence of earthworks here also (see below, 76). The trench was much too limited to answer any questions on the extent or even the direction of a possible earth rampart. The relatively steep slope seems a poor location for any such construction running northeastward, and any defensive line to the northwest would be more effective above the scarp and boulder tumble just uphill.[26]

Indications reminiscent of the earth bank at the East Tower were found in 1972 in the continuing excavation of the Northeast Command Post.[27] A deep sounding inside the building went through the outer slope of a mass of red earth that rested at 0.60 mbsl on a thin layer of pebbles over more red earth.[28] The outer limit of the rampart, if that is what it is, lies about 7.50 m inside the line of the Classical curtain. Too little of the earthwork and its pebble base was recovered to determine its exact orientation, that is, whether it paralleled Avenue A or B.

In 1974, a deep cutting was made in Avenue C, about eight meters northwest of the Southeast Gate. Rudolph in his season report described a layer of pebbles over red earth "which extends about 2 meters to the north of the 4th century street line ending 1 meter short of its southern edge," or about 6 meters in width; he dated both pebble layer and earth below by pottery evidence to the 6th century (Rudolph 1973/1974, 267). Having himself observed the excavations at the Northeast Command Post and the East Tower, he likened the Avenue C findings especially to the latter and commented on the evenness of the layer and the lack of any signs of traffic. In conclusion, he suggested that all three might have been parts of an early defense system.

The trace of these early walls is based more on theory than fact. The evidence now available suggests that there was an Archaic circuit around a small settlement near the harbor and another, probably quite separate, around the acropolis and Industrial Terrace. The place of these enclaves in the history of the fortifications is discussed in the final chapter.

---

[25] HP 900, a black-glazed miniature Corinthian handleless cup, early 5th century, was found at the bottom of the Classical wall. Several obsidian blades (e.g., HS 279, HS 280, HS 339) were found just above the dark earth, which contained one Archaic sherd.

[26] HP 899A,B, Corinthian Geometric fragments, may have come from the Industrial Terrace (see below, 49, note 19).

[27] The walls were cleared in 1962 (NB 1.1, 1.2). Deeper soundings in 1972 (Trench 135/375), possibly to bedrock, reached earlier levels at 1.2–1.24 mbsl in the western corner of the building.

[28] In her final report in 1976 (NB 130/375, 38), B. A. Goldhor concluded that "a six and a half meter wide surface [of pebbles or stones] running in a northwest–southeast direction" appeared in this trench and in trenches 130/370, 135/365, and 135/375 as well, the elevations within a 20-cm range. It seemed too wide for a road but was perhaps "the foundations of the ancient sea wall" or an open public area. The surface was associated with Archaic material.

– CHAPTER THREE–

The Towers and Gates

Towers both rectilinear in plan (here called square, although they are never exactly so) and curvilinear (part or full circle, called round) occur along the Halieis circuit wall. The square towers may not all be contemporary; the round ones, on the other hand, probably do belong to the same building program. The gates for which there is any measurable evidence are all associated with towers with the exception of the East Gate. Tower **16**, which is square, is accompanied by a small gate. In their latest and now most recognizable form the main gate towers are round, but it seems probable that all had rectilinear predecessors, either towers or simple bastions. In theory the tower is subordinate to the gate, but because they are better defined and on the whole easier to comprehend, the towers take the lead here, beginning with those rectilinear in plan. Where appropriate, the discussion of any gate follows. To present the facts as directly as possible, both stages of the gates associated with the round towers are discussed together with the latter. The East Gate is discussed with the square towers with which its form has more in common. The gates that have no associated towers and the posterns come last.

The Halieis towers occur at the expected places (Fig. 19): at significant changes of direction in the trace, at intervals in long stretches between these points, and at the gates. The distances between towers are roughly 100 to 120 meters, except on the north side where some intervals are much less; Towers **12** and **13** are less than 40 meters apart. The bastions in the Northeast Wall are about 55 meters apart, and the interval between Towers **16** and **17** is only slightly more.[1]

The locations of the major gates follow the layout of the streets within the town and presumably also the roadways outside, although these cannot be so clearly demonstrated. Avenue B and Avenue C each end at a gateway in the Southeast Wall (Fig. 18). At the other end the former connects with Street 8, very likely also a major thoroughfare, at the main land gate; there the traces of the ancient roadway have been found offshore. Lawrence's observation (1979, 304) that Greek planners preferred to place gates "midway on a long, more or less straight, frontage" applies both to the East Gate and later to the Southeast Gate; his remark (1979, 303) that, if the traffic were equal on two routes, each would have a gate, describes the rationale for their coexistence.

The Square Towers and Their Gates

These towers are of two basic types: some had hollow chambers at ground level (Towers **12**, **13**, **16**, and quite possibly **17** and **18**), while others were solidly filled (Towers **2**, **5**, **10**, and **19**, and the predecessors of Towers **6**, **9**, and **11**). Those in the second group were probably all built of mud brick above a base of conglomerate orthostates, a common Greek type. The stone base followed the outline of the tower; any projection outward or,

[1] Lawrence gave the length of a bowshot as 30–35 m, somewhat less for the bolt-projectors used in the 4th century (1979, 381), but Martin (1947/1948, 99, note 1) put the average range of an arrow at 75–80 m. Winter (per lit.) gives the effective range as probably not more than 50–55 m. The small nontorsion catapults that became common before the middle of the 4th century are given a range of 200–300 m by Ober (1987, 570).

For the purposes of this volume, towers are considered to have had appreciable projection, whether inside the curtain or out, on the order of 2.50–5.00 m. After the earliest period, a hollow story at the walkway level sheltered sentries and defenders, who may have used the roof as a fighting platform. Bastions, on the other hand, projected only the minimum amount. They were designed to augment the fighting area at walkway level, whether at the East and Southeast Gates or along the Northeast Wall. Whatever shelter was provided may have been only of wood and reeds above the masonry parapet, since the space seems too limited for any but hand-held catapults. For the unequal projection of the towers in the Northwest Wall, see below, 32.

less often, inward interrupted the wythe of the curtain.[2] In its earliest form, such a tower rose no higher than the curtain, any tactical advantage being derived from its projection. If the walkway passed behind the tower (on the side toward the town), as at Towers **2–4**, **12**, and **13**, a structure on the upper level need not have interrupted it.[3] Two-story towers, with a chamber at the upper level, were probably the general rule in the 5th century, owing to the obvious advantages in protecting men and equipment, as well as the value of the added height of the roof as a vantage point.[4] The access would have been from the walkway, often reached from a stair located near the tower; hollow towers with ground-floor access were a later, largely 4th-century development.[5] There is no evidence at Halieis as to whether any of the towers were continued above the walkway, either in mud brick or some sort of half-timbered construction, but the use of such an upper story was common practice by the 5th century (Winter 1971, 153–54). Whether the walls of the hollow towers were carried at least as far as the walkway in stone cannot be demonstrated; the level top of the stone base course in Towers **12** and **13** and the lack of any masonry tumble in their vicinity suggest that the upper walls were of mud brick.

*Tower **1*** (Fig. 1)

Southward from the shore of the harbor at the northwest corner of the trace, there is a small knob at the top of the first steep rise, now largely bald bedrock at the edges but crowned with a few shrubs and pine trees. The commanding position overlooking the harbor entrance, as well as the moderate change in the direction of the trace at this point, suggests a logical place for a tower. The Admiralty chart (Pl. 1), which is difficult to interpret in detail, seems to show a rectangular tower, or even a gate, projecting outward.[6] The

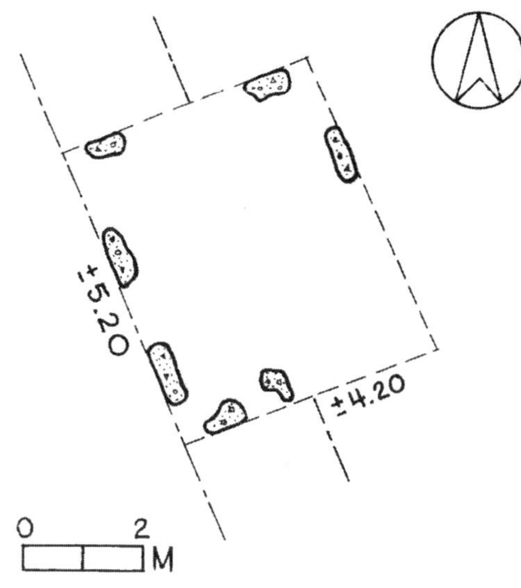

*Fig. 1. Tower **1***

existing remains, on the other hand, indicate a projection on the inside of the wall just south of the angle. The evidence consists of some conglomerate blocks, very much eroded, which are scattered about the crown of the knob, enclosing an area considerably smaller than the bedrock outcropping (see below, 46, note 4). Two of these blocks appear to be in situ and form a straight line on the southwest, the same line that is continued southeastward as the wall trace. Two other blocks probably mark the return on the southeast, and a northern corner can be made out, but the remainder is little more than rubble. It seems clear, however, that a small square tower, just over five meters wide and projecting northeastward (inward) for somewhat less than five meters, once occupied this spot.[7] The core was probably solid, of rubble and earth. The natural

---

[2] This economical system that used the minimum of cut-stone blocks applied also to bastions and sometimes to wall access.

[3] Thucydides (3.22) made a point of the towers in the siege wall around Plataiai, which went from face to face so that the guards walked through them.

[4] Winter 1971, 152–53. Adam (1982, 48) pointed out that the hollow ground floor made it possible to defend the area close to the foot of the wall from arrow slits, but filled towers were used down to the Roman period, possibly because they were less vulnerable to battering rams as well as simpler to construct.

[5] Winter 1971: towers hollow at ground level were built at Mantinea (240; time of Epaminondas) and Gyphtokastro (162, note 44; last third of 4th century) but were unusual before the Hellenistic period; cf. Lawrence 1979, 223. Thucydides (2.18)

described the refugees in 431 taking shelter in the "towers of the walls," which Winter (1971, 162) interprets as perhaps the earliest instance of chambers at ground level. The southeast-angle tower at Phyle, variously dated from the end of the 5th (Winter 1971, 139) to the middle of the 4th century (Lawrence 1979, 175), is sometimes considered to be a special case because the steeply sloping terrain required a story of solid masonry below the hollow chamber at the level of the courtyard.

[6] For the oval enclosure also shown in this area on the Admiralty chart, see below, 43.

[7] NB 616, 20 records the outer face of the wall as "continuous as far as dump [of road scrapings] against knoll" and places the remains of the tower inside that line.

height of the knob may have made a curtain-height tower of four or five meters sufficient, but the practical advantages of an enclosed structure at walkway level make a good argument for a second story, an argument strengthened by the need for height where there was no outward projection. The walls of the tower, like the curtain, were surely mud brick, although a structure above the walkway level may have been of wood or half-timber, its roof providing a lookout if not a fighting platform.

A tower contained wholly within the trace is unusual and contradicts the normal purpose of towers in fortification systems.[8] This would be, of course, to command a view of the outer face of the curtain and to defend it with flanking fire, as well as to provide a position of the greater strength resulting from more massive construction and perhaps greater height than the curtain. The predecessor of Tower **6** on the acropolis appears to have had no outward projection, and the structure designated Tower **8** very little.[9] Protected by the curtain rather than the reverse, they may have had the important primary function of watch posts, but they would also have provided fighting platforms.

Tower **2** *(Fig. 2; Pl. 2b)*

Southeastward 120 m along the trace are the remains of a rectangular tower, roughly 5.60 m wide and projecting 3.25 m outside the wall. The location on the flat-topped ridge is at the head of a wide vale dropping down to the rocky shore (Fig. 17). It has no direct relation to the hypothetical West Gate, about 20 meters to the south, but would have overlooked it. The projection of the tower is not at right angles to the curtain either north or south of it. Its front wall seems to face more directly down the slope, the south wall toward the gate.[10] The outer wythe of the curtain appears to be bonded into the north side of the tower. The inner wythe here is missing; Williams recorded "smoothed bed-rock" just north of the tower

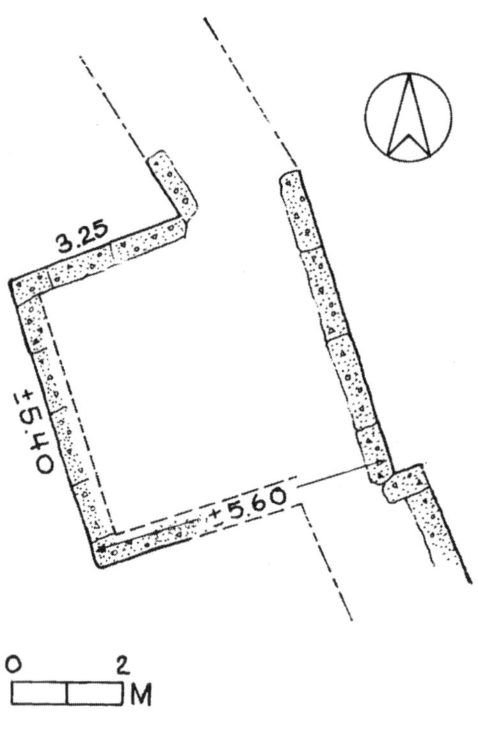

Fig. 2. Tower **2**

corner, where the wall block would have been.[11] He also noted that the remains of the rubble fill in the tower appeared continuous with that of the wall. The inner wythe of the curtain proceeding southward is offset inward (eastward) by 0.50 m. The outer wythe and the adjoining part of the south wall of the tower are missing; there may have been continuous fill on this side as well. The northwest corner is well preserved and slightly rounded, with no sign of drafting. The blocks, 0.45–0.50 m wide, are well fitted with approximately vertical joints; where they could be measured on the lower west side, they are about 0.70 m high.[12]

---

[8] Lawrence (1979, 380) described inward-projecting towers as "an alternative setting, rare after the fifth century (when it occurs at Halieis on flat ground)." He was presumably referring to the Phase 5 tower on the acropolis, where the ground outside the circuit wall is the broad, relatively flat top of a ridge that declines gently to the south. This square tower is now dated 410–390 by Williams (n.d.). Lawrence interpreted an increase in the wall thickness of the stockaded camp at Helicon as "probably . . . a solid tower of inward projection" (1979, 163).

[9] See below, 24. It is possible that the superstructure in these cases, above the level of the curtain, was designed for height

rather than strength and was of a less substantial nature, such as the "half-timber" work discussed by Winter (1971, 153–154).

[10] For a discussion of the shapes and positions of rectilinear towers, see Winter 1971, 198–200; Winter credited the engineers of the 4th century and Hellenistic Period with the development of more sophisticated designs and their practical application.

[11] NB 22, 105. The plan (Fig. 2) is based on this sketch with some additions.

[12] Detailed examination of the blocks even on the outer side would have required removal of some of the soil and dense overgrowth; the existence of a socle is therefore undetermined.

Tower 3 (Fig. 3; Pls. 3b, c)

As the trace runs southward, following the ridge and climbing steeply to the next terrace, it shifts again from just west to just east of south. Tower **3** lies immediately beyond the angle, roughly 100 m along the wall from Tower **2**. Like Tower **2** it is not aligned with either of the adjacent sections of curtain but faces southwest toward the mouth of the channel into the harbor (Fig. 17). The north corner was exposed by a ditch for an irrigation pipe; the first block of the northwest wall can be seen bonded into the curtain. At the west corner, natural erosion has exposed the angle block; its top was dressed back 0.06–0.08 m on both faces for 0.44 m to define the corner in a manner recalling the more sophisticated drafted corners of the East Gate and the East Tower (Tower **10**). The full height of the blocks on the southwest side could not be learned without excavation, but especially in view of the fact that they lie below the level of the nearby blocks of the curtain, they have the appearance of a socle course at the low point, carrying a course of orthostates above it.[13] The overlap of the blocks at the north corner indicates that the tower and the first block of the curtain to the north are contemporary. The block that bridges the angle between the curtain and the tower is about ten centimeters higher than those on either side. Between this corner and the next section of curtain to the southeast, there is a 20-meter gap where the blocks of both wythes are missing.[14]

Tower 4 (Figs. 18, 19; Pls. 4a, b)

A large knoll defined by the 35-meter contour marks both the high point of the West Wall and the southwestern extreme of the city enclosure.[15] Outcroppings of conglomerate and tumbled boulders ring the steep edge. The position, a little over 100 meters in a straight line from Tower **3**, is an important one, providing the best view of the outer end of the long channel leading to the harbor (Fig. 17). It would seem an excellent site for another tower, but despite

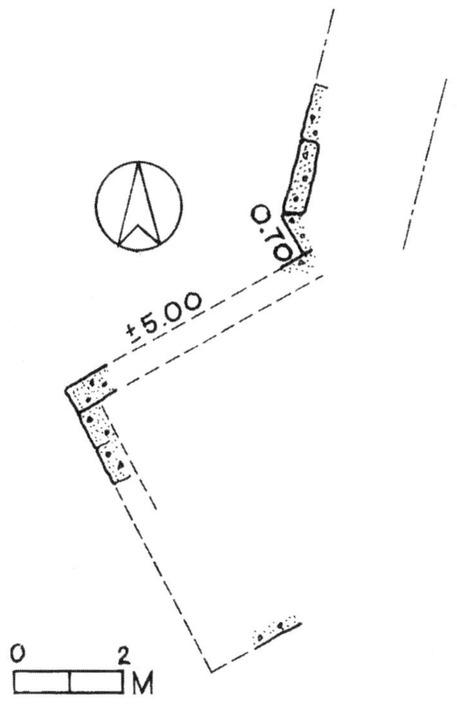

Fig. 3. Tower 3

repeated visits, the ground whether fallow or plowed had failed to reveal to me any trace of one. Cooper, however, recorded on his general topographical survey in 1974 a trace of the south corner of Tower **4**.[16] The tower is located approximately where one would expect to find it and appears to have projected seven meters or more from the curtain; there is no evidence for the width.[17] This is considerably more than that at any of the other towers, and the connection to the curtain is unknown. The importance of the position might explain the unusual projection, but it places the front farther down the slope where a higher foundation would be necessary, and the stretch of curtain

---

[13] Compare the stepped socle of Tower **6** (Pl. 5b).

[14] The dashed line indicating the south corner in Figure 3 is based on a dashed line on Cooper's survey plan. I cannot confirm any indication of the southeast side of the tower, but it was presumably approximately as shown.

[15] Note that the contour line surrounding this knoll has been incorrectly labeled "40" rather than "35" on McAllister 1972, ill. 3

and has been omitted entirely on Boyd and Rudolph 1978, pl. 87.

[16] The outline of the tower is shown on Boyd and Rudolph 1978, pl. 87.

[17] As Cooper recorded the corner, the tower is set facing somewhat more to the south than the face of the curtain behind it, so that the projection would be greater on the northwest side than on the southeast.

to the northwest commanded by the longer side of the tower is a relatively short 24 m.[18]

Tower 5 and Its Gate (Figs. 18, 19)

Tower **5** is located at the southwest corner of the acropolis defenses and roughly 120 meters from Tower **4**; it now appears to be entirely within the circuit wall.[19] It was probably associated with a gate controlling the roadway on the west side that climbed steeply to the summit (see Williams n.d.); any remains of the gate would lie just west of the acropolis excavation area. The arrangement would be the standard one with the tower on the right of the approaching attacker. The position of the south face is not known, but it is a reasonable assumption that it was flush with the end of the West Wall, if it did not project beyond it. Restored on this basis, the tower would measure roughly eight meters on the west face or approximately eight meters square, about the same size as Tower **10**.

The Phase 5 Tower (Fig. 21; Pl. 5a)

The great square tower on the acropolis that preceded Tower **6** was built against the interior face of the existing fortification wall and so was entirely inside it. The details of its construction and the circumstances that may have dictated this unusual arrangement will be discussed in Williams n.d. Suffice it to say here that the orthostates of its base, in trapezoidal style with stackwork, were set on poros plinths. The fill of the core was found level with the top of the base. There is no indication that this tower was ever associated with a gate; there would have been no particular reason to have one at this location where it would only have provided a weak point in the acropolis circuit.

Tower 7 (Fig. 9)

Whether a square tower, more than 120 meters from the one on the acropolis, preceded round

Tower **7** at the east end of the Industrial Terrace has not been determined. The round tower was set directly on bedrock that is now barely covered, and the excavations that exposed the houses inside the circuit did not extend this far. North of the tower are blocks that show above the current surface, some apparently in line with the inner face of the curtain, but another line about a meter farther north and running a little less south of east has yet to be interpreted. It may be the remains of an earlier form of the tower or of some access, stair or ramp, to the walkway. The position is certainly one where a tower would be expected, immediately overlooking the valley to the east and marking the angle at the southern end of the southeast section of the trace (Fig. 19).

Tower 8 (Fig. 23)

The upper part of the Southeast Wall is exceptional in that for most of its length it apparently consisted of hollow chambers (the Chambered Curtain) rather than the usual solid curtain. Midway in this stretch, the largest of these rooms projects 1.04 m beyond the rest on the outer side of the fortifications and was identified as Tower **8** on Boyd's plan (Boyd and Rudolph 1978, pl. 87); it would have measured about 8.30 m deep and 8.70 m parallel to the trace.[20] The inner façade is continuous with those of the other rooms, all of which run beside a hard-packed road surface separating them from a group of houses. The small projection is even less than the 2.20 m of the bastions in the Northeast Wall (below, 52, 64); it would seem to be merely an architectural feature, too little to serve the practical purpose of controlling the face of the curtain. If at an earlier stage the curtain was of the usual double-wythe form, 2.50 m to 3.00 m wide, the line of the inner wythe remaining the same, such a tower would project 5.00 m like those in the West Wall. The trenches sunk in 1970, however, provided no evidence for such a possibility.

A tower at this point, together with Tower **9**, would have divided the Southeast Wall in

---

[18] Tower **4** might have been about the same size as Towers **1** to **3** but thrust out from the curtain like those in the Northwest Wall. Alternatively, the tower might have been larger (cf. Tower **10** at 8.08 × 8.25 m), but if it was directly connected to the curtain, it would have been the largest of all the square towers except possibly Tower **11**. It is also possible that the block is not in fact in situ but has shifted downhill. Optimistically, one might hope that clearing away a few centimeters of the open field here, at the boundary of the archaeological zone, would answer some

of these questions.

[19] The line of the west and north faces as shown on Figure 18 is based on Cooper's survey working plan. When I looked for these remains in October 1980, they were so heavily overgrown with holly oak that I could only confirm that there was a pile of masonry there.

[20] With these dimensions, it would have surpassed Tower **10** in size. For an alternative interpretation see the discussion of the Chambered Curtain, below, 64–65.

thirds, each stretch 100 to 120 meters long. Outside the large room, there was a layer of debris "solidly packed, with numerous Corinthian-style roof-tile fragments" (NB 112, 8). Two tower-tile fragments found inside in one corner (below, 65) might have come from the curtain.

The Predecessor to Tower 9 (Fig. 25; Pls. 7b, 8a, b)

Tower **9** was preceded by a rectangular structure on the northeast side (the right and unshielded side of an attacker) of the Southeast Gate, a bastion in form rather than a full tower. It was 7.20 m wide but projected only a little over two meters from the face of the curtain.[21] Constructed of large conglomerate orthostates 0.60 m high with roughly dressed faces on the exterior, it was bonded to the curtain at the northeast end; there are small uncut filler stones of conglomerate and limestone. This course rests on an irregularly projecting base of large unfinished conglomerate blocks with at least one small filler. Together the two courses form a wallbase just over a meter high that rests on sterile red earth. The interior of the bastion is filled with large untrimmed blocks of conglomerate and earth, while the wall at the same level is packed with earth and rubble. The line of stretchers for the base of the outer side of the curtain is interrupted for the length of the bastion. Behind the southern half of the bastion and extending at least a meter farther to the southwest, large blocks outline a trapezoidal base that terminates the curtain and projects about a half meter on the town side; the structure formed the northeast side of the gate.

On the opposite side of the gateway, the lowest course of masonry projects outward at least as far as on the northeast and may have carried a similar bastion, but the presence of the modern road has made it impossible to determine its full extent. Since the form of the gate apparent today is the one modified to include the round tower, they are discussed together below.

The East Gate (Fig. 4; Pl. 11c)

The East Gate lies about midway between the Southeast Gate, at Tower **9**, and Tower **10**. It is the only one of the principal gates (that is, those wide enough for carts), for which measurable remains are known, that is not associated with a full tower. Inside the city wall, Avenue B made a direct connection with the Hermion Gate (Fig. 18). Outside, perhaps joined by the road from the Southeast Gate, the continuation of the city street passed the Demeter sanctuary and the necropolis on the way to the south shore of the promontory, a distance of two or three kilometers (Fig. 17). It may have been the importance of this thoroughfare that decided in favor of the East Gate when the Southeast Gate was blocked (see below, 37–38). On the other hand, it was apparently considered close enough to Towers **9** and **10** to serve without the addition of a new round tower when others were added to the system.

Surface remains are visible in a vineyard just east of and at a level somewhat lower than the modern road. The position of the passage, about 4.30 m wide, is clearly defined, although only a part of the plinth course for the side wall is left on the southwest. On the northeast, a small bastion is outlined by a continuous series of conglomerate plinth blocks. It measures 7.20 m in the direction parallel to the trace and projects about five meters from the line of the curtain, which was not cleared at this point in consideration for the vineyard. The bastion has a further extension about 2.40 m square at the outer end of the passage. The construction is all of a piece and tightly fitted, although the stretchers at the outer end are thicker. The east corner of the projection is drafted.

The projection would not have made as strong a frame for a gate as the main block, and no indication of a gate at the outer end of the passage has been recognized. If the design was not merely to give a weightier appearance to the opening, it may have been to add to the length of the passage.[22] Assuming that the gate building extended an equal distance on either side, the space at the walkway level, spanning the opening, would be slightly larger than that provided by the bastions along the Northeast Wall. It is possible that the passage was unroofed, with only a lintel beam above the gate itself at the inner end, so that the defenders could rain missiles from above. A timber walkway, easily removed in an emergency, would connect those on the wall on either side. Access to the walkway from street level was more

---

[21] Approximately 2.05 m at the southwest end, 2.20 m at the northeast.

[22] Aeneas Tacticus (39.3) recommended the use of a portcullis to trap the enemy in the gate passage or to block the passage quickly while the gate itself is being closed and barred. A barrier such as he described, however, of stout timbers reinforced with iron, when drawn up would effectively block any outward-facing openings in the limited space over the gateway.

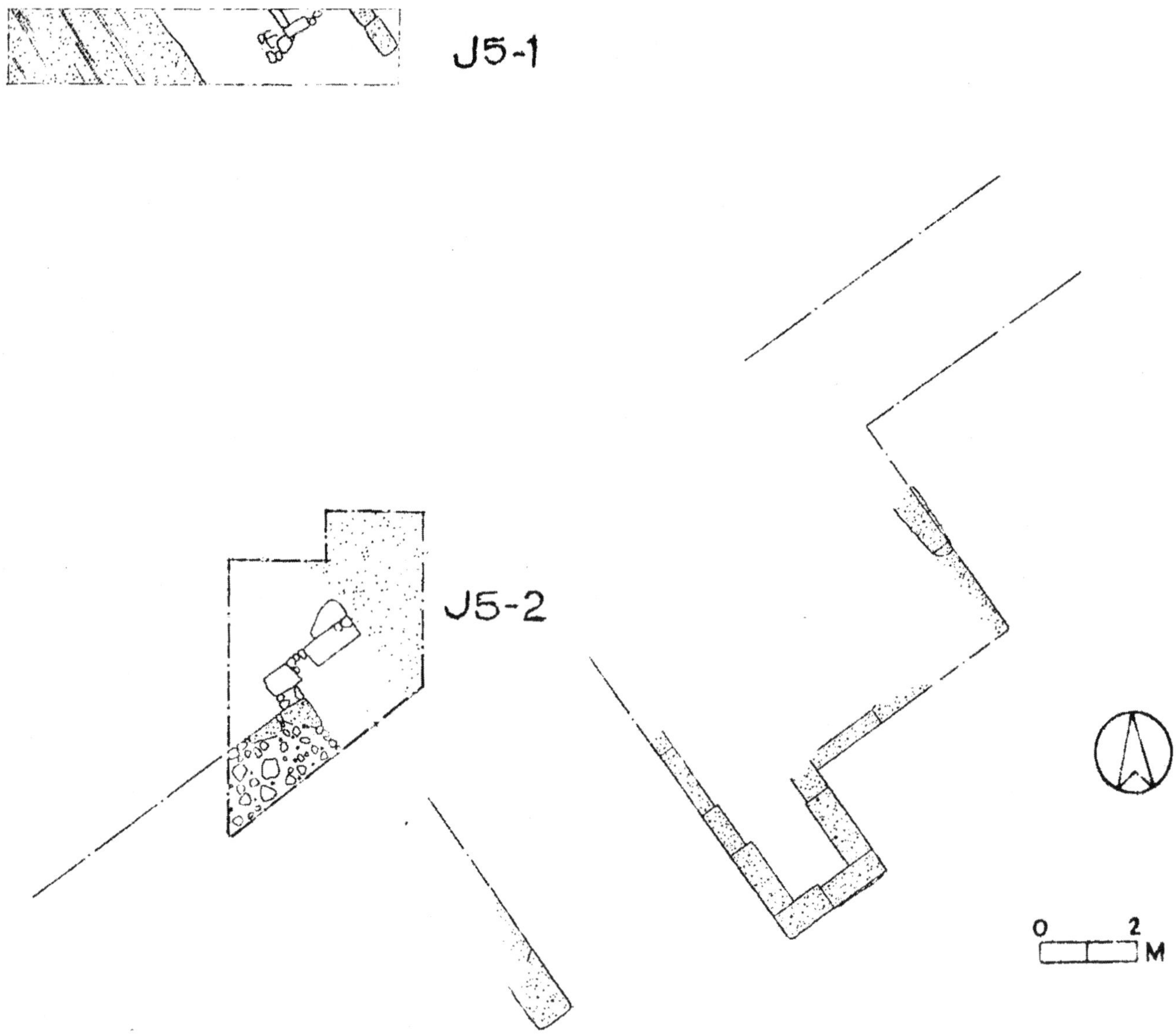

Fig. 4. East Gate with Trenches J5-1 and J5-2

likely to be at Tower **9** or **10** than at the gate, but since only a few centimeters of the street face (on the southwest side of the gateway) has been cleared, the question remains open.

Trenches J5-1 and J5-2 (the former about ten meters away on Avenue B, the latter just inside the wall) exposed wheel ruts in the ancient street that ran toward the Hermion Gate, demonstrating that the gateway was ample for wagon traffic.[23] The road metal was of pebbles and white clay, covered with broken tiles and, near the East Gate, mud brick. A bronze arrow point of the three-edged type known as Scythian was found in this fill.[24]

On the southwest side of the gateway, some blocks were uncovered that belong to the inner part of the gate structure. Two large conglomerate

[23] Section J5, Trench 1 (8.0 x 1.5 m east–west). Trench 2 was extended twice, the second time as far south as the modern retaining wall along the road would permit, resulting in an irregular shape 4.00 m wide (east–west) and a maximum of 6.50 m long over all. The ruts were more marked in Trench 1, either because the street carried traffic to and from Street 1, as well as through the gate, or because the gate passage was better maintained.

[24] HM 543. See Snodgrass 1964, 153; Sulimirski, 1954, 282ff. The Halieis example is small, with a cast socket. While most examples found in Greece have been in 5th-century contexts, sometimes directly connected with the Persians as at Marathon, a great variety of types and sizes found at Olynthos are assigned to the siege of 348 (Robinson 1941, 397–98). For arrow points dedicated on the acropolis, see Dengate n.d., chapter 8.

orthostates, paralleling the inner face of the defense wall, extended more than 2.20 m as the outer wall of a small recess beside the passageway, on which they impinged some 0.80 m. They were separated from each other and from the base blocks of the city wall by gaps filled with small stones. The wall-base blocks for the curtain end 0.85 m short of the passageway; any stones that may once have finished the open end of the core, or any stretchers from an upper course, are now missing. There is no evidence for the position of the gate itself and its frame. Since gates always opened inward, it should have been at least two meters away from the inner end of the passage, so that the open leaf would not obstruct traffic along the wall. Presumably it lies outside the trench under the modern wall along the road.

There is a striking difference between the well-cut and closely fitted blocks of the outer part of the gate and the haphazard work at the inner side of the recess, but this masonry was no doubt stuccoed over on the city side of the opening. Beside the orthostates at the level of the road metal, there was a hard floor of earth and pebbles.[25]

Embedded in the hard earth floor were two fragments of a small marble half-column base of the torus-and-cavetto profile associated with the Corinthian and Ionic orders; it belongs to the first half of the 4th century (Fig. 5).[26] Since the gate appears to be of a simple straightforward design, presumably the engaged column came from some public structure in the adjacent (unexcavated) quarter of the town.

*Tower **10*** (East Tower) (Fig. 26; Pls. 12a–c, 13a)

Commonly called the East Tower, Tower **10** is the largest of the unmodified square towers that can be conveniently measured, 8.08 m (southeast side) by about 8.25 m (northeast side).[27] The exterior

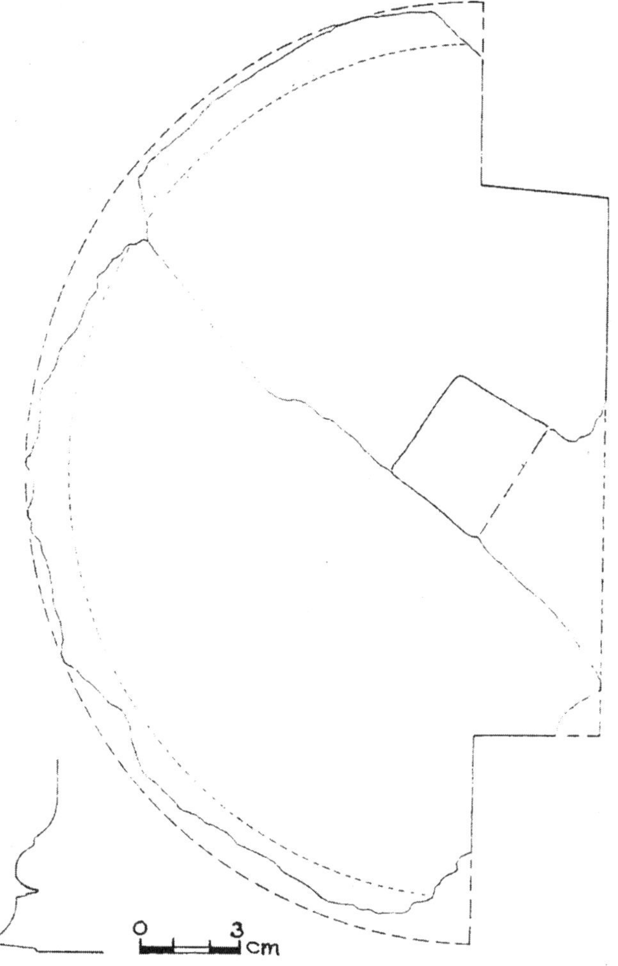

Fig. 5. Marble column base HS 275

projection is about 2.25 m from the curtain on both the northwest and southwest sides; that on the inside at the west corner is over 3.00 m. The wall base consists of massive conglomerate blocks that form the orthostate course, 0.60 m high and laid flush (that is, without setback) with a poros socle 0.25–0.35 m thick. At the north and east corners and presumably along the northeast and much of the southeast side, this plinth course rests on

---

[25] This surface is described in the trench notebook as a floor over soft, sterile red earth. Its location at the inside of the curtain should place it in the service street, which it has been assumed ran along the inside of the wall from Tower **9** to Tower **10**. If, however, Street 1 ran from the Southeast to the East Gate on the line of House 7 (see below, 78), the free space between the wall and the street might have been as much as three or four meters wide.

[26] HS 275. Ionic engaged-column base of white marble. Diam. 0.267 m, max. pres. H. 0.058 m. Two joining fragments. Half-circle with projection 0.155 m wide, 0.037 m deep at center back. Cutting ca. 0.035 m square set diagonally at center. About 0.015 m of unfluted shaft preserved, diameter ca. 0.23 m. At 8–9 times the diameter, the restored height of the column would be 1.84–2.07 m. Close to an Ionic base of stuccoed poros from Perachora (Payne 1932, 243),

placed by Shoe at the end of the 5th century (Shoe 1936, 147, pl. LXVI, 6) but also reminiscent of a group at Nemea dated no earlier than the mid-4th century. See Hill 1966, 33 and fig. 6. C. K. Williams II tells me the relieving surface on the bottom is found on examples at Corinth. It should be noted that marble is rare at Halieis; it is likely that the base was imported in finished form.

[27] It is not possible to give measurements for Towers **5** and **19** without clearing away heavy overgrowth and tumbled masonry. The Phase 5 square tower on the acropolis would have been wider (9.00 m) but not so deep (6.50 m), unless the measurement includes the fortification wall against which it was built; see Williams n.d. The square tower at the Hermion Gate, preceding round Tower **11**, appears to have been over eleven meters square. The size of Tower **4** is unknown.

compacted soil.[28] The tops of the conglomerate blocks are dressed to an even horizontal plane, but the joints on the northeast side are not vertical; the masonry style is trapezoidal. Next to the north corner block is a gap, the lower part of which is neatly filled with a small block of limestone (Pl. 13a). The rest of the gap may have been filled with another such block or with several stacked slabs in the manner of the stackwork in the Phase 5 tower on the acropolis (Pl. 5a; see Williams n.d.). The south and north corners are drafted (Pl. 13d); a few of the blocks show irregular finishing on the face, leaving a quarry-finish projection on part of the surface (Pl. 13c). The east corner is destroyed, even the plinth reduced to chalky traces in the earth.

No permit was acquired to excavate on the northwest and southwest sides, inside the circuit wall, but three blocks showing above present ground level mark the west corner. Their top surfaces are 0.80 m above the tops of the ortho-states on the outer sides of the tower; they probably represent the upper of two stretcher courses. The top surface of the block at the north corner is dressed as though to receive the first block of such a course on the northeast side. It is not possible to say how high the masonry continued. The prominent position, heavy foundation (see below), and partial course above the orthostates argue for masonry at least to the level of the walkway. No fallen blocks remain as evidence, but since the uppermost course is incomplete, it is clear that at least some blocks have been carried off.[29] The core, which in the center remains to the level of the orthostates or higher, is composed of water-worn stones and gravel with earth, rather than of mud brick.[30] Inside the face blocks on the southeast side of the tower large blocks of poros and conglomerate are visible, similar to those filling the bastion preceding Tower **9** (Pl. 7b).

A number of trenches were dug at right angles to the outer sides of the tower, in part to investigate the unexpectedly deep foundation first noted in Trench B at the south corner.[31] Those on the northeast (E, F, G) produced very little besides deteriorated mud brick and stones, except for a camp-fire pit near the north corner.[32] Many tile fragments were found toward the east corner. On the southeast side, the pottery finds increased, especially toward the south corner. In addition to more tile and small pieces of bronze, there were black-glazed sherds, some datable to the 4th century, and other pottery including Late Roman spirally grooved ware.

Trench B revealed a much deeper tower foundation than found anywhere on the site (Pl. 13b). Five courses of poros underlay the plinth course, beginning at an elevation of 1.00 mbsl at the bottom. Although the southwest side of Trench B was laid out 0.50 m from the south corner, which thus was not actually exposed, it was clear from the broken jointing of the courses that the deep foundation continued that far; in the trench the plinth block and those in the second and fourth courses below it (foundation courses 2 and 4) appeared as headers about 0.50–0.60 m wide. The bottom course (foundation course 1) consisted only of one large block at the corner, its top not horizontal, and a small one next to it to the northeast. The extra foundation courses did not appear in Trench K; Trench L, between B and K, was not carried up to the tower face. In the latter, however, there was evidence of a foundation trench with a bottom elevation of 0.14 masl, stopping no more than 3.50 m from the south corner. It appears, therefore, that foundation courses 2 and 3 stopped just northeast of Trench B, while 4 and 5 extended a meter farther. Nothing is known of the foundations on the southwest side of the tower, but they were probably supplemented at least as far as the face of the curtain, a distance of about 2.25 m.

A hard-packed white strosis was obvious in the trenches along the northeast side of the tower.[33]

---

[28] The trench supervisor for the 40-cm extension to Trench E, on the southeast face of the east corner, wrote, "In clearing the area once occupied by the corner block, we notice that the block and the next one on the SW face seem to have been set on hard-packed reddish earth which is clayey enough to have been the ruins of mud-brick" (NB 511, 71). It should be noted, however, that the large Trench A dug in the field 60 m to the east produced nothing but similar red earth, characteristic of the bottom land and perhaps a source for the mud brick in general use at the site.

[29] The East Tower is quite close to the current road entrance to the site and to the shore. Its blocks would have been visible and accessible throughout its post-Classical history. Mud brick found close to the tower might be fallen from a parapet at the walkway level.

[30] Compare the mud-brick core of Tower **6** and its predecessor on the acropolis (Williams n.d.). If the outer wall was continued up in mud brick above the height of the masonry wall base, Tower **10** might have had a mud-brick core above that point.

[31] Trenches B and E (at right angles to the southeast and northeast sides of the tower, respectively) were dug in 1968 (NB 511); the remainder in the East Tower area were dug in 1970.

[32] No floor or finds were associated with the fire pit. The hearth level (0.41 masl) was about 0.70 m below the modern surface, just below the bottom of the socle course.

[33] Robert Giegengack, consulting geologist for the Halieis excavations in 1970, pointed out that lime would be carried down through relatively loose soil until it reached a precipitation level, formed by a denser material. There is no strosis of road metal.

It began at the tower face a little above the bottom of the plinth course and sloped away rapidly. Below it the earth was soft brown or red-brown with pebbles and, in Trench B, what may have been poros working chips. The angle of the slope suggests that this was a use level, rather than a prepared roadway beside the tower, that represented the ground level contemporary with Tower **10**. The red earth found below the strosis contained Archaic pottery and may be contemporary with the earth rampart in Trench U (see above, 18). Red earth with stones, found above the white strosis in Trench B and also on the northeast side, may have come from either the curtain or the demolished tower itself.

A possible position for a gate or postern at Tower **10** would be on the southwest side, at the junction of Avenue A and Street 1, but the presence of one is not very likely.[34] The natural drainage of the town site would have reached a low point here. The drop toward the northeast in the level of firm soil is indicated by the descending courses of the curtain-wall base in Trench O (below, 51–52). The excavated areas, however, did not include that just south of the tower where there might well have been a drain through the Classical fortification wall. The distribution of pottery in the trenches near the tower suggests that habitations were limited to the inside of the trace as now preserved and that there was some similar barrier in Late Geometric or Archaic times. The greatly increased amounts of sherds along the southeast side of the tower and especially near the south corner might represent the detritus from a street drain. Furthermore, the more regular face blocks on the southeast, laid with vertical joints in contrast to those on the northeast side, and the special deep foundation at the south corner may have been constructed either originally or as a repair, made after the tower had partially collapsed, to counter a soil condition affected by drain runoff.

Several slabs of shelly limestone were found in the vicinity of Tower **10**, reused as cover slabs

for Late Roman/Early Byzantine graves.[35] Some are in the general form of coping or geison blocks (that is, the top surface slopes down to the front edge), but the only one with a profile similar to the Tower **6** coping blocks (see Williams n.d.) was found in a field about 200 m to the east.

The Predecessor of Tower 11 (Fig. 28)

The Late Roman/Early Byzantine bath,[36] the remains of which can be seen just above the surface of the water near the shore, was partially cleared in 1965 (see below, 85). Virtually nothing is known about the rectangular structure incorporated in it other than what can be made out from the aerial photographs. It appears to be a square tower that preceded round Tower **11**; the sturdy construction employed heavy stretchers, with one header on the southeast and two on the northeast to tie back into the presumably solid core. It no doubt should be considered part of the adjacent gate, which is discussed below in connection with the round tower. It seems to have been about 11.60 m square, making it the largest in the circuit (compare Tower **6** at about 9 x 6.5 m and Tower **10**, a little over 8 m square).

Towers 12 and 13 (Figs. 6, 7; Pl. 19)

The small square towers **12** and **13** defended the North Wall, which faced directly on the harbor.[37] (A small square structure east of Tower **12** is clearly an addition, probably of the Roman period when the fortifications were no longer in use; Fig. 36 and Jameson 1969, 327, fig. 6.) The towers are 5.10 m and 5.80 m wide and project 4.80 m and 4.60 m, respectively, from the outer wall face. The walls were built of conglomerate orthostates 0.50–0.60 m thick and lined by others about 0.30 m thick. These orthostates rest on a floor of polygonal blocks, also conglomerate, which in Tower **13** extend to the south face of the curtain, at a level about 2.20 m below the water's surface.[38] A large

---

[34] While there are exceptions, major gates were generally placed at the center of straight stretches of wall. The Southeast Gate takes this position on the long southeast side of the circuit and was supplemented by the East Gate, only about 50 meters from the East Tower. A postern or sally port so close to the East Gate seems unnecessary.

[35] Rudolph 1979, 297–301, Graves 1 (Trench H) and 2 (Trench J). Since the shelly limestone is easily transported, too much importance should not be attached to the places where it has been found. The location at the East Tower of a group of graves needing cover slabs is as likely to have been responsible for their presence as a first use on the East Tower itself.

[36] Jameson 1969, 339, pl. 90. Rudolph (1979, 304) put the date before the second half of the 6th century of the present era.

[37] Tower **12** was investigated by Frost and Owen in 1965, Tower **13** by Jameson's underwater teams in 1967 and 1968 (Jameson 1969, 334).

[38] At the time of these underwater investigations, official Greek datum was not established at Halieis, and all measurements were taken from the surface of the water. Jameson has since determined the Classical water level to be about 2.40 m below the present surface, or 3.25–3.45 m below Greek datum (see below, 86–87).

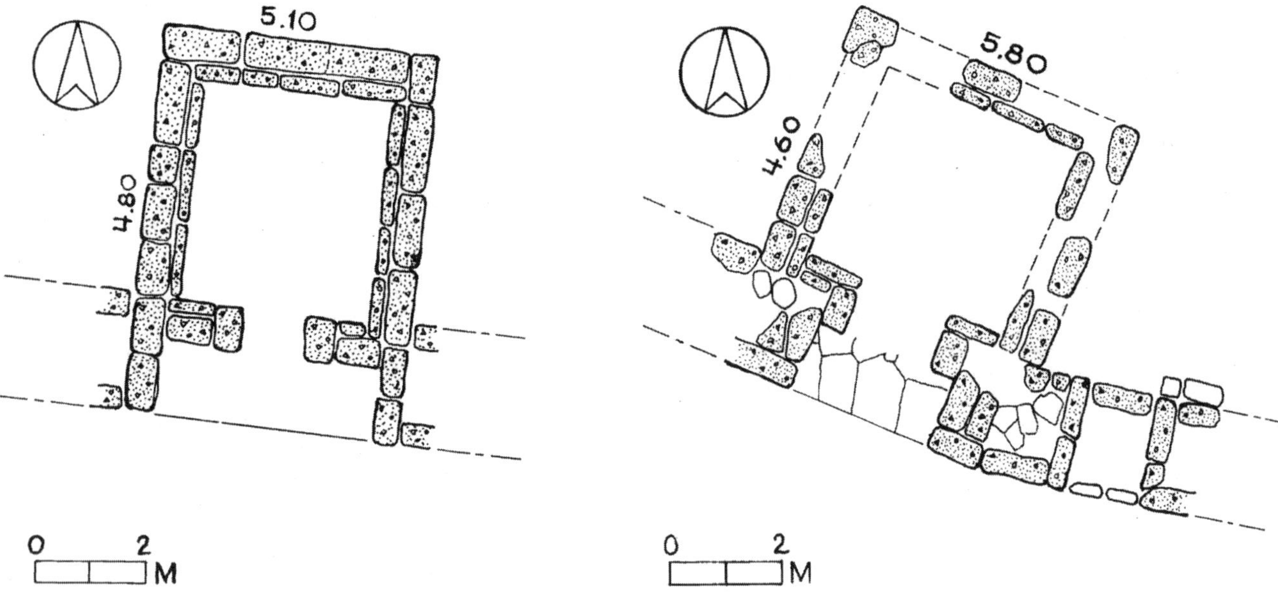

Fig. 6. Tower **12**   *Fig. 7. Tower* **13**

Corinthian tile fragment was found nearby. In each case, a door 1.20 m wide on the side toward the city gave access to the hollow ground floor, but the construction is not identical.

The inside face of the entrance wall for Tower **12**, for which the plan is well preserved, is aligned with the outside face of the adjacent curtains; the outer blocks of the side walls carry across the curtain, forming an entry recess the width of the tower chamber. The doubled orthostates of the spur walls at the back of the recess are terminated by large cross-blocks that form the door jambs. The tower is a unit completely separated from the adjacent curtains. It is hardly surprising that no evidence was found for a street or other ground outside the entrance; a structure parallel to the curtain, however, and no more than six meters to the south was recorded by the underwater team (Fig. 36). There was no basis on which to date it, but its presence may indicate the width of open land area adjacent to the curtain.

Tower **13** is not so well preserved but appears to have been constructed integrally with the curtain. The inward angle of the curtain appears on its south face, just to the east of the entrance, but it has no particular relation to the tower; immediately east of the angle is a small postern or drain (see below). On either side of the entrance the curtain continues as far as the back of the jamb block; these are set against the outer face of the narrower orthostates that line the

chamber. The entrance recess is consequently restricted to about 2.60 m. Both the outer and inner blocks of the west side wall appear to be bonded to the curtain; those on the east seem to stop at the outer face, but at least one block is missing there.

Although it differs in detail the construction of both towers indicates that the inner and outer wall blocks are contemporary. It is possible that the outer blocks were carried to the height of the walkway and that the interior was lined with mud brick above a conglomerate base course. It is more likely that the inner blocks were added to the usual single row of the filled towers augmenting the walls to carry the weight of the fighting platform, with or without an installation of light artillery, and that the full thickness of the wall was mud brick.

The polygonal blocks forming the entrance-way floor of Tower **13** stop in line with the south face of the curtain at a level about 3.00 mbsl; below the paving at this point, Jameson reported "at least some 0.40 m. of heavy gravel below which begins gray, calcareous mud" (Jameson 1969, 34). The unusual construction detail of stone paving apparently running under the wallbase may be explained as a platform foundation required by the location, where there was neither bedrock nor securely compacted soil. We do not know the distance from the water at that time; even in the sheltered bay the towers may have been subject to seasonal storms. The construction may be compared with that of round Tower **14**, but

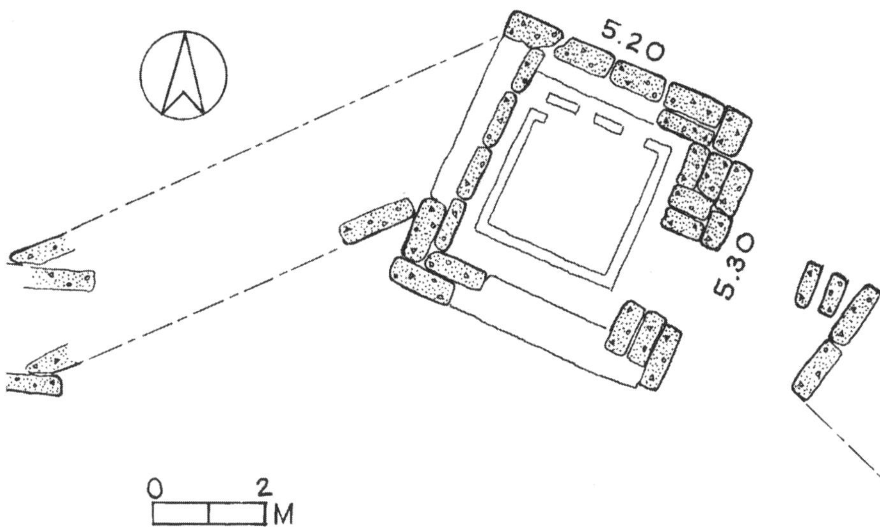

Fig. 8. Tower **16**

because these towers were hollow, the platforms were finished as floors.

The distance between the towers is the shortest in the circuit, only about 40 meters. Jameson suggests that the head of the harbor might have come just east of Tower **13**, which would have guarded the beginning of the mole running west to Tower **14.**

Tower **15** (Fig. 29)

At the west end of this section of the North Wall lies the Harbor Gate with its round towers **14** and **15.** If there was a rectangular structure preceding Tower **14,** no indication of it was found in the underwater excavations. The remains of Tower **15** are heavily covered with rubble and broken Roman pottery, washed down at the shore line. A confusion of straight walls on the landward side may include the remains of a rectangular predecessor. It is possible with close study of the aerial photograph to read a square tower there,

one side of which appears as the thinner straight wall continuing the curving one at the southeast. The doubled orthostates, thinner on the inside (west), are reminiscent of Towers **12, 13,** and **16**; a predecessor could have been about the same size, somewhat more than five meters square. It is also possible, however, that the straight section of wall at the southeast side of the round tower is an adaptation of the tower's plan to some adjoining structure.[39]

Tower **16** *and Its Gate* (Fig. 8)

Tower **16.** Known only from the aerial photographs and several underwater inspections, Tower **16** has a hollow chamber on the ground floor; it was entered at the east side from Street b (Fig. 18 and Boyd and Rudolph 1978, pl. 87), which passed out of the city to the shore through the adjacent gate.[40] The tower is approximately 5.30 m square; its double walls, reminiscent of Towers **12** and **13,** are a little under a meter thick.[41] On either side of the doorway the tower wall is reinforced on the

---

[39] It is difficult to make sense of the blocks on the east side of the tower in the aerial photograph even though they are in shallow water; they are tumbled about and in part covered by the heavy deposit of late amphora sherds. There seems, however, to be a wall or at least a foundation that runs out along the southeast side of the tower to the Projection (see below, 42).

[40] The entrance to the tower faces the end of the curtain terminating at the passageway and so is within rather than on

the inner side of the wall. It is on the correct side for a sally port, set in the right flank of the tower (facing out). Winter (1971, 240) cited the sally ports in the towers at Mantinea as examples of this design, arranged so that the shielded side of the defenders was presented foremost as they exited.

[41] The plan previously published as Jameson 1969, 326, fig. 5 was produced almost entirely from the aerial photographs, supplemented with control measurements made by divers and a sketch plan made by Owen and Frost.

outside with a third line of orthostates. The projection of the tower itself is very slight, perhaps a meter beyond the gate on the east side and half that on the west, where the curtain swings out nearly to the outer corner, but unlike Tower **8**, which also projects only a little, it is set at the apex of a sharp outward bend in the trace. A similar arrangement occurs at Tower **18**. This means that the walkway did not pass on the inner side of the tower, as it did at the small towers **2–4**, **12**, and **13**. Passage past this point could only be made through the tower, as would have been the case at the larger Tower **10** and perhaps Tower **5** and the square predecessor of Tower **11**.[42] An interior ring of narrow blocks shows clearly on the photograph and divers' drawings.[43] The central area was not tested. It is possible that the tower was built on a platform base like those suggested for Towers **12** and **13**, but that this one was left rough, to be covered by a wooden floor supported on the narrow ring blocks. A similar detail may have been used in the Northwest Command Post.

*The Gate at Tower **16**.* The smallest of the gates is just east of Tower **16**, which would have been on the attacker's right. Like all the buildings now submerged on the north side of the city, it is obscured not only by silt but by a heavy growth of weeds and sea creatures. It seems clear, however, that it was in line with Street b and that a door opened into the street at the side of the ground-floor room of the tower. Two large cross-blocks form the end of the curtain opposite this door, and two more, parallel to them and close together, probably belong to a drain at the side of the passage, leaving about 1.50 m clear. Since the curtain is terminated and the tower entrance is, in effect, within the width of the curtain, there must have been a true gate rather than a simple postern tunneled through the circuit wall.[44] The gate would have been too narrow for a cart or a well-loaded donkey and led only to the foreshore, but there may have been a strategic advantage in the ability to make a sally behind anyone attacking the Harbor Gate.

*Towers **17** and **18*** (Fig. 18)

The aerial photographs show faint indications of Tower **17**, about 70 meters from Tower **16**, and a clear outline of Tower **18**, some 80 meters beyond. Both towers are nearly engulfed by the outswing of the curtain on the east, yet project four meters or more on the west.[45] The purpose would seem to be to guard against attackers approaching from the direction of the harbor mouth, presumably by boat, and to keep watch on the curtain to the west. Tower **18** is roughly the size of Tower **16**, but it is not possible to say from the aerial photograph whether the ground floor was hollow or filled.

*Tower **18A*** (Fig. 18)

None of the survey drawings have shown any tower at the extreme northwest angle of the circuit, but that there was one there is a virtual certainty.[46] The westernmost section of the Northwest Wall that can be seen in the aerial photograph angles outward into the harbor, where the intersection with the West Wall calls for a tower close to the shore. Its presumed position overlooks the inner end of the harbor entrance passage and would have made it a convenient source of material for the builders of the Porto Kheli quay opposite. It may have been square like the others in the Northwest and West Walls, or it may have been a round tower, as Williams suggested the Admiralty chart indicates (below, 43; Pl. 1); that would have interesting implications for the extent of the remodeled circuit.

*Tower **19*** (Fig. 31)

Almost at the center of the site, just above the low scarp where the known remains of the Middle Wall terminate, is Tower **19**, now much overgrown by brush and shaded by a large locust tree. As the curtain descends the slope, the trace jogs to the east between two terraces; on the lower level, jutting out north and west of the angle, there are blocks forming the northwest corner of the

---

[42] The unequal projection and the interruption of the walkway recall the tower at the southeast angle of the fort at Phyle; Wrede 1924–1925, Abb. 11.

[43] To my knowledge, no information about the elevation in relation to the doorsill is recorded.

[44] Lawrence (1979, 304) gave the maximum opening for a postern as 1.50 m.

[45] Three towers at Phigaleia (Blouet 1833, pl. I: two towers east of K, one west of gate N) have similar plans. These three have

the greater projection on the right (facing outward), while the tower at Phyle (note 42 above) like those at Halieis has it on the left. The choice was presumably determined by the direction from which an attack might be expected.

[46] The point of land in question is private property attached to a villa and lies outside the archaeological zone. In our 1970 survey, wary of trespassing, we did not venture closer than the landward side of the villa buildings.

rectangular structure. Two blocks approximately at the southeast corner were uncovered in the excavations in Area F5, but it is uncertain whether they were in situ. As nearly as can be made out for the dense overgrowth, a mass of earth and rubble is heaped behind the northern side of the tower, which would be comparable in size to Tower **10**.

The short east–west stretch between the tower and the lowest preserved section of the curtain (in Area F6) seems a possible place for a postern, but the foundation of the curtain is continuous over the interval and parallels a drop of about a meter. It is more probable that there was a gate farther down the slope, where the modern road, very likely following the ancient line, runs westward below the scarp. The gate would have been overlooked by the tower, whose existence must indicate that the region on the west side of the wall was or could be enemy territory.[47]

The Round Towers and Their Gates

While "square" (that is, rectilinear) towers continued in use throughout the Classical and Hellenistic periods, "round" (that is, curvilinear) towers were apparently considered an improvement at Halieis. Curvilinear towers are known as early as the 6th century[48] and were often preferred at gates and at sharp angles in the trace.[49] Various reasons have been suggested for their popularity. It was easy enough to build them in mud brick or the rubble masonry of earlier construction, not so easy in cut stone. The corners of square towers might hide attackers from the view of defenders on the curtains (Rusch 1997, 748), and when heavy artillery came into use in the Hellenistic period, the corners inside a tower became waste space. It has also been suggested that a curved form would be harder to damage with a ram or missile than a rectilinear one where the corners were vulnerable (Lawrence 1979, 38), but that advantage probably applies principally to those constructed of stone, that is, a missile would be more likely to bury itself in mud brick than to bounce off, no matter what the shape. The

choice of round towers for an ambitious building program at Halieis was no doubt based on a combination of perceived advantages, not least of which may have been a desire to appear *au courant* (Fig. 35).

Of the six round towers, three (**6**, **9**, and **11**) clearly had rectangular predecessors.[50] On the acropolis, the Phase 5 tower did not project beyond the face of the curtain; Tower **6** appears to have been in the form of a complete circle, set into the core of its predecessor on the same axis, its center a little in front of the intersection of the projected lines of the curtain on either side (Fig. 21). Towers **9** and **11** were only a little more than half circles wrapped around the earlier structure; the center in each case appears to have been located at the face of the core tower. In each case, the diameter of the round tower was not much greater than the width of its predecessor. Of the others, Tower **14** was also a complete circle, but it was probably part of an entirely new construction at the Harbor Gate. The remains at Tower **15**, forming only part of a circle, were not cleared on the south side; there may have been a square tower there, but it would have been small, like the others in the northwest section of the trace.[51] At Tower **7** the existence of a predecessor remains to be determined. The ground floor of Tower **6**, and probably Towers **7** and **9**, was filled; that of Tower **15**, and possibly Towers **11** and **14**, was hollow.

The first of the round towers, in size, importance, and probably date, is Tower **6** on the acropolis (Pls. 5b, c). It is fully described and discussed in Williams n.d. The gate for the acropolis enclosure is not associated with it but located instead at the west side, adjacent to Tower **5**. The other round towers, **7**, **9**, **11**, **14**, and **15**, are taken up in order; they are presumably contemporary with each other and part of the same remodeling program as Tower **6**.

Tower 7 (Fig. 9; Pl. 6b)

Tower **7** is the smallest of the group, only 6.80 m in diameter; the plan constitutes about three-fifths of a circle.[52] Its location at the sharp change in the

---

[47] The course, history, and purpose of the Middle Wall are open to various interpretations; see below, 54–56.

[48] E.g., Halai, 6th-century tower: Goldman 1940, pl. III.

[49] Winter 1971, 194–95; Winter (1986, 415) held, however, that no "round" towers (e.g., the oval tower at Peiraieus) had been convincingly dated to the 5th century.

[50] For the possibility of a round Tower **18A**, see below.

[51] Cf. semicircular tower R2 at Plataiai, whose diameter at ca.

12 m is more than double the width of the square tower it encircles (Aravantinos et al. 2003, 294–95, fig. 6). The square tower was somewhat over five meters wide, comparable to the small ones at Halieis.

[52] While small in relation to the other towers at Halieis, the diameter of 6.80 m may be compared to that of the round tower at Phyle, 6.00–6.50 m (Wrede 1924–1925, 191).

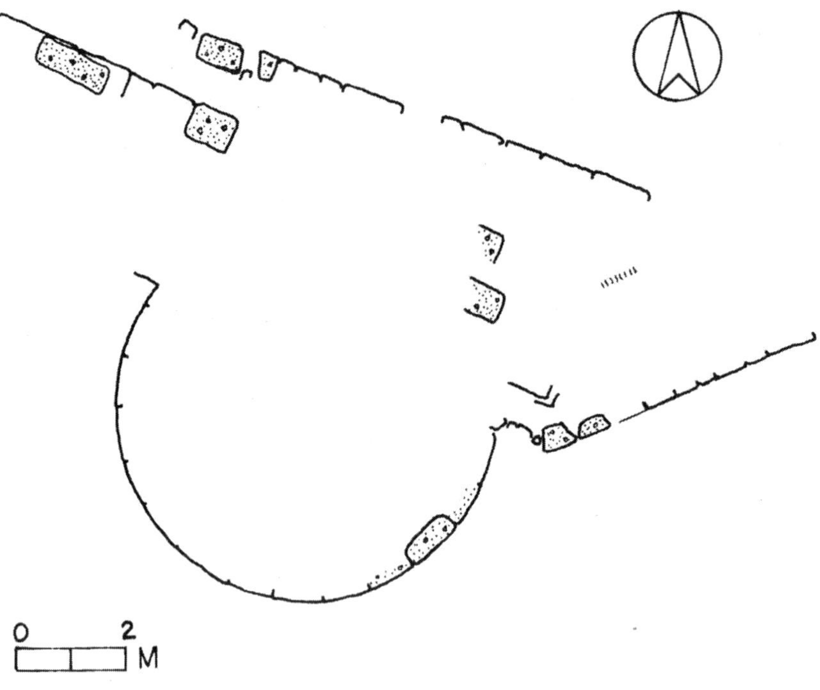

Fig. 9. Round Tower **7**

direction of the circuit from the southern to the eastern boundary of the city, at a point where it is possible to view the terrain to the south as well as the valley to the east, probably accounts for its inclusion in the rebuilding program (Fig. 35). It should be safe to say that if the course of the circuit predated its construction, there would have been an earlier tower of some sort, but the surrounding area was not excavated, and the blocks apparent on the surface provide no definite evidence.

The remains of the tower were cleaned and drawn, but not excavated, in 1962.[53] The conglomerate socle is not bonded to the outer face of the city wall, which is preserved on the east side in a few small irregular blocks. Inside the socle blocks, the excavators found "an interior floor of bedrock and heavy pebbles" (NB 3, 146). The presence of bedrock indicates that the outer blocks are indeed a socle and not a wall base with only

the top showing. Once the original base was removed, a solid core, if there were one, would soon wash away. No remains of the super-structure, such as the coping blocks of Tower **6**, have been identified. Several rectilinear blocks of the light shelly limestone that were found in the excavation of the adjacent buildings on the Industrial Terrace would have been easy enough to transport downhill from the acropolis and may have originated there.

Tower **9** *and the Southeast Gate* (Fig. 25; Pls. 7a, b, 8c)

Tower **9**. To the right of the Southeast Gate on entering, Tower **9** stands in the canonical position on the unshielded side of an attacker. Here, however, there is no question of an earlier square tower: as at the East Gate, a rectangular bastion of conglomerate blocks, around which the round

---

[53] The work was supervised in part and the plan drawn by Williams; his drawing provides the basis for Figure 9 with some additions from my survey in 1971. Although most of the tower has been reburied, the outline can be seen, especially on the

aerial photographs. Apparently the blocks north of the tower were not all cleared; some visible in 1972 are not shown on the 1962 plan, while some on that plan are no longer visible.

tower is wrapped, was originally considered sufficient to guard the entrance (above, 25). It was set about a meter northeast of the jamb of the gate and extended 7.20 m along the curtain, at which point the blocks of the round tower overlie the line of the bastion. The northernmost preserved block of the bastion does not appear to have a square corner and may have been trimmed to accommodate the blocks of Tower **9**. These continue around it as shortened headers rather than changing to a stretcher as at the southwest side. A block on the northeast side of the bastion that bonded with the curtain was cut down to receive the overlying course of the round tower. Various smaller blocks, some of them cut and presumably reused, filled the gap between the curtain and the lower courses of Tower **9**. The blocks of the bastion rest on the same pebble layers as those of the later round tower (below).

A line of stones across the curtain, about three meters from the southwest end of the bastion, seems to mark the northwest face of a structure that terminated the curtain at the gate. Large conglomerate blocks mark the line of the face along Street 1, set out about 0.40 m from the inner face of the curtain. The southwest wall formed the side of the gate; since it continued the line of the houses along Avenue C, it formed an acute angle with the curtain. It is possible that there was a chamber here, over this structure and the space back of it (behind the old bastion, at the end of the curtain), that was used in connection with the gate. The blocks that now form the base along the street do not suggest that the wall was carried higher in stone. No access below the level of the walkway is evident.

Tower **9** is approximately 8.00 m in diameter and just over a half circle at the base; set directly against the earlier bastion, the center of its arc is on or at the face of the orthostate course of the earlier structure. The highest preserved course, level with the blocks of the bastion, consists of wedge-shaped headers of conglomerate about 0.38 m high and 0.90 m long.[54] Beneath them on the outside a lower course of conglomerate stretchers

and a poros socle can be seen, the latter scarcely above the ancient road level.[55] Inside, the course below the headers is of poros, again in wedge-shaped headers, dressed down on the outer half to receive the top course; these blocks extend inward another 0.80 m, their joints offset from those above. Like the blocks of the earlier bastion, the poros headers rest on compacted earth over layers of pebbles, small ones over others the size of a child's fist. The earth has been dressed to accommodate the uneven bottoms of the blocks. The choice of the wedge-shaped headers in Tower **9** (and Towers **11** and **14**), in contrast to the heavy orthostates of Towers **6** and perhaps **7**, may be due to the difference in the subsoil: Tower **9** is built on sterile earth, Towers **6** and **7** on bedrock.[56]

The outside face of the tower is handsomely hammer dressed and appears more regular than that of Tower **6**. The hairline joints are vertical where they have been exposed; in the short stretch that could be uncovered, there was no need for downward stepping, and there are no fillers. The last block on the southwest, which encloses the south corner of the earlier bastion, is a stretcher twice the width and half the depth of the wedge-shaped headers. Its northwestern half is the full height of the stretcher and header courses; the other half has been notched to lap over the rough-faced lower base course. A straight block, also a full-height orthostate but oddly offset from the round tower by a few centimeters, completes the northeast flank of the gateway at the level of the headers; it bridges the original interior corner between the bastion and the gate structure. Two conglomerate socle blocks, each with a corner jutting out in casual irregularity, support these two blocks; they may be part of the base course for the predecessor, left in situ when the round tower was built. Since their tops are at the level of the ancient road metal, they would not have presented any obstacle to traffic.

No bricks could be identified in situ on the round-tower headers, which were covered by only a few centimeters of soil. Careful trimming of the outer edge of the first wedge-shaped header on

---

[54] Wedge-shaped headers (the long sides not parallel but tending to converge, so that the inner end is narrower than the outer) were used in at least one of the semicircular towers of the West Wall in the Potters' Quarter at Corinth. Stillwell (1948, 56–57, 62, pl. 18, b) argued on excavational grounds for a late 5th-century date. Similar blocks may be seen in the semicircular towers at Phigaleia (dated second quarter 4th century by Winter, 1971, 111–12 note 23) and in the round tower at Phyle (Wrede 1933, 167).

[55] The curved blocks on the southeast side of Tower **9**, at the surface of the modern road, were the first to be noticed. The road could not be interrupted for excavation, but it was possible to clear the southwest third of the arc down to ancient road metal and to clean the tops of the rest of the blocks enough to record them.

[56] Tower **15**, with a ground-floor room, is a special case. It is not known where bedrock lies there, but it is probably considerably below the tower foundations; these are not only submerged but buried in detritus.

the southwest side of Tower **9** looks like a guide surface by which the course was leveled (it is remarkably even), more probably for stone than for brick; there is a similar treatment on the north corner block on Tower **10** (above, 28), where there was at least one more course.

About 50 meters to the west opposite Meter 960 is a small rectangular structure defined by conglomerate orthostates (Fig. 24; Pl. 9d). Its purpose and date are unknown; it has no connection with the fortifications. Isolated inside it stands a curved conglomerate block that recalls the wall base of Tower **6**, or perhaps more closely, the header-and-stretcher construction of Tower **15**. It measures 1.38 m on the chord of the outside arc and is about 0.34 m thick; the height is not now visible. The end joints are not cut on radial lines, and the inside curve is somewhat irregular, making the arc look sharper than it really is. It is not possible to reconstruct Tower **9** with a hollow first level, like Tower **15**, since there is no entrance at street level; the line of orthostates beside the gateway and along Street 1 is at least a half meter in height. It is possible, however, that there was an upper course of orthostates resting on the wedge-shaped headers (cf. Towers **14** and **15**) and forming an outer shell (as in Tower **6**) for the solid fill within; the irregularity of the inner curve in that case would not have mattered.

The Southeast Gate. The Southeast Gate is one of three considered important enough to merit a round tower for its defense, although Tower **9** here is smaller than the other round gate towers. Inside, the gate connected directly with Avenue C, which has been shown in the excavations to run northwest at least to Street 3, where it may have forked (Fig. 18). Avenue C apparently divided the built-up area of the eastern part of the city in two, the lower flatter ground to the northeast, the steeper slopes rising to the principal escarpment

on the southwest; it may have followed the Archaic defense line (see above, 17–19) and possibly served as the route to a civic center.[57] Outside the gate, a road on the same general line would have passed above the sanctuary of Demeter,[58] on the way to the quarries and the necropolis[59] in the valley where the modern road now goes to Kosta, the mainland harbor closest to the island of Spetsai (Fig. 17). Close outside in the relatively fertile bottom land is a well.[60] In sum, the users of the Southeast Gate were probably going about local business.

On the southwest side of the roadway across from the round tower, a socle of poros, projecting about 0.25 m and carrying a course of undressed conglomerate blocks, continues outward to the southeast at least 1.70 m beyond the line of the curtain (as extended from northeast of the gate), at which point it disappeared into the scarp of the trench;[61] there is no setback from the gate opening. It is possible that this socle also carried a projecting bastion, although it would have been unusual to have the greater projection on the attacker's left. The distance between the early bastion on the northeast side of the gate and this socle is just over four meters (they are not quite parallel). The form of the original gateway resembles that of the East Gate, where the bastion is also 7.20 m wide and projects as much as a full tower (Fig. 4).[62] The passageway now preserved at the East Gate is 4.30 m wide.

Two massive blocks (Fig. 25; Pl. 9a), as wide or wider than they are high and with the same fine hammered finish as the blocks of Tower **9**, rest on an intermediate course of conglomerate; they make a square corner that projects beyond the line of the curtain only to the same extent as the bridging offset block on the northeast. The corner block, laid as a stretcher along the passageway, is partly supported on an undressed stretcher deeply notched to receive it. The top of

---

[57] Blocks of a large building or complex recorded on the survey at right angles to Avenue C and some 30 meters to the southeast suggest the location of one or more public buildings.

[58] Stone blocks outlining a rectangular building were visible at the time of the excavations. On a higher terrace to the south was a scarp of earth containing many votive miniatures including piglets. These were mentioned by Philadelpheus in his field notes, now stored in the archives at Indiana University. See Jameson 2004. Additional references are Jameson 1969, 340–41 and Jameson et al. 1994, 424, site A 15.

[59] See Dengate 1976. Wheel ruts have been noted about halfway to the necropolis (Fig. 17). Trench A, 60 m due east of Tower 10, and Trenches C and D, about 70 m southeast of the East Gate, failed to reveal any trace of a road (Jacobsen 1970), but the exact

line is hard to predict.

[60] At the time that the 1962 topographic plan showing the property lines was made, this well in Field 31 was of such importance that it was recorded at the end of a long easement through neighboring properties. 1t is on the line where tradition places a seasonal stream.

[61] The modern road severely limited the investigation of the southwest side of the gate and outer end of the drain.

[62] The bastion at the East Gate projects more from the face of the curtain on the northeast side because the line of the wall (as restored) bends somewhat to the north. Very little of the outer part of the opposite side of the gateway shows above ground; it is not possible to say how far it projected.

this second block is as much as 0.15 m below the corner block and may belong to an earlier structure. The first block on the outer face, next to the corner block, is bonded with the side wall of the drain that parallels the passageway a meter to the southwest (below, 59–61); the drain-wall block is deeply notched to receive it like the stretcher along the passageway.

The line of the outside face could be followed from this corner toward the southwest, within the limits of the excavation trench, only as far as the drain, leaving a number of unanswered questions. If an earlier projecting structure, indicated by the socle course and the conglomerate blocks it carries, was removed when Tower **9** was built, was it replaced by another round tower or bastion, offset to the southwest presumably at least to the other side of the drain, or does this line represent the face of the curtain? The line, beginning about two meters outside the line of the curtain on the northeast side of the gate, would be turned outward very slightly but certainly not enough to command the exterior of the gate.[63] It would not parallel the blocks along Street 1 that appear to represent the inner face of the fortification.[64] The existence of a second round tower seems unlikely, considering the lesser importance of its position on the shield side of attackers and the fact that a single tower was considered sufficient at the Hermion Gate. The location of the drain would make it awkward, though not impossible, to construct a round tower on that side of the gate.

The roadway through the gate, including the ridge and gutter at each side produced by long use, is over three meters wide, but the large pivot blocks that preserve the cuttings for the gate sockets (one still retaining some of the lead used to hold the bronze insert) reduce the clear passage to 2.20 m; the opening flares slightly as the road descends toward the outside.[65] The blocks are of the regulation two-level form, the inner, lower level for the leaf pivot, the outer, higher level for the jamb post (Pls. 9a, b). The sockets measure 0.09 x 0.10 m (southwest) and 0.13 x 0.17 m (northeast;

actually 0.13 x 0.11 m with a 0.06 m extension).[66] The socket was made for a bronze insert (ληνός or ὅλμος; cf. Winter 1971, 258), leaded securely in place; the square shape ensured that it would not twist in position under the torque applied by the friction of the turning pivot, set in the stile of the gate leaf.[67] The sockets as preserved are very shallow; no greater depth would have been necessary since the great weight of the gate leaf would have kept the pivot in position. The upper end of the stile with the corresponding pivot would have been set into the lintel, in this case presumably of wood.

A frame would have been necessary to limit the outward swing of the gates to the closed position. The jambs would have rested on the outer, raised part of the base blocks, shielding the pivoted stile from the outside. In this instance, however, the usual sockets to hold wooden jambs are lacking. It is conceivable that the upright part of the frame was in courses of stone, even if the lintel was wooden.

There is no indication of a sill; the road metal continues in a steady downward slope out through the passageway. The difference in size of the two socket holes suggests that the leaves may have been unequal in width,[68] a large leaf on the northeast, filling perhaps two-thirds of the opening (about 1.25 m wide), and a narrower (about 0.95 m wide) on the southwest. The large leaf could be kept closed except when carts or heavily loaded animals needed to pass. A vertical bolt to fasten the fixed leaf would be dropped into a cutting in a stone sill or at least in a substantial block embedded in the roadway for this purpose. Because no such block was found, it is possible the sill was wooden, no longer preserved. There is no evidence to show whether the socket blocks are contemporary with the bastion or with Tower **9**; they could have been reused.

Across the passageway and set against the outer ends of the jamb blocks is a row of three large poros blocks; the choice of material suggests either that they were reused or more probably, in view of their great size, cut in haste from the

---

[63] Winter (1971, 212) suggested that "swinging the wall outward along the slope above the gate" sometimes served as a substitute for a gate tower, but the slope and the angle here are too gentle to qualify.

[64] For the line followed by the northeastern half of the Chambered Curtain, see below, 67.

[65] Lawrence (1979, 303) gave the average width of gates intended for cart traffic as 2.70 m to 3.50 m. The Southeast Gate seems to have had minimum dimensions for its class.

[66] The smaller (southwest) cutting is some 20 cm farther from the blocking wall than the other, distances fixed by the lengths of the pivot blocks, which abut the blocking wall. While the position of the gate is indicated by the pivot holes, the longer block kept the blocking wall from aligning exactly with it.

[67] For a discussion of typical arrangements for the pivoting and fastening of gates, see Lawrence 1979, 250–53.

[68] For a discussion of unequal gate leaves, see Lawrence 1979, 254.

relatively soft material.[69] Alone, they seem a thin line, more suitable as a barrier for wheeled traffic than for resisting a battering ram, but excavation produced no trace of a second wall or fill other than fallen mud brick. These blocks would, however, have made a sufficient base for a mud-brick wall built against the outside of the gate.[70] If plastered like the rest of the fortifications, its vulnerability would not have been apparent from the outside.

The remains on the southwest side of the gate are difficult to interpret. Proceeding inward from the block at the square corner, the tops of the next two conglomerate stretchers are progressively lower and are continued by a low wall of rubble and mud mortar. The second block from the corner lies next to the southwest jamb base block; the third is leveled with the second by a row of tightly fitted small stones. A conglomerate orthostate, which appears to be in situ, rests partly on the third conglomerate stretcher and partly on the rubble wall. The space between the drain and the gate passage is level with the second stretcher and is packed with rubble and earth. None of this construction equals the workmanship of the round tower and the square exterior corner opposite it.

Excepting a few large Corinthian pan tiles and one large Lakonian cover tile of unusually thick section, there was little ceramic material in the fill of the passageway. Diagnostic pottery was limited to some blisterware fragments found on the road surface at the inner end. There were no traces of coping blocks like those associated with Tower **6**. Several thick squared pieces of shelly limestone can be seen in the terrace wall along the modern road, and one was found beside the northeast socket block, but there is nothing to indicate how or where they were used.

At the inner (southwest) corner of the gateway are four wide, shallow steps (Pl. 9c); the top step, of sandstone, is a reused cover slab from the drain that ran through the curtain about a meter southwest of the passage (see below, 59–61). The bottom step, also sandstone, projects into the gate passage and is curved at the corner, as though to ease the turn to the left into Street 1; the

southeast end of the step is missing. There is a small conglomerate block at the northwest end of the poros second step, a sandstone one at the other, both somewhat higher than the tread; perhaps these were bases for door posts. The poros third step is damaged at the southeast end and pieced out with a higher block of shelly limestone at the northwest. The actual corner is now a pile of rubble; conceivably it is a deteriorated conglomerate block. Between the corner and the first cover slab of the drain, more or less level with the drain cover, is a small square limestone base.

Beyond the drain along Street 1, the corner of a room was exposed, apparently the northeastern end of the Chambered Curtain. If the bottom of the drain was level with the street, the floor of any chamber above it would have been about 0.60 m higher. The whole area when excavated was seen to be filled with fallen mud brick. It is not clear whether there was a guardroom on this side of the gate or whether the construction at this corner was originally solid at least to the level of the walkway. The corner steps, which are wide enough to suggest public rather than private access, seem too casual in their construction to belong with the fortifications; they may represent some late reuse of the area after the gate had been blocked or fallen into disrepair. Moreover, because many of the drain cover slabs are missing and one was reused for the top step, the drain must not only have been out of use but exposed when the steps were built.

*Tower **11** and the Hermion Gate* (Fig. 28)

*Tower **11**.* This tower is wrapped closely around the north corner of its square predecessor, using wedge-shaped headers like those of Tower **9**. Like Towers **14** and **15** it is 9.20 m in diameter.[71] There was no investigation of the basis for this conglomerate course, the top of which is now just at the surface of the water. Although the tower itself would have been on dry land, the harbor was not far away across a gentle slope. If the construction was similar to that of Tower **9**, the Classical water level would have been only about

---

[69] They probably are what Aeneas Tacticus (32.5) called a wagon-filling stone (λίθος ἁμαξοπληθής), in this case up to 1.30 m long, 0.50 m wide, and about 0.70 m high, even larger than those in the Spur at the Harbor Gate (below, 42).
[70] Lawrence mentioned the practice of blocking nonessential gates in times of danger (1979, 248–49), citing the instruction of

Aeneas Tacticus (28.1–2) that when a city is afraid of attack every gate should be blocked except the least accessible (to the enemy).
[71] Compare the diameter of Tower **6** on the acropolis at 10.85 m; see Williams n.d.

1.50 m below the socle. Bedrock is assumed to be well below the ancient ground level in this place, which would have been part of the valley-bottom land, and stone foundations might have been carried deeper in this instance. The use of the wedge-shaped headers appears to be linked to construction on compacted soil as opposed to the more certainly stable bedrock (see above, 13). Although there is no evidence for a course of orthostates above the headers and a hollow ground floor, it is possible that all three waterfront towers (**11**, **14**, and **15**) were similarly constructed, if not Tower **9** as well.

The Hermion Gate. Land travelers coming from the north or, nearer at hand, from the sanctuary of Apollo, would see the Hermion Gate first. Traces of a road were found in shallow water running northeastward from the gate for some 35 meters. The road probably paralleled the shore and, turning northward, passed east of the sanctuary race course on the way to Hermion.[72] Inside the town, the road continued as Street 8, just beyond the terminus of Avenue B.[73] The remains of the gate are obscured by the small Late Roman/Early Byzantine bath that was built on top of them (see below, 85) and are difficult to examine because they are now submerged. The aerial photograph provides the best view, although it cannot make the relative elevations clear. While admittedly speculative, some cautious observations can be made.

The square tower to which Tower **11** is attached borders the roadway and forms the northwest side of the gate in the classic relationship, on the unshielded side of the attacker. The line of the curtain can be seen clearly as it approaches from the southeast; there is no sign at all of any tower on that side. The position of the actual gate is uncertain. A single block is visible against the southeast side of the square tower; it is aligned with a structure across the gateway that parallels the Northeast Wall, perhaps an access

stair and guard room (see below, 59). If the gate was at this point, it would have been deeply recessed. Inside the curtain and across the roadway from the tower are two walls that form the southern corner of a rectangular area of the same orientation, which differs noticeably from that of the overlying bath. The enclosure seems to be related to the road and its continuation in Street 8, rather than the lines of either the North or the Northeast Wall;[74] these, when projected, intersect at the square tower about two meters inside its east corner. The walls of the enclosure appear no heavier than those of nearby houses, but it may still have served some of the purposes of a gate courtyard, providing a second line of defense and a mustering place for troops just within the main gate.[75]

It is now impossible to make out the connection with the curtain of the North Wall.[76] Nevertheless, the fact that both the square tower and especially the round one attached to it appear to be well outside it suggests that the gate structure was extensive. The purpose in the outward projection of the round tower may have been to permit a clear view of the outer face of the Northeast Wall as far as Tower **10** and of the North Wall as far as Tower **14**, as well as of any activity along the east shore of the harbor and the road from Hermion. The apparent retention of the square tower in the remodeling program may have been to provide additional space for the defenders and their stone- or bolt-throwers.

*Towers **14** and **15** and the Harbor Gate* (Figs. 29, 36; Pl. 19)

*Tower **14**.*[77] The form of the tower is a complete circle. It is built of wedge-shaped conglomerate headers like those of Towers **9** and **11** but with a solid core of untrimmed pieces of conglomerate that form a platform base, similar to those suggested for Towers **12** and **13**. They do not, however, give the appearance of a floor. The solid

---

[72] Cart tracks in the bedrock can be seen today at the edge of the water near the sanctuary and have been detected underwater farther south in aerial photographs (Jameson 1969, 338, fig. 8; Jameson et al. 1994, 48–49).

[73] Street 8 has been tentatively indicated parallel to Streets 3–7. Remains visible in the aerial photographs of buildings just to the northwest suggest that the street was wider than the others, the line on that side closer to that of the gateway. This was probably a major avenue.

[74] Aeneas Tacticus (15.3) wrote of assembling the defending forces at the gates, one or two companies at a time, in preparation for sallies against the enemy. This rectangular area may have

been such a mustering place, just within the main gate.

[75] Winter (1971, 217) put the development of the courtyard gate at the beginning of the 4th century.

[76] See below, 53, for the connection of the Hermion Gate to the North Wall, on both earlier and later traces.

[77] Figure 29 relies heavily on the aerial photographs. It cannot be stated too strongly that accuracy under these conditions is difficult to achieve. The photographs, while revealing much detail, vary from shot to shot depending on what the divers were able to clear and what the currents had buried or reburied in the silt. I take responsibility for their interpretation where actual measurements were not available.

core of boulders may have continued in brick or rubble to the walkway level, or, if the lowest story was hollow, they may have been covered with a layer of clay or with slabs. The headers, 0.20–0.25 m high and currently about two meters below the water surface, rest at 3.20 mbsl on poros blocks, 0.40 m high, that carry through to the outside face and rest on yet another course of poros. If the Classical water level is correctly estimated to have been about 3.60 mbsl (see below, 86), or about 2.60 m below the present surface, it came roughly at the top of the lower poros course. Throughout Halieis, poros plinths are found at ground level.

The top of an orthostate base course 0.60–0.70 m high resting on the headers would have been even with the top of those in Tower **15**. The diameter is 9.20 m, the same as that of the other waterfront towers, **11** and **15**. The blocks on the east side are set in to permit a bond with the end of the North Wall curtain approaching from the east (see below, 53). On the southeast side of the tower additional poros blocks continue the line of the widened quay to form the northeast side of the gate, opposite the Platform (below, 42). The exact line of the shore in the Classical period is unknown but can be estimated to have been about ten meters from the tower (Fig. 19).

Tower 15. Twenty meters to the southwest a second tower, also 9.20 m in diameter, guarded the other side of the Harbor Gate. The remains are not only submerged but are heavily covered with rubble and sherds of late Roman amphoras, washed down from the shore. About two-thirds of a circle can be seen, together with a confusion of straight walls on the landward side. The construction of the round tower is of conglomerate orthostates set as headers and doubled stretchers, the latter separated by a space to form a hollow wall about a meter thick. The top of this wall is at about 2.50 mbsl, with an opening on the south side toward the town. The nature of the foundation has not been discovered but may well have been similar to that of Tower **14**. The regular finish on the interior of the tower wall, which is if anything thicker than those of Towers **12** and **13**, indicates that Tower **15** was hollow at ground level. If the ground-level story may be said to begin with the conglomerate blocks above the socle, those of Towers **6** and **9** were filled solidly. The situation

at Towers **11** and **14** has not been determined; there is no evidence remaining for Tower **7**. The apparently exceptional design of Tower **15** together with the importance of its central location suggests that its purpose may have been similar to one mentioned by Aeneas Tacticus (11.3) at Chios. He spoke of the ship-sheds and stoa adjacent to the tower "in which the magistrates took their meals," a description that might well apply to Tower **15** at Halieis.[78]

The Harbor Gate. The gate between Towers **14** and **15** must have been as important to the town as the Hermion Gate, if not more so. It opened directly on the shore and saw the daily passage of those going to and from the boats in the harbor. The twin towers that guarded it suggest the intention to present an imposing appearance and to offset the vulnerability of the gate. Its design, however, is peculiar to its location and difficult to interpret or to parallel.

The gap between the twin towers is reduced to about seven meters by a construction (hereafter, "the Projection") that runs northeast from Tower **15** for eleven meters and by a single row of poros blocks on the southwest side of Tower **14**. The conglomerate blocks of the Projection that remain rest on a course of poros and are 3.00 mbsl at the northern end, roughly even with the headers in Tower **15**. They are 0.25 m high, laid flat, and are tightly fitted with rather irregular joints to form a surface 3.25 m wide and about 6.00 m long ("the Platform") at the northeast end. Between the Platform and Tower **15**, the Projection narrows to about 1.20 m. It is not bonded to Tower **15** and so could have been built subsequently, but it is probably contemporary. There is no evidence to suggest what sort of structure may have risen above the Projection to close this interval in the fortifications.

At the northeast corner of the Platform are three cuttings, one small hole each in the north and east blocks and one overlapping the joint (Fig. 10b). The small holes are 0.15 m by 0.25 m in plan, the larger 0.30 m by 0.50 m; all are 0.20 m deep. The block on the east face is rectangular and is joined to an irregular block behind it by a double-T clamp. This clamp is not only unique in the Halieis construction known at this time but is among the few known to exist in Greek fortifications before the Hellenistic period. It is

---

[78] M. H. Jameson brought this passage to my attention in connection with a discussion of the mint and other public

buildings associated with fortifications.

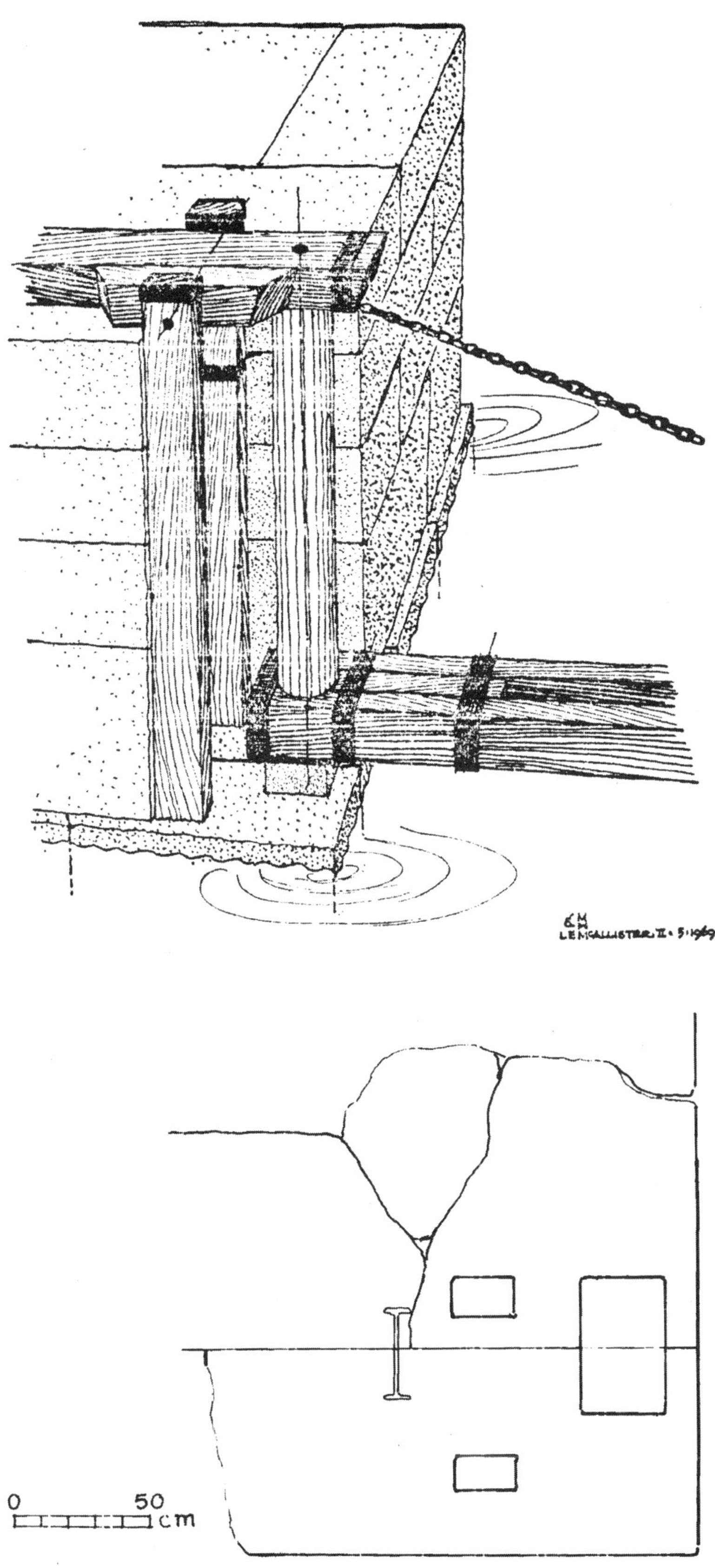

Fig. 10. (a) Reconstruction of the Harbor Gate. (b) Cuttings for the Harbor Gate

noteworthy that these generally occur in waterside construction.[79]

While the cuttings are reminiscent of those regularly found on pivot blocks in classical gateways, they differ in important respects because of their special location. The large cutting is 0.50 m from the east face but only 0.10 m from the end of the Platform; it straddles the joint between two blocks, a weak arrangement for which the clamp was intended to compensate. Sockets in pivot blocks are normally square and shallow.[80] The additional length across the joint would give the insert, presumably fine-grained stone, greater purchase so that it acted like a dowel. The eastern of the other two cuttings is approximately centered on its block (partly exposed but clamped). The western, in a less vulnerable location, is aligned with the west edge of the large cutting.

The most striking difference between these and normal gate cuttings is their relative positions, with the smaller cuttings to the side rather than outside the main pivot.[81] A possible reconstruction calls for a stone insert in the large cutting, with an appropriate socket for a pivot of bronze in the bottom of a vertical post (Fig. 10a).[82] According to this proposal, two vertical beams as high as the masonry construction on the Platform were anchored in the smaller cuttings by tenons. Courses of stone must certainly have continued higher than the usual orthostate course in this exposed location; the alignment of the cuttings suggests that the masonry was flush with their west and south sides. The pivot at the top of the post was set in a horizontal beam sandwiched between the two verticals and anchored back into the main mass of the masonry. A boom was formed of two parallel horizontal members attached on either side of the pivot post and bound together

at intervals throughout their length, perhaps with metal straps. Additional support was provided by a chain from the top of the pivot post to a point two-thirds of the way along the boom. (A second chain at the one-third point would further counteract any tendency to sag and accord with common present-day methods of boom support.) The natural tendency of the boom would be to pull the top of the pivot post outward, with an accompanying inward thrust at the bottom. The top is restrained by the beam embedded in the wall, the bottom by the socketed pivot block. There is no stress on the relatively weak outer margin of the conglomerate blocks at the northern edge. The rectangular stone insert braces against the masonry to the west when the boom opens inward to the east, while leaving clearance for the back end of the boom. The offset position of the eastern socket provides more stability for the open position.

The additional construction at the south side of Tower **14** might have supported a pivot block for a second leaf or boom for the gate, but this would have required an anchor post within the opening. It is more likely that a post here secured the free end of the boom swung from the south side of the gate. No sill or road metal was found in the gap between the Platform and Tower **14**.

From the Projection a wall runs southward on the east side, passing to the east of Tower **15**. It appears to align with the lowest (nearest) preserved section of the Middle Wall, but this association may be illusory. A wide spur wall (the "Spur") of large poros blocks in two courses runs westward from the Projection for seven meters, bonded in 4.50 m south of the end where the cuttings are and resting on conglomerate rubble. The top of the upper course lies at 3.20–3.25 mbsl, the top of the lower course at 3.60–3.70 mbsl. Two blocks of the upper course, 1.25 m by 0.80 m and

---

[79] Winter (1971, 136, note 37) wrote that clamps prior to the Hellenistic period were probably confined to the slabs of the walkway and gave Messene as an example. Although Thucydides (1.93.5) mentioned as a remarkable detail the clamps used in the Themistoklean walls of Athens and Peiraieus, E. Vanderpool wrote (per lit. 2/3/72), "I know of no archaeological finds to illustrate it." The only clamps of that period that have so far come to light are in the Kerameikos along the bed of the Eridanos (Noack 1907, 153–55). In discussing the walls of Peiraieus, Judeich (1905, 139, note 4) referred to a 5th-century wall at Parion in the northern Troad where the face is bonded to the fill with wooden clamps. Clamps in harbor works were recorded by Georgiades (1907, pl. I, fig. 4) at Lechaion. Paris cites the harbor at Mytilene, the mole at Knidos, and the quays at Kenchreai (1915, 10). Only two clamp cuttings were reported at Eretria by Pickard (1891, 378): one is a T, the other a hook,

both at the junction of the mole and the round tower at the southwest corner of the circuit. At Thasos, swallow-tail clamps were used in both the schist blocks and those of marble that topped them in the Archaic seawall, which the excavators took to indicate that at least one course of schist was above the water line (Archontidou-Argyri et al. 1989, 55–56).

[80] Lawrence in his discussion of these installations gave the size of the socket in a gate at Eleusis as 0.11 m square and 0.03 m deep (1979, 253).

[81] See the description of the blocks at the Southeast gate, above, 37.

[82] Louis E. McAllister Jr was the principal author of this reconstruction, which first appeared in Jameson 1969, 335–36, fig. 7. This type of barrier is frequently found today at road entrances to state parks and the like.

0.35 m high, remain in place at the east end. A dislodged block at the west end and traces of the rubble foundation at 4.00 mbsl suggest that this spur originally continued even farther.[83]

There are many questions raised by Towers **14** and **15** and the gate between them; the answers cannot depend solely on this presentation of the physical remains. A full discussion of the Harbor Gate, together with the North Wall and the adjacent areas to the north and south, is given by M. H. Jameson below (chapter 7). It draws on other information from the underwater investigations and refers to the history of the fortifications and the site as a whole.[84]

Tower 18A

The Admiralty chart (Pl. 1) shows an oval enclosure occupying most of the stretch between Tower **1** and the north shore, an area currently covered by a 20th-century villa. A large oval tower is so improbable that it suggests the delineator, in transcribing the surveyor's notes, mistook the contour of the knob for a structure. (It might also be noted that the chart shows the acropolis enceinte as a large square enclosure, only one corner of which, the Phase 5 tower, would have been visible.) Williams (n.d., note 18), however, took the oval as an indication of a round tower. The location indicated on the chart, not only close to a square tower (perhaps Tower **1**, although it is shown projecting outward) but short of the actual corner of the trace, seems unlikely, but the possibility of a round tower lower down at the northwest angle of the fortifications has important implications, discussed in the final chapter.

Gates of Unknown Form

There are several places in the defense circuit where small gates might have been a convenience for passage to daily labors outside the walls. There is insufficient evidence, however, to decide whether they would have been gates or posterns (see below, 44).

The West Gate (Fig. 20)

There is no sign of a major gate in the whole length of the West Wall. This is hardly surprising, for not only would there have been only local traffic on this side of the city but this stretch would have been most vulnerable to surprise attack from raiding parties landing in one of the small coves along the long entrance channel to the main harbor (Fig. 17). On the other hand, in peacetime a passage through the West Wall would have been a great convenience.

About nine meters south of Tower **2**, the inner wythe of the defense wall apparently terminates in a cross block. After an interval of about eleven meters the wall can be found again farther south, with at least one block projecting beyond the outer face. This would have been the logical place for the gate; the natural route across the ridge is indicated by the present-day track, which, just south of Tower **2**, branches off the modern road and continues down the west slope to coves along the entrance channel. The road to this point has taken the natural line across the site; very likely it marks the ancient route as well, continuing either Avenue C or a hypothetical Avenue D higher up the slope all the way from the Southeast Wall. The remains now visible support the hypothesis of some sort of structure south of the opening and just where the direction of the curtain changes, on the unshielded side of an attacker. Hardly more than a postern, not even on the order of the East Gate but overlooked by Tower **2**, it would have been relatively easy to defend or even to block entirely in times of unrest.

Gate East of Tower 4

The possibility of a gate between Towers **4** and **5** is discussed below (47).

Gate on the Industrial Terrace (Fig. 22)

About at the center of the curtain on the Industrial Terrace, where there is a slight angle in the line of the inner wall, there are two large plinth blocks of poros. They appear to be socle blocks, like those used elsewhere in the circuit, but their top surface is higher than the bottoms of the stretchers to the west. Immediately to the east, the wall blocks are missing; where they resume after more than two meters, a cross block connects the innermost and middle lines of the wall.

---

[83] The measurements taken by the divers indicate a slight slope down to the west, no more than 5–10 cm in 7.00 m, which could be the result of natural settling.

[84] For an account of the curtain and mole between Towers **13** and **14**, see below, 53.

A small trench opened next to the plinths failed to shed any light on their use.[85] They lie considerably above the level of the adjacent Terrace buildings, although their material suggests that they were originally at or below grade. They may, however, have been used like the much larger blocks at the Southwest Gate (above, 37–38), as a basis for a mud-brick construction blocking part of the gate opening in the inner line of the curtain. A smaller gate would have remained, at least until the wall was rebuilt on the outer line (see below, 49), at which time a new gate or postern may have replaced it. Considering that there is no other known opening on the south side of the circuit, it would have been convenient to have one here, but since there are no visible remains at the center of the outer wall, the evidence is lacking even to suggest what form it might have taken.

Posterns

If a postern is defined as an opening (a short tunnel) through the curtain sufficient for the passage of a single armed man, the break in the curtain east of Tower **13** is the only candidate at Halieis, although there may have been others that have not been identified. The opening at Tower **16** (Fig. 8) has been classified as a small gate because of its relation to the tower doorway (above, 32). The relative positions are similar, but the doorway of Tower **13** (Fig. 7) is on the south and faces into the city, while the opening in the curtain is alongside; nothing is known of the street pattern inside the wall at this point. It is possible that the opening, which is about 0.60 m wide, was for a postern in the form of a tunnel through the curtain and little over the height of a man.[86] Two blocks, in line with the curtain, now bar the inner and outer ends of the passage; the outer block is somewhat the heavier of the two. Such a postern, which like the gate at Tower **16** led only to the foreshore, would have been a convenience but unnecessary except as a sally port; it was apparently blocked like the Southeast Gate and filled with rubble like the rest of the curtain.

The narrow opening as seen in plan also suggests a drain, similar to those identified in the Northwest Wall (see below, 62).[87] Two blocks, one square and one oblong, adjacent to the passage on the outside, seem to be in situ, but their purpose is unclear. They may not be structural at all but represent debris from the wall or blocked postern, or an extension of the drain outside the wall.

It has been suggested (Jameson, per lit., 2001) that there was a postern in whatever wall rose above the Projection at the Harbor Gate. It would have provided access to the area between the Spur and the curtain west of Tower **15**, perhaps an advantage in dealing with hostile seamen barred at the gate. Others are suggested for the interval between Towers **4** and **5** (below, 47) and on the Industrial Terrace (above, 43–44), which are mentioned above as possible locations for gates, and in the upper Southeast Wall (below, 50). The evidence now available, however, does not support the general use of posterns for military purposes in the Halieis circuit, such as were increasingly common after the middle of the 4th century (Winter 1971, 143–44). It may be that the Halieis fortifications were what McNicoll (1986, 309) called a "passive circuit with few posterns," perhaps more appropriate where the number of defenders was small.

---

[85] Trench 910/150, immediately inside (north-northeast of) the poros blocks; it was limited by the southern archaeological boundary, which runs across the blocks. Remains of mud brick, notably of dark gray like that found in early levels on the acropolis, were found below the blocks, suggesting an earlier earthwork. There was no sign of a road surface.

[86] Lawrence (1979, 304) gave a meter as the average width of posterns, with a range of 0.80–1.50m. Compare posterns at Gyphtokastro (Winter 1971, 239–40, fig. 254).

[87] The drain at the Southeast Gate is 0.81 m wide. Adam (1982, 45) notes that at Thasos and Oiniadai drains attained the size of a postern.

– CHAPTER FOUR–

The Curtains and Related Structures

There is so little left of the curtains at Halieis that in most places not much more than the trace can be made out. The identifiable remains of stairways, bastions, and drains can be described, however, as well as those few sections that have been excavated or otherwise deserve special comment. For the purposes of this catalog of elements, the sections of the curtain are taken up in the same order as the trace (above, 14–15), without regard to their place in the chronology of the site. Locations along the curtains identified by meter numbers are shown on the key plan, Figure 19.

The Curtains

The usual construction of the curtain base is in two wythes of conglomerate, filled with rubble and earth. It is assumed that the exposed stonework was only one course high, sometimes set on plinths, because very rarely is more than one course preserved; the principal exceptions are on slopes where the courses are stepped and overlap.[1] Thus, where the curtain is described as "a double-wythe wall," since that is all that remains today, it is important to remember that the expression applies only to the base and that probably no more than a meter above the ground

the construction changed to solid mud brick coated with plaster. It may be assumed that the curtain was crowned with a walkway protected by a parapet. The walkway may have been surfaced with crushed tile or stone, which would be less slippery than tile or stone paving as well as less costly.[2] The parapet would have been topped with tiles, the tower tiles described above (7). Where the wall base was stepped on slopes, the walkway and parapet must have been inclined or stepped, depending on the gradient. At such steps in the walkway, there would have been terracing stones.

The West Wall (Figs. 18, 19; Pl. 2a)

The construction of the West Wall base appears uniform throughout: large, trapezoidal, quarry-faced blocks nearly twice as high as wide were set with the outer wythe on bedrock wherever possible but provided with a leveling course of small blocks as necessary; this often projected like a socle.[3] Plinths were used for the inner wythe, presumably where bedrock dropped below the base level established on the outer side.

The northwest angle of the circuit wall, probably defended by a tower, must have been at

---

[1] The blocks of this base in the following descriptions are properly called stretchers rather than orthostates if they are no higher than they are wide, but it is not always clear in the fieldnotes whether this appearance reflects their original shape or is due to lack of excavation. In most cases it is clear whether the top surface is still preserved. Thus with the exception of a few places duly noted, the base blocks were probably orthostates, sometimes on plinths. It is possible that at least in some places there was a second course above the stretchers to make a higher base.

[2] Winter also mentioned wooden planks and waterproof cement as possible finishes (1971, 150), but considering the extent of the curtains and the cost, these seem less likely for Halieis.

[3] At about Meter 130, three meters south of the stair, the outer blocks are recorded (NB 741, 9) as 0.55 m wide, 0.35–0.40 m high, the inner 0.40–0.50 m high, 0.80–1.20 long. These are the exposed heights; there was no excavation. Opposite the southern end of the stair (called a ramp in NB 22, NB 516; see below, 57), one of the blocks in the outer wythe, here a little lower than the inner, was noted with a sketch (NB 516, 20–21). The block is close to 0.60 m high; its top is about 0.15 m higher than that of the one adjoining on the south. A ledge 0.34 m wide has been cut down about 0.21 m on the outside. The effect is similar to the projecting socle or leveling course noted elsewhere, but no horizontal joint was apparent.

the water's edge, at or just west of the boundary line between the archaeological zone and the modern villa on the point opposite the town of Porto Kheli. The scarp that forms the present shoreline shows bedrock rising vertically five or six meters, overlaid with a meter or more of soil, but there is no sign of the fortifications. More stone than usual was probably used to make the transition from one level to the other, but the blocks are gone, whether to the Porto Kheli quay as rumored or elsewhere. The northernmost remnant of the West Wall could be found in 1972 in the garden of the villa just outside the archaeological boundary: a conglomerate block jutting out in a downhill direction from the wall of a small outbuilding. With a few other blocks, which were shown on the 1962 topographic plan, the lines of both faces could be made out as far south as Tower **1**. Although the double line is shown with confidence on the 1962 survey, there was little to be seen in 1970. Whether from long years of exposure or an inferior source for the stone, the blocks had for the most part degenerated into broken lumps and gravel.

The following section of the wall, 2.78 m wide and in crumbling condition in 1970, is now marked only by tumbled rubble.[4] As it follows the crest of the ridge, bedrock is close to the surface, but clearing away the rubble might clarify the trace. There is no reason, however, to doubt the 1962 drawing, which has been used as a source for Figure 18, even though this section could not be verified in subsequent surveys.

Beyond the hypothetical West Gate (above, 43) a good stretch of the wall is preserved at about Meter 275 (Pl. 2d). The blocks of the outer wythe now measure 0.50–0.65 m in height and 0.40–0.50 m in width; they were well fitted but are now badly eroded. On the inner side, the present ground level is even with the tops of the blocks for much of the stretch. Both wythes probably rest

on bedrock; the total width is 2.22–2.28 m. At one point, the inner wythe steps down toward the north 0.14 m, but a larger step of 0.50 m just to the south is probably due to a missing block. The block below it, still in situ, represents a lower course necessitated by the drop in ground level. As the top of the wall base stepped down with the continuing northward descent, this lower course would become full height, the upper being first reduced in height, then eliminated altogether.[5]

At Meter 310 (Fig. 11; Pl. 3a), because there is a natural scarp (a small drop in the level of the bedrock) on the east side of the ridge, the ground falls away rapidly from the inner face but is at present level on the west side with the tops of the outer blocks. While some of the inner ones have tumbled inward, other conglomerate blocks still cling precariously to the crumbling bedrock, serving as a retaining wall for the plowed field to the west. The joints are not vertical, and as well as can be judged without cleaning, neither are they perpendicular to the face. Where the bedrock declines toward the north, two courses are used; a full-height block has been carefully notched to overlap the lower course. The blocks of the inner face are 0.50–0.57 m wide. The width of the outer blocks could not be determined, but that of the full curtain is 2.30 m.

As the wall continues south of Tower **3**, some sections are missing and others overgrown, but enough remains to define the meandering trace. In places, the outer face is marked only by a

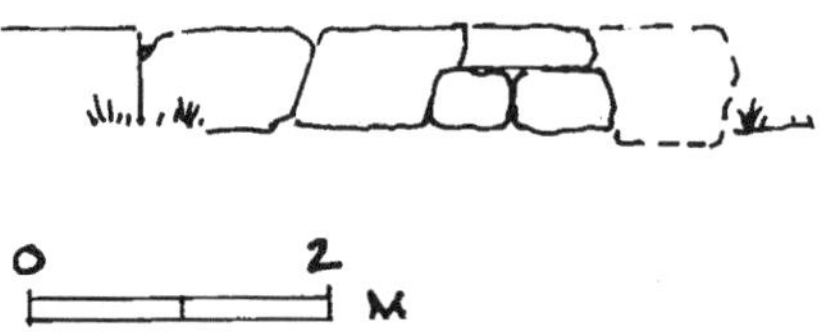

Fig. 11. Portion of the West Wall at Meter 310, east face of the inner wythe

---

[4] Before 1970, the road leading to the villa on the point reached the West Wall south of Tower **2**, passed between it and the structure immediately to the east, and continued along the ridge toward Tower **1** at a distance of several meters from the wall. At some time following the 1970 excavation season, the field east of the wall was sold, and this right-of-way was shifted to the west. A road scraper dispatched for this purpose passed between Tower **2** and the adjacent structure, removing all trace of the curtain just south of the latter and seriously damaging the tower by skinning off the outside face of the conglomerate blocks at the north corner; their remains are in situ but too shattered to measure. The crumbling blocks of the next section of wall to the north were reduced to the level of the road surface or dislodged from their positions, and the resulting debris was

shoved into a great heap against the rock outcrop at Tower **1**, burying the north end of this section of curtain. The possibility of recovering the plan in detail by excavation is slight since bedrock is very close to the surface of the road, especially at Tower **2**. In 1970, there was time only to record the trace, without detail. A series of aerial photographs had been taken, but their usefulness is limited by the patches of dense overgrowth. Williams made notes on Tower **2** and the interior projection near Tower **1** in 1965 (NB 22, 103–5). The plans shown here are a combination of these notes with the 1962 and 1970 surveys, supplemented where possible by my notes of the remains apparent in 1971 and 1972. The indications on the 1962 topographic plan are not reliable for actual dimensions.

[5] Compare the wall base for Tower **6** on the acropolis (Pl. 5b).

bedding of short, scrappy conglomerate blocks, sometimes in two courses and often set in a cutting in the bedrock, apparently to make a broader and more level bed for the now missing orthostates.[6] The bend at Meter 365, which follows the natural contours, is accompanied by a thickening of the wall to more than three meters.[7] The widened section is that closest to the top of a broad gully or hollow that descends rapidly to the west shore.

Across the knoll at Tower **4**, the remains of the wall are very fragmentary. Small blocks of conglomerate and bedrock cuttings mark the line, which here runs northwest–southeast and is largely overgrown. Descending the knoll on the southeast side, the outer wythe makes a definite angle. From this point, the wall continues in a more easterly direction to the acropolis.[8] The construction appears to be the same, with the bedrock here left higher between the wythes and occasionally supplemented on the outer side by small blocks in a leveling course (Pl. 4c). This bedding or bedrock projects 0.18–0.28 m on the outer side; in the only measurable spot, the width of the curtain itself is 2.56 m.

At Meter 510, where the tops of the inner blocks are now level with the ground, there is a cross block bonded into the inner wythe; there is no other such block recorded in the West Wall except at the West Gate. A modern footpath runs across the trace here at the low point of the crest between the western valley inside the circuit and the slope down to farther coves along the entrance channel. Although it might seem convenient to have a postern on the southwest side of the city, there is now no appropriate break in the outer wythe. Finally, some twenty meters short of the

acropolis, surface traces of the wall have disappeared entirely; the line is assumed to have run straight to Tower **5**, located on the inner (north) side of the curtain.

Despite its erratic course and comparative length, the West Wall was conceived as a whole, built at one time, and apparently remained without modification. Doubtless it was best preserved where deepest buried; the northern section was already in poor condition before it was so badly damaged in 1970–1971. There are few places where the style of the masonry can be appreciated, the exceptions being at Tower **2** and Meter 310 (Fig. 11). It is basically isodomic, if the term can be applied when there is usually only one course; any irregularity of the coursing is due to the terrain rather than to style.

The Acropolis (Fig. 18)

The stages of the defense wall across the south side of the acropolis are discussed in Williams n.d. The abrupt drop that limits the acropolis on the west, north, and northeast diminishes and disappears on the east so that the slope is continuous to the scarp at the west end of the Industrial Terrace. East of Tower **6** the wall trace turns northeast, descending gently on a diagonal across the sloping ground. A short line of blocks showing on the surface about midway in this stretch is in line with the latest wall face at Tower **6**; others to the north belong to the Phase 6 wall face (Fig. 21). At Tower **6** these lines are diverging but here seem to be parallel, about two meters apart. The outer line is continued by a rubble leveling course but peters out before reaching the scarp.

---

[6] This construction results in the false suggestion of an outer facing later added to the first wall. Such a facing would have been too narrow (0.15 m) for any sort of construction except a revetment, unheard of at this time and place. The detail is visible at many locations along the West Wall, including the damaged section between Towers **1** and **2**, and appears again on the Industrial Terrace (see below, 48–49).

[7] The widening seems to be accomplished by an irregular curve that connects two straight sections of unequal width in a continuous if clumsy construction. Cooper (Plan of site 1972, 1974) and Boyd (Boyd and Rudolph 1978, fig. 1, pl. 87) were properly skeptical of any curves and in their finished plans showed the sections as straight, meeting at a very wide angle; certainly in the Classical period, such walls, even when apparently meandering, are usually composed of straight sections. The working plan embodying Cooper's survey notes (1970), however, is not so definite. I returned in 1972 to verify my own findings. The stretch in question, represented on the inner side by plinths, was heavily overgrown with holly oak and could only be surveyed by taking offset measurements from

a base line. Reaching under the branches at arm's length, I took as many measurements to the apparent inner face of the wall as possible, arriving at the results shown in Figure 18. Since the blocks may well be in a crumbled state, I do not believe the question can be resolved without removing the bushes, which were too dense even to permit measurements through them to the opposite (outer) face of the wall. I recorded the total width as 2.87–3.23 m, quite possibly including a projecting socle.

[8] Cooper and Boyd have recorded offsets in this stretch, where the straight sections meet and overlap. My reconnaissance in 1980 found that some of these jogs were covered by bushes and could not be verified. The curtain here traverses a slight depression between the knoll at Tower **4** and the acropolis; the ground is nearly level, falling off gently on either side. The offsets are too slight, and their location too level, to have served any practical purpose such as the indented trace of late Classical and Hellenistic systems (Winter 1971, 117). They would have had a stabilizing effect in connecting neighboring sections of the curtain, or they might be the remains of a socle for an added facing like that of Phase 7 on the acropolis (Williams n.d.).

There is no indication of an enclosure wall for the acropolis on the east side. It might have been at the drop to the Industrial Terrace, where the angle of the trace changes. Three conglomerate blocks on the east slope above this point, which now act as a retaining wall for the soil to the west, are probably part of an independent structure.

The Industrial Terrace (Fig. 22; Pl. 6a)

At the bottom of the east slope of the acropolis, there is a sharp drop of several meters followed by a number of ledges in the bedrock; some, at least, are probably cuttings but represent more than one stage of wall building. The defense wall turns southeast to follow the flat-backed ridge along the south side of the Industrial Terrace. The remains present a confused picture, not simplified by olive trees, the roots of which have shifted a number of blocks from their original alignment. Although buildings on the central part of the terrace were excavated in 1962 and 1965, the fortifications, with the exception of Tower 7, were left untouched at that time and have never been cleared.[9]

Between the scarp at the west end of the Industrial Terrace and Tower 7, a length of some 60 meters, the ground drops nearly six meters. The change in elevation was accomplished by a series of shallow steps, not obvious now because of missing blocks. Those that remain are partly exposed and are arranged along three main lines of wythes. The innermost (northern) and middle lines are not straight but form a shallow recessive angle near the midpoint. The outside line runs straight but is missing at either end.

The innermost line is the best preserved. It is built of conglomerate orthostates that vary in length from 1.02 m to 1.34 m, with one or two limestone blocks at the west end. The blocks are not all tightly fitted: two gaps of 0.25 m are now empty, while at the east end there are small fillers of both conglomerate and limestone still in place. At the small trench 910/150 near the center of the run, the orthostates rest on a socle course of cut conglomerate plinths about 0.35 m thick. There are three large blocks of poros at the angle in the center, set so that their tops are higher than the bottom of the adjacent socle.[10] The tops, now only a little above ground level, are much worn, but their preserved thickness is at least 0.35 m; their width is 0.60–0.75 m.[11] Parallel to the inner line at the west end and a meter or so to the north, there are two conglomerate stretchers with a nearly square limestone block at either end (below, 57–58). They slope so steeply on the ground below the acropolis scarp that they are more likely to be connected with the defenses than with a building.

To the east of the poros plinths, a cross block, not bonded into either wythe, lies between the innermost line of blocks and the single remaining block of the outer wythe of the innermost wall; the outer line is continued by crumbled remains nearer Tower 7. At the eastern end of the inner wythe, near Tower 7 where the present ground level is lower, the orthostates rest on plinths of conglomerate and sandstone that run on a slightly different orientation. Parallel to them about a meter to the northeast and extending still farther, a short row of blocks can be seen directly behind Tower 7.[12]

The middle line is preserved in three separate sections and represents the inner wythe of a different wall. At the west end, the blocks appear to merge with and to be fitted to those of the innermost line. Farther east, but still short of the center angle, there is a stretch of large blocks somewhat irregular in width; the finished side is the one to the north. East of the center angle, a few stretchers are visible. They might seem at first to form a south-facing outer wythe for the inner wall line, but they are not parallel to it; their line converges with the inner line about at Tower 7.

The outermost (southern) wall line, which parallels the middle line, is best preserved in the western half but even there is badly weathered; sometimes it is only represented by the leveling course of small blocks, often eroded to rubble. These blocks were probably outside the face of the

---

[9] See Jameson n.d., chap. 3, for the excavations on the Industrial Terrace. The buildings seem to belong to the late 4th century, contemporary with the pottery of Deposit VI and architecture of Phase 6 or 7 on the acropolis.

[10] In 1976, a small trench was sunk, under my supervision, to investigate the two plinth blocks at the center of the innermost wall; see above, 17. The possibility that there was a gate or postern of some sort at the center of the Terrace is discussed above, 43–44.

[11] The thickness of these blocks is even now somewhat more than that of the adjacent conglomerate plinth (about 0.30 m); they were probably at least 0.40 m thick originally, perhaps considerably more. They do not approach the size of the blocks barring the Southeast Gate (about 0.70 m high), but they have apparently remained exposed for many centuries, while those at the Southeast Gate were well buried.

[12] See above, 24, for the possibility of a square tower preceding Tower 7. See above, 34, note 53, for the investigation of walls in this area.

wall, in the form of a projecting socle;[13] they give the misleading impression that the wall was as much as three meters wide. In the eastern half, the line is nearly obliterated; there are a few blocks that, with a cross block, form a slight projection from the line, as well as a few other scraps of uncertain purpose.

A number of large Corinthian pan tiles of the type known as tower tiles (above, 7) have been found on the surface outside the line of the curtain as well as in the excavations of the Industrial Terrace buildings; one remains where it was found, reused as a floor tile (above, 7).

The relative chronology of the Industrial Terrace defense walls, based on the available evidence, is not so clear as it might be. At a minimum, a cleaning of the whole stretch should be instructive. There appear to be at least two distinct lines for the curtain, perhaps with several stages adjacent to Tower 7. A common practice in the design of Greek defenses, if the old wall was not to be replaced and terrain permitted, was to add later walls outside the earlier, economizing on time and material by straightening angles in the trace rather than adding them, unless they were sharp enough to create a strategic advantage. On this premise, the innermost line should be the inner wythe of the older wall, perhaps originally with a postern at the center and overlooked by a square tower at the corner of the trace.[14] The later line of the outermost wall would run straight to Tower 7. It is not possible to say how much of the older wall might have been reused and how much dismantled. No indication of road metal was found in Trench 910/150, either along the wall as a service street or running downhill from the poros plinths.

The Southeast Wall (Figs. 23, 24)

Tower 7 is not exactly at the corner, where the trace turns sharply to the northeast, but rather immediately to the west of it.[15] The outer wythe of the curtain now consists of small blocks of conglomerate and sandstone, which presumably constituted a leveling course;[16] the line can be followed for some way as it slants down the slope to the scarp. Near Tower 7 (Fig. 9), a few blocks of an inner wythe are visible, at a distance of about 2.25 m (outside face to outside face). Other blocks close by follow the orientation of this section of the curtain, which differs from that of the Terrace buildings. The latter seems determined by a general plan for the area, perhaps including one or more unexcavated buildings to the west and based on the direction of the natural drainage rather than the line of the trace.[17]

Surface remains of the Southeast Wall stop about seven meters northeast of Tower 7 and begin again only below the scarp at the bottom of the terrace. A short stretch below the scarp presumably connected with the upper end of the Chambered Curtain.[18] A trench (H4-5) across the trace, about three meters below the scarp, exposed two large conglomerate blocks of the outer wythe, the uphill one (wall block 4) set 0.45 m higher to accommodate the slope and doubled on the inside by another squared block (wall block 5) 0.50 m wide and at least 0.70 m long (Fig. 12). This block remains unexplained; it must indicate a different structure, probably connected with the major change in level at the scarp, whether or not it included access to the walkway. Three courses of conglomerate blocks found at the north end of the trench might be part of the crosswall at the upper end of the Chambered Curtain (see below, 65). Rubble characteristic of the core of a double-wythe wall was found beside the lower block of the fortification wall (wall block 6), extending inward about a meter, or roughly in line with wall block 5.[19] Beyond this was a layer of yellowish-brown clay about 3 meters wide covering the underlying red soil as far as a line of rubble just south of the crosswall blocks, but there was no sign of an inner wythe. At the south end, outside the fortification,

---

[13] Compare the socle of small stones that extends the bedrock in places along the West Wall, above, 47.

[14] For the possibility of Archaic walls on the Industrial Terrace, see above, 17–18.

[15] Compare Tower 3, above, 23, Fig. 3.

[16] It is possible that this leveling course belongs to a refacing of the curtain, such as occurred on the acropolis (Williams n.d.), extending it slightly beyond the tower base.

[17] The orthogonal plans of late Classical and Hellenistic cities often disregarded the lines of the trace, although when space was at a premium, as along Avenue A at Halieis, buildings might be fitted into quite irregular plots.

[18] This structure, the direction of which shifts slightly to the north, forms the greater part of the upper Southeast Wall; since it differs so markedly from the double-wythe wall used for the rest of the curtains, it is described in the following chapter, under Attached Military Structures.

[19] Pottery found adjacent to wall block 4 included cooking-ware lopas fragments (knob and rim) HP 1027 (350–325); in the small-stone wall core north of wall block 6 were found coarse- and cooking-ware fragments including amphora HP 1029, some poor black-glaze and Corinthian sherds, and one red-figured sherd. Corinthian Geometric amphora fragments HP 899A,B (dated "no earlier than the late 8th century" by K. De Vries, NB 112, 29) found near the surface may have washed down from the Industrial Terrace.

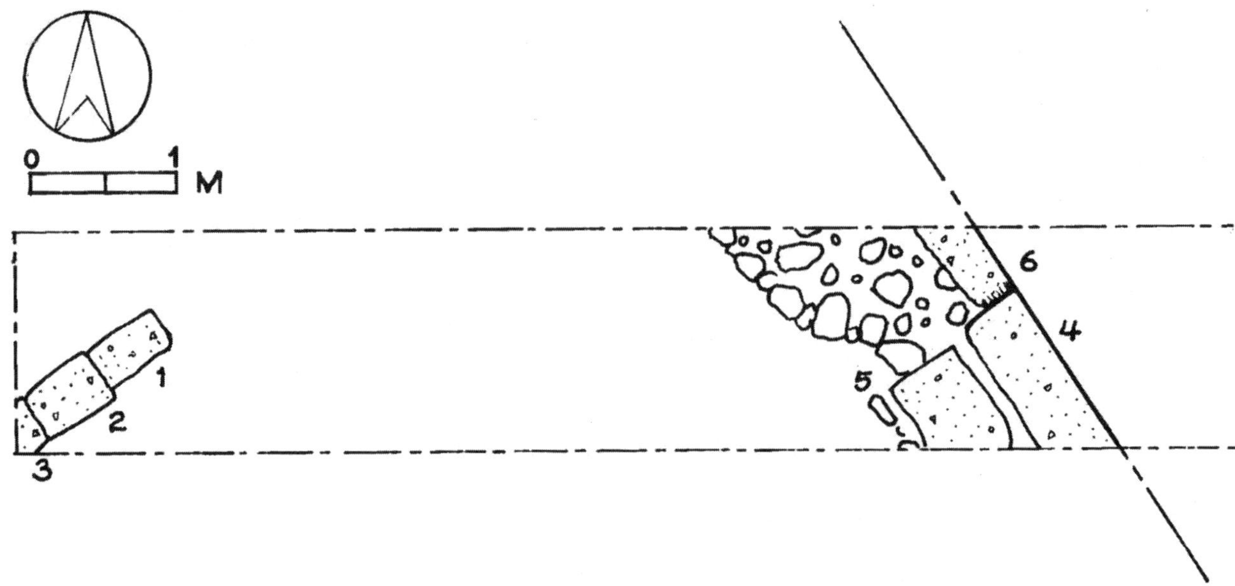

Fig. 12. Trench H4-5

there was a heavy tile fall in which tower tiles predominated, with other Corinthian-type tiles and a few coarse and cooking-ware sherds.

The principal surface remains of the upper Southeast Wall stop at a small scarp some 22 meters downhill from Tower **8**. Three small rock-cut steps descend the rock face just outside the wall (Pl. 6c). As the line of wall blocks is continuous at that point, the steps must belong to a period either before or after the visible fortification system. If the line of the modern road, which may well follow that of an ancient one, were continued along the 10-meter contour across the site, it would cross the trace at this point and descend to a valley where local tradition records a seasonal stream. There is no sign of such a watercourse now, but the valley may have contained springs or an ancient well used frequently enough to make it worthwhile to ease the way up and down the low scarp. If the steps belong to the Archaic or earlier periods, there probably was no wall here at that time.

Because the Southeast Wall is on earth or earth fill in its lower part (see above, 18–19, for the earlier earthwork), rather than on bedrock, the lack of firm bedding required a change of construction using a heavy foundation topped by conglomerate stretchers.[20] These may in turn have carried other stretchers or orthostates to make a

sufficient base for the mud brick wall above, but for these there is no supporting evidence. Beyond the Southeast Gate, the characteristic double-wythe wall appears again, beginning on the inner side of the rectangular bastion, at the northeast end of the trapezoidal structure (above, 25, 35). From Tower **9** past the shrine, for which the curtain serves as the back wall, the blocks of the outer wythe were cleared: they are conglomerate stretchers, 0.60 m wide and 0.40 m high at the most. Only their faces are dressed, in a manner similar to the tower blocks if not so smoothly finished. Four of the six visible joints are wider at the top than at the bottom and are filled with neat stackwork of conglomerate or split-face blue limestone. These are small blocks, not slabs; the joint behind them is filled with earth and small stones. The other two joints are on either side of a low block of conglomerate, only 0.18 m thick, perhaps a piece of patchwork. The tops of the large blocks are not even; the highest is finished level on top, the others only roughly so. They were probably brought to an even height with a layer of small stones, such as formed the top layer where this face runs behind the bastion and Tower **9**.[21] The inner wythe of the curtain behind this foundation is composed of large conglomerate blocks filled in with split limestone.

---

[20] This construction is apparent at intervals all along the lower Southeast Wall (see Meter 1015, East Gate, East Tower Area).
[21] Compare the layer of small stones on top of the orthostate on the southwest side of the passageway, above, 38. This layer

would seem to prepare for mud brick without a course of orthostates. See the description of the curtain at the East Tower below.

Northeast of Tower **9** a trial excavation near Meter 1015 in 1970 (Trench I5-1) revealed a double line of large conglomerate stones with earth-and-rubble fill between, running northeast–southwest in the southern half of the trench. This formed the foundation for a stretcher course, a few blocks of which show nearby on the surface to the southwest. The inner wythe was clearly defined by two large blocks with dressed surfaces on the exposed side and top. Both blocks extended into the trench walls, the larger at least 1.40 m in length. The top of the northeast block lies about 0.08 m lower than that of the other; a space between them is filled by a small unworked stone. The core contained some large stones, measuring as much as 0.90 m in the largest dimension, as well as smaller stones and earth; two sherds of 4th-century black-glazed ribbed ware were found in the top layer.

The outer wythe was less definite than the inner, consisting of two large unworked blocks and rubble; these should be considered a foundation for a stretcher course. There was no sign of a foundation trench. The foundation blocks are about 0.50 m high; the width of the curtain at this point measures 2.40 m. Two joining red-figured sherds found among others at the level of the bottom of the blocks give only a general indication of the construction date.[22] Below the blocks of the inner wythe, the soil contained much sand and gravel, as well as small stones, resembling a river-bed deposit, in stroses sloping slightly downward away from the inside face of the wall.[23] The stones, however, which also appeared in the scarp, did not occur at any level in a uniform layer over the whole trench, nor was there any sign in this small area of road metal adjacent to the wall.[24] At the level of the foundation, there were signs of mud brick with stones and some roof-tile fragments. The tiles were generally Corinthian; tower tiles were represented, mostly in the upper part of the tile fall. The datable sherds found with them were of the 4th century, with ribbed decoration.

The construction of the wall at the East Gate appeared to be the same, but only a short stretch was uncovered in Trench J5-2 (Fig. 4), and that may have been part of the gate building rather than the curtain.

Three of the trenches (M, O, and U) opened in 1970 in the East Tower Area cut across the line of the fortification wall, exposing a foundation of large conglomerate face blocks with stone and earth fill (Fig. 26). The construction is the same as that uncovered at Meter 1015, but the large blocks, roughly dressed on the top and exposed face, are more closely fitted. The top of the wall foundation, here 2.50–2.55 m wide, slopes down as the ground drops to the northeast.

In Trench U, a cut made across the wall showed that the core and face blocks were as much as 0.61 m deep; they rested on a mound of sterile red earth (see above, 18). Presumably, the same construction prevailed for most of Trench O. The large blocks, however, were missing on the outside in the northeastern part of the trench; the line was continued by smaller stones in a leveling course that descended in two steps to a point about 0.325 m below the top of the inner face.[25] The rubble core also dropped to the lower level but at the same time went considerably deeper. In Trench M, the bottom of the rubble core was found about 0.70 m below the top of the outer blocks. Above the rubble, the remainder of the core consisted of red earth or deteriorated mud brick in Trench M, of dark earth and pebbles in Trench O.

The slope established by the top surface of the inner foundation face at Trench O, when projected, meets Tower **10** at the level of the top of its conglomerate orthostates (Fig. 26, longitudinal section). Ground level over that interval, however, dropped as much as the height of those orthostates in addition, or about 0.60 m. The difference would have been accommodated in two or more steps, so that the foundation for the curtain would meet the tower at the plinth level. The height of the stretchers on that foundation is unknown, but a comparable

---

[22] HP 902 (Trench I5-1, basket 8), probably mid-5th–mid-4th century.

[23] Similar stroses of material were found in the trenches near Tower **10**. See above, 18.

[24] A number of Archaic pottery sherds were found in dark soil in a small patch in the center of the trench (e.g., HP 900, a miniature handleless black-glazed Corinthian cup, 500–480), below the level of the foundation course; the remainder of the lower levels was virtually without sherds or other finds. Below the dark earth, the soil was red and sterile. If there was an early earth rampart on this side of the town (see above, 18–19), it seems likely that it was further to the southeast (77–78) and that these sherds attest general occupation rather than specific fortifications.

[25] Late Roman / Early Byzantine burials have been found throughout the area, on both sides of the wall (Rudolph 1979, 297–301). One was beside the upper step in Trench O, another in an amphora just inside the wall face at the north corner of the trench. The larger blocks may have been removed when these graves were dug, if they were not already missing.

juncture is preserved on the east side of Tower **6** (Pl. 5c; NB 22, 116; Williams n.d.). There, the first block of the curtain matches the orthostate in height (0.62 m); the convex face suggests that it was originally cut for the tower. It rests on the tower socle and a block of comparable height (0.17 m, on bedrock), with a small filler block between. Two more blocks of the curtain base were exposed below the coursed mud bricks of the wall, set at socle level; they are each nearly a meter long and 0.60–0.65 m in height, fitted but not squared. A similar detail employing at least one orthostate for the curtain to match that of Tower **10** is a reasonable restoration. If the southwest side of the tower had a full upper course, that also may have been matched at the beginning of the Northeast Wall.

Inside the defense wall, the excavators uncovered parts of a series of houses with pottery ranging in date from the late Geometric period to the early 4th century.[26] A layer of packed stones found near the top of the wall foundation in Trenches O, M, and T (but not in U) may have been a street or court paving from the last period of occupation. The nearest building, of very humble construction, is below this latest paving and must once have run right to the inside face of the fortification wall; a 4th-century house with a fine plaster floor preserved a distance from the wall of at least 3.50 m.[27]

Tiles of various sorts were found throughout the area. Pieces of heavy Corinthian tiles were found on both sides of the wall. A conspicuous quantity of these lay on the paving near the top of the wall blocks in Trench O; one large fragment was used to cover the mouth of the amphora used for a Late Roman/Early Byzantine burial in that trench. Other tiles of different sizes were Lakonian in shape and fabric, some with a black wash.

The Northeast Wall (Figs. 18, 19)

From Tower **10**, the wall trace runs straight northwest to the Hermion Gate and Tower **11** with only a slight drop in level. About half of this curtain is now submerged, the top of the wall blocks lying barely a meter below the present sea level. Excavations in 1962 and 1972 partially investigated a short section adjacent to the Northeast Command Post near the middle of the run, just at the edge of the water. For the southeastern part, a few blocks, some showing only in the modern road surface, serve to confirm the line of the trace. In contrast to other parts of the fortifications, the Northeast Wall is conspicuous in its regularity. Three small bastions divide the curtain, here about 2.50 m wide, into roughly equal sections.[28] They project outward from the wall face 2.20 m, are 7.30 m long, and are spaced 53.50 m apart from each other and from the west side of the Hermion Gate (that is, from the square predecessor of Tower **11**). The outer face of the curtain is not continuous behind them; they are merely intermittent wide parts of the wall and perhaps served as arrow-shooter (man or machine) emplacements. Some superstructure would have been needed to roof artillery machines, but its walls may have been only an upward continuation of the mud-brick parapet topped with a wooden roof. The latter might also have served as an open fighting platform with a parapet.[29]

In 1962 a single trench was run toward the shore through the Northeast Command Post at about the midpoint of the building. A "series of bricks in a fragmentary state" was reported in situ about 3.50 m from the central base (Fig. 27).[30] The location, which cannot be pinpointed, should be about on the

---

[26] For instance, Trench P, NW Well, contained HP 774, a cooking-ware jug similar to Attic examples dated 460–440, and HP 776, an eschara stand similar to Attic examples dated 460–390. Trench P NW contained HP 691, a louterion rim fragment similar to an Attic example dated ca. 430–415. Trench M, west extension, contained HP 693, an Attic Type A skyphos fragment dated 400–375.

[27] In Trench O, the paving was seen to turn up against the wall. As there is no foundation trench, it is probable that the wall blocks were originally exposed for much of their height (note the same height for the orthostates of Tower **10**, above, 27) and that the mud brick covered by this paving comes from the destruction of the earlier house. The room in Trench R with a fine plaster floor contained 4th-century pottery, including an Attic red-figured hydria (HP 924), a black-glazed kantharos (HP 813), and a cooking-ware lopas (HP 872). It was probably contemporary with the stone-and-pebble paving, although being farther up the slope, the elevation of the floor is about 0.45 m higher.

[28] In 1976, the width at the drain beside the Command Post was measured as 2.45 m. The Northeast Wall is not as straight as it appears at small scale. Cooper's survey shows that it was probably constructed in several segments, perhaps from bastion to bastion, that are not perfectly aligned.

[29] With a roof platform, these bastions could qualify as towers of shallow projection, designed specifically for artillery (Winter, per lit.). Compare the projection (2.20 m) with that of Tower **10** (2.50 m). See below for discussion of the access stair and the Command Post at the central bastion.

[30] Trench T, NB 1.1, 113. Not all the various trenches are shown on Williams's end-of-season plan. This one, called the Base Trench, was "ca. 1.50 x 4.00 m" and was cleared to a depth of 0.40 m below the surface " . . . ca. 3.50 m north of the central column base," near the center of the trench and 0.20 m below the surface, "were a series of bricks (touvla) in a fragmentary state." The bricks were recorded as 0.05 m thick and at least 0.31 x 0.25 m in length and width. The acropolis bricks seem to have been thicker, e.g., those in Tower **6**, 0.41–0.435 long and averaging 0.077 m thick (Williams n.d.).

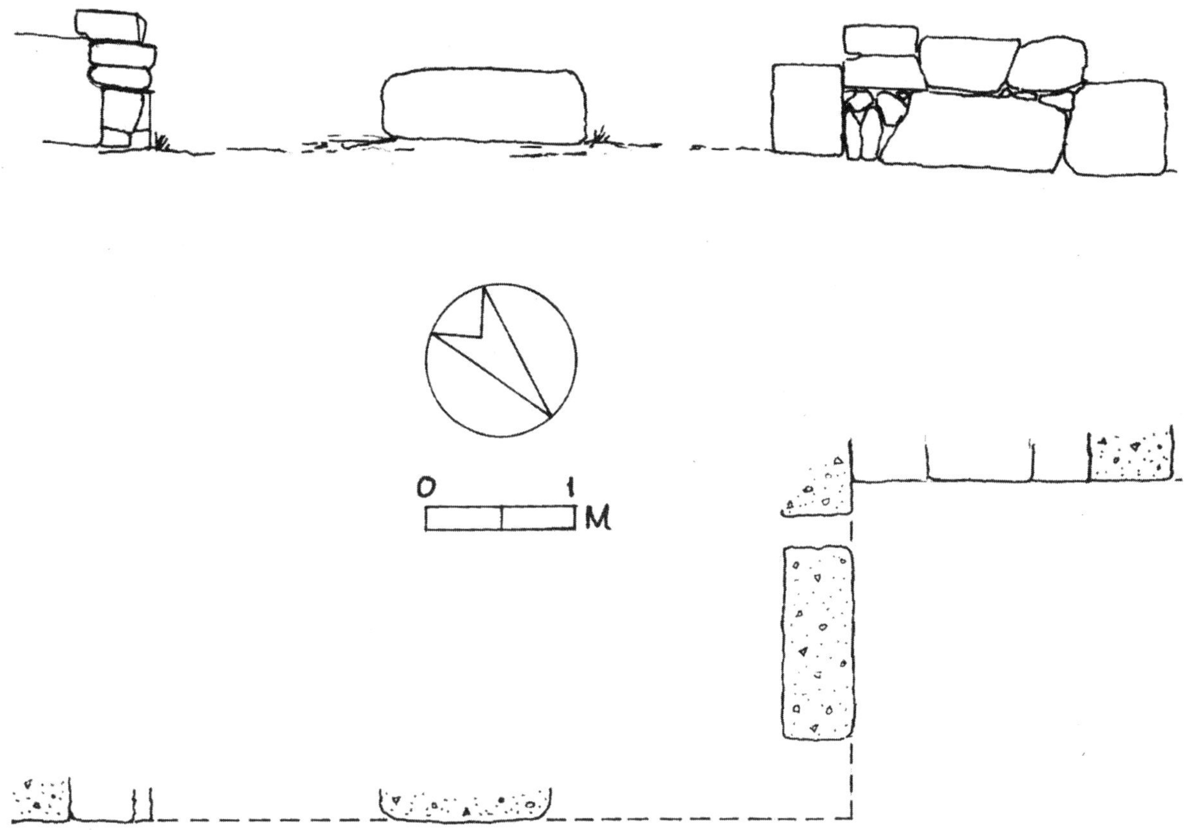

Fig. 13. Center bastion, Northeast Wall, elevation and plan

line of the outer wythe of the curtain. The bricks could be from either the curtain base or the bastion.

The center bastion shows signs of repair (Fig. 13, Pls. 15b, c). The two large conglomerate orthostates of the original northwest side remain, bonded deeply into the face of the curtain. Only one orthostate of the curtain is preserved. The gap between this block and the bastion is filled with small scraps, which were also used to repair the face of the bastion near the east corner. Two roughly fitted limestone stretchers, possibly reused, and two conglomerate blocks carry the curtain base some-what higher than the adjacent bastion orthostates.

The North Wall (Fig. 19)

The connection of the square tower at the Hermion Gate to the curtain of the fortification wall running westward is now lost or buried under the remains of the Late Roman/Early Byzantine bath overlying Tower **11** (Fig. 28). On the aerial photographs a continuous line of blocks can be seen running southwestward toward the shore. This long wall has been interpreted as the face of the curtain on an earlier trace (see above, 16), but it is not possible to make out any details.

The curtain following the later northern trace, extending from Tower **11** to Tower **14** and including Towers **12** and **13**, is now entirely submerged; it enclosed a large area presumably of strategic importance. The connection of this curtain to Tower **11** would have been indirect, using the end of the earlier southerly curtain as an intermediate link to avoid a blind pocket formed by an acute angle. It also was built as a double-wythe, rubble-filled wall, about 2.50 m wide. The outer wythe is bonded with Tower **14** on the east side; the last block is overlapped some 20 centimeters by the wedge-shaped header outside it (Fig. 29). On the inner side of the wall, the excavators found a line of large rectangular poros blocks, lying about 0.25–0.35 m below the level of the outer wythe. The south face of this course is over 5.50 m away from the north face of the outer wythe, so that at the west end it wraps around the south side of the tower. The blocks were traced 90 meters eastward from Tower **14** (about 15 meters east of Tower **13**), continuing in a straight line even when the trace is angled more to the north. It was published by Jameson (1969, 333) as the retaining wall for a mole, enclosing a small harbor, on which the fortification wall was built (see below, 92).

The Northwest Wall (Figs. 18, 19)

As it passes the Northwest Command Post west of Tower **15**, the curtain, which forms the north wall of the building, appears to be narrower, perhaps two meters in width (Fig. 30).[31] After a gap of 25 to 30 meters where only the bare outline can be made out in the aerial photographs, a third, intermediate line of blocks appears between the two outer faces, continuing around the inward bend of the trace at Meter 1665 between Towers **15** and **16** (Fig. 30). The overall width appears to be a constant 2.50 m or even less. On the west side of the bend an additional structure on the inside of the wall may have been a stair (below, 59); the intermediate line of blocks extends beyond it in both directions. The purpose of this middle wythe is not clear. Perhaps it was intended to strengthen the vulnerable interior angle of the curtain; the width of outer and intermediate wythe together is too slight ever to have served alone as the fortification.

The curtain between Towers **17** and **18** appears in the aerial photograph to be curved, but more probably it was built in a series of straight sections.

The Middle Wall (Figs. 18, 19)

The Middle Wall can be traced at intervals from the acropolis halfway down the hillside almost to the modern road. Below this point there are no indications of its existence. The longest stretch in the upper part skirts the west side of the acropolis, running almost straight north after apparently originating at Tower **5**; this section is discussed above as the western trace (17; Pl. 16a).[32] Above

the scarp at about the 25-meter contour there are blocks that have been surveyed and assigned to one or more lines of wall, but none have been cleared. Parallel blocks at the 30-meter contour show an overall width of about two meters; they appear to align with others upslope that form the eastern trace (above, 17). Above the parallel blocks, a wall runs crosswise, not quite at right angles and extending farther to the west. The group was interpreted by Boyd as a right-angle bend in the western trace. Von Harl (1970 season summary) referred to a structure "in the middle of the upper terrace" that suggested to him the outline of a tower, perhaps these same blocks. Since a tower would rarely have been built at an interior angle, it would have to belong to the eastern trace.

The best-preserved section is about half way from the acropolis to the shore, on the two sloping terraces (middle and lower) above the modern road (Fig. 31).[33] In 1962, Williams spent a day clearing the surviving blocks of the wall on the middle terrace "to certify its existence."[34] The southern end was cleared again in 1970, and the excavations in Sections F5-6 opened trenches at the bottom of the middle terrace, where the downhill trace jogged to the east, as well as on the lower terrace.[35]

At the southern end of the middle terrace the wall runs straight downhill (Pls. 16b, c, 17a). It emerges at right angles from a near-vertical scarp several meters high, along the line of which the western trace coming down from the acropolis has shifted some 12 meters to the east. The ground slopes downward from the scarp at a considerable angle that lessens only slightly over the northern part of the middle terrace, dropping altogether some 5 meters in the 30-meter distance; the lower-

---

[31] For the Northwest Command Post, see below, 70; for the drain beside it, see below, 61–62. The divers extended their operations to include this area.

[32] I am dependent on Cooper's survey working plan for details of the section of the western trace northwest of the acropolis, which I have seen but not measured. On the plan, intended to record location rather than exact sizes of blocks, the width scales 2.5–3.0 m. The western wythe here is virtually continuous. The eastern, more heavily covered with detritus from the acropolis edge and consequently overgrown with shrubs, is represented by only a few blocks. No cross blocks are indicated, but there is little slope.

[33] The northern terrace (in Section F6) lies between the 15-meter and 17-meter contours, the southern terrace (in Section F5) roughly between the 17-meter and 22-meter contours, at the high scarp. Von Harl referred to these in his "Concluding Report" as "lower" and "middle," reserving "upper" for the much longer but more problematic stretch above the scarp. These are the designations used here. Williams excavated only on the middle

terrace; a reference to the "lower stretch" probably means that just south of Tower **19**.

[34] "A run of 30.05 meters" (NB 5, 134). The long trenches were then refilled. About seven meters near the center of the stretch was left untouched because it passed close to an olive tree. Williams noted "an excavation needed to examine wall construction, chronology, and relationship of surrounding [buildings] to it." In 1970, when the southern end of this run (at the high scarp) was cleared again (NB 122, 13–15), sketch plans were made by Von Harl and David and Barbara Blackwell. My survey notes were made the following year (NB 516, 43), but some of the blocks had been reburied.

[35] Trench F5-1, 1.5 m wide, crossed the wall near the northern end of the upper segment. The exposed blocks of the 12-meter section on the lower terrace, which continues downhill on a line offset about 8 m and angled more to the east, was surveyed in 1970; two trenches (F6-3, F6-4), each 2 m wide, crossed the northern end.

terrace segment drops about 2 meters in a 15-meter length. The builders accordingly used a compartmented curtain construction not found elsewhere at Halieis but well known at other sites. The cross blocks, bonded into one wythe and butted against the other, served to keep the fill of small stones and earth within the cavity from sliding downhill. As other steep sections of the outer circuit at Halieis were built without this device, however, it may be the added strength thus given to a relatively narrow wall, 20–30 percent narrower than in most other places, was a contributing factor in the choice of the construction system.[36]

On the middle terrace, the contrast between the two wythes is immediately apparent.[37] The eastern is formed of conglomerate orthostates 0.31–0.32 m wide and 1.47–1.67 m long; no height is recorded, but there is a step at each joint.[38] Presumably owing to the minimum depth of his excavation, Williams did not say whether other stones, earth, or bedrock lay beneath the orthostates. About 11 meters from the south scarp, where the orthostate is missing, a single block roughly 0.60 m square extends somewhat east of the line of the wall. The western half of the block has been trimmed down to carry the missing orthostate, apparently at a place where there was a low point in the bedrock or the subsoil was too soft. The next block to the north on Von Harl's sketch appears after a gap, in the proper interval for an orthostate, but it is shown wider and at the same level as the parallel plinth in the western wythe. Although both Williams and Von Harl restricted the poros plinths to the western wythe, this block may again have filled an exceptional low or soft spot. Where Trench F5-1 crossed the wall, one orthostate of the eastern wythe was missing; the remaining one was set directly on soil without plinth or socle.

The western wythe on the other hand is represented by poros plinths up to 0.65 m wide and uniformly 1.20 m in length.[39] As they ascended the steep slope, some of these overlap. The conglomerate blocks remaining on the plinth course are 0.40–0.43 m wide, 1.20–1.40 m long, with some shorter fillers. Where the south end was cleared, two conglomerate cross blocks were exposed at the level of the plinths; they presumably carried orthostates like one in situ in Trench F5-1. They were bonded into the western wythe and abutted the eastern, creating compartments the length of two orthostates. The total width of the curtain is only 1.70 m in sharp contrast to 2.25–2.50 m usual elsewhere at Halieis.

At the bottom of the middle terrace, the trace jogs again to the east. A few conglomerate orthostates and some cuttings show the line of the return, which was set on a ridge of bedrock; one of the blocks was reused, apparently in situ, in the wall of a mid-4th-century house. There is a row of conglomerate blocks that parallel the east–west line of the jog at a remove of about 0.90 m to the south. The size of the blocks (up to 0.50 m by 1.00 m) distinguishes them from the rubble used with mud mortar in the 4th-century house walls. They may represent the outer line of a stair tucked into the corner to provide access to the curtain at Tower **19** (see below, 59).

Tower **19** guards the jog in the trace between the terraces, but there is no sign of any gate or postern. On the lower terrace, the compartmented construction of the defense wall continues at a width of 1.65 m (Pl. 17c). At the south end, the first two preserved blocks of the eastern wythe are of limestone.[40] Two others now lie diagonally across the cavity giving the false impression of cross blocks bonded into the eastern side; as the core slipped away, they shifted to lie more directly

---

[36] The compartmented wall, with cross blocks bonded into one or both faces, is a development of the more primitive use of headers to bond the faces to the fill. It is already known at Oiniadai (late 5th or early 4th century; Winter 1971, 236), where the cross blocks occur regularly every 2.50 m (Powell 1904, 146), but becomes general in the 4th-century header-and-stretcher style of masonry (Tomlinson 1961, 133–140), e.g., at Phyle, Gortys, Messene, and Mantinea. The technique was particularly favored in sea walls, e.g., at Lechaion and Delos (Paris 1915, 13 and note 1). The cellular construction of the acropolis wall in Phase 4 was not the same; the crosswalls were of rubble masonry.
[37] The sections of curtain on these two terraces are the only ones at Halieis where blocks of both wythes have been cleared and can be compared. Although Trenches O and M in the East Tower area and I5-1 southwest of the East Gate crossed the foundations of the curtain, no blocks of the wall base are preserved there.
[38] Von Harl recorded the steps as 15 cm in height (NB 122, 13),

but the levels noted on each block on his sketch indicate drops of 0.32 m, 0.26 m, and 0.21 m, proceeding from south to north. These figures suggest that the conglomerate blocks could have been standard stretchers 0.40 m high, but Williams and Von Harl referred to them as orthostates. At Halieis, orthostates are regularly 0.60 m high but are 0.35–0.40 m rather than 0.30 m in width, even for house walls.
[39] Von Harl's measurements, roughly standard for poros plinths. Williams recorded lengths of 0.26 m and 0.53 m, as well as 1.21 m, but the short pieces may have been next to the cross blocks.
[40] Williams recorded other limestone blocks (NB 5, 133–34): "At one point on this west face, at lowest level of wall (not certain that this set of blocks rests on bedrock) are two well cut limestone (grey) rough hammer dressed blocks that appear to be reused material." These blocks have not been identified and may lie in the refilled trench between Trench F5-1 and the cleared blocks at the south end of the upper terrace.

with the slope. A true cross block remains in situ, bonded into the western wythe in Trench F6-3.

The exceptionally narrow width of the wall on both these terraces would have left little more than a meter at most for the walkway. The width might be increased, either permanently, using overhanging slabs as at Messene (Adam 1982, photo 61), or in a removable form with planks on scaffolding, even without additional supporting piers.[41]

Under a tile fall against the west face, Williams reported finding lamps that can be dated to the later 5th and early 4th centuries.[42] In Trench F5-1 a 4th-century coin of Hermion was found in the upper part of the stone fill between the wythes.[43] A piece of a heavy Corinthian pan tile appeared under one of the orthostates on the middle terrace, one of only a few such among many Lakonian tiles from the trenches. If it was used on the wall, it is from an earlier stage, but the excavators found no indication of an earlier wall or any repairs to the visible remains.

The Middle Wall, which apparently had only one tower and even though reinforced with cross blocks used less material, does not suggest a defense against outside forces armed with 4th-century artillery. The possible reasons for its construction, the question of its trace north of the excavated section, and its relation to the rest of the fortifications are discussed in the final chapter.

Access to the Walkway

There must, of course, have been some regular access to the walkway, or parados, at the top of the curtain. Where there were towers with a hollow ground floor, an interior ladder or stair served the purpose, but where these were not available, some sort of exterior access was required.[44] While ladders could be used where convenient and as conveniently cast aside to impede access to the city by any enemy who scaled the wall, when several armed defenders, carrying weapons, needed to go up or down, some more permanent construction, whether stair or ramp, would be provided.[45] There is no evidence for the height of the curtains at Halieis. Philo (1.12) prescribes a minimum of 20 cubits (about 9.25 m) to exceed the capacity of scaling ladders; this would include the height of the parapet.[46] The height of the walkway from the ground on the inside might be about two meters less, or even as little as 4.50 m as at Messene (Lawrence 1979, 345). Lawrence stated that one access should be provided for each stretch of curtain so that troops would not need to pass through the towers; he added, however, that the stairs were often located at the towers, with the landing at the door to the chamber at walkway level (1979, 345–46). On the other hand, stairs at gates were considered poor defensive planning, since they would make it easy for any who forced the gate to gain access to the walkway.[47]

Whether or not entirely of stone, the stairs were commonly constructed parallel to the curtain, to save material and to avoid interfering with the passage of troops at the foot of the wall. Stone steps were supported by a ramp of earth and rubble, which was contained by a stone or mud-brick flanking wall like those of the curtain wythes. On a slope, the run usually started at the higher end, reducing the number of risers to a

---

[41] See Winter 1971, 143–45, for a discussion of Philo's ἴκρια (80.31–32) and wooden scaffolding.

[42] NB 5, 132–33. HL 19, BG lamp, Howland Type 21 C (Athenian Agora IV), last quarter 5th well into early 4th century. HL 20, BG lamp nozzle, Howland Type 23 A (?), late third quarter 5th into first quarter 4th century. Von Harl wrote in his 1970 summary that a date post quem is given by the remains of an early 4th-century house in Trench F5-1 overrun by the compartmented wall. It seems likely, however, that he based this conclusion on the large conglomerate block at the west end of Trench F6-2 that was dressed down for the orthostate crossing it. This block, with the others in line to the east of it, probably belongs to a wall-access stair rather than an earlier house wall (see below, 59).

[43] HN 1970-4. See below, **165**, 135.

[44] Winter (1971, 149) cited Gyphtokastro as an example of this distinction.

[45] Winter 1971, 149: ἀναβασμός or ἀναβαθμός is the general term used for steps but does not define the construction used. The alternative term κλίμακες was used to denote permanent

stairways but was certainly originally applied to ladders or fixed wooden stairs. While "ramp" is often used in archaeological writing, owing to the disappearance of the actual step blocks, I have been unable to find any example of ramped access except at the Dema Wall and at Miletos. McNicoll (1997, 14) wrote that "ramps to the wallwalks were probably quite common" (presumably in the Hellenistic period) as they were useful for moving artillery machines, but he could cite no example in Asia Minor except for the southern cross wall at Miletos. However useful, to accommodate machines they would have needed to be wider than a stair (the smallest stone thrower was ca. 2.5 m wide), as well as longer, making much more of an interruption to the passage beside the walls.

[46] Winter gave the average height of Classical walls (including parapet and merlons) as 7.00–9.50 m, citing Phyle (ca. 8.50–9.50 m) and Messene (ca. 7.00–9.00 m).

[47] The well-documented stairways at Thorikos are a good example of this principle, all set at a distance from the gates or posterns. See Mussche 1961.

minimum (Lawrence 1979, 345). The width, Lawrence wrote, is "generally uniform"; ranging from less than a meter to nearly two meters, it needed to be sufficient for two men with equipment.[48] There seems to have been little care in the preserved examples to make the treads or risers uniform; treads range from 27 to 35 cm, risers from 23 to 28 cm (Martin 1947–1948, 112, fig. 3, note 5).

Access at Meter 130 (Figs. 18, 19)
At Halieis, where the stone masonry of the curtain was limited to a base course, any remains of a stair would appear as no more than a projection on the inside of the wall. At Meter 130 there is such an addition, indicated by a line of blocks now barely visible in the modern road.[49] Extending over 11 meters, the wall base that they form projects 1.50 m from the inner wall face at the north end and 1.18 m at the south; the ground here is now virtually flat.[50] The structure is about the length required to reach a walkway at an average height.[51] If the bottom of the stair was at the south end, the greater projection at the north end may have been designed to give the high stair greater stability, perhaps even allowing the face of the supporting ramp to be battered, or to widen the landing at the top.

In the Halieis type of earth-and-stone-fill construction the inner wythe at a stair might be interrupted, as here, if stair and curtain were constructed together; the bastions are similarly designed (above, 52). This system would, in effect, rely on a stone base only on the outer sides where the mud brick was exposed to the elements. The surface remains do not show any inner wall blocks in the interval (a single piece of conglomerate now visible appears to be bedrock), but excavation would be necessary to be sure. A break in the wall line is implied by Williams's sketch and seems to show clearly on the aerial photographs, despite

the indication to the contrary on the 1962 topographic plan.

An alternative to a stair is suggested by a similar construction at Thorikos near the main gate in the north wall (Mussche 1961, 184, pl. IV:E). Its length is 5.40 m, its projection 1.20 m at the east end, 1.50 m at the west; this canted position is described by the author as "irregular." Enough is preserved to show that this was not a stair but an enlargement of the wall for the defense of the adjacent gate; no explanation is given for the cant. At Halieis, in contrast to Thorikos, there is no sign of a gate between Meter 130 and Tower **1**; the outer wythe is continuous as far as the knob. It is also conceivable that this inner buttress formed an access landing, reached by a ladder.

*Access East of Tower **4*** (Figs. 18, 19)
Descending the southeast side of the knoll at Tower **4**, the trace turns at an angle toward the acropolis. On the level ground at the bottom, there is again a projection on the inner side of the wall. Connected to the main curtain by a slanting wall on the west and a right-angle jog on the east, the projection is 0.83 m wide and measured 3.07 m along the curtain. The outer wythe is continuous, but the inner is interrupted. This construction is both shorter and narrower than the one at Meter 130, but the wall may not have been so high here.

Access on the Acropolis
Two sets of stairs from the Phase 6 barracks to Tower **6** and to the earlier wall are described in Williams n.d.

Access on the Industrial Terrace (Fig. 22)
Near the west end of the Industrial Terrace a short, steeply sloping line of blocks appears north of the inner line (above, 48). There are two conglomerate stretchers with a nearly square limestone block at either end. It is difficult to say in their uncleared

---

[48] Seven examples of stairs at Thorikos (*op. cit.*) average 1.15 m in width, ranging from 1.15 m to 1.50 m. Lawrence, in stating that there are no known traces of wooden handrails, remarked that they would have impeded men carrying equipment. For two men passing each other, moving at any pace with equipment, a meter seems impossibly narrow; it is, in fact, the dimension found in posterns designed to pass one man at a time (see above, 44, note 86).
[49] For the state of the remains see above, 46, note 4.
[50] NB 22, 103. The notes describe the remains as a socle of conglomerate one course high. No dimensions are recorded for the height and width of the blocks; the height was probably not completely preserved or visible even then. No attempt was made to look for the bottom of the blocks or to discover on what they

rested. The notes for the 1970 survey (NB 514, 92) give the length as 11.69 m and the southern projection as 1.17 m. On the 1962 topographic plan, the projection scales ten meters by one meter at each end, but the cant is obvious on the aerial photographs.
[51] At Thorikos the stairs vary in length from 3.50 m (Stair T, without landing) to 8.75 m, depending on the length of the landing at the top as well as some variation in the height of the wall. Making a very rough calculation, with treads of minimum width (27 cm), 11 meters would allow for 33 treads and a generous landing over two meters long; 25 treads would be possible at maximum width (35 cm). The height attained by 34 risers (23–28 cm each) would be ca. 7.80–9.50 m, by 26 risers ca. 6.00–7.25 m.

state whether they are parallel to the inner or to the middle line of wall. A connection with the latter, which is interpreted as the inner wythe of an outer curtain, is suggested by a single crosswise block that projects from the curtain inward toward these four blocks rather than toward the outer wythe. The remains are too tenuous to support any reconstruction, but they may have been part of some access to the walkway at the point where the wall climbed the scarp to the acropolis.

A few unexplained blocks north of Tower **7** (Fig. 9) may also be remnants of a stair (see above, 24).

Access at Tower 8
The possibility of stairs in Tower **8** is discussed with the Chambered Curtain (see below, 65).

Access at the Southeast Gate (Figs. 24, 25)
There are two additions inside the wall just northeast of the Southeast Gate. The first is now reduced to five large poros slabs and a fill of large stones and earth behind them.[52] Its length is about 3.35 m, its projection about 1.30 m from the face of the trapezoidal structure on the northeast side of the gate; their northeast ends are aligned. Even at the steepest proportion of tread to riser (27/28 cm), a stair on this base would have risen only about 2.50 m from the street level, conceivably for access to a room on an intermediate level, over a solidly filled ground-level base. The poros slabs have no structural connection with the gate or curtain; in more sophisticated surroundings they would be taken for a monument base.

Barely a meter further along the inside of the curtain, there is a substantial foundation 1.60 m wide and exposed for 8.50 m.[53] Its face is built of conglomerate blocks with joints irregularly wider at the top than at the bottom; these are filled with small untrimmed conglomerate blocks or limestone cobbles. The character of the masonry is similar to that of the outer wythe of the curtain at the shrine (see above, 50) but less carefully executed. This structure appears to be the base for a well-built flight of steps, probably stone treads set in a mud-brick ramp, with a mud-brick facing like the rest of the curtain. At the southwest end, there is a platform of

somewhat smaller blocks, 0.85 m deep and the full width of the stair, like a bottom landing. The remaining length, even if no greater than what appeared in the trench, would provide for a minimum top landing of 0.80 m and 22 treads about 31 cm wide, rising between 5.75 m and 6.45 m to the walkway, if it was level with the landing. The block next to the bottom landing along the face is considerably deeper than wide, with two dressed faces, as though to provide a cornerstone at the beginning of the rise.

The continuous inner face of the curtain may provide a clue to the unorthodox position of this stair so close to the Southeast Gate. It appears to have been added to the original construction, quite possibly after the gate had been permanently closed.

Access at Tower 10 (Fig. 26)
The line of the Northeast Wall runs southeastward straight from the Hermion Gate past the Northeast Command Post, and several blocks visible on the surface indicate that it continued to Tower **10**, where it would have met the northwest face at a slight angle. Two large conglomerate blocks lie on a line parallel to the curtain (that is, at right angles to the northwest face of the tower), starting about 1.50 m from the west corner of the tower and about 1.80 m from the assumed line of the curtain's inner face. It is possible that another block actually bonded with the face of the tower, but its presence cannot be determined without at least clearing the point of intersection. It seems likely that there was a stairway here, set in the corner between tower and curtain; it would provide access to the walkway and perhaps to an upper room in the tower. The arrangement is similar to that at Tower **19**, except that here the stair is at right angles to the tower rather than to the curtain.

Access at the Northeast Command Post (Fig. 27)
The visible remains on the inside of the curtain from Tower **10** almost to the Hermion Gate include no structure that might provide access to the walkway with the possible exception of the Northeast Command Post. The base course for the curtain is absent for the 10.20 m width of this building, but its line is paralleled at a distance of

---

[52] There are three blocks set parallel to the wall and a fourth at right angles across the southwest end, the fifth filling the space behind it. The northeast end now appears open or unfinished; the last block is hollowed out on the inside as though it had been cut originally for the mouth of a well.

[53] An extension on the east side of the excavation trench, intended to pursue the line of a drain crossing Street 1, revealed a casual line of small stones not quite at a right angle, apparently running across the end of the stair less than a meter more to the northeast. This little wall seems quite different in character and probably overlies any further evidence of the stair.

about 1.20 m by a socle of small stones, providing little more than a leveling course. The length, if continued across the building, would be adequate for a stair to the walkway, strategically located midway between Towers **10** and **11**. The presence of a stair contemporary with the bastion would explain the absence of a base course for the curtain (compare the stair at Meter 130). It appears that the base course for any such stair, at one time leveled by the preserved socle course, has been entirely removed along with almost all the orthostates for the walls. The stair could have been accessible both from within the building and from the northwestern section of Avenue A.[54]

Access at the Hermion Gate (Fig. 28)
The preserved blocks of the inner wythe stop 6 meters southeast of the Hermion Gate; the last 1.70 m is overlapped by a wall that adds nearly a meter to the width of the curtain. This wall is composed of stretchers, but headers extending toward the curtain, on either side of the third block from the gate passage, suggest that the structure was filled solid. The aerial photograph shows the fill of the fortification wall at full width as far as the western of the two headers even though the blocks of the inner wythe are missing. Between the line of that wythe and the parallel wall, however, no fill can be seen; perhaps it was of mud brick rather than rubble. It is possible that this was a bastion strengthening the gate, with an access stair, but this would be counter to the rule against stairs at gates.

It will be noted that no point of access has been suggested for the long stretch of the North Wall. Towers **12** and **13** seem too small for internal access except by ladder. Towers **11** and **14**, however, are large enough and must be assumed to have provided access for both the guards and light armaments.[55]

Access at the Northwest Command Post (Fig. 30)
A passage along the west side of this building (see below, 62) was interpreted by Jameson as a ramped access to the walkway, with a widening at the north end for a landing just inside the line of the curtain. At that place the defense wall has an opening between two cross blocks that suggests a drain; perhaps drain and ramp were combined.

The use of a ramp, rather than an inside stair, may be linked to the movement of artillery from the main street to the wall. Apparently as a consequence of this choice, the Northwest Command Post is shallower than its northeast counterpart by the width of the stair (see above).[56]

Access at Meter 1665 (Fig. 30)
The last identifiable location for a stair along the Northwest Wall is at the strong interior angle at Meter 1665, between Towers **15** and **16**. Three lines of masonry are preserved at the angle, which was further augmented by an interior projection that may have carried a stair. As at the locations at Meter 130 and the Northeast Command Post, the line of the wythe on the city side is interrupted; the length of the projection is about 10.20 m and the additional width somewhat over a meter.[57] The structure would have strengthened the vulnerable interior angle but obstructed the passage along the service street.

Access to the Middle Wall (Fig. 31)
A row of conglomerate blocks set on bedrock parallels the east–west jog of the curtain on the south side of Tower **19**. They are only approximately rectangular, about 0.40 m wide and as much as 0.60 m long. Despite their irregular shape, from their size alone they seem more akin to the blocks of the curtain than to the rubble walls of the houses in the area. The block at the west end has been cut down to make a bed for the block of the curtain that once crossed it. Another, similarly trimmed, was reused in the house built over the eastern part of the row. This one might, in fact, be the now-missing block from the curtain, turned upside down. The row of irregular blocks probably formed the base for a wall supporting a stair, about a meter wide and four meters long that provided access to the curtain and to Tower **19**. Its location south of the jog allowed it to start a meter or more higher than the base of the tower on the terrace below.[58]

The Drains

The Drain at the Southeast Gate (Fig. 25; Pls. 10a, b)
Just 1.30 m southwest of the Southeast Gate, a large drain runs through the curtain and the

---

[54] For the possibility of a stair over the drain outside the Command Center, see below, 61, note 64.
[55] Compare the bastion at Thorikos, above, 57.
[56] It should be noted that at the southwest corner of the Command Post, the narrowest point, the width of the "ramp"

between buildings on Frost and Owen's plan scales barely two meters.
[57] These dimensions are of necessity approximate since they are scaled from the Frost and Owen plan of the underwater remains.
[58] Compare the access stair at Tower **10**, above, 58.

structure behind it. It is positioned close to the corner where Street 1 crosses the end of Avenue C. The wider, chambered form of the curtain used higher up the slope seems to end here at the gate building, and Street 1, which runs along the inside face of the curtain, jogs to the east along with it. The natural drainage on Avenue C would run either directly into the drain or through the gateway. At the same time, surface water running down the hill from the upper part of Street 1 would pass close by the inlet. If the streets were in good repair, the gutters channeled most of the runoff to the drain.

The drain itself is 0.90 m wide and runs parallel to the southwest side of the gate passage at a distance of about 1.30 m. It is constructed of large conglomerate orthostates, 0.165–0.20 m thick, about 0.60 m high, and varying from 0.44 m to 1.45 m in length. It was originally roofed with slabs of sandy conglomerate, 0.50–0.80 m wide, several of which were found in situ.[59] The floor at the inlet was at the level of the street gutter and for the first 0.30–0.35 m was composed of compacted cobbles resembling road metal. The main part of the drain, of which nearly eight meters have been cleared, was paved with slabs of conglomerate. The outer end, which now lies under the modern road, could not be explored, but before reaching the limit of the trench, the floor changed again to broken stone or bedrock. The drain continued into the scarp; at this point it was already a meter beyond the outer face of the square south corner of the gateway, but the position of the outer face of the curtain as it continued southwest is not known.

At the inner end, by good fortune the first cover slab as well as the floor slab was preserved in situ (Pl. 10c). In each there were two rectangular cuttings measuring about 0.03 x 0.035 m, the longer dimension across the drain. A slope was cut to the side of the northeast floor socket and the southwest cover socket. One end of a bar could be seated and then the opposite end hammered sideways into place. The upper sockets are now slightly to the south of those below, but this is presumably owing to a very small shift in the position of the cover slab. Vertical bars inserted in these slots, 0.565–0.57 m in from the inner opening, would have divided the channel in three, preventing the passage of anything larger than about 0.32 m (the center interval). A heavy rain would have produced a torrent down the upper stretch of Street 1, supplemented by the runoff from Avenue C, which would have been drained in part down other cross streets. The bars at the inner end of the drain would have kept it clear of branches and other debris, as well as acting as a safety measure for goats, sheep, dogs, or small children. An examination of the outer end, where bars might be expected to prevent the ingress of an enemy, produced no traces of any cuttings as far as now cleared, nor any masonry dividers of the opening.[60]

The barrier at the inner end of the drain at the Southeast Gate at Halieis would have provided an eventual deterrent to anyone trying to crawl through, but unless the bars were leaded in place, the slope at the side of the sockets (see above) would have allowed them to be removed fairly easily, perhaps to clean the channel; if the drain was buried in the solid structure of the gate building, there may have been no other access. Lawrence (1979, 271) cites accounts in Strabo (15.1.21) and Diodorus (19.45) of flooding at Rhodes caused by blocked drains, which often narrowed toward the outer end, making it difficult to clear obstructions.[61]

The details of the drain at the Southeast Gate, including a carefully laid floor and walls bonded into the blocks beside the gate, must have been required by its location under a structure planned with the gate, of which there is now little evidence. Its extent inside the curtain seems to have been determined by the depth of this

---

[59] This sandstone was undoubtedly chosen because it weighed relatively little and was easily cut in slabs, but elsewhere it does not seem to have been used to carry any great load. The slabs now missing may have been taken to cover graves (see above, 10) or to use as floor slabs; compare a 4th-century building, possibly commercial, found in Trenches 165/210, 165/215 (10, note 24).

[60] Dr. Von Harl brought to my attention an account in Polybios (4.57) of the drunken gate guard at Aigira, surprised by an Aitolian deserter who entered the city through a water channel (διά τινος ὑδρορροίας). At Megara Hyblaia, a large drain fitted with grills to keep out the enemy replaced an earlier channel sometime in the 6th century (Tréziny 1986, 188). Sockets for bars at the mouth of drains were found at Pergamon (Conze 1913, I,

ii, 203) and at Thasos, where they were set in lead (Garlan 1966, 612; 1967, 272). At Amphipolis six triangular piers subdivided large water channels into seven, each 20 cm wide at the opening; square sockets provided for a bar in each subchannel (Lazarides 1975, 63–71, dwg. 5). These drains would have needed an access at the inlet sufficient to allow cleaning from time to time.

[61] Neither the drain at the Southeast Gate nor the one beside the Northeast Command Post (see below) appears to narrow at all. Other possible drains mentioned here were underwater off shore and are only apparent for the short passage through the curtain; there is no obvious indication of narrowing. A 4th-century example of a grill at the inlet end was found at Thasos (see note 60 above).

building together with the Chambered Curtain. Although the drain would silt up very quickly without regular cleaning, sherds found in the fill (Trench 990/350, 1976) ranged from 5th-century red figure to Roman rouletted ware.

The Drain at Tower 10
For the possibility of a drain on the southwest side of the tower, see above, 29.

The Drain at the Northeast Command Post (Fig. 27)
A drain similar to that at the Southeast Gate runs through the Northeast Wall just east of the Command Post. It emerges from the present bank at the shore, about 5.50 m beyond the outer face of the curtain. In 1962, the conduit was cleared for about 1.20 m in from the mouth, where work was halted for fear of danger to the workman.[62] The internal width at the top of the outlet is recorded as about 0.95 m; the side walls were more than a half meter high. In the excavation trench adjacent to the Command Post, three large poros slabs were found covering the conduit roughly between the two wythes of the curtain;[63] two more slabs were cleared outside it. The interval between the two cover slabs outside and the three inside is only about 0.35 m, a minimum for wall-base blocks; it is filled by two conglomerate blocks with a joint at the center of the span. No investigation was made of the walls or floor of this part of the drain or the way in which the curtain blocks bridged the channel, nor is the ancient ground level known in relation to the slabs outside the curtain.

No sign of the inner wythe of the curtain was recorded. Two blocks at the northwest side of the drain are dressed down to carry cover slabs a meter further inside the curtain. The poros plinths along the side of the Command Post terminate against them. Together with the blocks that back them, they may have framed the inlet at this point. On the available evidence, it is hard to explain why the inlet was projected inside the line of the curtain.[64] The drain is positioned approximately on the line of Street 4, which would direct storm runoff as far as the little square in front of the Command Post. If the gutter feeding the drain began at street level near the front of the building, like the drain at the Southeast Gate, its floor would have been roughly level with the Command Post plinths, which Halieis building practice put approximately at ground level. At the back of the building, the elevations of the plinths and the cover slabs are not recorded, but the latter cannot be higher by much.[65] The thickness of the slabs may be estimated from a photograph as at least 0.40 m, and the floor of the drain was probably down another 0.60 m. Running in the open space beside the southeast wall, some sort of channeling would have been required along the side of the building, probably involving a deeper foundation beneath the poros plinth course, only the top of which was exposed in the 1962 excavation.

The Drain at the Northwest Command Post (Fig. 30)
There are indications of other possible drains in the part of the curtain that is now submerged. Nothing is known about the gradient of Avenue I, which runs more or less parallel to the modern shore line and, less closely, to the Northwest Wall; it may have been negligible. The chief surface runoff doubtless came down the intersecting streets, although their grade was probably slight. Some of the openings in the curtain align with streets, but this was apparently not consistent; the street pattern was not always maintained between Avenue I and the fortification wall. Along the west side of the Northwest Command Post, at about Meter 1623, is a passage that bends to the west at midpoint and is enlarged where it meets the curtain; the curtain is pierced by a small opening that is divided in half by a single block at right angles to the line of the wall. On either side are short returns and blocks doubling the outer wythe. It has not been possible

---

[62] The mouth of the drain is described (NB 1.1, 79) as "rock-cut." Bedrock should be well below this level; the natural cementing action of the groundwater so close to the shore would have made it very difficult to distinguish close-fitted blocks. The bank at the edge of the water is bordered at its base with "beachrock," a lime formation with some similarity to bedrock that may have developed since the rise in sealevel in post-Classical times.

[63] The dimensions of the cover slabs (NB 1.1, 159) from south to north: ca. 1.54 x 0.60 m, 1.46 x 0.56 m, 1.50 x 0.60 m.

[64] It has been suggested that there was an access stair here, paralleling the curtain and rising over the drain. While

theoretically possible, there is as yet no evidence for or against. If it existed but was removed when the Command Post was built, the base might have been retained to avoid a corner that would trap runoff water.

[65] No routine elevations were taken during the 1962 excavations; the depth of the various walls and blocks were recorded as measured down from the surface. While the cover slabs of the drain are said to be "parallel with or slightly below the surface of the earth" (NB 1.1, 159), the Ionic capital HS 6 "lay on the suspected stylobate [plinths], ca. 42 cm below surface of earth" (NB 1.1, 39).

to study the remains except in plan in the aerial photograph together with the plan produced by Frost and Owen; the relation to ancient street level is unknown.

Jameson has commented that the walls of the passage seem heavier than necessary for a drain and suggests that they were the retaining walls for a ramp (above, 59). The adjacent building is not so deep as the Northeast Command Post, with little room for an interior stair behind the central column (below, 70). The opening in the curtain must still be accounted for, however, and the parallel walls, which leave a triangular space open next to the Command Post, suggest a channel. The side walls may have served a dual purpose, ramp above and drain below, opening from a courtyard between the large building and Avenue I, approximately opposite the end of a possible Street e.[66] The bend in the channel suggests that the opening in the fortification wall was already there when the ramp and the Command Post were constructed.

Other Drains Now Submerged (Figs. 18, 30)

At the east side of the postern at Tower **16** (Fig. 8), there are two parallel blocks at right angles to the curtain that seem best explained as subdividing the mouth of a drain (see above, 60, note 60); the position is in line with Street b. Three more openings can be made out in aerial photographs: one at Meter 1720 just west of Tower **16** and two between Towers **17** and **18** at Meters 1785 and 1820. The first is at the end of a wide street or court, the last apparently not. No remains inside the curtain near Tower **17** were recorded by Frost and Owens nor can any be made out on the aerial photograph.

Finally, the opening in the wall on the east side of Tower **13** (Fig. 7) may have been for a drain rather than a postern.[67] This opening is very narrow for a postern, although carefully constructed and as carefully blocked. On the other hand, while nothing is known of the levels or streets inside the wall, there was probably not much slope. If an inner harbor was close by, that would have been the natural recipient of any surface drainage.[68]

---

[66] The existence of this street is entirely hypothetical; it was not shown on Boyd's topographic plan (Boyd and Rudolph 1978, pl. 87).

[67] See above, 44. When the requisite dimensions for a postern and for a drain passage through the curtain are so close, there is room for debate about the correct designation, especially for those now submerged. The opening at Meter 1720, however, is so close to the gate on the other side of Tower **16** that it seems unlikely to have been for a postern.

[68] The possible presence of the harbor nearby leads to the suggestion that this opening served to equalize the water level in the event of a storm from the northwest. Jameson suggests that the inner end of the harbor was between Towers **12** and **13**, which would support this proposal.

– CHAPTER FIVE–

Attached and Adjacent Structures

There are several structures built against or as part of the curtain walls that must be considered to have some defensive purpose. Their presence is worth comment because such construction was often specifically forbidden or at least controlled. A free space between the fortification wall and the buildings inside it was a normal requirement, both to permit rapid movement of troops in an emergency and to guard against treachery from within. Philo (80.15) specifies 60 cubits for a right-of-way inside the wall, a width sufficient to permit the movement of wagons and artillery but perhaps more generous than normally achieved. A similar space was often required on the outside as well. An inscription at Ephesos prescribes 40 feet inside, 50 feet outside (Maier 1959, I, 238–41). Nevertheless, as Winter (1971, 125, note 60) points out, the precaution of a reserved space was not always observed: houses along the west edge of the North Hill at Olynthos are built up to the thin city wall, the intervening space roofed over.[1]

At Halieis those buildings that are known to be part of or directly attached to the defense wall seem not to be houses, and some may have had public as well as military functions. Inside the circuit wall, these include the Chambered Curtain of the upper Southeast Wall, the Northeast Command Post with the mint, and the Northwest Command Post or arsenal, as well as the major structures on the acropolis (see Williams n.d.). Several unattached structures immediately adjacent on the inside of the circuit were probably also military in function. Two non-military buildings were found outside the curtain: a small shrine was built against the outside face, and the Southeast Building, of unknown purpose, was immediately adjacent.

The Chambered Curtain (Fig. 23)

When the Southeast Wall appears below the main scarp that divides the eastern part of the town from the Industrial Terrace, the trace has swung in, running slightly more to the north and continuing straight downhill. Not far from the scarp a trench (H4-5) was dug in 1970 across the line of the fortifications (Fig. 12; see above, 49–50).[2] At the north end of the trench, at the line of the inner wall of the Chambered Curtain, three blocks of a crosswise partition appeared that may mark the uphill end of that structure. Three courses of the wall remain, built up to retain the higher ground to the south.[3] At the base on the northeast side was a layer of small-stone rubble.

As it descends the slope, the defense wall verges on a low scarp above the valley to the southeast. The grade is fairly steep: the difference in ground level from the main scarp to the next low drop, a distance of about 65 meters, is more than seven meters. Considerable stepping would have been necessary here and is evident in the outer line of the wall, well preserved in the northern part of this section. The blocks are conglomerate stretchers, varying in length from 1.08 m to 1.70 m, with the majority between 1.22 m and 1.40 m. In three cases, blocks less than a

---

[1] Robinson and Graham 1938, 39–41, pl. 110). Winter (1971, 164, note 44) suggested that the space between the houses and the city wall may have been used for barracks.
[2] This area is contained in Section H4 on the 1970 grid (N 6900–7000/E 16200–16300). Crossing the Chambered Curtain were

Trenches H4-1, 2, and 5 (NB 112).
[3] A nearly complete Attic one-handler (HP 729, 450–425) and a red-figured fragment from an open shape (HP 1028) were found east of the crosswall, presumably within the room.

meter long were used to fill out the horizontal run of the step; in at least one case a block 0.21 m high was used beneath a stretcher to compensate for the drop. The height and width of the blocks is about 0.40 m and the step half that or less. In the present state of preservation, it is hard to say whether the exterior faces were bossed or merely quarry faced. The tops were dressed smooth and slope slightly downhill. As they have not been cleared, it is not known what lies under the stretchers.

This section of the Southeast Wall is not the filled double-wythe wall used elsewhere for the fortifications but is formed by a series of rooms, about seven meters deep with a continuous northwestern wall along a street. Much of the plan of the upper part can be made out from the surface remains, supplemented by information from some of the trial trenches, but it was not apparent that it probably continued as far as the Southeast Gate until that area was excavated in 1974 (Trench 990/350). The total length would have been at least 130 meters. Blocks showing on the surface at irregular intervals mark off rooms varying in width from 2.30 m to 5.90 m with a uniform interior depth of about 5.20 m. Other blocks paralleling the front and back walls indicate at least some interior subdivision.

Across the street (here 3.7 m wide) along the northwest side of the building were other structures whose remains show scattered across the sloping ground extending to the northwest. Some of these were investigated in Trenches H4-4, 6, and 7 and have been identified as houses by the finds, which date ca. 350–300.[4]

Near the center of the Chambered Curtain a large room projects 0.90–1.00 m beyond the outer wall face in the manner of a tower (Tower 8). The interior dimensions are 7.80 m in width and a little over 7.00 m in depth. One trial trench

extending uphill to the west was laid out across the wall bordering the street.[5] A second, short trench, at right angles to the first, crossed the same wall a little farther to the northeast.[6] This wall as excavated consists of conglomerate stretchers 0.35–0.40 m wide, set on bedrock, sometimes with packing, or on poros blocks,[7] themselves on a thin layer of soil or directly on bedrock, the stretchers they once carried gone. There are also cuttings in the bedrock, where even the poros blocks are missing. Despite its varied nature, the construction seems to be of one period: the choice of bedding for the large regular blocks depends on the terrain. An intermediate wall parallels the northwestern side of the room at a distance of about 2.10 m; its line is indicated by one partially excavated block of conglomerate and others that show on the surface. The width of these blocks varies from 0.40 m to 0.50 m, notably greater than that of the street wall or crosswalls of the Chambered Curtain but similar to the blocks of the back wall on the southeast. The northwest faces of the intermediate-wall blocks are aligned, as are the southeast faces of the back-wall blocks, as though they represented opposite faces of an independent structure.[8] The space on the street side suggests the location of a wooden stair, easily reached from the entrance.[9] Two small poros blocks running crosswise between the intermediate and northwest walls represent the southwest wall of the tower room. The evidence available provides no clue to the location of doorways.

Only a small corner of the big room was investigated; the bedrock drops off abruptly about a half meter northwest of the intermediate wall. The upper layers in the trench were fallen mud brick and Corinthian-style tile fragments. The sherds were chiefly of cooking ware and

---

[4] Parts of five rooms of the house in H4-4 were exposed and produced the most inventoried finds, which support the domestic character of the area. Black-glazed table ware includes an oinochoe (HP 895), two kantharoi (HP 724 and HP 1026), two skyphoi (HP 894 and HP 1024), and two saltcellars (HP 720 and HP 755). There are a few fragments of cooking-ware vessels (two lopas lids [HP 716 and HP 1018] and a chytra [HP 1019]) and fragments from at least seven plain-ware amphoras, probably used for storage. Six pyramidal and three conical loom weights suggest household weaving. Iron utensils, a probable spit handle (HM 537A,B), a possible sickle blade (HM 532A,B), and nails (HM 502A and HM 544) are other household items. A bronze ring (HM 501) is probably a furniture attachment. A simple bronze phiale or bowl (HM 647) may have been used for table service.

[5] Trench H4-1 (10.0 x 1.5 m) east–west, across the west corner and parallel partition of the room, together with the full width of the roadway.

[6] Trench H4-2 (2.00 x 1.0 m) north–south.

[7] These poros blocks are regularly described by the excavator as small. They do not seem to be the same as the plinths used elsewhere (see 9).

[8] Well-shaped blocks of irregular width, aligned on the exterior face, were also used for the plinth course of the Northeast Command Post, although those are of poros. The specification would have been for a minimum width but with all faces finished.

[9] The width of 2.10 m seems generous; compare the stair proposed for the Northeast Command Post, above, 58–59, set at the back of the room and perhaps over two meters wide.

Corinthian fabric, with some black-glazed ware and two tower-tile fragments.[10] Just above bedrock, by the poros crosswall blocks, there was part of a pyxis lid of "Corinthian fabric with concentric bands in purple and (spotted) brown paint" (NB 112, 14). A piece of iron plate and small iron fragments perhaps from an ax-head (HM 493) were found with bronze fragments and 4th-century pottery above the bedrock cuttings for the northwest wall.[11]

The wall on the outer side of the Chambered Curtain wherever it appears on the surface consists of a single row of stretchers. Generally, they are no thicker than those on the inner side, although at the "tower" room the outer blocks vary from 0.45 m to 0.50 m wide. For this reason, it seems unlikely that there was a true tower here at all, if by that term a full second story even of mud brick is implied; the towers with hollow ground-floor chambers on the north side of the city (Towers **12**, **13**, and **16**) have doubled walls.[12] The projection of the "tower" room about a meter beyond the curtain seems very little; it would be barely sufficient for an arrow slit and for observation along the face of the main wall. While there is no abrupt drop on the outside, the ground falls away steeply to a small valley, only to climb again to an even greater height on the farther side. The terrain is scarcely suitable for battering rams; the position is vulnerable rather to a surprise attack by foot soldiers or to missiles lobbed over the wall from some distance.

Nevertheless, the wider blocks of the intermediate and back walls of the "tower" room do suggest walls more substantial than the crosswalls and carrying a heavier load. The span is not excessive, but the beams may have supported a substantial fighting platform with some sort of shelter for light artillery machines and their operators. A stair at the inner side would have provided access.

Downhill to the northeast, there was no excavation or even clearing of the sparse surface remains. The Chambered Curtain is apparent again at about Meter 955 where there are two rows of conglomerate stretchers. The finished faces for both are on the exposed southeast side, the inner row lying about 0.40 m higher than the other. One block of the outer row appears to have a bossed face and at the northern end a drafted margin. The outer row drops down twice, in steps of 0.09 m and 0.20 m, as it proceeds northeast. No steps are apparent in the inner row, but there are two large gaps in the line of four blocks. The stretchers are 0.41–0.48 m wide; the rows are 0.53 m apart. About 5.50 m inside the inner row of blocks is a third, its level 0.40 m higher, indicated by two separated stretchers 0.35 m thick, the dimension commonly used at this site for house walls and for the inner wall of the Chambered Curtain. Together these three rows appear to represent its continuation at a width of 7.25 m. The reason for the double outer wall is not evident; it might indicate a repair or rebuilding. Surface cleaning, if not excavation, might assist in finding an explanation.

It is theoretically possible that the Chambered Curtain was preceded by the usual double-wythe curtain. If its inner wythe followed the inner line of the Chambered Curtain, a tower (8.30 x 8.70 m) slightly larger than Tower **10** might then have been built on the lines of the later Tower **8**, projecting the customary five meters beyond the outer wythe. Admittedly, the sampling provided by the 1970 excavations was small and traces might have been few after rebuilding, but at Tower **8** there was not even a bedrock cutting to support this suggestion. If the outer wythe ran on the line of the intermediate wall, the earlier curtain would have been about three meters wide rather than the usual 2.50 m. An outer wythe set where the bedrock drops off would have produced the usual

---

[10] HP 652, a Corinthian miniature kotyle, and HP 1012, a fragment of Attic red figure, as well as Roman spirally grooved ware and modern sherds, were found immediately below the surface. HP 1013, an Attic black-glazed echinus bowl (350–325), came from the second pass; HP 1014, a black-glazed mug (late 5th/early 4th century) came from the third. Cooking ware and poor quality black-glazed sherds were found in lower levels, but fewer of Corinthian fabric. (It is possible that some of the pale fabric was "Eastern Peloponnesian," not much discussed in 1970.) Two conical loomweights (HC 289, HC 290), probably 4th century, were found in Trench H4-1 inside the big room.

[11] Iron plate fragments (HM 493A,B, 7.2 x 6.2 x 1.1 cm) and ca. 13 others with a convex curve on the finished edge, lentoid in section (possibly an ax head), and pieces of iron scrap. Ca. 24 bronze sheet fragments (HM 499) 0.001 m thick.

[12] Towers without a solid core at least to the walkway level are rare in the early 4th century; see above, 21. The east tower at Phyle (Wrede 1924–1925, pl. V) has a solid story beneath the room at interior ground level, owing to the abrupt drop in the terrain, and may be considered a special case; the walls of the chamber are doubled in thickness. The numerous examples of towers with hollow ground-floor chambers from the Hellenistic period show the doubled walls required for greater strength, both to carry upper stories of masonry, frequently with artillery emplacements, and to withstand attack from battering rams. See Winter 1971, 176.

width, but the excavator did not regard this drop as a cutting.[13] The outer wall of the Chambered Curtain was not tested except at the extreme southern end, possibly uphill from its first room. The rubble characteristic of core fill found beside the outer-wythe block 6 (see above, 49) is the only indication that a double wall might have existed there. The logical line for such a wall would be that of the outer wall of the later rooms, connecting smoothly with the wall on the Industrial Terrace and following the southeastern edge of the lower terrace. If, however, such a large tower, presumably filled solidly at the ground-floor level, already existed, it is improbable that it would have been demolished to be replaced with the lighter-weight construction of the Chambered Curtain. It is also more likely that a large square tower would have been built at a gate or where the trace changes direction significantly, rather than in the middle of a straight run of curtain.

The purpose of the Chambered Curtain remains to be determined. However unlikely it may seem that a structure with so light an outer wall could be a fortification, it is even less probable that houses on so regular a plan (one room deep and over 130 meters long) were the product of private enterprise. It seems equally improbable that artillery would have been installed at ground level at Halieis. If the usual double-faced curtain ever existed in this stretch, it was completely dismantled and replaced with a deliberate and orderly building; the irregularity of its spaces may have been due more to the steep site than to haphazard planning. Defense against an external force seems to have been a secondary consideration.

These rooms contrast with the neat divisions of the casemated walls at Teke Kale (Caria), for instance, or the barracks at Phylla Vrachos in Euboia.[14] Although the sizes of the spaces vary, they probably were used in some manner for the maintenance of the defensive forces. Shelter was provided in the wall for the Peloponnesian troops besieging Plataiai in 429.[15] At Olynthos, on the west side of North Hill, the space between the wall and the houses was apparently roofed (and was sometimes part of the house), but even these thin city walls (0.80 m) were double the width of the house walls and of the outside wall at Halieis (Robinson and Graham 1938, 39–41, 69–70, fig. 1). Barrack accommodations have often been identified in the ground-floor space of towers.[16] Philo of Byzantion admired and recommended a design that he called Rhodian (80.45): walls constructed as hollow vaulted chambers that could be used to house troops but that could be quickly filled in when under attack. His plan consisted of a corridor seven cubits (about 3.25 m) wide, off which rooms ten cubits square (each holding seven beds) alternated with solid construction also ten cubits square; the outer wall was three cubits (about 1.40 m) thick. Lawrence stated (1979, 363) that there was nothing in Greece that answered this description and doubted that Philo's theory had ever been put into practice. Winter (1971, 162–64 note 44), differing with the excavators who took them for artillery emplacements, cited the ground-level chambers at Miletos (Von Gerkan 1935, 56) and Herakleia at Latmos (Krischen 1938, no. 51 on plan; pp. 16, 17, fig. 13, bottom right) as examples of barracks.

The three-room building on the south side of the acropolis has been identified as barracks and arsenal, and the structure on the west side as a mess building (Fig. 21; Williams n.d.). Perhaps a dozen at most could be accommodated on couches, fewer in the barracks, suggesting that the company there was a small elite guard. Other buildings adjacent to the West Wall and Tower **19** may have provided support for the sentries on watch, but most of a citizen force would have been lodged at home

---

[13] See above, 24–25. The abrupt drop in the bedrock apparent in Trench H4-1 was not described as a cutting by Hitzl (NB 112:5). The distance (0.40–0.80 m) recorded from the east scarp of the trench does suggest that the drop and crosswall were parallel, since the wall crossed the trench diagonally. Wall blocks set on the line of this depression might have formed the outer wythe of a 2.50 m wall along the street.

[14] Teke Kale: McNicoll and Milner 1997, 41; the spaces are 4.05 x 3.77 m, sufficient to house four men at 3.82 m² per man. Phylla Vrachos: Coulton 1996, Coulton 2002. Freestanding in the open area of the fort, Building 3 is 112 m long and 7 m deep. It consists of rooms 4.5 x 5.9 m in four groups of five with narrow passages between, "the most carefully planned Greek barrack building known" (Coulton 1996, 161). Coulton (2002, 111) places both construction and relatively short-lived occupancy in the late 6th or early 5th century. Lawrence (1979, 176, 177 fig. 30, giving the

name as "Filla"), calculated that the rooms would hold "not less than 12 men apiece," but Coulton (2002, 41) gives 12 as the maximum, 9 if their palliasses were ranged along the walls, for a total of 180 to 210 men. At 5.20 m the inside depth at Halieis is less, but the length of some 120 m (not counting "Tower 8") is more. Because of the irregular widths of the rooms occupancy can only be estimated; it seems likely that about 200 men could be accommodated if the entire structure was used for barracks.

[15] Thucydides (3.21) described the two walls built around the besieged city as sixteen feet apart with towers at intervals of "every tenth battlement," extending from one face to the other so that the guards passed through them. There in bad weather the guards could watch, sheltered by a roof.

[16] E.g., Ephesos, Tower 9 (McNicoll 1997, 95) and Tower 41 (ibid. 99–100).

when off duty. A sizable contingent could be housed and fed in the Chambered Curtain. Excavation so far has not provided many clues to the specific uses of the rooms;[17] pieces of iron and bronze found in the area suggest that metalworking may have been one of them.[18] Tower **8** might have housed a workshop where arms and armaments could be repaired. It seems more likely, however, that this larger room was an intermediate "command post" containing stairs to a fighting platform above, in a more pedestrian fashion recalling those attached to the Northeast and Northwest Walls. Other rooms may have served as barracks, combining the facilities provided by the barracks and mess building on the acropolis. At other sites where barracks have been identified, no separate mess facilities have been noted.

The Chambered Curtain continued as far as the Southeast Gate, but the manner of the connection between the two is not yet clear. Boyd suggested on his site plan (Boyd and Rudolph 1978, pl. 87) that the last section narrowed at Meter 955, the outer wall following the inner of the two found there as far as the gate. The final piece of the inner wall appears to have been exposed in the excavations immediately southwest of the gate. A wall of rubble rather than stretchers is set back from the face of conglomerate plinths and may belong to a later reuse. Throughout, the upper stretch of Street 1 runs farther from the outer face of the curtain to accommodate the width of the rooms. Where they stopped, the street jogged to the east to continue along the Lower Southeast Wall. The houses at the intersection with Avenue C were similarly affected.

The Northeast Command Post and Mint (Fig. 27; Pl.14a, b)

The Northeast Command Post.[19] Inside the Northeast Wall, roughly opposite the center bastion, there is a large building that has been partly excavated.[20] Its overall dimensions are about 10.20 m in width and about 10.50 m in projection from the line of the inner face of the defense wall. A course of well-fitted poros plinth blocks 0.50–0.60 m wide (nearly a meter wide at the south corner) and carefully aligned on the exterior provided a foundation on three sides. On the southwest, fragments of red and yellow plaster were found along the inside face. The fourth side was formed by the inner face of the curtain, which is not preserved.

About 1.20 m inside the line of the curtain and parallel to it, there is a socle or leveling course of small stones. Only the northwestern part of the floor was cleared (in 1962), exposing a stretch of the socle about four meters long that stops 0.80 m short of the plinths on the northwest side. Its purpose is obscure, but it may indicate the area occupied by a stair to the level of the walkway (see above, 58–59).

The relationship of the side walls to the curtain is not obvious; only the line of the outer wythe is certain. On the northwest, the plinths stop 2.75 m from this line; a rectangular filler block, slightly offset toward the interior of the building, reduces the gap to 2.45 m, which approximates the standard for the width of the curtain elsewhere in the Northeast Wall. At the foundation level on this side at least, there was no bonding of building and curtain, but the blocks of the inner wythe are not preserved.[21] The situation on the southeast side

---

[17] Loom weights (above, 65, note 10) suggest domestic occupancy but may belong to a later reuse of barrack space.

[18] In addition to the pieces of iron and sheet bronze (see above, 65, note 11), a large piece of iron slag (ca. 15.00 x 14.9 x 5.8 cm) was found with the Corinthian tile fragments in Trench H4-1. Six pieces of iron bar (HM 519) and a bronze ring (HM 506) were found in the area of the roadway in Trench H4-3. It should be pointed out, however, that metal scraps and bits of slag are common in these excavations, in domestic areas and as a component of road metal.

[19] Because of its shape, with remains of masonry walls on three sides, this structure was soon nicknamed "House Pi," a designation that appears in earlier notes. It has been variously identified in reports as a council chamber (Young 1963), a barracks or arsenal (Jameson 1969a, 330), and a mint (Rudolph 1973–1974). It may at one time or another have deserved all these interpretations but has been given this title for convenience.

[20] The walls were cleared in 1962 under the supervision of T. W. Jacobsen (Trench T, NB 1.1, 1.2), with assistance from M. H. Jameson and J. H. Young (Jameson 1969, 328, 329–30). Deeper soundings in 1972 (Trenches 130/370, 135/375; Rudolph 1973–1974) revealed earlier levels in the area of the western corner of the building. In

1975 (Trenches 135/375, 135/380) and 1976 (Trench 135/380) small soundings in the western quarter and in front of the building were carried to greater depth in compiling evidence for the mint and earlier structures. The renewed excavations in 1972 and 1976 were restricted to the western side by the boundary of the field under permit. The area investigated included the entrance and the central base but did not extend to the fortification wall or to the northeast side of the building. See Context Summary, 116–26, below.

[21] The ground falls off steeply to the narrow strip of shingle at the water's edge. No remains of the curtain have been exposed between the angle at the center bastion and the part to the northwest that is now submerged. The north extension of the North Trench, which followed the northwest wall of the building, was "continued to the sea at a depth of ca. 40 cm." through "comparatively soft earth" that suggested to H. S. Robinson the presence of a collapsed drain (Trench T, NB 1.1, 77). "The last 2.40 m. [beyond the end of the stylobate] were then dug to a deeper level" producing "many small stones." There would have been no need for a drain on the downhill side of the building; the stones were presumably fill from the curtain. Foundations for the curtain may lie still buried northwest of the trench, which was only a few centimeters wider than the stylobate.

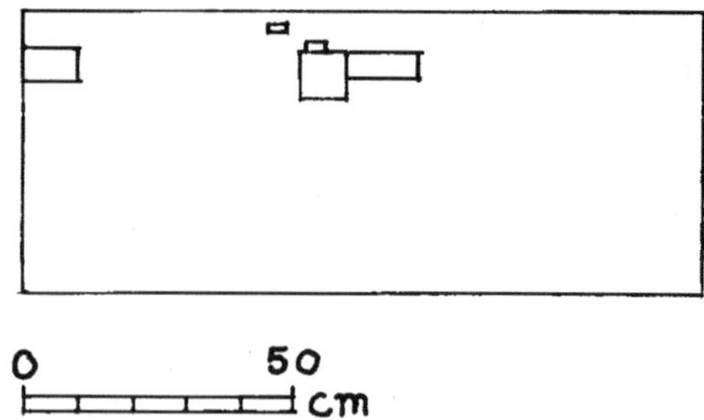

Fig. 14. Northeast Command Post, doorsill

is complicated by the presence of the drain that passed through the curtain just outside the building (see above, 61). The orientation of the blocks at the northern end remains the same, but the alignment and coursing change. In the middle of the northernmost preserved block a change in the level of the top surface comes at a distance of about 2.70 m from the outside face of the curtain, suggesting that this block was bonded to the fortification wall.

Almost at the center of the southwest side a sandstone doorsill measuring 0.50 x 1.25 m remains in place on the plinth course (Fig. 14).[22] Toward the inner side, there is a group of cuttings at the center and another at the left (western) end, but no corresponding one on the east. About 45 cm to the east, a square base of sandy stone was found apparently in situ on the plinth.

Of the orthostate course, there remain only three conglomerate blocks 0.60 m high on the southeast side, where they showed above ground level before excavation, and none at all on the northwest or southwest. The lengths (from the north) are roughly 1.75 m, 2.00 m, and a short 0.80 m, next to the now missing corner block; the width is about 0.44 m. At the north end of the middle block, the last 10–15 cm have been cut down as if to accommodate a block in the next course.

Two plinths on the northwest side and one on the southwest carry dowel holes. An Ionic capital (HS 6) of shelly limestone (Pl. 15a), lying

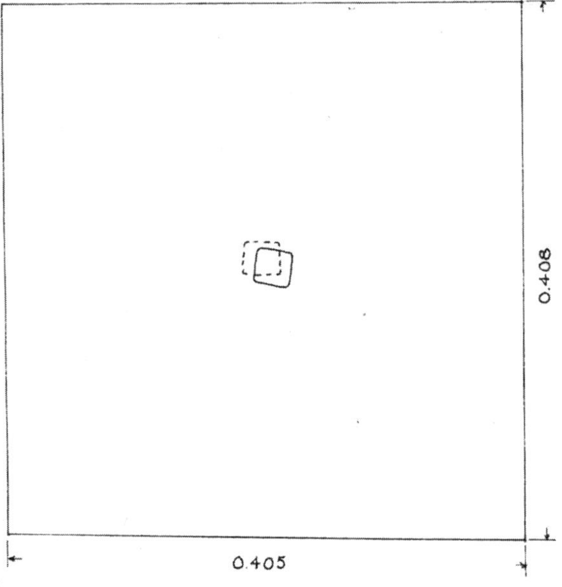

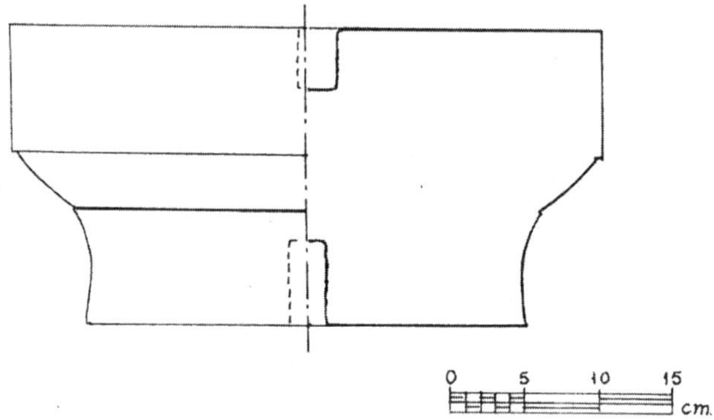

Fig. 15. Doric capital of shelly limestone, HS 381

on one of the plinths on the southwest, and its unfluted elliptical engaged shaft, immediately outside, came to light in 1962; they may have decorated the facade.[23] In the center of the building a poros base about 0.70 m square and 0.28 m thick marks the location of the only interior support for

<hr>

[22] In the mess building on the acropolis, the plinths on the southeast side change from poros to narrower sandstone blocks, perhaps an indication that the latter were above grade. This fine-grained stone would undoubtedly wear better than the softer poros and could be finished more smoothly than conglomerate.

[23] Notes by Jameson (Trench T, NB 1.1, 82) describe the stone of "the engaged column and bases" as "sandy grey." The half-column is backed by a pilaster 0.18 m square and 1.63 m long; the combined depth is 0.29 m. On one end a square cutting with traces of lead is centered on the half-column (ibid., 86). The depth of the threshold block is 0.50 m; that of the "base" is not recorded but was apparently the same. The difference between the depth of the column+pilaster and that of the sandstone blocks is only

0.10–0.11 m, too little for a wall behind but appropriate for a setback in front. To explain the 0.45 m gap between the threshold and the "base", the entrance might be imagined with a central door of two leaves, flanked on either side by engaged columns on molded shelly-limestone bases set directly on the plinths, and beside them above sandstone "bases," narrow openings fitted with grills, these in lieu of any windows. The capital is only 0.12 m high, and the height of any molded base is unknown. Cf. HS 275, marble Ionic base found near the East Gate (above, 27). The doorway would have been only about 2 meters high. Perhaps the half-columns were raised on piers 0.60 m high like the orthostates.

the roof. It rests on a poros subbase 0.34 m thick and about 1.20 m from side to side, set in poros chips. The subbase projects about 0.25 m in front; the back side was not excavated, but an equal projection would yield a subbase roughly 1.20 m square. The size indicates that it carried a considerable load.[24] The subbase was surrounded by a packing of poros working chips and apparently rests on fallen mud brick, contemporary with the earlier rubble house walls.[25] This relatively soft substratum explains the use of such a substantial base. A Doric capital (HS 381) of shelly limestone (Fig. 15), found inside the building in the 1972 excavations, may have crowned the central column.[26] While it seems clear that the space was covered, the single-width orthostates make it likely that it was by a roof rather than a second story. Their substantial width and the dressing on the top of one suggest that the walls were of stone for the full height. The fact that so few wall blocks remain is not surprising; it is noted above in connection with Tower **10** that the location near the water and the modern road would have made it easy to make use of the remains as a source of building material.

At first glance there seems to be no relation between the central bastion and the Command Post. The building roughly coincides with the bastion on the northwest side but extends some two and a half meters farther on the southeast, its width limited by the presence of the drain. The southeast plinth course is aligned with the cover slabs. The limiting factor on the northwest is unknown. There is no clear necessity for alignment with the bastion; the plan may have been determined by the parallel structure on that side, if that was already in place. The area proposed for the stair, however, as revealed by excavation almost exactly corresponds to the bastion. Unfortunately, the restrictions on the excavated area leave unknown both its terminus and any foundation for the inner wythe at that point. On the basis of available evidence, it appears that the Command Post was constructed after the curtain

and drain were in place and was adapted to the latter at the east corner.

It seems likely that the existing stair, now enclosed in the Command Post, was not removed but retained, not only as a convenience but as a structural part of that section of curtain (see above, 58–59). There must have been a base for the mud-brick fortification wall and its walkway, either the usual parallel inner wythe or the stair base substituting for it. The small stones of the leveling course laid at floor level would have carried a base course of stone blocks to provide a solid foundation even if sheltered.

Narrow passages separated the building from its neighbors on either side.[27] That on the southeast ended at the storm-water drain through the curtain; blocks exposed in 1962 appear to block passage along the curtain to the southeast. There must have been more open space in front of the entrance on the southwest, perhaps as much as 13 x 15 m,[28] suitable for mustering the changing guard but not for public gatherings of any size. Wheeled vehicles would have been completely blocked along Avenue A, leaving the little plaza out of the way of general traffic.

The Mint. One purpose of this building is suggested by coin blanks found there, from which the building has been identified as the city mint, but it is by no means certain that it was originally constructed for this use.[29] It was published by Jameson as an arsenal or barracks (1969, 330). The hollow ground floor, single width orthostates, and the lack of relation to the bastion outside the curtain make it unlikely that the structure was carried above the height of the walkway as a tower. On the other hand the possibility of a stair at the rear of the building suggests that the occupants had need for direct access to the walkway and bastion above. Fragments of the heavy tower tiles found both inside and outside the wall in this area are the finest examples found to date and show the characteristic pale green slip.

---

[24] The subbase (NB 135/380, 17), which was only half exposed, presumably consisted of two blocks, each 0.60 x 1.20 m (a common block size at the site), set side by side. This arrangement would parallel that in the Northwest Command Post (see below, 70).

[25] The stratum below the subbase contained nothing that could be dated later than the 5th century. The fill around the blocks belongs to Lower Town Level B (4th century).

[26] Found upside down, about a meter inside and approximately level with the threshold block, in fallen mud brick (NB 135/

375, 10–11). If not from interior partitions for the mint (see below), the mud brick might have come from a parapet or other structure on the roof.

[27] The passageway on the southeast was 2.80 wide, that on the northwest only 1.50 m.

[28] Very little of the area south of the building has been excavated. The trenches (130/370, 135/370) near the west corner revealed only rubble house walls along a road at a lower (and presumably earlier) level. See above, 19.

[29] For full discussion, see chapter 8, below.

Nearly two millennia later, Andrea Palladio recommended that the mint and prison be built beside the fortification walls (1977, III.16). Vitruvius, on the other hand, placed the treasury, prison, and senate house adjacent to the forum (5.2.1). The "forum" or agora has not been identified at Halieis; the small open space in front of the Command Post, in a domestic quarter, is more probably a mustering place for troops than a civic center. In any case, the coin-producing activities of the mint, to which public access was presumably forbidden, might well be separate from the treasury. A building originally constructed as a command post and arsenal, a securable location, may have accommodated the activities of the mint from time to time. The size of the city and the number of surviving coins suggest that this was an intermittent occupation.

The Northwest Command Post (Arsenal or Prison)
(Fig. 30)

A building apparently similar to the Northeast Command Post is set against the Northwest Wall at Meter 1620. It is now submerged and known only from aerial photographs, verified by divers who did some clearing. It measures about twelve meters in width and eight in inward projection from the curtain and, like its counterpart, has a central column subbase, made of two slabs (Jameson 1969, 330). It differs, however, in that the inner face of the curtain, here somewhat thinner, continues as its back wall. The free walls are of doubled orthostates, suggesting a second story. There is also an inner line paralleling the north and west walls that appears similar to the inner circuit in Tower **16** (Fig. 8), perhaps a construction detail for the interior floor.

The purpose of this building is entirely a matter of speculation, but it was presumably public and very likely connected with the defenses, especially if the building was two-storied. If access to the curtain was provided by the stair or ramp alongside on the west, a simple wooden stair or ladder would have been adequate to reach the upper floor. The shallower depth of the space in comparison to the Northeast Command Post may have been found adequate because there was no masonry stair to accommodate. Jameson considered the structure a barracks or arsenal like its counterpart against the Northeast Wall. Perhaps it also served as the

prison, especially if the civic center was in the vicinity.[30]

Other Associated Structures, Attached or Adjacent

While those structures attached to the city walls on the inside have been shown to have had a primarily military purpose, there are several built near or actually against the curtain where this cannot be certain or is clearly not the case. Their presence is worth comment because non-military construction of this sort was often specifically forbidden. A free space between the fortification wall and the buildings inside it was a normal requirement, but a similar space was often specified on the outside as well (see above, 63). Inside the circuit at Halieis are the buildings at Tower **2** and at the Middle Wall, which may have been built for military use. Outside, there is the curious shrine northeast of Tower **9**; other remains that are near enough to warrant some consideration are at Meter 1015, not far from the shrine.

Buildings near the West Wall (Fig. 20; Pl. 2b, c)

A few walls that remained in the vicinity of Tower **2** in 1970 indicated the presence of several structures of undetermined date; the appearance of their conglomerate blocks suggests that they were contemporary with the fortifications. The area is more level than the ground to the east, which falls away with few signs of habitation until the slope eases toward the bottom of the western valley. Without excavation there is no way to determine whether these were private or military structures, but one, directly opposite the tower, may well have been a barracks.

The plan, as it appeared in 1970, is rectangular, about 4.50 x 9.00 m, the long axis running parallel to the curtain; the north corner and the northeast side are missing, nor is there any indication of a door. The conglomerate blocks are preserved one course in height (up to 0.48 m visible) with large vertical joints, set upright on bedrock in the manner of the curtain; at the southeast end their width can be measured as 0.48 m. The upper walls were probably of mud brick. The construction is similar to that of the tower, heavier than normal for domestic purposes. From the west corner a wall continued northwest

---

[30] See above for the recommendations of Vitruvius. The adjacent ramp and drain are described above, 59–61.

toward Tower **1**; it is composed of heavy conglomerate blocks like those used in the defense wall. Its line gradually approaches that of the curtain, which is not preserved in that stretch. At the northern end it is only 1.50 m away from the line of the inner face, but any connection such as a stair or ramp would have blocked the service passage at the foot of the wall.

This heavy wall is paralleled at 0.78 m by a narrow, rectangular structure 3.00 m wide and at least 24 meters long; its blocks are only 0.35 m thick, the size generally used for house construction. Only the southwest and northwest walls and the return at the north corner of this building are preserved.

From a point close to the south corner of the first building, a wall ran a short way westward toward Tower **2**, then turned a right angle to proceed southward paralleling the curtain at an interval of about 2.50 m. Recorded where it bordered the modern track in 1970, this wall has been completely removed by a roadscraper.

The rectangular building opposite Tower **2**, similar to it in construction, may have been a barracks or other military service building. The location is sufficiently distant from the built-up area of the west valley and along the shore to have made it convenient, if not strictly necessary, to provide some support facilities. It is noteworthy, however, that the entrance to this building, as well as to the long one north of it, was apparently in the unpreserved side facing toward the town but away from the defense wall.

Other structures with light walls of conglomerate blocks are shown on the surface survey farther north (Boyd and Rudolph 1978, pl. 87); they seem to parallel the curtain but at a distance of three or four meters and may belong to private houses. Unfortunately, there is no available evidence whatever as to their date; considering their appearance and location, they are almost certainly ancient and probably Classical.

The Building near the Middle Wall (Fig. 31)

On the lower terrace at the Middle Wall (Area F6) are the remains of a substantial building set close against the rising bedrock to the south. The blocks showing above ground were cleaned of weeds and grass. The walls consist of conglomerate blocks about 0.30 m wide and varying in length from 0.75 m to 1.75 m. The east wall extends for more than four meters, the west wall for more than eight. A little to the north, a trench (F6-3) was laid out across the building and the defense wall, exposing a line of small blocks filled out with stones to the same scant 0.30 m width. It appears to be a foundation for the continuation of the west wall to a total length of at least 11.70 m; the width of the building at the south end is just over five meters. The southeast corner blocks are missing, but the rest of the south end wallbase is preserved.

A small room 2.40 m (north-south) by 2.70 m in the southwest corner is partitioned off by similar or slightly thicker blocks. There is a door 0.80 m wide in the north wall of the room, opening toward the center of the building. Trench F6-3 also exposed two neat rubble walls at right angles, possibly foundations for other divisions, as well as fragments of red wall plaster.[31] These interior walls suggest that the building continued to the north. The west wall, however, while 2.50 m away at the south end, gradually approaches the east face of the defense wall. In Trench F6-3 these walls are only 1.30 m apart, close to a minimum if passage along the curtain was to be maintained; there was no room for a pathway across the south end. The position of the entrance is not evident. If it was at the end of the preserved blocks in the west wall, it would have been at a rather constricted point.

The quality of the construction in this building far surpasses that in the houses, earlier or later, on the middle terrace to the south. It is much closer in character to the defense wall. The blocks, though thin, are not reused but well cut, carefully aligned, and apparently set on a solid foundation course. The structure, somewhat larger than the one opposite Tower **2**, may have been used in support of the sentries in Tower **19**, perhaps combining living quarters and storage.

The Shrine (Fig. 25; Pl. 11a)

Less than five meters northeast of Tower **9**, a small shrine was built against the outer face of the fortification wall.[32] The two remarkable aspects of the building, its orientation and location, remain unexplained. The doorway, which occupies virtually the whole of the front wall, faces

---

[31] On bedrock under the east-west wall was an amphora containing three sherds (HP 800): A, a red-figured body fragment (5th to mid-4th); B, body fragment, late Type A skyphos (?, mid-4th); C, flaring rim, Peloponnesian mug (?).

[32] The structure was excavated in 1975 (Boyd and Rudolph 1978, 353–55). Identification as a shrine was based on its orientation with a door opening eastward, a possible offering platform in the center, and several miniature kotylai among the finds.

southeast. The side walls do not appear to be aligned with any other structures in the vicinity; their angle most closely approximates that of the northeast side of the gateway and Avenue C but deviates even farther than they do from a right angle to the city wall. Although the plan strongly suggests that the curtain was built across the back end of the shrine, cutting it off at an angle, the excavators found no indication of any earlier structure that lay under the fortifications and reported that the cement floor "displays no trace of resurfacing." The cut-conglomerate socle or wall base had no underlying plinths, perhaps because the weight of the walls was not enough to require a spread footing. The base presumably carried mud-brick walls topped with a roof of the Laconian tiles found in the area. Nevertheless, even if the shrine as preserved today entirely postdates the circuit wall, some compelling reason must be sought that would require it to face southeast (rather than the more familiar approximate east) and at the same time not allow it to stand clear of the curtain.[33]

The location, right against the curtain, is surprising. Its roof would have provided a handy step for any enemy attempting to scale the wall. Although its proximity to the Southeast Gate suggests some relation between the two, it is not really at the gate but separated from it by the bulk of the round tower or the earlier bastion. The votive niche that Boyd suggested as a possible predecessor (Boyd and Rudolph 1978, 355, note 26), if it were associated with the gate, would surely be set somewhere in the gate structure, while if it were merely set in the mud-brick curtain, it would have no important orientation of its own.

That the shrine was built in this place and at this angle argues strongly for a predecessor, whose perpetuation included its location and orientation. While the pottery found within the shrine was "typical of the 4th-century wares found at Halieis," the limited investigation below the cement floor at the foot of the curtain produced "a small amount of pottery as early as the 7th century." Although Boyd was inclined to associate this material with earlier fortification construction,

it might equally well stem from habitations or an earlier shrine, whose structure was curtailed when the present curtain was built. Perhaps the fact that it was overlooked by Tower **9** outweighed any threat from a military point of view.

In the discussion of a possible trace for a lower Archaic circuit (below, 77), it is suggested that the line of the earthworks discovered in the East Tower area might have continued straight past the East Gate as far as Avenue C, only later shifting slightly more to the west. Such a line would have run outside the shrine as excavated, which would be virtually at right angles to it.[34]

The Southeast Building (Figs. 18, 19; Pl. 11b)

The remains of a substantial building appear on the surface east of the modern road, at a lower level and less than four meters outside the southeast wall at Meter 1015/1020, between the shrine and the East Gate. Enough conglomerate stretchers remain to give the outline, eight by thirteen meters or more in extent and approximately parallel to the curtain. Other blocks indicate at least one interior division. There are no visible signs of other structures in the vicinity, nor can it be associated with the roads that led to the Southeast and East Gates. Most puzzling are traces of walls, showing at the surface of the modern road, at right angles to the northwest wall of the building and coming within 2.50 m of the curtain. The block at the east corner preserves carefully trimmed faces, with a strange protruding tongue on the end (southeast face).[35] Despite its proximity the association of this structure with the fortifications seems doubtful because it lies outside the circuit. Possibly it was connected rather with the shrine, only some fifteen meters to the south.

The Service Streets

Passage along the fortification wall at ground level was a normal requirement, both to permit rapid movement of troops in an emergency and to guard against treachery from within (see above, 63). The open spaces along the Halieis walls have already

---

[33] Boyd suggested that the orientation was "a conscious effort to have the structure open eastward in the fashion of most Greek temples," in other words, that the relation of the shrine to the curtain had been distorted as far as practicable.

[34] Jameson pointed out (per lit. Nov. 1, 2002) that there is no obvious reason why the specific location could not have been

shifted, such restriction generally being reserved for "wells and springs and where lightning struck."

[35] Cooper noted a similar instance in the west valley and suggested that they were lifting bosses; the end position is unusual, and the size seems excessive, but I have no alternative to propose.

been mentioned in passing. Where there has been no excavation that might reveal a road surface, there is still information that can be drawn from the position of visible building remains.

Between Towers **1** and **2** the survey shows a series of walls that indicate a service street paralleling the curtain, in most places about seven meters wide, though hardly more than two meters near Tower **2**. For the rest of the West Wall, there are no signs of structures (other than stairs) built against it, but the visible remains are sparse, and there was probably less pressure to fill all available space than in the densely built-up sections along the waterfront.

The barracks building on the acropolis is constructed against the defense wall, a position responsible for its identification (see Williams n.d.). There is no evidence for the wall in the rest of the acropolis circuit, but the whole area is so small communication from one section to another would not have been a problem.

The buildings on the Industrial Terrace have their own orientation, which makes the open space inside the defense wall less obviously a passage. The southern corner of the two eastern buildings in each case lies about three meters away, but no road surface has been identified. A footpath along the wall rather than a street is possible.

The best known service street is the one paralleling the Chambered Curtain, revealed in the excavations in Area H4. It was limited on the opposite side by houses built with reused blocks and rubble and containing 4th-century pottery. The street was fully 3.50 m wide and was characteristically covered by a "vast roof-tile fall." Outside Tower **8**, there was a large amount of deteriorated mud brick and a layer of debris near the bedrock cuttings for the front wall, "solidly packed, with numerous Corinthian-style roof-tile fragments," that showed signs of fire.[36] The road surface was here partly bedrock; the northwestern side had a metaling of small stones set in lime mortar over a packing of stones and loose soil.[37]

This street has been identified at intervals from the upper end of the Chambered Curtain to the Southeast Gate at Avenue C. After a slight jog, it continues as Street 1. The width at the house northeast of House 7 is 5.20 m, allowing ample room for the access stair; the clear width is 3.50 m. Boyd restored this section as a wide avenue

paralleling the fortification wall. No trace of its limits appeared in the trenches at the East Gate, however, and it is possible that it ran parallel to Street 2, diverging from the curtain on the line of the houses at the Southeast Gate, at least as far as Avenue B. The space along the curtain would have increased in width as it progressed toward the East Gate and was doubtless heavily traveled. Between that gate and Tower **10** the evidence is even less clear. The 4th-century houses southeast of the tower preserve a narrow passage, although earlier structures beneath them would not appear to have done so (see above, 52). Boyd showed a narrowing of the street beyond the intersection with Avenue B, but it is possible that it continued parallel to Street 2, northwest of the houses in the East Tower area.

Close to the inside face of the wall in the northwest part of Trench I5-1, between the Southeast and East Gates, the soil appeared to be half mud brick and half small stones uniform in size, probably fallen from the upper part of the wall. A meter or so away from the wall the soil was lighter in color and the stones in it were more varied in size, but there was no sign of road metal. The same conditions appear to prevail along the wall at the East Gate, although the metal of Avenue B passing through the gate is well preserved (Fig. 4).

Without excavation at the west corner of Tower **10**, there is no information on the junction with Avenue A; it is tempting to restore a small open area to allow clearance for the west corner of the tower and the adjacent stair. The survey records only one block (on the line of Street 2) along the line of the Northeast Wall as far as the Command Post. Avenue A, a broad street some five meters wide, may reasonably be restored here although without tangible evidence. It would correspond to the following section known to run from the Northeast Command Post to the Hermion Gate, separating the fortification wall from the houses that lie between it and the road from the East Gate (Avenue B). On the southeast side of the Command Post, however, there are walls exposed at the end of the 1962 Main Trench that, like the Post itself, would block the avenue. Not enough was cleared to determine the extent or nature of the building or buildings, but the construction, of substantial dressed blocks, some on plinths, is similar to that of the Command Post

---

[36] NB 112, 5–6. For the most part, the tiles in the fall were of Lakonian shape in a red fabric.

[37] Finds below this paving were few; the pottery consisted of sherds of coarse ware and cooking ware, five black-glazed sherds, and the base of a Corinthian skyphos decorated with light-brown rays on a green slip (NB 112, 12).

and the better adjacent houses and is presumably contemporary.

The removal of an early rampart may have provided the reserved space for the two sections of Avenue A, which contrast conspicuously with the irregular passage inside the Northwest Wall. The aerial photographs clearly show a service street or space of varying width separating the Northwest Wall from the submerged remains of the houses. West of Tower **16** these seem to run parallel, but to the east the line of the houses is quite irregular, leaving some spaces more open. The structure at the inward bend of the curtain (Meter 1665) would block passage entirely, were there not a small recess in the house wall at that point. The tumbled blocks apparent in the aerial photograph may have come originally from a wall on the other side of the passage.

A minimum space about a meter wide was preserved along the east side of the Middle Wall on the lower level in Area F6, if indeed the wall is contemporary with the building there. Only when this part of the fortifications was abandoned was a house built over the access stair and against the east–west stretch just to the south in Area F5 (see above, 59).

CHAPTER SIX

The Development
of the Halieis Defenses

Many questions have been raised here in the course of describing the remains. Some, like the nature or even the existence of Tower **18A**, may never be answered. Meanwhile, however, a tentative history of the Halieis fortification systems can be presented, based on the information at hand.

Greek fortifications, as a category of structural remains preserved to this day, are singularly disappointing when the discussion turns to their date.[1] Often the most conspicuous feature of an unexcavated site, they crown the skyline or can be traced over a relatively barren landscape by the thorny growth that has been left undisturbed to cover them. They are imposing and majestic in their testament to the mason's skill, even when reduced to a single course of stone, for their silent witness to the man-hours represented by their trace, measured not in ancient feet but in modern kilometers. It is sometimes possible to determine a sequence of phases from plan and construction, but their specific date often eludes us, with the exception of those civic projects that attracted enough notice from ancient writers to be mentioned in literary references and where the identification of the extent remains with the text can be assured. Any historical or literary references must, of course, be taken into consideration. While chance plays a part in their preservation and their accuracy, when taken together with the social and political picture of the times gathered from many sources, these accounts will help to make a proposed dating more or less acceptable.

The field archaeologist's traditional approach through excavation can prove sadly frustrating and has not often been attempted.[2] Since it would be pointless to tackle more than key elements, such as gates and towers, or interesting features like stairs, through-wall drains, and noteworthy adjacent structures, the investigation of the greater part may be limited to surveying, often without even the benefit of brush removal so that the trace may be properly recorded and described. The sinking of spot trenches may depend on success in acquiring the necessary permits, on the terrain, and often, on the cost of removing the overburden of fallen masonry in large units. And when all is done, what can the digger hope to find? Successive construction and destruction of the Halieis acropolis wall and associated buildings have provided an unusual stratigraphic record. Ordinarily there is no occupation debris except that washed into through-wall drains, and stratified floors are limited to the rare guard room. Frequently the wall is founded on bedrock without construction trench or backfill. If the wall is hollow, the fill is likely to be rubble brought from elsewhere on the site; if anything datable is found in it, its significance will be questionable since the deposit is unlikely to be sealed. In the more remote stretches, only the builders or the sentries would have left any artifact; while a chance coin might be found, no one would carry fine ware there, and coarse ware

---

[1] This shortcoming is shared by many ancient fortifications throughout the Mediterranean wherever they are unaccompanied by specific attribution to a political regime, through literary or epigraphical text.

[2] If the list is restricted to those possibly contemporary with Archaic and Classical Halieis, whose glory days extended little past the middle of the 4th century, the following examples may be noted. Fortifications excavated in conjunction with urban sites: Argos, Corinth, Gorytsa, Halai, Plataiai, Stymphalos, Thorikos. Isolated forts excavated: Phyle, Phylla Vrachos.

is rarely helpful when the excavator is hoping to identify the quarter century, if not the decade.[3]

There are other ways through which the physical remains may suggest a date. For much of the trace at Halieis only the weakest of dating methods, that of style, is available to make the connection between most of the circuit and the well-studied remains on the acropolis. Style, whether of military design, construction, or finish, can sometimes be supported by comparison with other sites where a sound chronology has been established.[4] But where the fortifications run close to the occupied areas within them, the streets and houses even more than the public buildings, there is hope for stratification of finds that may date the walls by association. At Halieis the remains in the houses in both the northeast and northwest quarters, and again in those at the Middle Wall, are crucial in this connection. In addition, the town plan may be unexpectedly informative.

When all the available information and various approaches are combined, at Halieis there are still far too many gaps to date any section or feature of the fortifications with certainty. The conclusions presented here include conflicting situations that a choice of solutions fails to resolve. Nevertheless, this tentative outline of the fortification history is given in an attempt to provide an overall view, although its elements may be rearranged, adjusted, and reinterpreted in future.

The Archaic and Early Classical Circuits
(Fig. 32)

The scant evidence for the earliest fortifications outside the acropolis suggests that some sort of wall also existed on the south side of the Industrial Terrace as part of an enclosure augmenting the protected area on the hilltop, which is only about a half hectare in extent (above, 18). This lower terrace would have provided storage space for supplies in a limited emergency but was probably not large enough to house the general populace.[5] There is no evidence at this time for any other part

of this defense. The terrain suggests that it surrounded the terrace and returned westward on the north side, along the line of the scarp roughly at the 25-meter contour and above the tumble of boulders at the bottom of the Terrace slope.[6] No specific investigation has been made to look for traces, but it is very doubtful that there would be any. A wall of mud brick, laid on bedrock or a bedding of small stones, would have soon washed away when it was no longer maintained. Above the boulders now seen northeast of the terrace (Pl. 18a, b), more than likely there would have been only a palisade composed of thorn branches and brambles like the barriers used today to control the routes taken by sheep and goats traveling from one terrace to the next. The line proceeding to the west may have cut across the contours to run along the 35-meter contour, or even higher, or followed the 25-meter contour in a wider sweep to the north depending on the area required (whether, for instance, live stock was kept in the enclosure). The link back to the upper circuit may have been on the line of the eastern trace of the Middle Wall, close under the drop on the north side of the acropolis. The date suggested by the pottery from Trench 910/150 on the Terrace would make this wall coeval with Phases 1-2-3 on the acropolis, before the general destruction there about 600–590 (Deposit II). The 1962 and 1965 excavations found virtually no signs of Terrace habitation earlier than the 4th century, but the remains uncovered were close to bedrock. The area downslope just above the scarp remains undug.

Although it was suggested at the time of excavation that the ambiguous discoveries in Trench H4-5 (at the south end of the Chambered Curtain) might indicate early earthworks, it is much more likely that any return westward would be higher up, above the scarp at 25 meters. The sherds dating as early as the late 8th century could easily have been washed down from the Terrace (see above, 49, note 19).

A second circuit around a small town site near the shore is dated by the associated pottery

---

[3] Stamped amphora handles might prove the exception, but such containers would be more likely in kitchens and dining rooms. A red-figured sherd found in an undisturbed position in the foundation trench for the Isthmian gate at Corinth brings the date close to 450 that on literary evidence and finds from adjacent graves might have been set twenty-five years earlier (Carpenter and Bon 1936, 116), but black glaze alone will say little more than "classical."

[4] See above, 11. Throughout the following discussion, there are repeated references to the Phases (1–7) of architecture and Deposits (I–VII) of pottery on the acropolis; for these see the

chart (chapter 9 below) and Williams n.d. There are also references to Levels A–E in the lower town; for these see Boyd and Rudolph 1978, 334–35.

[5] It has been noted above (48) that no defense wall has been identified on the east side of the acropolis (Williams n.d.), which suggests that the two areas were combined at an early date.

[6] This line for the early defenses was proposed by J. A. Dengate in the course of discussion at Indiana University in May 2000. A mud-brick wall on a socle, similar to those on the acropolis, would be more appropriate to the steeper upper slopes than the earth rampart restored for the lower town.

to the 7th century and early years of the 6th (Lower Town Level D), before the acropolis destruction (see above, 18–19). There is clear evidence of domestic occupation near the East Tower at this time, continuing through the 6th century (Lower Town Level C). The defense wall was in the form of an earth berm, probably topped by a palisade, running on the line of the later stone-based curtain between Tower **10** and the East Gate. The construction seems more primitive than the early walls on the acropolis, but it may have been chosen because the terrain was relatively flat and there was ample space and plenty of available material. Another segment of this circuit was found in trenches sunk at the Northeast Command Post. Although the section is short, probably this stretch ran parallel to Avenue A. There has been no excavated evidence to indicate how far the line extended; it might well have been as far as the later Hermion Gate. Finally, a single test trench in Avenue C again suggested to the excavator the traces of the same sort of rampart. Avenue C is known only for 65 meters or so, but at least for that distance, it also runs parallel to Avenue A.

When the earthwork defenses were constructed and how long they were maintained is unknown. Any scheme for a wall trace based on this slim evidence must be highly speculative. It is possible, however, that there was an early earth rampart, following much the line of Avenue A but somewhat inside it, that turned southwest a little more than 90° at the site of Tower **10** to run toward the East Gate. The area enclosed would have been bounded on the south along the line of Avenue C, parallel to the northern limit. Its orientation may be termed A–C. There is at present no evidence to show whether the line on the southeast ran straight past the position of the East Gate to a point outside the Southeast Gate before turning westward, although this appears likely.[7] The terrain slopes gently to the northeast, but there are no topographical restrictions on a layout that might at first seem surprisingly regular. The position of the northwest side of the enclosure likewise is unknown.[8] The maximum area enclosed might have been more than three and a

half hectares, roughly the same size as the later town between Streets 1 and 8 and Avenues A and C, if, for the sake of argument, it extended as far west as the Hermion gate. Finally, the position of the gates in this rampart can only be guessed. The principal ones may have been in the same general locations as the East and Hermion Gates, communicating with the harbor and the road to the cemetery. A track between them, corresponding to Avenue B, might then have formed the main street for the community.

The relation of the lower enclosure to the augmented acropolis enceinte remains uncertain; as proposed here it would have presented little deterrent to a determined attack. If the chief threat was from seafaring marauders, as Snodgrass (1986, 129) posits for the Archaic fortifications in the Aegean islands, the berm and palisade would have been sufficient to discourage or delay them while the inhabitants rallied to the defense of the small settlement, with retreat to the upper, more defensible enclosure possible if necessary.

It is doubtful that there will ever be enough evidence to show the disposition of structures within the Archaic enclosure and whether or not it followed a plan on orientation A–C. The diagonal line of Avenue B suggests a pragmatic approach with fixed points at the gates at either end and perhaps a wooden tower (see above, 18, note 24) at the site of Tower **10**. Once the rampart was in place, the random grouping of houses or other buildings, garden plots, and open ground within would have filled the space, but that there was an orderly arrangement of lots and lanes is far from certain.

The Combined Circuit (Fig. 33)

At some point in the early 6th century (Level C), a new orientation based on Avenue B was deliberately chosen for a regularized town plan (Fig. 17).[9] The reason for the shift was undoubtedly a practical one. It is likely that structures of one sort or another already lined Avenue B and that small lanes ran away from the main street more or less at right angles. The road would have made a major

---

[7] The shrine, which now appears outside the fortification wall and oddly oriented, would be inside such a rampart and approximately at right angles to it.

[8] It is tempting to try to deduce the line from the scattered bits of wall in the western part of this area, known either from excavation trenches or the surface survey (where the remains are almost certainly later), but in most cases the stretches are too short and continuity is lacking.

[9] Rudolph proposed the beginning of Level C (1984, 144) for the origin of the orthogonal layout of the streets (Boyd and Rudolph 1978; Boyd and Jameson 1981). The evidence adduced for the early date of orientation B comes largely from five test pits, of necessity deep but limited in lateral extent. Other tests and published discussions of the Halieis layout are cited in Rudolph 1984.

interruption in a formal plan on the A–C orientation, yet it was essential to the internal traffic between the two main gates and could not be eliminated. Seven insulae were laid out along this base line with cross streets at intervals of 100 Greek feet.[10] This process might have begun at either end, and at first it would appear that the wider blocks between Streets 1 and 2 shown on Boyd's plan are the result of space left over. Consider, however, a theoretical Street 1 beginning at Tower **10** and laid out parallel to Street 4.[11] It would run well inside the East Gate, whose position was fixed, but reach Avenue C about where it does now, on a line preserved in House 7 and its neighbor.

The old circuit of earth ramparts may have continued to enclose the new layout of streets and house lots, but it would have been found inadequate by the Tirynthian refugees, arriving not long before the Athenian attack in 460. It may have been this influx that gave the impetus for the next stage, a single circuit enclosing both the acropolis and the lower town. The connecting wall on the southeast would have continued the line of Street 1 up the slope to the main scarp and the site of Tower **7** on the Industrial Terrace. When the earth ramparts became obsolete, their course would be undeveloped ground, the natural line of broad avenues.[12] With the removal of the rampart on the line of Avenue C, the continuous southeast fortification wall would make a gate desirable at the end of its replacement roadway. At the same time, the presence of Avenue C might have determined the location of a large structure, surveyed but unexcavated and of unknown date, south of the avenue and on the A–C orientation. Whatever its purpose, it would now be within the fortified circuit.[13]

There is too little evidence to fix the relative dating of the new town plan and the combined circuit. As presently understood, there is a gap of some twenty years in the history of the acropolis defenses, from the destruction at the beginning of the 5th century to the construction of the first masonry wall in Phase 4.[14] This phase may well have included a wall on a stone base carried around the lower settlement and up the slopes to connect with the acropolis circuit. A number of Peloponnesian cities, including Corinth, Epidauros, and Sikyon, are know to have come to the defense of Halieis at the time of the Athenian attack in 460/59. Conceivably they had already aided the Tirynthians and local populace in the design and construction of the new circuit.

It is reasonable to suppose that the move to a single circuit implies a new type of defense, if only because an earth rampart could not be used on the hillside. The next step would be a wall, presumably mud brick on some sort of stone base, such as was now in use for the upper enceinte. It must be recognized, however, that while towers and gates might be remodeled or even rebuilt, to reconstruct the curtain from the ground up together with its crowning walkway would be a serious undertaking, unlikely to be assumed short of major disintegration or destruction. Therefore, the curtain based on the double line of orthostates that is apparent today is almost certainly the first real fortification wall in each section, although varying in date, to remain essentially unchanged except perhaps for the Middle Wall.

The combined circuit in the form of a stone-based wall, I suggest, ran southeast from the Hermion Gate to the site of Tower **10**, outside the rampart that would leave cleared space for Avenue A.[15] The intervening bastions seem to be integral with the curtain. The East Gate must have had some substantial structure, because its position was maintained together with the old trace from Tower **10**. From there, however, the wall angled in to the junction of Street 1 and Avenue C, newly created by the removal of the earth rampart. The circuit ran uphill to the Industrial Terrace where the older, more northern line of defense wall on the south side may have continued this circuit to the acropolis. A small tower, after the fashion of

---

[10] Boyd and Rudolph 1978, 340.

[11] That the streets as excavated are not perfectly straight should surprise no one, but since the cleared sections of Streets 3, 4, and 5 are virtually parallel, Street 4 is taken here as the basis.

[12] There is an obvious comparison to the trails that in many places in the United States have taken over the right-of-way of defunct railroads. According to Michael Jameson (per lit. 2001), in Beijing thoroughfares now run where old walls and gates have been leveled. The possible line of a rampart paralleling Street 8 would not be apparent. Much of the street is now underwater, and the southwestern part may have merged with the open area of the later agora (see below, 81, note 27).

[13] It is difficult to make out the pattern of other structures in the middle ground between the 5-meter and 20-meter contours; the actual extent of the formal streets is unknown, whatever the theoretical layout. The orientation of the scraps of wall apparent on the survey should be read with caution; without excavation it is hard to tell whether they have been dislodged.

[14] Stonework 0.50–1.00 m high is preserved; it is probable that the upper part of the wall was still of mud brick.

[15] The evidence adduced for this section of rampart is not very exact; the small area identified lies several meters inside Avenue A. The rampart would have been retained until the new wall was built, and a working space might have been maintained between them. No such accommodation would have been needed at Avenue C.

those in the West Wall, would have marked the turn near the site of the later Tower **7**. The Phase 4 defense on the acropolis used a cellular masonry base with rubble crosswalls, a detail not repeated elsewhere on the site. It was built at some time before the Athenian attack about the middle of the 5th century before Deposit V on the acropolis and corresponds to Level C in the lower town. Hypothetically, other small towers might have existed at the sites of Towers **11** and **10**. The line on the west is not so easy to determine. It may have followed the eastern trace down hill to meet with the northwestern side of the lower Archaic enceinte. The exact trace of the connection is debatable. It might have turned sharply southeast-ward to follow the steep drop above the modern road, or angled more gently across the relatively level ground to the northeast. Possibly a gate marked the northwest end of Avenue C.

An explanation for the Chambered Curtain is more difficult. This long barracks building would be unnecessary if the town guard was composed of local citizens, who could be expected to go home when they were off duty, and the relatively light outer wall suggests that the commander was less concerned with an attack from without than an uprising within. These factors imply the presence of a foreign garrison. In addition to the short-term presence of the Peloponnesians, there were two Athenian occu-pations, one soon after the failed first attempt in 460 and one in 423. The sympathies of the population might be expected to be anti-Athenian and Argive but pro-Spartan and Peloponnesian.

The apparent lack of any earlier upper southeast curtain is puzzling. If one existed, it would seem expedient to build the barracks against it. If it did not, the Chambered Curtain would be the first link between the upper and lower enceintes, more likely with the earlier date than the later. The units of the three-room structure on the acropolis identified as barracks and arsenal (Fig. 20) are larger than those of the Chambered Curtain (excepting Tower **8**).[16] The building,

combined with stairways to the walkway and Tower **6**, has been dated by Williams to acropolis Phase 6 (Williams n.d.). It would appear to be an improvement over the Chambered Curtain, much as the Northeast and Northwest Command Posts seem to be upgraded versions of Tower **8**.

The Square-tower Program (Fig. 34)

The fortification system that included major towers **5**, **10**, **11**, and **19**, which may be called the square-tower program, is the first that is clearly defined by the visible remains. (The hypothetical tower preceding Tower **7** could be associated with them, or like the East Gate and the bastion preceding Tower **9**, could belong to the first stage of the combined circuit.) These towers have been associated with the Phase 5 tower (predecessor of Tower **6**) on the acropolis, dated by acropolis Deposit V to the very end of the 5th century (410–390) and equated with Lower Town Level B (early).[17] The tie is not a strong one, however. The acropolis tower is exceptional in its interior position and very likely its function, and the chief similarity other than shape lies in the general style of the masonry, which includes some stackwork between the conglomerate orthostates, a possibility also on the northeast face of Tower **10**. In its very exposed position, Tower **10** may have been of stone to the walkway level.

If the square-tower program is considered independently, there is no reason why it could not have provided the towers for the hypothetical stone-based circuit during architectural Phase 4 on the acropolis. On the other hand, the square-tower program may have been separate from and subsequent to the construction of the stone-based curtain, replacing any small towers, which would have been obliterated in the process.[18] If the combined circuit of stone-based curtain was contemporary with Phase 4, the square towers and the western trace of the Middle Wall would then correspond to Phase 5 and the rectangular acropolis tower.[19] With the rise of the town's

---

[16] The width of the eastern rooms, 1 and 2, is 6.20 m, and that of room 3 is about 4.30 m; the depth for all three is 6.35 m. Contrast the depth of the Chambered Curtain rooms at about 5.20 m, the widths varying from 2.30 m to 5.90 m.

[17] Williams found no evidence for an absolute date for the Phase 5 architecture. The bulk of the pottery in Deposit IV is late 5th century in date with little if any from the 4th. The coins J. A. Dengate dates late 5th or early 4th (per lit. 24 February 2003). See below, chapter 9.

[18] The bastion preceding Tower **9** appears to bond with the curtain but only minimally.

[19] The use of poros plinth blocks (as well as stackwork) in the Phase 5 Tower and Tower **10**, and also in the Middle Wall and the Northeast Command Post, has already been noted. Although the significance for dating has not been sufficiently studied, it seems likely that this construction system was introduced in Phase 5. Reused poros plinth blocks were used for the acropolis barracks building, very likely from the western half of the Phase 5 tower, which was dismantled to make room for the barracks. The toichobate of the mess building, dated to Phase 5, was also poros, although somewhat more casually constructed. See Williams n.d.

fortunes, the small towers and the principal gates would have been rebuilt on a grander scale closer to the turn of the century.

In attempting to reconstruct the square-tower circuit, Tower **5** should be the starting point. Its remains, now tumbled blocks covered with brambles, reveal no details, but they appear to lie inside the line of the West Wall as it approaches the acropolis. Two reasons for its construction would be, first, its juxtaposition to the acropolis gate, assumed to exist although the excavations did not include it, and second, its location at an angle in the trace. At the gate, the tower would have been in the canonical position, on the right hand of anyone entering. The major square towers, with the exception of the one on the acropolis, all occur at significant angles in the trace. If that principle may be taken as basic to the program and Tower **5** lies at a corner, then the continuing curtain is that on the north side of the gate, running along the west side of the acropolis toward Tower **19**, on the line of the western trace of the Middle Wall (above, 17).[20]

On the same principle, Tower **19** should mark a significant change of direction in the trace or guard a major gate, if not both. No sign of a gate was apparent in the excavations or the cleared areas adjacent (above, 33); it should have been downhill from the tower or, if the trace turned sharply, on the east side. As long as there was a separate upper circuit, whose trace is mostly conjectured, it is possible that there was a strong point such as a wooden tower on the site of Tower **19** and that this marked a sharp angle and the low point of the upper enclosure.[21]

Unfortunately, no remains on the lower levels have been identified to indicate how the circuit was closed between Towers **11** and **19**. It is suggested above that a small square tower might have preceded Tower **15** (31). It could have been the terminus for an earlier trace for the North Wall running southwest, then west, from the Hermion Gate, approximating the present shoreline (17). A northward extension of the Middle Wall, which appears to align nearly with the southeast side of this tower, would have

completed the square-tower circuit. Tower **15** would have been constructed over its predecessor and largely obliterated it.

A better solution would disregard any structure at Tower **15** and require a wall parallel to Street 8 for which the section at Tower **11** is the only evidence, but it would include all the large square towers. It may be noted that if the 4th-century agora, whose site is still the subject of speculation, lay between the eastern and western sections of the lower town, it would have been outside such a square-tower circuit. Its development might well have obliterated some of the early fortification wall, even reusing the masonry.[22]

A first stage of the square-tower trace might soon have been succeeded by one with small square towers not just at the site of Tower **15** but at Towers **14** and **13** as well. Continuing the wall to the large square tower at Tower **11** would enclose a small harbor and an area for the commercial center. Access to the western valley might have been continued through a gate about at the line of the modern road.

If there was a major tower at each point where the trace changed direction significantly, a large square tower might be expected as a predecessor to Tower **7**. That none has been identified may be owing to subsequent demolition combined with the lack of excavation to clarify the blocks that remain north of the round tower. On the other hand, the size of the tower might well have been less than that of the others in the square-tower program, just as Tower **7** is the smallest of the round towers. Perhaps its proximity to the acropolis made a larger tower seem unnecessary.

Of the sections of curtain that made up the square-tower circuit those from Tower **5** to Tower **7** and from Tower **9** to Tower **10** are self evident; the section dimly seen in the aerial photograph running southwest from Tower **11** should be added. The long straight wall between Towers **10** and **11** follows or parallels the line proposed for the Archaic circuit. Only the central bastion has been examined with any care; it appears to be

---

[20] There is no evidence for an earlier form of the Middle Wall on the middle terrace except for the fragment of tower tile found under one of the wythe blocks, but it is not unreasonable to suppose that the whole stretch from Tower **5** to Tower **19** was rebuilt at the same time.

[21] It is possible that the upper Middle Wall on the eastern trace was originally constructed for the combined circuit, if not for the older upper enceinte, and retained until the wall on the western trace replaced it in the square-tower program.

[22] There must have been a marketplace of some sort for the Archaic village, very likely somewhere along Avenue B. With the unification of the upper and lower enclaves, it might have been relocated more centrally, but a close connection with the waterfront seems probable. The open area in front of the Northeast Command Post, at least as it still existed in the 4th century, seems too small, but houses may have encroached on it if it was replaced by a new agora.

bonded to the face of the curtain and contemporary with it. The Northeast Wall bastions are not unlike the somewhat larger bastions at the East and Southeast Gates and could also belong to an earlier stage preceding the square-tower program. The Chambered Curtain would have formed the closure of the square-tower circuit between the Southeast Gate and Tower **7**.[23]

Despite the 1962 and 1970 excavations in Sections F5 and F6, the Middle Wall remains puzzling; the construction seems oddly idiosyncratic. It appears well built, and the use of compartments, unique at Halieis, can be explained by the steep grade. The only other stretch of curtain to approach the same grade is the Upper Southeast Wall, where the crosswalls of the Chambered Curtain perform a similar function by retaining any terracing fill. The reduced width requiring less material might suggest urgency but also a disregard for artillery attack. The house built over the stair at Tower **19** points to abandonment in the first half of the 4th century. Williams (NB 5, 135) took the limestone blocks, two of them "at the lowest level of wall" (NB 5, 134), to be reused and concluded from them that "this city wall was not part of the city's original fortifications," but wrote that the lamp he found beneath the tile fall also indicated that the wall was not built in the latest phase. Limestone blocks were used for unskillful (presumably late) repairs to the Northeast Wall, but also appear in the walls on the Industrial Terrace. Neither the quarry nor a preexisting building on the town site has been identified as a source for the limestone. While the limestone blocks of the Apollo temple across the harbor would have been available after its destruction in 460, a source nearer at hand for these occasional blocks would seem more likely. It is unclear whether Williams's determination that the blocks were reused was based on more than the difference in material. The excavated stretch of the Middle Wall may have been built in the late 5th century, perhaps even as a realignment at the time Towers **5** and **19** were constructed. The use

of a poros plinth course recalls the construction of the Phase 5 tower on the acropolis and Tower **10**, as well as the Northeast Command Post.

The Western Defenses

It has been said that the second half of the 5th century is not represented by the pottery in the eastern part of the city,[24] but while examples are sparse, they are not entirely lacking. There may have been a general reduction in population, or, if their houses were damaged in enemy attack, many of the inhabitants may have chosen to rebuild in another part of the site. Certainly by the late 5th century the inhabitants had begun to build at the foot of the western valley.[25] They introduced a pattern of streets duplicating that in the eastern section but again with a shift in orientation. The area of gently sloping ground was more limited than in the older quarter. Avenue I, which roughly followed the shoreline, would have been the established route to the western point, but the road was not so straight as Avenue B, perhaps because it was not determined as the shortest route between two gates. Information about the eastern extent of this new development is almost entirely lacking. It may be noted, however, that a reconstruction on paper of seven blocks like those in the eastern quarter would bring the boundary, Street h, in line with Tower **13**. The wall between Towers **13** and **14**, which may have determined the new orientation, is mentioned above in connection with the square-tower program. It came as close as possible to the shore line of the main harbor and sheltered the inner harbor.[26] Whether the eastern section of Avenue I and the unexplored area from Street e to Street h in the center of the site adhered more strictly to a formal plan or like the blocks to the west were influenced by structures already in place is a matter of conjecture. The section of the North Wall between Towers **11** and **13** would be merely a connecting link, with Tower **12** approximately at its midpoint.[27]

---

[23] The rockcut steps, just outside the line of the Southeast Wall and at the east end of a hypothetical track across the middle of the site (50), could have been made either before the creation of a single circuit at whatever date or after the abandonment of the Chambered Curtain.

[24] E.g., Boyd and Rudolph 1978, 335; Rudolph 1984, 139.

[25] Boyd and Jameson 1981. Cheilik's House (Jameson 1969, 328) on Street d represents the only excavation west of Tower **15**. The finds range in date from the late 5th century to the late 4th, as do those of the much more extensively excavated eastern half

of the lower town.

[26] For the 4th-century shoreline see the Key Plan, Fig. 18. This relation of the western layout to Tower **13** was pointed out to me by Michael Jameson.

[27] It has often been suggested that the Classical agora, yet to be identified, lay somewhere in the central area. It may have been within the triangle bounded by Streets h and 8 and the wall between Towers **11** and **13**, in space reserved for it between the old and new sectors.

The new quarter, like the older, is not likely to have been left long without fortification. To protect this section the line of defense now had to include the whole of the western valley, running along the high ground south and west of the town as well as along the extent of the shore line, in other words, the trace of the Northwest and West Walls. Although the land suitable for building did not reach even as far as Tower **18**, a Tower **18A** on the point at the harbor entrance would have had a strategic value. The construction of the new defenses must have postdated that of Tower **19**. The Middle Wall, forming the west side of the square-tower enceinte, was no longer needed, and the lower stretch, where carts had access, was undoubtedly dismantled and the base blocks reused elsewhere. Tower **19** and the curtain running south to Tower **5** would have fallen into disrepair, but the terrain would have made salvaging the base blocks much more difficult and their removal less important.

From its appearance, the West Wall, from Tower **1** to Tower **5**, might be the oldest part of the masonry-based circuit.[28] Characteristics that are dated at other sites from the 5th to the beginning of the 4th century include the meandering trace along the high ground, generously enclosing developed and undeveloped areas so that they could not be overlooked by enemy attackers; the double-faced stone curtain base of trapezoidal blocks and occasional stack-work, filled with earth and rubble, the upper part of the wall presumably of mud brick; the ortho-states set on bedrock or at best small stones forming a leveling course; and the small rectangular towers (**1–3**), solidly filled at ground level and bonded to the curtain, at wide intervals yet calculated to keep all attackers within bowshot. Tower **4** was at an important location but one where the trace shows a gradual change in direction rather than an angle; it may have been the same as the others or perhaps larger. No special measures were taken to resist rams. Only with the advent of torsion-artillery machines in the 4th century were these elements generally found wanting. So little masonry is preserved above ground level it can hardly be said to have a style, but the impression is early, or at least old-fashioned, rather than late. The Northwest wall

appears somewhat later and more sophisticated, its towers hollow at ground level and thrust out from the main line of the curtain. The West and Northwest Walls, however, are each dependent on the existence of the other and must be coeval. The improved, and more expensive, design of the latter may have been determined by its more prominent position along the waterfront.

The nature of the first closure between Towers **15** and **14** is unknown; there is no evidence to reconstruct curtain, harbor works, or gate. Tower **15** would not be needed between Towers **19** and **14** if not in connection with the harbor entrance.[29] The wall that runs alongside Tower **15** and out to the Projection might be part of an earlier construction, but at right angles to the Northwest Wall rather than oriented with the street plan.

The Northeast Command Post could have been constructed at any time following that of the Northeast Wall. Its construction details suggest a date no earlier than the major square towers. It is somewhat grander than the large room in the Chambered Curtain (Tower **8**) that might have served a similar purpose, but the latter was very likely earlier and more hastily built. The construction of the Northwest Command Post similarly assumes that of the Northwest Wall. Both command posts appear to have been fitted to drain passages already extant in the adjacent curtains. It should be noted that each post is sited at about the midpoint of the wall bordering their respective town quarters.

The Round-tower Program

Sometime before the middle of the 4th century, there was a major rebuilding program that again concentrated on the east side, from which an enemy was most likely to make a land approach. Probably Tower **6** and the barracks on the acropolis were the first elements to be constructed, followed by round towers **7**, **9**, and **11**. These towers may have appeared up-to-date but were still able to accommodate only the smallest torsion stone-throwers.[30] The Southeast Gate was updated and possibly the Hermion Gate as well.

The new towers were intended to present a bold face as well as to augment the previous defenses. The impression they give now, certainly

---

[28] I am much indebted to Frederick A. Winter for pointing out to me that the West Wall could from its appearance be as late as the beginning of the 4th century.

[29] Jameson, however, proposes that the entrance to the harbor

was at first open the full 20 m (below 92), to be constricted later by the construction of the Projection.

[30] Ober 1987, 569–604.

the same when they were new, is that of a prosperous town at the high point of its history. It may be noted, however, that no round tower was added to either Tower **19** or Tower **10**. Since the Middle Wall was not then in use, there would be no need for any renovation of Tower **19**. Remodeling Tower **10**, if in contrast to the other square towers it was already built of stone at least to the walkway level, would be more difficult and less imperative.

It is possible that there was a round Tower **18A**, although at the shoreline junction of the Northwest and West Walls rather than higher on the headland as the Admiralty chart suggests (see above, 43). It would have completed the impressive waterfront face of the town, visible from the higher ground to the north as one approached from inland, and strengthened an important defensive position. Its presence would also indicate an important role for the western loop in the 4th-century defense program, otherwise primarily concentrated on the eastern part of the town.

The relation of the western defenses to the round-tower program is focused at the Harbor Gate. Unlike Towers **6** and **11**, and perhaps Tower **7**, that were added outside their predecessors, round towers **14** and **15** must have been constructed over anything earlier. It is to all intents and purposes impossible to determine whether the submerged remains of Tower **14** contain an earlier structure, in the manner of Tower **9**. It is possible that, with much effort, remains could be recovered of some rectilinear structure preceding Tower **15** (see above, 31), but it may have been a small tower like Tower **16**. Such a history might explain the curious arrangement of the wide-set towers at the Harbor Gate.[31]

The most likely sequence would put the western expansion in the late 5th or early 4th century, perhaps contemporary with Phase 5 on the acropolis, but the fortifications might not have followed immediately. This would make the square towers no later than the Phase 5 tower and indicate a short life for Tower **19** before the construction of the western defenses at the turn of the century. The more elementary nature of the West Wall might indicate either that it was the first part built or that it was completed in haste with

greater economy. The Harbor Gate with Towers **14** and **15** would be dated with Tower **6** and acropolis Phase 6 to some time in the first part of the 4th century.

The Fortifications Abandoned

Late in the 4th century certain measures indicate a shortage of manpower and possibly also of funds.[32] The acropolis walls were strengthened (Phase 7). The south wall on the Industrial Terrace was straightened, and a facing may have been added to the east wall there. The Chambered Curtain barracks, absent an occupying garrison of any size, may have been taken over for ordinary domestic use. The Southeast Gate was blocked, and clumsy repairs were made to the center bastion in the Northeast Wall. If there was a gate on the Industrial Terrace it may also have been blocked at this time. The houses (Lower Town Level A) were remodeled with used material and inferior workmanship. The northern section of the Middle Wall had long been dismantled, and houses had been built over the ruins of the central section adjacent to Tower **19**.

J. A. Dengate has suggested that the southern section of the Middle Wall may have been used as part of an expanded acropolis enceinte in the late 4th century, carried eastward in the form of a simple palisade, to protect the small garrison of an occupying force on the acropolis and Industrial Terrace. The enclosure would be much the same as or slightly larger than the one hypothecated for the Archaic period. The traces of any palisade would be just as hard to find, but there are several abrupt drops in the slope, one of which might have been incorporated in such a barrier. There is no way of knowing how much of the upper part of the Middle Wall might still have been usable. The Chambered Curtain would have been outside this circuit, but perhaps the contingent would have been too small to need it.

Nevertheless, by the end of the century Tower **6** was overthrown (Deposit VI), and the acropolis was abandoned. Jameson (per lit. 2003) suggested that bringing the defenses up to date with stone curtains and artillery installations appropriate to the Hellenistic period would have required better

---

[31] A tower such as Tower **15** at a re-entrant angle is unusual, but the location is a weak point in the defenses and important for the defense of the Harbor Gate. If there was no earlier tower there it is more difficult to understand why the round tower

was not built closer to Tower **14**.

[32] Rusch (1997, 725) gave a figure for each watch of one defender for every three meters of circuit.

material than conglomerate, such as limestone. This would have been not only beyond the means of the townsfolk but quite possibly counter to the interests of the hostile power responsible for the destruction, who may have preferred not to have a defensible harbor at such a strategic point. While the pottery and other finds indicate that the lower town was at least partially occupied by a few inhabitants into the next century, there are no more chapters in the history of the fortifications.

– CHAPTER SEVEN–

Submerged Remains of the Town and Its Immediate Vicinity

MICHAEL H. JAMESON

The information derived from the study of the submerged remains at Halieis has proved valuable but subject to inevitable limitations. It may be helpful to set out briefly the history, aims, and methods of their study.

Before the project began, the sea's excavation of walls along the shoreline was evident to even the casual visitor. When the surface was calm and the sun's reflection not too glaring, more walls could be seen further out from shore. The British Admiralty chart of 1838 (Pl. 1) showed what is now a reef some 30 m offshore as the tip of a tongue of land projecting northwards into the bay. From the beginning of the project, mapping of the underwater remains was a prime goal. (For the coastal history of the southern Argolid and the Aegean, see Van Andel and Lianos 1983 and Jameson et al. 1994, 194–210.)

The contribution of each season's work may be summarized as follows[1]:

1965. In the excavations' second season, Frank Frost and David Owen undertook to record what could be seen without excavation (NB 15). Cleaning was confined to a room of a Late Roman/Early Byzantine bath on the reef. Using only mask and snorkel, Frost and Owen mapped by measurement and triangulation the essential features of the visible remains. This map was supplemented

and corrected in the following years through further study of unexcavated remains, both on shore and in the sea, by Marian H. McAllister, Frederick A. Cooper, and Thomas Boyd, making use of invaluable photographs from balloon-suspended cameras taken by Eunice Whittlesey and Julian Whittlesey (on the techniques used, see the Whittleseys' description in Jameson 1969, 332–33).

The 1965 season showed that the curtain of the city walls extended northwest from the last traces on land in the northeastern sector of the town for some 100 m, ending in a complex in which a large, circular tower (Tower **11**) of Classical date (to judge by its resemblance to other round towers in the circuit) marked the location of a gate, which we named the Hermion (Hermione) Gate since the road running through it followed the route to that city to the northeast of the Halias. Partly covering the tower was a small bath complex of Late Roman/Early Byzantine date (see below, 95–97). To the west the city wall could be seen continuing for another 65 m, with a small rectangular tower (Tower **12**) at ca. 50 m, before disappearing under mud. From this point to where the wall could be seen once again running roughly parallel to the shore in the western sector of the town there was a gap of ca. 180 m.

[1] We are grateful to the patience, ingenuity, and good humor of many who, in addition to the authors, worked in various seasons on the submerged fortifications and other structures in the vicinity of the town: William Donner, Frank Frost, Stephen Hallin, Anthony Jameson, M. P. Johns, Karl Kilinski, Ralph Mason, Christopher McNaught, Patrick O'Kane, D. I. Owen, Susan Owen, Cynthia Patterson, Richard Platt, Helen Pratt, Richard Pratt, Rick Preuss, Geoffrey Robinson, Peter Smith, Ian Storey, Rick Van Berg, Eunice Whittlesey, Julian Whittlesey, and John Wollerton. The captain of the indispensable kaïk was Mitsos Tringakis to whose knowledge of Porto Kheli Bay and its octopus we are much in debt.

1966. In an attempt to fill this gap, Harold Edgerton conducted a sonar survey and located a series of anomalies below the seabed, ca. 30–35 m north of the North and Northwestern Walls. Markers were left at these points for future investigation.

1967. One of our principal aims this season was to resolve the question of the gap in the walls. To that end we used two-meter-long range rods to probe for the continuation of the walls under a coating of mud and a pump with an adjustable nozzle manufactured by the Roberto Galeazzi company of La Spezia, Italy, to blast away mud that had accumulated on top of the walls. The equipment was operated by divers using a hookah system for air. We were able to determine that the line of walls coming from Tower **11** and the Hermion Gate had a second small, rectangular tower in its course (Tower **13**). The wall's angling to the north increased at Tower **13** and ended in the large round Tower **14** at ca. 160 m west of the Hermion Gate (Fig. 36, Pl. 19). Twenty m to its south lay a second round tower, Tower **15**, into which was tied the eastern end of the wall north of the west side of the town, the Northwest Wall. The gap between the towers was narrowed to 7 m by a platform ("the Projection") projecting northeast from Tower **15** with cuttings for a gate or boom on the upper surface of its northeastern corner and on the north by a line of poros blocks running east from the south face of Tower **14**.

By the end of the 1967 season the area enclosed by the wall running from Tower **12** to Towers **13**, **14**, and **15** had proved to be a roughly triangular space of some 1,000 square meters. In this space no constructions were observed either by divers or in the balloon photographs. The contrast with the buildings crowding up toward the city wall to the east of Tower **11** and west of Tower **15** suggested that the triangular enclosed area was an open space, either an agora or a harbor.

1968. There was further cleaning of the new gate and the nearby towers with portable dredges using the "eductor" principle (see Jameson 1969, 331–32) and continued use of balloon photography. Approximate limits of the open area east of the Harbor Gate were determined. A hypostyle building just outside the Hermion Gate was examined (see below, 93–95). The easternmost of the anomalies located by Edgerton in 1966 was investigated by divers who found the source of the readings in rubble at 1.00–1.20 m below the modern seabed.

1970. Underwater study shifted to the northeast of Porto Kheli Bay where the sanctuary of Apollo was identified (*The Sanctuary of Apollo*, The Excavations at Ancient Halieis, 4, forthcoming). Work in this area continued in 1971 and 1973; a small-scale investigation planned for 1974 was cut short by events in Cyprus.

1972. Harold Edgerton, on returning to Halieis, confirmed and marked three of the anomalies he had detected in 1966.

1973. A team of divers dug trenches at two of the anomalies marked the previous year (compare Fig. 36 and below, 87–89). Another test was dug in the area we have termed "East of the Harbor Gate" (below, 87). This test furnished valuable stratigraphy and, at the lowest point reached, a wooden post of Late Bronze Age date.

In evaluating the data and interpretations presented here it would be well to bear in mind some of the peculiar problems of shallow water archaeology. In the muddy basin of Porto Kheli Bay the chief problem is the obscurity at depths of ca. 2 m caused by the mere presence of divers and greatly aggravated by excavation or clearing of mud, stones, or weeds. In addition, the unstable sides of trenches make it difficult for others to confirm what a diver has reported. Usually only one diver could work at any point. By the time the project turned its attention to the submerged sanctuary of Apollo a number of solutions were being devised that will be discussed fully in the fourth volume of this series of publications. Most of the work reported here was done in the project's early years.

The Undersea Elevations

Interpretation of the submerged remains requires an estimate of both the sea level at the various historical periods for which archaeological remains have been found and of the level of the seabed at these same dates (see Fig. 37).

The initial work of mapping and cleaning the submerged parts of the town and its fortifications was done with elevations calculated from the surface of the sea on the working day. The first season, 1970, in the Northeast area, which proved to be the sanctuary of Apollo, we continued to use sea level as zero. Starting in 1971 the sanctuary of Apollo was mapped into the grid of the town by F. A. Cooper and T. D. Boyd. Elevations from then on were based on Greek datum for sea level established by the Hellenic Army Geodetic Survey (referred to as mbsl — meters below [mean-standardized] sea level; Cooper 1987, 10–14, and below, Appendix C). Mean Sea Level of Corinth (Poseidonia) was 1.3060 m in 1962. Subsequently, the Survey switched to Mean Sea Level of the Kavalla station. The excavation of the anomalies detected by sonar in 1966 and 1972 and the study of the stratigraphy in the area East of the Harbor Gate, both conducted in 1973, recorded depths from Greek datum. In fact, the actual sea level at Porto Kheli varied from day to day but at all times was well below Greek datum. The cuttings on the Projection for the Harbor Gate were measured as –2.00 and –2.15 m. A variation of 15 cm in measuring the surface of a body of water at different times may be regarded as inevitable and trivial. Comparison of measurements from surface to seabed in the area East of the Harbor Gate in 1968 and 1973, the first from the actual surface, the second from Greek datum, shows a difference of 1.17 m. In view of the need to factor in the usual difference between Greek datum and actual sea surface in comparing elevations, we add arbitrarily 1.00 m to all elevations using the sea surface and suggest that they may be regarded as accurate to within ±0.50 m. Depths in the following discussion are given as mbsl unless otherwise specified. All elevations are negative.

The deepest level and earliest date in the submerged areas were determined by the discovery of a wooden post in the unbuilt-upon area East of the Harbor Gate (between Towers **14** and **15**). The post was found in the course of a study of the stratigraphy of the area in 1973 (NB 750, 2304–15). The trench was 15 m southeast of the cuttings at the Harbor Gate between Towers **14** and **15** and 11 m south of the city wall between Towers **13** and **14** (see Fig. 36). The modern seabed was at a depth of 3.12 m, below which were 0.70 m of clay-like mud containing Late Roman/Early Byzantine pottery fragments (Fig. 37).[2] From 3.82 to 4.72 m gravelly soil contained many small sherds of finer pottery, including some with traces of black glaze and one miniature kotyle. Because the sherds were very small, the most we can say of their date is that they derive from the most

substantial periods of the town's occupation, Archaic through Classical (ca. 700–300). At the bottom of this stratum gravel gives way to pebbles in whitish clay followed by thick, gray clay. Below 4.72 m a single large fragment of coarse ware at 4.97 m (HP 2109, a poorly preserved pithos rim) was the only pottery encountered.[3] At 5.67 m the top of a wooden post was found. The post, from a fir tree (*Abies*), extended to 6.42 m. The wood from this post (P-2065), which was not carbonized, was radiocarbon dated at MASCA at the University of Pennsylvania (Lawn 1975, 203) to 1160 B.C.E. ± 50; in 1967 the dating was calibrated by the Wiener Laboratory at Cornell University to ca. 1345 B.C.E., with 95.4 percent confidence for between 1500 and 1190 B.C.E.[4] A date in the Late Bronze Age may be regarded as secure.

A trench in 1968 in the entrance of the Harbor Gate yielded similar information, except for the absence of a Late Bronze Age level (NB 504, 67; see Fig. 37). The modern seabed lay at 3.20 m. Between 3.20 and 3.60 m there was Late Roman/Early Byzantine pottery. Tile fragments stopped at 4.10 m. Gravel and small, water-worn sherds appeared between 4.20 and 4.40 m and sterile, light gray clay thereafter. In comparison with the 1973 trench ca. 15 m to the east, we find (bearing in mind the different measuring of depths) that Late Roman/Early Byzantine pottery extends only to 3.60 m rather than 3.82 and that the stratum of gravel and small sherds below this level is 0.20 m thick and not 0.90 m. The gray clay starts at 4.40 m rather than 4.72. Most of the discrepancies are probably to be attributed to the crudeness of measuring, especially before the determination of Greek datum, but the thinness of the gravelly stratum in the entrance, 0.20 m compared to 0.90 m, may be accounted for by ancient efforts to dredge the entrance, if we follow the hypothesis of a sea gate, discussed below, 91–93.

The Anomalies

In 1966, Harold E. Edgerton of the Massachusetts Institute of Technology, assisted by Sarah Dublin Slenczka and E. Loring, made a preliminary sonar survey in Porto Kheli harbor. It had been hoped

---

[2] As elsewhere at Halieis, the Late Roman/Early Byzantine pottery consisted primarily of spirally grooved amphora fragments. Cf. Rudolph 1979, 304.

[3] W. 0.102 m, L. 0.236 m, Th. 0.042 m. Munsell 5YR c/1 (gray). Many large inclusions. Outer surface broken away. Small part

of rim preserved. Flattened upper (?) surface. Surfaces seem to have been smoothed by fingers; traces of horizontal smear marks preserved. Outer face of rim may have been convex.

[4] We are most grateful to Dr. Elizabeth Ralph and to Professor Peter Kuniholm and their associates.

that the sub-bottom profiler used by Edgerton could solve the puzzle of the gap in the line of the walls north of the town but it proved not to be effective at such shallow depths. His survey, however, did locate a number of anomalies at greater depths under the seabed in Porto Kheli Bay, north of the submerged walls and thus outside the line of fortifications. A test trench in 1968 at the easternmost anomaly found rubble and tile fragments at 1.10 m below the seabed. In 1972 Edgerton returned and, assisted by Bruce Bevan, Karl Petruso, and Priscilla Murray, reconfirmed the location of the three easternmost anomalies for which he left markers on the seabed. In 1966 three more anomalies had been noted between 50 and 90 m north of the Northwest Wall. But in 1972 it was investigation of the eastern anomalies, north of the curtain between Towers **12** and **14**, that he recommended, one reason being their shallower elevation. The locations of the western anomalies were not confirmed but it is not clear from Edgerton's 1972 report whether this was attempted. No markers for them could be located in 1973. The three western anomalies are still shown on Edgerton's 1972 chart, identified as found in 1966, but the third from the west is accompanied by a question mark. The sonar readings seem to show that the western anomalies began to be detected at ca. 7.5 m (= 8.5 mbsl). If these are man-made constructions originally at or above sea level they must go back into the Early Bronze Age (with a rise of 0.15 m a century, at least some thirteen centuries before the Late Bronze Age post at 5.67 m).[5]

In 1973 a team of divers (Cynthia Patterson, Stephen Hallin, Ralph Mason, and Geoffrey Robinson) dug test pits at two of the markers left by Edgerton (Fig. 36; NB 750, 2300–2303, 2311–12). Lines of conglomerate rubble proved to be the source of the anomalies recorded by sonar, about 30–35 m north of, and hence outside, the North Wall and some 60–70 m from the present shoreline. The first trench (located at N7276/E16225, Fig. 36, Anomaly 1) was on the easternmost marker, ca. 30 m north of Tower **12**. Seabed was 3.60 m (Fig. 37). The first 1.00–1.20 m below the seabed consisted of sterile, gray clay. In the next ca. 0.30 m (4.80–5.10 mbsl) were numerous Late Roman/ Early Byzantine sherds, bone fragments, and fruit stones (later determined to be olive pits). Between 4.75 and 4.95 m came the line of rubble in a single course,[6] no more than two stones wide, running northeast/southwest. Pebbles, medium and small, were noticed around the rubble. The line of stones is referred to in the notebooks and reports as "the Edgerton anomalies" and for convenience we continue the neutral designation, "the Anomalies." Late Roman pottery and organic matter were described as found above and "around the edges" of the stones. A single fruit pit is mentioned as under a piece of poros limestone (not identified as part of the line of rubble). Neither pottery nor wood serves to date the laying down of the line of rubble. Aside from the one pit (which was too small to be dated separately), no pottery or wood was reported below the stones. The rim of a small jug or a chytra (HP 2079) was found at about the level of the bottom of the stones but not under them.[7] To 5.75 m, the deepest point reached in this test, there was sterile gray mud.

A second test was dug at the third marker from the east (Anomaly 3), ca. 70 m northwest of the first (coordinates N7285/E16190). At a depth of 4.94 m nine pieces of conglomerate rubble were uncovered, at most 0.16 m high. The stones formed an acute angle, one line running northeast/ southwest while three other blocks joined them from the north. Late Roman/Early Byzantine pottery, less than in the first trench, was found above the stones.

These flimsy lines of rubble cannot be described as constituting a wall, mole, jetty, or even, as in preliminary reports, a "sea wall" marking the shoreline (Jameson 1973–1974 [1979], 264), for which the remains are ill suited. A single course of rubble was observed at the lowest level of the spur projecting from the structure south of the Harbor Gate. Here, we suggest, we have traces of foundations for mudbrick constructions near the shoreline. With the rise of the sea level only the stones at the base of the walls survived. The two small trenches are insufficient to reveal the plan and character of these constructions, whether they formed a continuous wall (Edgerton conceived of the anomalies as a single continuous phenomenon) or are traces of separate structures of varing dates.

---

[5] For Final Neolithic and Early Bronze Age remains on the acropolis at Halieis, see Pullen 2000.

[6] The impression recorded in 1968 NB 504 of a double layer is at odds with the more systematic record of 1973 NB 750.

[7] HP 2079, Unit 128-1700, about one-third preserved. H. 0.062 m, W. 0.061 m. Fine, sandy clay, Munsell 10 YR 7/3 (very pale brown). Inside, wheel-ridging. Globular body, slight flaring rim.

The organic matter found with the pottery on and around the rubble provides Late Roman/Early Byzantine dates. It included wood (P-2099) and olive pits (P-2098) that give dates of ca. A.D. 200 and 370 respectively (calibrated by the Wiener Laboratory), the later date being the time of production of the olive fruit and its pits. The preservation of the organic matter indicates that from the time of its deposit it had been in water continuously. The date of ca. 200 may be that of the cutting of the wood, which could antedate its lodging in the rubble by a long interval, but the olive pits of ca. 370 should be close in time to the actual deposit. By that time, if not earlier, the anomalies were below sea level but still open to deposition of pottery, wood, and so forth.

Evidence from a wooden post (P-2064) found in the submerged temple of Apollo 700 m to the north of the Anomalies in 1973 shows that the Late Roman/Early Byzantine sea level was, in fact, considerably higher. The post, not carbonized, was found reaching from 2.80 to 3.20 m. As with the Late Bronze Age post in the inner harbor (above, 87), its preservation indicates continuous submersion. Its ^{14}C date of ca. A.D. 480 (calibrated by the Wiener Laboratory) suggests that when the organic matter at the Anomalies was deposited, the surface of the sea was more than 1 m above the rubble, a preferable hypothesis to supposing that there had been an extraordinarily rapid rise in sea level of ca. 2.00 m in about a century.[8] The Early Byzantine buildings investigated by Frost (1977) at Phourkari, near the eastern tip of the Argolid peninsula, are at the lowest points 1.20 m below the surface of the sea, that is, 2.20 mbsl.

If the rubble of the Anomalies was laid down on dry land, sea level at the time of construction was below 4.95 m, let us say ca. 6.00 m or lower. The post east of the Harbor Gate showed a sea level of 5.67 m or higher. These considerations point to an early date for the Anomalies, Late Bronze Age or Early Iron Age (cf. Fig. 38). From ca. 1300 B.C.E. (post east of the Harbor Gate) to ca. A.D. 480 (post in the Temple of Apollo), the minimum sea level rose from 5.67 to 2.80 m, an average rise per century of 0.15 m. We do not suppose the rise was in fact so regular and we repeat that for both posts we are speaking of minima. Nevertheless, the figure of 0.15 m allows us to see that we are in the right vicinity. A

thousand years after the date of the LBA post, at the time of the latest fortifications, the minimum sea level would be about 1.50 m higher, that is, ca. 4.17 m. Our tests furnished maxima of 4.00 and 4.72 m. The level of the rubble at the Anomalies, 4.95 m, presumably on dry land, suggests a sea level that existed some time between the Late Bronze Age and the Classical period. The presumed Archaic–Classical date of the jug or chytra found at the level of the bottom of the rubble is consistent with a date before the end of the Classical period as is a sea level below the level of the rubble. If we postulate a sea level of ca. 6.00 m, we are closer to the Bronze Age than the Classical for the laying down of the rubble.

Much later, the Late Roman/Early Byzantine occupation with many traces of buildings along the shore (see Fig. 38; Rudolph 1979) deposited considerable debris in the bay. The presence of rubble in the seabed close to shore may have served to catch and hold organic material. Fuel for the bath nearby is an example of the need for quantities of wood to be brought to the site.

The levels containing Late Roman/Early Byzantine pottery at the Anomalies and East of the Harbor Gate are not the same. At the Anomalies the stratum is from ca. 4.80 m to 5.10 m. East of the Harbor Gate it is from 3.12 to 3.82 (these are the measurements made in 1973; a deep test in the entrance of the Harbor Gate in 1968 yielded much the same information, with Late Roman/Early Byzantine pottery at ca. 3.20–3.60 m). The lowest point of the second area's deposit is about 1.00 m above the beginning of the Late Roman/Early Byzantine deposit at the Anomalies, that is, the seabed east of the Harbor Gate was higher than at the Anomalies. A second stratum, a gravelly layer with small sherds, some of which are Archaic or Classical, at a depth of 3.82–4.72 m in the 1973 trench, 4.20–4.40 m in the 1968 trench in the entrance, is absent from the Anomalies, aside from a single sherd from a jug or chytra.

Chronology of the Harbor Gate Area
(Figs. 37, 38)

In the Late Bronze Age sea level was at least 5.67 m or somewhat higher. A wooden post fixed into the seabed (for mooring a boat or perhaps attaching fishing nets) was ever after immersed in salt water. This area was never dry land or the

---

[8] This was the information furnished to Jameson et al. 1994, 199–200 and table 3.7, where earthquakes are offered as a possible

contributing factor.

wood would have rotted away, which is not to say that there was always sufficient depth of water to serve as a harbor. It is significant, however, that while Late Roman/Early Byzantine structures were built along the shore of the bay to the east, none were found in the enclosed space East of the Harbor Gate (Fig. 36; cf. Rudolph 1979, 296). In the first millennium B.C. the sea level continued to rise and silt accumulated in the form of heavy gray clay of the same composition as the Late Bronze Age seabed. There was found a single coarse-ware sherd, a pithos rim, probably of Archaic or Classical date (HP 2109). For a long time there seems to have been little traffic in or close to this sector. The next stratum of gravelly soil represents deposits prior to the Late Roman/Early Byzantine period. Substantial habitation of Archaic through Late Classical times spanned the years from ca. 700 to 300. In that time and for the four or five centuries without permanent habitation that followed, the seabed was between 4.72 and 3.82 m (4.20 and 3.60 m in the entrance), levels open to deposition of pottery. Above 3.82 and 3.60 m Late Roman/Early Byzantine pottery begins to appear.

The stratum of gravel may be of similar date to the gravel layer (0.40 m thick, Jameson 1969, 334) found under the conglomerate blocks in the lower course of Tower **13**, below which is sterile gray clay (NB 504, 67; compare above, 30). Gravel was noted also under the Southeast Wall, northeast of Tower **9** (see above, 51). The quarrying of poros and conglomerate blocks for the latest line of the North Wall, the one we see ending at Tower **14**, may have involved digging in a gravelly area, perhaps the stream bed and valley to the east of the Southeast Wall.

In the 4th century B.C. the sea level was below the cuttings for the closing of the Harbor Gate at the tip of the Projection, at 3.00 m. The top of the Spur on the west side of the Projection, consisting of two courses of poros blocks on a third course of rubble, was either at or close to ground level, or, if we are dealing with a sea gate, sea level, as was the line of poros blocks along the south face of the North Wall (compare above, 86). A short wall projecting out from an important defensive tower makes no sense for fortifications whether on dry land or on the waterfront. The Spur (described above, 88) is best understood as a retaining wall, whether its upper surface was dry land or seabed. The upper surface of the upper course of poros was 3.25, of the second course, 3.70, and of the rubble below it ca. 4.00 m. If this

was a sea gate, the 4th-century sea level was between ca. 3.25 m and ca 4.00 m. As for the seabed, in the Classical period, ca. 480–338, it was no higher than 4.40 at the entrance (4.72, fifteen m to the east) since it is at this point that gravel and black-glazed sherds begin to appear. While no higher than 4.40, we cannot say how much of the 0.95 m of clay below, between the beginning of the next stratum and the upper tip of the Late Bronze Age post, was deposited in the historical period, nor how much of the gravelly stratum may have been deposited after the town was abandoned (little if any, if we are correct in associating the gravel with the final construction phase). With the sea gate hypothesis, at the time of the latest fortifications the minimum depth of water at the entrance would have been between roughly 0.60 and 1.00 m.

Comparison with elevations in the sanctuary of Apollo at the northeast of the present Porto Kheli Bay shows that the elevation of the northern starting line of the stadion in the 4th century was 3.00 m, the same as that of the cuttings at the Harbor Gate (Plan of the Sanctuary, November 1973). The lowest point on the plan is 3.46 m, the top of a block on the western side of the rectangle supporting the viewing stands. A chart of the seabed of present-day Porto Kheli Bay (Fig. 39) shows that the contours here are widely spaced, that is, that the gradient is very gradual (as much as 325 m from the modern shore to the 4 m contour, 250 m from the 3 to the 4 m contour; contrast the steeper gradient at the Harbor Gate, from shore to 3.00 m in 150 m). The Archaic and Classical buildings in the sanctuary could have been very little above sea level and still some 200 m or more from the contemporary shoreline. If the bottom of the block serving as a support in the stadion viewing stand is taken as above sea level, a minimum depth for Classical sea level is ca. 3.76 m (3.46 + ca. 0.30 m). We have seen that the constructions around the Harbor Gate point to a level between 3.60 and 4.00 m.

By the time the abundant Late Roman/Early Byzantine pottery began to be deposited, the seabed in the Harbor Gate area had built up to 3.60 (at the entrance), 3.82 (at East of the Harbor Gate). Outside and to the north of the North Wall, at the Anomalies, the Late Roman/Early Byzantine seabed was ca. 1.50 m below that in the area of the Harbor Gate, no higher than 5.30 when Late Roman/Early Byzantine pottery began to be deposited. The Late Roman/Early Byzantine sea level is shown by the well-preserved wooden post

(P-2064) in the Apollo temple to have been 2.80 m or higher ca. A.D. 480.

The Harbor Gate

The problem of this gate, whether it was a land gate opening onto the shore or a sea gate giving access to a small, enclosed harbor, may be considered under three headings: (1) the relation of the gate to sea level and seabed in the 4th century B.C.; (2) the construction and placement of the gate; (3) the relationship of the gate and the empty area to its east to the plan of the rest of the town.[9]

(1) We have shown above why we believe that at the time of the final phase of the fortifications the sea level was between 3.60 and 4.20 m and the minimum depth of water at the entrance was roughly between 0.60 and 1.20 m. In the 7th century, when the settlement at Halieis was becoming more substantial, the ground level or seabed was no higher than ca. 4.20 m in the entrance (4.72 m, East of the Harbor Gate) since it was from that point that Archaic–Classical sherds began to appear. This leaves a very shallow depth of water for a harbor. It needs to be emphasized, however, that the figures are minima, but even as minima they cause, in our view, an insuperable difficulty in interpreting the gate as on dry land (see Figs. 37, 38).

After the construction of the last, 4th-century gateway, 0.40 m of Late Roman / Early Byzantine deposit, starting at 0.60 m below the bottom of the gate, accumulated in the entrance way. Below that was a 0.20 m stratum of Archaic–Classical date. This last, it could be argued, was fill deposited in the construction of the gate or in the centuries before the gate was built rather than material deposited during the use of the entrance. But the next 0.40 m of Late Roman / Early

Byzantine pottery cannot be so explained and the possibility of a robber trench later filled with pottery of the time is disproved by the corresponding stratum in the open area East of the Harbor Gate where robbing is not plausible. It is inescapable that there was an open space of between 0.60 to 1.20 m under the bottom of the mechanism for closing the entrance. Leaving such a gap below the bottom of the wooden leaves of a gate at this large and highly exposed entrance is inexplicable.[10]

(2) The placement and the construction of the gate also point to a sea, not a land, gate. The design of land gates aims to dominate the approaching enemy by means of projecting towers, preferably on the assailant's unshielded right side, or by flanking walls creating a passage through which the attackers must go to reach the entrance itself (Winter 1971, 208–9; McNicoll and Milner 1997, 6; Adam 1992). If a land gate is hypothesized here with the shore of the harbor just outside the gate to the west, we have to suppose that at this most vulnerable spot in the whole system the gateway is exposed with one tower to its north but the other, which could dominate the unshielded right side of the assailants, 12 m away to the south. (For the vulnerability of gates by the shore, note Aeneas Tacticus's recommendation, 10.8, that vessels be required to drop anchor only at specified gates.) All other towered gates at Halieis, in the manner of most Greek gates with towers, have towers on the left side of the entrance, thus dominating the unshielded right side of attackers.[11] If this were a land gate why not place the entrance to the north (right) of the south tower (Tower **15**)? Instead, the entrance is to the south (left) of the north tower (Tower **14**) because against approaching vessels there was no advantage in dominating one side rather than the other while farther away from the

---

[9] Consideration must be given to the brief but sharp dissent to the interpretation of an enclosed harbor by Frank Frost (1985) who wrote without benefit of details from more recent investigations. His view that an inlet or embayment close to the north shore of the town site "could not have occurred naturally by any known principle of geomorphology" is not shared by the scientists we have consulted (cf. Jameson et al. 1994, 54, n. 13). Simply lowering the sea level below the modern contours will not recover the depth between ancient sea level and seabed that permits the presence of a harbor. Finally, the comment by an experienced researcher that "it does not feel like a harbour" is not to be dismissed out of hand but does not lend itself to examination or refutation.

[10] A gap sufficient to show the presence of men and horses within the gates of Amphipolis is mentioned by Thucydides (5.10.2).

Lawrence (1979, 256) supposes there was generally a closer fit "though pivots were often considerably above the floor." At the Silenos Gate at Thasos, where the pivots were 0.30 m above the floor, a double row of blocks served as a stop. On pivots at Halieis, see above, 37.

[11] There are examples of towers on the left side of the approaching enemy, as at Oiniadai and Kydna (Adam 1992, 18–19), where the terrain requires assailants to approach with their right flank exposed to the curtain. At Halieis, the East Gate (see above, 25–27) has what has been called a small "bastion" rather than a tower on its left side. Its opening, however, is considerably narrower, 4.30 m compared to 7 m at the Harbor Gate, which, whether on land or sea, was clearly a much more important and vulnerable entry to the town.

shoreline the channel was deeper and less liable to silting. It is possible that an earlier version of this entrance extended the full 20 m between Towers **14** and **15**, closed by chains and nets (cf. Garlan 1974, 388–89) and that the 7 m entrance we see now, closed by a boom, was a modification made for greater safety.

The cuttings at the northeast corner of the Projection (Fig. 10b) accord with no example of a fortification gate known to us. Instead, the reconstruction of a boom proposed by Louis and Marian McAllister in our first publication of this gate (Jameson 1969, 334–36) and described above (40–42) seems the most plausible solution. Such a boom is mentioned by Aeneas Tacticus (53.2): "Just before Chios was betrayed, one of the archons, joining in the betrayal, persuaded his fellow archons, saying that since there was peace they should pull the harbor's *kleithron* on to land and dry it out and pitch it." Garlan (1974, 388–89 and fig. 67, 388) illustrates and comments on a metal chain, a *halusis*, which is supported by buoys and anchored to the seabed, as described by Philo of Byzantium, *Mech. Synt.* 5. C. 52.[12] If the harbor entrance had once been 20 m wide, that is, the whole distance between Towers **14** and **15**, such a chain would have been used to close the opening. The angled wall east of the Projection may have been used by men hauling the boom open.

(3) The course of the North Wall west of the Hermion Gate and Tower **11** is clearly meant to enclose a larger space than would a direct connection to the Northwest Wall, beginning at Tower **15** (Figs. 18, 19). From Tower **13** the line of the wall angles further to the northwest. Within the space enclosed by the North Wall west of Tower **13**, the Harbor Gate, and the construction to its south (the Projection) no constructions of any date have been detected. A line of white poros blocks runs parallel to and south of the North Wall for ca. 105 m, ending on the west at the south face of Tower **14** and on the east half way between Towers **12** and **13**. It lies between 2 and 3 m south of the south wythe of the North Wall at a depth of 3.20 m (as measured in 1968). We have suggested that it served as the foundation for a mole on which the North Wall rested (Jameson 1969, 333; it was not determined whether a corresponding line of blocks was placed off the north face of the North Wall). Frost (1985, 65) speaks of "a long,

straight outerwall with its footings underwater" as unparalleled. Moles, however, are common enough and whether they angle in, out, or are curved depends on the space they are designed to enclose.

The empty space east of the Harbor Gate and south of the North Wall is regarded by Frost as an agora. The absence of any larger structures on its margins, as one would expect for an agora, is an argument from silence and cannot be pressed. Blocks from such buildings would have been conspicuous and easily robbed out. Another difficulty derives from the detection of an earlier line of the North Wall that ran southwest from a square predecessor of Tower **11** at the Hermion Gate perhaps to a square predecessor of Tower **15** (see above, 31). To see the empty space as an agora one would have to suppose it was an addition to a preexisting agora further south since it cannot be imagined that the city lacked an agora up to this time. A civic rather than a military purpose for this final revision of the fortifications would be surprising.

The use of a chain to control the entrance to Porto Kheli Bay, ca. 350 m at its narrowest today (somewhat less in the 4th century B.C.), would have been impractical and unparalleled (cf. Lehmann-Hartleben 1923, 74). The doctrine that warships were always or by preference beached nightly has been shown to be untenable (Harrison 1999). The closed harbor proposed for Halieis would have provided shelter for a few vessels (triremes are thought to have been about 37 m in length and less than 4 m in beam, Morrison and Williams 1968, 285) and permitted the foreign garrison that seems most likely to have manned the walls at this time to maintain communications with its home base whenever a chance to slip out offered itself.

Limenes kleistoi, "closed" or "closable" harbors, are not uncommon, appearing often as a secondary harbor, smaller than the principal commercial harbor of a town (Lehman-Hartleben 1923, 65–74; Blackman 1982). Most, to be sure, are known primarily from textual references and have not been explored carefully. But another example may be added: Zangger (1994, 232–35) has investigated the harbor of Asine at the upper end of the Argolic Gulf. A wall, composed of roughly hewn cubic blocks of 0.20–40 m to a side, now

---

[12] Aeneas Tacticus (8) says such barriers are treated in his *Paraskeuastika* and therefore omitted from the *Poliorketika*.

Chapters 51–62 of Philo of Byzantium *Mech. Synt.* 5. C discuss protection against attack from the sea (Garlan 1974, 313–14).

mostly submerged, runs for some 200 m along the west side of Kastraki, once an island, later a fortified hill, leaving a gap of less than 50 m between the southern tip of the wall and the land. Zangger, who dates the wall to the time of the Hellenistic fortifications, believes that "It would be highly unlikely that this basin was used as a port, because it is so small and shallow [today 3 m at most to judge from p. 235, fig. 15] that even navigating a canoe in it is difficult." Rather he suggests that the submerged wall may have "been an extension of the Hellenistic defence system, providing protection from approaching ships" and perhaps also serving as a quay. The Hellenistic fortress at Asine, now dated with the reoccupation of the site to the late 4th or early 3d century (Penttinen 1996), was not the work of a local population for its own defense any more than the walls at late Classical Halieis. At both sites the utility of a small protected harbor should not be overlooked.

In the light of McAllister's observation on the remains at Tower **11** (the Hermion Gate) (see above, 16), the sequence of the city walls in this area can be conjectured as follows:

(1) The antecedents of the surviving North Wall (west of Tower **11**) and Northwest Wall (west of Tower **15**) and their relationship to the Middle Wall (at present known only as far north as Tower **19**) are unclear. McAllister (above, 80) sees two possibilities: (a) that traces of a wall running southwest from Tower **11** and the Hermion gate, parallel to Street 8, came up to a hypothetical square predecessor of Tower **15**, as did an extension of the Middle Wall from Tower **19**. (b) But in the absence of any surviving trace of an earlier tower or of walls coming up to it from the east and south, she thinks it more likely that the wall running southwest from the Hermion Gate ended at Tower **19**. In either case the area enclosed by the later North Wall and Towers **12–15**, including the Harbor Gate, lay beyond the fortifications at this time but would have been reached by a gate also providing access to the western valley.

(2) The stretch of city wall angling WNW from Tower **11** was built out into the bay, probably at the time round Tower **11** replaced the rectangular tower at the Hermion Gate. This line ended at the round Tower **14**. An opening of ca. 20 m, flanked on the south by round Tower **15**, was left for entering the harbor enclosed by the new wall.

(3) The harbor entrance was narrowed to 7 m by building a projection out from Tower **15** at the tip of which a boom was set. Significantly the remaining entrance is at the northern end of the 20 m opening. Silting at the south end of the entrance, a problem perhaps addressed by the spur wall running out from the Projection, could have made the wider entrance usable only at the north end. The smaller entrance, with Tower **14** on one side of it, would have been easier to control than a 20 m opening. Silting has rightly been seen as a threat to an enclosed harbor (Frost 1985, 65). The town may have been abandoned less than fifty years after the round tower phase of the fortifications and so perhaps before the more serious disadvantages of the harbor's design had been encountered.[13]

The exploit of the Spartan Aneristos in capturing Halieis with a merchant ship full of soldiers (Herodotus 7.137.2; cf. Jameson n.d., chap. 1) probably occurred in the third quarter of the 5th century and therefore before the three stages in the development of the harbor's defenses outlined above. The system of rectangular towers is dated to the end of the 5th or beginning of the 4th century (Phase 5) and the substitution of round towers (Phase 6) to before the mid-4th century. But from the earliest period of the town's fortifications it would have required protection along the shore,[14] with walls following roughly the same line as that in stage (1). The lesson learned from Aneristos may have led to the harbor gate, first wide and later narrow, seen in stages (2) and (3).

Two submerged buildings not related directly to the fortifications were examined in the course of our study of the walls and gates, a hypostyle building outside the Hermion Gate and a bath of Late Roman/Early Byzantine date, built over the old gate and its towers.

The Hypostyle Building
(Fig. 40, Pl. 19)

The presence of a rectangular structure with two rows of column bases in its interior was revealed by balloon photographs in 1967 and explored by divers in 1968 (NB 504, 49–51; Jameson 1969, 338 and pl. 91a). The remains were overlaid by heavy

---

[13] For the round tower program, see above, 82–83. On the acropolis, this is Phase 6 (Williams n.d.).

[14] For examples of walls along the shoreline of a harbor, cf. the large commercial harbor of Knidos (McNicoll and Milner 1997, 55, fig. 11, after Krischen 1938, pl. 2) and Seleukia Pieria (McNicoll and Milner 1997, 84, fig. 16).

deposits of silt, rubble, and beachrock, and no systematic cleaning or excavation was undertaken. The very tentative plan (Fig. 40) is derived largely from the balloon photographs supplemented by observations and measurements by divers; it supersedes earlier published plans of the submerged remains.[15]

The building is 20 m north of and outside the Hermion Gate and Tower **11**, on the west side of the main road leading from the gate to the sanctuary of Apollo and all the northern and western territory of the Halias, as well as, more distantly, to Hermion. It measures ca. 11 x 14.5 m oriented northeast/southwest with the long east side immediately adjacent to the road, ca. 7 m wide and composed of heavy gravel; the road is visible in the balloon photographs. The bottom of the wall blocks are at 2.80 mbsl. If the plan was based on the short foot of 0.278 m used in the stadion of the Apollo sanctuary (167 m ÷ 600 feet, Jameson 1972 [1976], 236; 1973, 229), it may have been conceived of as a rectangle of 40 by 50 feet (11.13 by 13.92 m; our measured length of 14.5 m would then be off by 0.58 m, which is quite possible).

The surviving parts of the walls consist of a rather patchy double row of thin, poorly preserved stretchers, averaging 0.25 m in height, resting on a rubble foundation. The thickness of the south wall is 0.75 m. The walls no doubt were continued in mud brick. Six column bases in two rows of three consist of two rectangular blocks of limestone, one above the other, under which is a block of poros. The elevations we recorded suggest that all three elements were not always preserved. At the central base on the west side where the top of the uppermost block is at 2.70 m, its thickness is 0.15 m and that of the next lower block is 0.10 m. Dimensions recorded were 0.59 x 0.59 m (about 2 feet square) and 0.59 x 0.68 m. The use of three blocks for each column base may have resulted from raising the floor level of the whole building at some point, adding a third block to the column bases, and replacing the columns. The columns were set ca. 4 m from the outer walls and ca. 3 m apart, center to center. A distance between bases of ca. 1.97 m was recorded.

Remains of a floor (described in the notebook as heavy, gray cement) were observed alongside the column bases. We interpret this as originally a lime floor, traces of which were also found in the temple of Apollo.

Inside the northeast and northwest corners were two rectangles ca. 1 m on each side, constructed of heavier blocks than the walls' stretchers. Exact measurements, which would have required extensive cleaning, were not obtained. One may compare the rectangular compartment in the northeastern corner of the middle room of the temple of Apollo in that god's sanctuary north of this building (Jameson 1973–1974 [1979], 262). Here they may have served as foundations for ladders to an upper floor. No entrance to the building has been detected. The east and west sides seem to be unbroken. Divers had the impression that there was an entrance along the north face but recorded no confirmation. A south-facing entrance would agree with the two temples in the sanctuary of Apollo. Marian McAllister has pointed out that the position of the column bases suggests a hypaethral structure possibly with a central hearth (which was not detected). It is noteworthy that no tile fragments were reported, in marked contrast to the many distinctive early Corinthian tiles of the temple of Apollo. The building may always have had a brushwood roof.

Black-glazed pottery was found at the level of the poros blocks underlying the column bases. Cleaning in the northern part of the building ca. 0.25 m below the sea bottom yielded a number of black-glazed sherds (the rim of a cup, body of an oinochoe, a cup handle, a krater[?] handle) and several Geometric or, more likely, Subgeometric sherds as well as ribbed black-glazed fine ware, coarse ware, and Late Roman/Early Byzantine spirally grooved ware, and some fragments of wood and metal. Most of the Late Roman/Early Byzantine pottery is just below the seabed and there is no indication of brick and mortar construction. Clearly, the building was in use in the Classical period. How much earlier the building may have been built is not shown by the 7th-century pottery since it may have come from early graves along the road, disturbed by the later construction of this building.

A military or commercial function for the building seems to be precluded by its location in an exposed position just outside the main city gate. A cult building is more likely but none of the pottery is characteristically votive (there were no examples of the otherwise ubiquitous miniature kotylai), though it would be consistent with a

---

[15] Schoder 1974, 88, publishes an oblique aerial view of the Hermion Gate area and identifies the building as a stoa.

building where meals were taken. Nor was an altar detected either north or south of the building, but no exhaustive search for one was undertaken.[16] The possibility of the building being a hostelry is worth considering. It agrees with some of the characteristics of Greek examples: it is on a road, near a sanctuary and a city gate (cf. Kraynak 1984, 26, 164–65), and close to the shore of the bay. It could have catered to visitors to the games held in the stadion. Its plan, however, seems to be unique. The one possible parallel, a Hellenistic building at the foot of Mt. Oros on Aigina associated with the cult of Zeus Hellanios, was restored as a columned hall, 19.50 x 29 m, with three rows of five bases by Welter (1938; Kraynak 1984, 147–49 and pl. LXI). Hans Goette (1999), however, has reexamined the remains and concluded that the columns formed a *pi*, with only the easternmost column in the middle row certain. The effect was of two stoas facing each other and joined at one end. To the west, there seems to have been an Archaic predecessor whose plan is not recoverable. Welter's identification of the building as a hostelry and dining hall for visitors to the sanctuary on the top of the mountain is plausible and is accepted by Goette, though regarded as unproved by Kraynak.

The Late Roman/Early Byzantine Bath
(Fig. 41, Pl. 19)

In the course of tracing and recording the remains in the sea in 1965, Frank Frost and David Owen realized that what lay under and around the small reef breaking the surface some 40 m offshore, lying over some of the fortifications at the Hermion Gate, constituted a bath building of tile, brick, rubble and mortar construction, and thus of Roman or Byzantine date. Because of the great difficulty in working just below the sea's surface, we did not attempt then or in subsequent seasons to excavate the remains or even to clean them extensively. Our aim was to establish the main outlines of the bath and the fortifications. Fig. 41 is a plan drawn by Marian McAllister showing the results of the work in the sea combined with the information derived from balloon photographs (Pl. 19). It is acknowledged that under the circumstances judgment on whether particular

blocks or walls relate to the baths, the fortifications, or both, is necessarily rather arbitrary. Interpretation of these remains has been helped by the publication of two roughly contemporary baths, near Zevgolatio in the Corinthia (Charitonidis and Ginouvès 1955) and at the Panayia site in Corinth itself (Sanders 1999). These are referred to in the following discussion as the Zevgolatio and the Panayia baths, respectively. The proliferation of small cubicles or basins, characteristic of these late baths, is discussed by Ginouvès (1955).

The bath complex, roughly 15 m square, lies 2 m south of the 4th-century circular tower. The *caldarium* (**C**), with its characteristic hypocaust heating system can be recognized on the south side of the building, the preferred location for this function (Vitruvius 5.10.1–2; Charitonidis and Ginouvès 1955, 105). Off of this room opened two oval and one square cubicles or wash basins (termed *baptisteria* in the description of the Panayia bath, "cuves-bagnoires" in that of Zevgolatio), **a**, **b**, and **c**, on the west, south, and east respectively. The construction is in brick and cement. The floor of **b** was cleaned and seen to be composed of square tiles, 0.53 m to the side and 0.03 m thick, scored with two sets of two or three lines, crossing each other[17] (cf. Höghammar 1984, 100, fig. 13, As3321), set in cement, and with discoloration showing where columns of round tiles, 0.20 m in diameter and 0.03 m thick, had stood to support the *suspensura*, the heated floor of the room. Tiles 0.27 m square and 0.03 m thick, found in the course of clearing cubicle **b**, may have constituted the floor of the *suspensura*. The Zevgolatio and the Panayia baths used smaller square tiles in the hypocaust and larger tiles for the *suspensura* floor. Cubicle **a** was not excavated but is thought to have resembled **b**. Cubicle **c**, on the east, was cleaned but the floor was not reached. Remains of the same types of tiles were found in it.

Immediately to the west of cubicle **b** is a rectangular space, **P**, 1.50 m on the north and east, 1.75 m on the west, at present open on the south side. This, perhaps together with the rectangular space to its east, may have constituted the *praefurnium* or boiler room that heated the air circulating in the hypocaust and the water for the *caldarium* (cf. Q2 at Zevgolatio and Sanders 1999,

---

[16] Compare the small shrine built against the city wall near Tower **9** and the Southeast Gate (above, 71–72). Although its construction is rudimentary, it is unmistakably a cult building.
[17] One example from two joining fragments was cataloged, HC

376 from 1965, NB 15, p. 155. Color: Munsell 10 YR 72 (very pale brown) to gray. It has two wavy grooves made with fingers on the surface.

454–55 at the Panayia bath). An alternative position for the *praefurnium* might be what we have interpreted as cubicle **a**.

The rectangular space north of **C**, 4.50 x 5. 50 m, together with the smaller rectangle, 3.50 x 3.00 m, adjoining it to the southeast, Rooms **X** and **Y**, were covered by the reef, now largely beachrock, and were not cleared. The excavators had the impression that after the bath's abandonment this part of the building had been deliberately filled in, to a height of ca. 0.75 m.

To the east and north of the larger rectangle are two curved cubicles, **d** and **e**, 1.50 x 1.74 and 2.45 x 2.25 m respectively. Cubicle **d** was partly cleared without reaching the floor. The same types of tiles as in **b** and **c** were encountered, though none were in place. It would be surprising if a hypocaust had continued this far from the *caldarium*. The smaller rectangle, room **Y**, to the south of **d**, may have served as a *tepidarium*, a transitional room to the *frigidarium* typically on the north side of the building and which may have been the function of **X** together with **d** and **e**. The long and narrow rectangular room on the northwest, **A**, 1.4 x 6.5 m, may then have served as an *apodyterium* or changing room, with the northern part as an entranceway (cf. Room E at the Panayia bath, 7.3 x 5.2 m).

Throughout the building were found fragments of marble revetment, 0.02 m thick, which had originally covered all or part of the interior walls, as at Zevgolatio and the Panayia site.[18] A fragment of slate in Room **d** suggests decoration of marble and slate, as in the *frigidarium* at the Panayia bath. A fragment of flat green glass in Room **c** (HV 12) points to windows of glass, again as at the Panayia bath. No traces were found that would indicate the heating of the walls by means of passages from the hypocaust formed by pipes, nippled tiles (*tegulae mammatae*) with projections or terracotta spacer pins to create a space within the walls, as, for example at Panayia and Berbati (Forsell 1996, 333, fig. 51). The same effect may have been achieved by leaving space between two parallel rows of bricks, as at Zevgolatio. No arrangements for bringing water to the bath or draining water out of it were detected, again as at Zevgolatio.

Date of the Bath

The southern Argolid saw intense settlement activity in the Late Roman / Early Byzantine period (ca. 400–650). There are simple burials and much pottery on the old town site of Halieis (Rudolph 1979), and at least sixty-six sites (second in number only to the Late Classical period) showing certain evidence of this period were recorded by the Southern Argolid Survey (Jameson et al. 1994, 229, 241; figs. 4.4, 4.22; full discussion of the evidence is projected for a volume to be edited by Mark Munn and Mary Lou Zimmerman Munn). The chronological range is determined by pottery and coins from excavation on land and the underwater and survey work. Coins found on land range from A.D. 270 (Aurelian) to 602–10 (Phokas). From the sea along the North Wall leading to Tower **14**, a coin of Constantius II (351–361) was found in 1968 (**333** NB 504, 71; see below, 140). Radiocarbon dating of wood found in the Anomalies and in the Temple of Apollo gives dates of ca. A.D. 200 for wood and ca. 370 for olive pits, both from the Anomalies, and 480 for a wooden post in the temple. Study of the very poor burials on land and the Late Roman / Early Byzantine pottery suggested that reoccupation of the site did not begin until the 5th century, flourished especially in the second half of the 6th century, and came to an end in the disturbances of the early 7th century (Rudolph 1979). The organic remains may suggest a somewhat earlier beginning of the settlement. A very characteristic type of amphora, attested in the 6th century in the Black Sea and the Eastern Mediterranean and well represented both in the sea and on land at Halieis (Jameson 1969, 340; Rudolph 1979, 305–9; cf. Frost 1977, 238, Phourkari), was manufactured at the survey site B-19 (if not only there), 4 km southeast of Halieis (M. L. Z. Munn 1985 [cf. Jameson et al. 1994, 443–44] where a coin of Phokas was found). Rudolph (1979) had seen the possibility of pottery production at Halieis itself at this time.

No pottery or coinage is securely associated with the bath building itself. Of the at least six other baths of this period in the northeastern Peloponnese,[19] only two have yielded useful information for dating, Asine and the Panayia

---

[18] An example found 5 m south of the city wall, between Towers **12** and **13**, was catalogued: HS 379, marble revetment slab from under ca. 0.30 m of mud, 1 Aug. 1968, NB 504, p.72, preserving one finished edge, Max. preserved length: 0.48 m, L. of finished edge, 0.209 m and Th. 0.021 m.

[19] Phourkari (Frost 1977), Methana (Mee and Forbes 1997, 142), Asine (two, only one of which has been published, Frödin and Persson 1938, 107–12, Höghammar 1984), Berbati (Forsell 1996), Corinth (the Panayia bath, one of several, Sanders 1999), and Zevgolatio (Charitonidis and Ginouvès 1955).

bath. Höghammar dates the Asine bath to after 400 C.E. and its abandonment to the early 7th century. The Panayia bath is thought to have been built in the first half of the 6th century and abandoned (or converted into a residence) in the second half of the 6th century. This would lower the dates proposed for the Zevgolatio bath, presumably to the 6th century. The Halieis bath is also likely to have been in use in this century though possibly built earlier.

The Late Roman / Early Byzantine return to Halieis can be seen as the establishment of a large landowner's estate, and the small bath as part of a villa for the use of the owner or manager of the estate. As for size, with the 15 m² at Halieis compare Phourkari, ca. 10 m², Zevgolatio about 16 m², the Panayia bath 18 x 12 m, and Asine ca. 18 x 14 m. Residences near the baths have been detected at Phourkari, Berbati, and Zevgolatio, while Asine and Corinth were small towns. The bath on Methana at survey site MS57 has been identified with hot baths mentioned by Pausanias 2.34.1 and, because of the presence of Eastern Sigillata A on the surface, dated tentatively to the 1st century C.E.; parallels (uncited) of the 1st and 2d centuries are mentioned (Mee and Forbes 1997, 142). Only the back wall, 15.50 m across, survives, roughly the same width as the Halieis bath. No settlement is associated with the site but it could have been a small private establishment nonetheless, the location having been determined by the presence of hot springs, if this is the site of Pausanias's hot baths.

At Halieis buildings of brick and mortar construction and others that take no account of the Classical city wall extend 30–60 m northwest and west of the bath (Pl. 19), indicating that this part of the shore was not yet under water, at least not in the earlier years of the Late Roman / Early Byzantine period. They would have been buildings auxiliary to the villa centered on the bath.

– CHAPTER EIGHT –

The Mint

JAMES A. DENGATE

The architecture of the Northeast Command Post and its identification as the mint, among other public uses, is discussed above, 67–70 (Fig. 27, Pl. 14a, b).[1] Its location and form indicate that it was an important structure for the polis of Halieis and not a private construction for the use of a wealthy citizen or citizens. Its location attached inside the fortification walls is relevant to its use. This chapter concerns the evidence found inside the building that indicates that this was the mint for the polis of Halieis. Whenever we had thought about the location of the mint for the Tirynthian and other bronze coins produced by Halieis,[2] we predicted that it would be nearby the undiscovered agora of the polis, like the Athenian mint near the Agora (Camp and Kroll 2001). This idea was supported by Vitruvius' (5.2.1) suggestion that the location of a city treasury should be near its forum. We would have thought Andrea Palladio's (1997, III. 16) sixteenth-century recommendation to build the mint beside the fortification walls anachronistic. Nevertheless, this is exactly where the first evidence for the location of the Halieis mint was found in 1962, the coin blank HM 6 (later correctly identified and renumbered as HN 1962-24, **1** in the catalog below).[3]

In 1972 the Northeast Command Post was excavated again, revealing concentrations of bronze scrap inventoried as HM 666 and HM 837. From these, twenty-seven coin blanks and flans were later extracted and given HN 1972 numbers (**2–24**, **25–27**, and **63** below).[4] This evidence was correctly identified in 1974 while looking for comparative material for the metals excavated from the Halieis Sanctuary of Apollo.[5] Wolf W. Rudolph, field director of the Halieis lower town excavations, welcomed the discovery of the Halieis mint and incorporated plans to focus on its excavation in 1975. At that time fifty-four more coin blanks and flans were excavated. In addition, two Tirynthian coins **254** and **282**, apparently partially struck, and a third misstruck Tirynthian coin, **292**, were found in the Northeast Command Post. In the open area between this building and Houses A and B, **281**, a double struck coin of Tiryns, was found and another partially struck example, **243**, was discovered in House A (see Ault 2005, 31 and 98). Thus the mint likely produced some issues, if not all, of the coinage of the polis of Halieis. The need for security probably determined its location in a substantial building that was constructed for public defense.

A preliminary report on the discovery of the mint at Halieis was presented at the annual meeting of the Archaeological Institute of America in Washington, D.C. (Dengate 1975). This chapter supersedes and corrects the information provided there. In 1976 work in the Northeast Command Post concentrated on deep soundings (see above, 19 and 69, notes 25 and 28) with no new mint debris discovered in these earlier levels. After that

---

[1] For ancient mints and minting, see Howgego 1995, 26–35. Object photos are by Reg Heron and Charles Gold.
[2] Tirynthian types were minted at Halieis for the local coinage. See Chapter 9.
[3] The coin-related objects are cataloged in this chapter and cited by bold-faced numbers **1–83**. The excavation coins are cataloged in Chapter 9 and numbered continuously from **84**.
[4] While I spent a little time in Porto Kheli at the site and

identified the coins from the excavations in 1972, I did not study the other metal finds in any detail at that time. Also extracted from HM 666 was **315**.
[5] I thank Tony Hackens for confirming the identification of the metal remains as debris from the mint at Halieis. We were able to compare both the Halieis and Argos groups in 1974 while he was working in Argos on the deposit of mint debris found there (see Consolaki and Hackens 1980, 289).

no later excavations of the mint or the Northeast Command Post were undertaken on land already owned for excavation. More of the building lies outside the property line to the east.

The evidence from Marian H. McAllister's study of the fortifications above indicates that the Northeast Command Post was attached to the inside of the northeast fortification wall interrupting the earlier town plan at this point.[6] This wall was a part of the first stone-based circuit (see above, 78–79) built either before or contemporary with the square-tower program (above, 79–81). The square-tower program is probably contemporary with architectural Phase 5 on the acropolis (see Williams n.d. and Table 7 in Chapter 9). Therefore, the construction of the Northeast Command Post could have occurred at the same time as Phase 5 or followed it, perhaps being as late as the round-tower program (see above, 83–84). This is in part because the similar Northwest Command Post (70) must follow the west expansion of the fortifications (81–82). This may be the same as or slightly precede the round-tower program (82–83) but does not have to be considered contemporary with the construction of the Northeast Command Post. Marian McAllister (*per lit.*) inclines toward placing the construction of the Northeast Command Post late in Phase 5 of the acropolis (i.e., around the end of the 5th century or beginning of the 4th) with the Northwest Command Post as a copy built thereafter, perhaps early in Phase 6 on the acropolis. The acropolis architectural Phase 5 is roughly equivalent to early Level B in the lower town (see below, Chapter 9, Table 7). The study of the fortifications, then, suggests approximately the same construction date as that derived from the preliminary study of the excavation evidence in the context summary (below), early in Level B or, at the earliest, the transition from the very latest Level C to Level B. Therefore, the Northeast Command Post would have been in use for one hundred years or slightly more. The drain and bastion preceded the Northeast Command Post, having been built with the circuit wall (Pl. 14b). The drain established the northeast limit of the building. The Northeast Command Post does not seem to have been constructed for use as a mint but rather the mint was later located there as a convenient and secure place for coining.[7]

The Excavations of the Mint

In 1962, parts of the interior of the building as well as all of the foundation walls around the perimeter were excavated in a series of trenches as part of Trench T. On the interior, the northeast side of the building was not cleared (58–59, Pls. 14a, 20a and Fig. 27). The rectangular area inside the walls of the building to the edge of the fortification walls is about 86.25 m square; if the line of stones defining a possible stairway is subtracted, the roughly square area remaining is about 72.25 m square.[8] The area of the three trenches excavated on the interior of the Northeast Command Post in 1972, 1975, and 1976 covers about 28.5 m square (although parts of two trenches extended over the southwest wall of the building to include areas outside). The 1962 excavations were conducted by different recovery and recording techniques than those of 1972–76,[9] when the rest of the building could only be partially excavated. Therefore the publication of the remains from the mint must consider the results of both phases of excavation.[10]

Initially the goal was to publish just the remains from the mint itself along with the coins

---

[6] For the early town plan see Rudolph 1984 and Jameson and Boyd 1981.

[7] The production of the earliest Halieis coins (see Chapter 9) occurs at about the same time as the construction of the Northeast Command Post. While it is thus possible for the building to have been made for use as a mint, minting of bronze coins is such a simple process that a special structure would not be necessary. Nor would a building constructed specifically for minting need the plastered walls and the elaborate capitals of the Northeast Command Post. Rather, the extant building, whatever its primary function, most likely provided a convenient location for the mint. The first issues, if minted shortly before the construction of the Northeast Command Post, must have been produced elsewhere on the site. If coins were not minted in the Northeast Command Post from the inception of the Halieis coinage, the Apollo head series may have initiated the minting in the building. The dating evidence for the building and the earliest coinage is not precise enough to determine whether it began there or not.

[8] The line of stones excavated in 1962 is probably only about half the length of the possible stairway to the fortification walkway. Although we cannot confirm that the stair was retained once the Northeast Command Post was constructed, there must have been access to the fortification walkway along the northeast stretch between the Hermion gate and Tower **10** (see above, 58–59). The stair could have been relocated over the drain at the northeast of the building (61, note 64).

[9] Ault (2005, 4–11) describes the excavation system used at Halieis for the land excavations from 1972 as well as his methodology in the study of the excavation records and finds. The exploratory season of 1962 used a system adapted by John H. Young from those used at the Athenian Agora and Olynthus.

[10] The northern and southeastern parts of the Northeast Command Post were only open in 1962 so that no photograph of the building combining these earlier remains with those opened during the later excavations was possible. Nor was balloon photography of the site done in 1962.

found in the building. These when compared with the other coins from the site (Chapter 9) clearly supported the suggestion made above that the local Halieis Tirynthian coins were minted in the Northeast Command Post. But as study progressed other related ideas about the context of minting and usage of coins at Halieis emerged. Bradley A. Ault (2005, 74–81) was able to identify the use of the rooms and draw other conclusions from the close study of the remains found inside the Halieis houses. Therefore it seemed worthwhile to provide more contextual information concerning the excavations in the area of the Northeast Command Post. To do this required a detailed description of the artifacts from each of the trenches in the mint area, which is included in the context summary appended to this chapter. This lists all the finds including the mint debris and the items in the catalog below as well as the coins cataloged in Chapter 9. Initially this context summary was only to include Levels A and B[11] of the mint area trenches, that is, from the time of the construction of the Northeast Command Post, but it was difficult to find a clear stopping point. The early material found in the deep tests made in this area is considered by McAllister in the description of the earlier fortifications of the site (see above, 19 and 69, notes 25 and 28). Therefore it seemed best to include all the material recorded from the trenches. The context summary includes all the levels in the trenches from the Northeast Command Post, in contrast to Ault's discussion of the houses, which concentrates on the remains from Levels A and A/B.

In 1962 a floor was cleared in the southwest corner of the building about 0.25 m below the surface (recalculated elevation of +0.55).[12] This floor level ranged from 0.06 m on the southeast by the surviving orthostate blocks to 0.12 m on the west of the doorsill below the tops of

foundation blocks (T. W. Jacobsen, NB 1.1, 61, with plan, 1–2) with recalculated elevations of +0.41 to +0.47 m (about the same as that of the elevations of the earth floor found in 1972 and 1975, which varied between +0.47 and +0.42 m).[13] The floor of the Northeast Command Post, and the area just outside it, was clearly identifiable from the numerous finds left there and because a layer of fallen roof tiles covered it.

The trenches in 1962 exposed the three surviving foundation walls, which suggested the name House Pi for the building. Part of the interior of the building was cleared at that time, including the central column base. The rest of the interior and part of the area outside was untouched until 1972, 1975, and 1976. But other parts of the open area southeast of the building (and inside it as well) remain unexcavated both in and outside the current field boundaries.

The Fire Pit

The excavation of the trenches in 1975 was directed toward understanding the mint while those done in 1962, 1972, and 1976 intended a more general exploration of the Northeast Command Post and its environs. Consequently this discussion relies primarily on details from the 1975 season, supplemented by the work done in 1976, 1972, and 1962. The mint debris was concentrated in a fire pit, or more correctly, a series of interconnected pits that extended east from almost a meter northeast of the center of the threshold block (Fig. 27 and Pls. 14a, 20a–c). This location allowed for light and ventilation when working near the fire.[14] A Doric capital of shelly limestone, HS 381, lay on the floor partially covering some of area of the fire pit excavated in 1972 (see above, 68–69, Fig. 15). The finds from the pit were not separated from those of the rest of the unit at that time but the significant ones were plotted individually on the plan of TR 135/375

---

[11] Table 7 in Chapter 9 lists these and the other lower town habitation levels with their general relationship to the acropolis architectural phases and pottery deposits including references.

[12] In 1962 elevations were taken by measuring down from the surface of the trench or from the tops of preserved blocks of the Northeast Command Post whose foundations reach an average height of +0.35 m. Using the 1972 elevations of the surface of the trenches excavated then (average of about +0.80 m) and the elevations of the building's blocks, the 1962 elevations have been recalculated by subtracting them from the actual surface elevations or block top elevations. Both elevations are given because it is impossible to know exactly what bench marks on the trench surfaces or which blocks were used to measure down from in 1962. The recalculated elevations are not to be

considered as accurate but do give some basis for comparison with the ones taken after 1971 when accurate bench marks were established. See Fredrick A. Cooper, Appendix C below.

[13] It is likely that the higher initial elevation of the floor given above taken from the surface of the trench merely reflects the inherent inaccuracy of this method. But it might be the level of the surface compacted during the Late Roman/Early Byzantine occupation at Halieis (see Chapter 7 above) and/or after the wall blocks of the Northeast Command Post had been removed.

[14] The ventilation would have been better if the entrance to the walkway at the top of the stair were open. If so this might support the possibility that the stair remained throughout the life of the building; see above, 58–59.

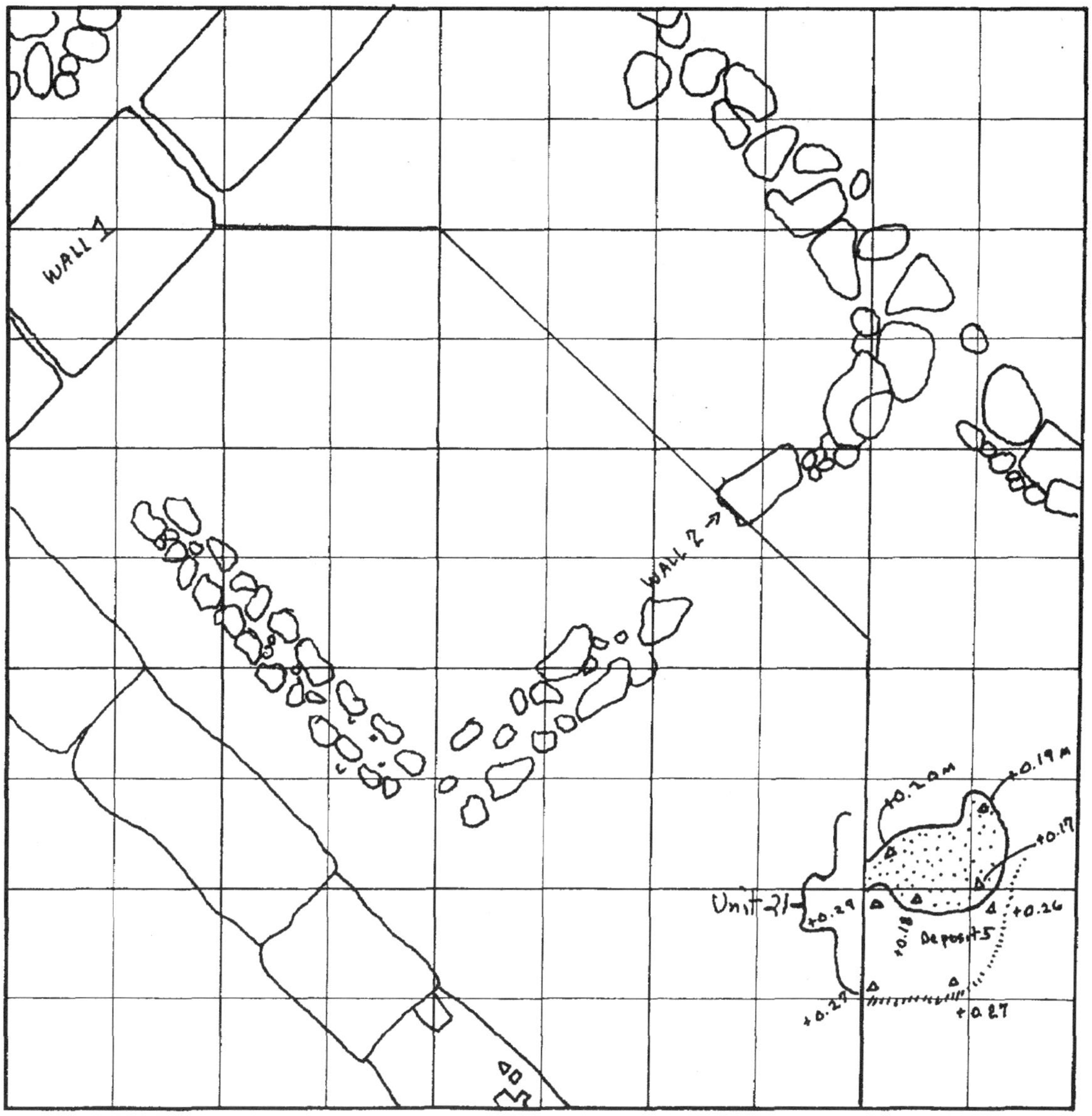

Fig. 16 a. TR 135/375. Fire pit excavation. "Deposit 5" is mud brick. Scale is half m per square.

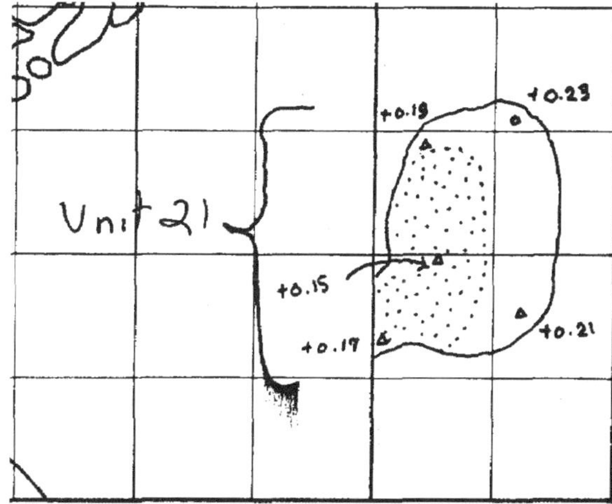

Fig. 16 b. Fire pit after removal of mud brick

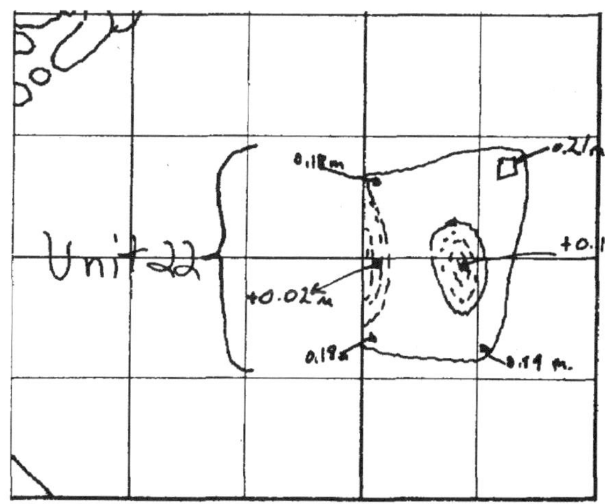

Fig. 16 c. Fire pit at end of excavation

unit 6 where HM 666 was found and below it, unit 9, where HM 837 was found (see the context summary below for details and Pl. 21a–e). In 1975 the rest of the fire pit was excavated in the east balk, units 19–23. The pit was irregularly shaped, as excavated in 1975, with deeper and wider sections of ash. Other parts were more ashy earth, indicating that successive fires, rather than a single fire, created the pit.

The concentration of mint debris was extended over no more than two square meters with the fire pit (or pits) itself being difficult to define because it was the result of a series of small fires on the earth floor of the building. The pit as it was fully excavated in 1975 formed an irregular oval of black, ashy earth about 1.80 m east to west by 0.85 m north to south. (Fig. 16 a–c and Pls. 14a, 20a–c record the uncovering of the pit.) The actual pit as excavated in 1975 had what appeared to be a mud brick, roughly 0.4 m on a side and 0.1 m thick, thrown over it at one point (excavated as unit 21 and outlined in Fig. 16 a). Perhaps it was simply clay tossed there to fill in part of the pit. It later became compacted to appear brick-like or actually was part of the usual mud brick used for wall construction at Halieis. Whatever the case, this "brick" was probably an improvised path over the soft ashy earth that would have been an obstacle to walking through the entrance. The location of the pit, with its good ventilation, had the drawback of blocking easy access. For this reason it seems probable that the fire pit debris was frequently cleaned out and the area refilled. This fire pit is probably the last of a series of fires on the earth floor of the building (Fig. 16 c). The mint debris and ashes were intended to be swept up later, the metal collected and recycled, and the pit refilled at intervals.

The elevations of the pit were from +0.36 m in 1972 to +0.02 m at its deepest in 1975. The earth in the immediate area of HM 666 was dry sieved in 1972 and all the earth excavated in the trenches dug in 1975 was dry sieved. This accounts for the recovery of more isolated mint scrap in 1975 than earlier in the parts where the earth had not been sieved in 1972 (or 1962). Probably more individual pieces of mint debris were scattered throughout the areas excavated but not sieved.

Along with the coin blanks and flans in the catalog below, the pit itself contained four bronze coins of the Tirythian type, Apollo head facing right (hereafter Apollo r.) **194**, **258**, **274**, **292**, and an Amphora/T tessera **315**, as well as a coin of Corinth **130**. For whatever reason, these were included with the rest of the metal debris in the fire pit. While one or two coins might be stray losses, the number indicates that these were part of the scrap intended for reuse. The pit also contained quantities of tiny bronze scrap, including drips and sheet fragments. All of the bronze would have been sorted out from the ashes and other debris to be forged into bronze rods.

More mint debris was found embedded in the earth on each side of the fire pit, 1975 unit 23, but not nearly as much as was found in the pit itself. Mint debris also appeared in TR 130/375 and TR 135/380. This other mint debris, not from the pit itself, may come from scraps lost during earlier minting activity.[15] Only an occasional piece escaped recycling, judging from the amount left in the ashy earthen pit. Probably what we have recovered from the fire pit itself is the actual debris from the last minting activity done on the site.

The Floor and Earlier Foundation Walls
As the accumulation grew, the soft ashy earth near the entrance would have become a hazard for users of the building, especially if quick and easy access to the stair and walkway of the fortification wall was required to defend the northeast section near the mint. Recall that the Northeast Command Post was added inside the fortification walls, interrupting Avenue A, a major thoroughfare. Earlier structures at the site were reduced to rubble foundations when it was constructed.[16] The highest points of these earlier foundations were encountered close to the floor level excavated inside the building, usually from about 0.02 to 0.12 m or more below the upper surface of the earth floor. As the earth floor was cleaned (and hence lowered) over time, it probably needed occasional resurfacing to bring it nearer the level of the top

---

[15] It is possible that the fire pit debris comes from a one-time use of the Northeast Command Post as a mint, possibly during an emergency near the end of the polis. But the metal scrap found in the earth below the floor outside the fire pit suggests repeated minting.

[16] At the time of excavation in 1972 and 1975, these rubble walls were interpreted as possible foundations for room dividers inside the building. But a large central column suggests that there was one main internal roof support and one large internal space. In addition, the earthern floor was above the highest level of the rubble walls. Finally, their plan is similar to the other foundation walls found immediately outside the building. This suggests an earlier complex of rooms, probably comprising a house or houses, that was destroyed before the construction of the Northeast Command Post. See Figs. 18, 27.

of the threshold block, +0.51 m. The elevations of the upper surface of the earth floor as excavated varied from +0.42 to +0.47 m. Thus the floor had been lowered in parts almost to the point where the tops of the rubble foundations below would have begun to protrude and low enough so that stepping up or down to the threshold block became inconvenient. It seems likely then that the earthen floor was nearly ready to be renewed at the time the building was abandoned. But the residents of Halieis may not have refilled the floor until the rubble foundations became real obstacles for using the floor and the threshold block a difficult step away from the floor level. Thus the floor could have become even lower before it was felt necessary to refresh it with new earth. Probably the need for easy access would intervene before this became too severe.

Since metal is heavy, it probably worked its way more deeply into the earthen floor whenever it was swept, but even pottery sherds were heavy enough to be embedded from daily use or cleaning inside the building. During excavation an unusual amount of metal was found on and directly below the floor, together with numerous pottery fragments. (See the context summary below.) This suggests that the floor had been cleaned regularly, probably renewed with earth (perhaps containing sherds and small fragments of roof tiles).[17] Each cleaning of the earth floor would likely push down more heavy objects. Consequently, the limits of the Level A and B activity in the floor of the building were difficult to determine and extended down to become intermixed with the fill used in the earlier structures destroyed before the construction of the Northeast Command Post.

The roof-tile fragments in the lower units were small compared to those from the end of Level A, suggesting that larger fragments had been removed for reuse elsewhere.[18] When the debris from these earlier structures had been removed, the building(s) were destroyed to the foundation level. A thin layer of debris may have been left as fill spread over the inside and outside of the newly constructed Northeast Command Post. This would have covered the foundations of the earlier walls below the earth floor of the new Northeast Command Post and the open area at its entrance.

The earlier rubble foundations were left in place. The use, cleaning, and resurfacing of the earth floor just above them allowed later but heavier remains to be pushed below the top of these rubble foundations. During excavation it was not possible to separate what was embedded in the floor of the building during its use, brought into it when refreshing the earth of the floor, or remained from the original fill left when the earlier structures were demolished. In general, the deeper the object, the earlier — with the caveat that heavier objects such as metal can be forced down by daily use and cleaning. The context summary below reports in more detail the excavation record.

The earth floor of the mess building on the acropolis also had finds embedded in it (see Williams n.d.). In House D, Ault (2005, 46 and 63) interprets the sherds in the *kopron* as debris from the cleaning of the house floors. At the Northeast Command Post, sweeping and resurfacing must have been done regularly to keep the floor level so close to the earlier rubble foundations. Probably the debris from sweeping the floor was dumped in the open area outside the door.

The Athenian Agora Mint

A parallel relatively close in time and location to the Halieis mint is found at Athens. Near the southeast corner of the Agora is a square building (27.20 x 28.90 m) containing fire pits with mint debris (Camp and Kroll 2001, 127–45). The building, constructed in the later 5th century, may or may not have been built specifically as a mint. It was certainly used for that purpose from the late 4th or early 3rd into the 2nd century. The earlier fire pits here have "large, thick-walled terracotta basins apparently set down into them, their inner surface displaying ample signs of burning" (135). The coin blanks (including some that were finished by flattening) and bronze debris are similar to the blanks and debris at Halieis (146–60). A bronze rod was reconstructed from an end and nine blanks (illustrated in fig. 20, 155) and metallurgical analysis of some of the blanks and Athenian bronze coins is reported (table 2, 152–54).[19] The evidence from the excavations of the Halieis mint is simpler. There was only one unlined fire pit excavated, the building covers less

---

[17] When refreshing earth floors in the Halieis houses, Ault (2005, 10–11) argues against much inclusion of sherds and this is likely to be the same for the Northeast Command Post.

[18] It is difficult to break up large roof tiles. Small fragments were probably the result of accidents during construction or demolition of earlier structures. At Halieis, collections of roof tiles were sometimes stored for reuse. See Ault 2005, 46.

[19] Metallurgical analysis of the Halieis examples has not yet been possible. Cf. Consolaki and Hackens 1980, 291–92, for neutron activation analysis of some of the Argive mint debris.

than half the area of that at Athens, and it is attached to the fortification walls, not free standing like the mint in the Agora. Even so, the Halieis mint joins the Athenian example as one of the few mints known from the ancient Greek world.[20]

The Bronze Blanks and Flans from the Mint

Bronze rods were first forged on an anvil with a groove. Occasionally the groove left lines projecting on the side as in **6**. The forged rod was then measured and scored as in **2**. Once scored, the cylindrical blanks were cut off, most likely with a chisel. (See Pls. 22–24.) The blanks were then hammered flat into the group I have classified as "flans." A flan in this context "is the metal disk of a coin, token, or medal as distinguished from the design or lettering stamped upon it." A blank is "a piece of material prepared to be made into something (as a key) by further operation."[21] In relation to coining, the two terms are broadly synonymous. But at the Halieis mint, there is evidence of two steps preparatory to the actual striking of the coins: 1. making the cylindrical sections from the forged rods; 2. hammering these into flat, thinner disks ready to be minted. The "blanks" found at Halieis are thus prepared from the forged rod to be made into flans, while the "flans" are the metal disks ready to be struck by the reverse die to impress it into the obverse die in the anvil to make a coin.[22] While the bronze objects found in the Northeast Command Post show both the cylindrical sections of the blanks and prepared disks of the flans, there are some that fall between the two,

partially processed blanks that have begun to be flattened into flans.[23]

That the ancients made this kind of distinction is shown by the two hoards of bronze flans from Olynthus. Nicholas Cahill suggests that these flan hoards might be evidence that minting bronze coinage was farmed out to individuals and done in their houses.[24] But he then points out that the sizes of the flans in the hoard are larger than the local bronze coin issues and further suggests that these hoards may be for counterfeiting foreign silver coins. At Halieis, coin production in homes, officially or unofficially, might have been possible. Ault (2005, 77–81) discusses the household economy with evidence for weaving and olive oil pressing found in the Halieis houses as well as on the Industrial Terrace (Jameson n.d., chapter 3). But minting at Halieis seems to have been a civic activity. The only mint yet discovered was located inside the Northeast Command Post, clearly a public structure attached to and planned as part of the improvement in the defensive system for the polis. This building was an appropriate location for the official mint of the polis. Here it would have been easier to control the metal and to provide security for the products. There is no evidence to suggest how the polis of Halieis managed the mint. But there must have been some procedure for organizing the minting. This is suggested by the different control marks on the issues of the Tirynthian coins, possibly identifying magistrates or contractors for these issues (see Chapter 9).[25]

Bronze coin blanks and flans similar to those from Halieis were found inside a temple built in the Classical period and used into the Roman

---

[20] These include Pella in Macedonia (Oikonomidou 1993); Nea Paphos on Cyprus (Nikolaou 1972a, 1972b, and Nikolaou and Mørkholm 1976, 9–10); Olbia in the Tauric Chersonese (Kostsyushko-Valyuzhinich 1914); and Thessalonika in the Late Roman period (Velenis 1996).

[21] Both definitions are from *Merriam-Webster's Collegiate Dictionary* (10th edition, 1998).

[22] What are called "flans" here are "finished blanks" for Camp and Kroll 2001, 155–59. Their usage expresses the further processing of the blanks before being struck as coins. Blanks and finished blanks, however, become easily confused or the two terms must be repeatedly used together. The use of two words, "blanks" and "flans," prevents confusion between the two phases of processing the segments of bronze rods before striking them into coins.

[23] Halieis provides evidence for only one way bronze coins were made in antiquity. For this way and others, see Hill 1922 and Hackens 1975 and examples cited by Camp and Kroll 2001, 158–60, and the following note.

[24] See Cahill 2002, 259–61, and Camp and Kroll 2001, 159, n. 34,

both with references to the Olynthus excavation volumes. These were in House B ii 6 (16 blanks and 14 flans) and A iv 5/7 (14 flans). Both hoards were found in containers; see Cahill 2002, 337, n. 94, correcting Robinson 1952, 403–4, pl. 173, nos. 23–25, who claims there was no evidence of a container. Robinson thought that these flans were cast because they were oval on one side and flat on the other. But this more likely indicates hammering into an indented oval surface on an anvil. Cahill does not discuss their manufacture except to point out that the houses with the hoards had no evidence for a furnace. But there were many ashes on the floor of room h of House A iv 7; see Cahill 2002, 259, fig. 59. Camp and Kroll agree that the Olynthus flans are hammered and not cast. They compare flans cast in a series, which have been excavated at Aï Kanoum (Bernard 1985, 83–84, pl. 11, nos. 225–34), Nea Paphos, and even the Late Roman matrices for casting them from Thessalonika (see references cited in note 20 above).

[25] This is only speculation for the small mint at Halieis. But we see it on a larger scale at Athens with the elaborate date and control marks on the massive Hellenistic new style silver coinage (Kroll 1993, 14–15, with references cited there).

Imperial times on the east side of the agora at Argos (Consolaki and Hackens 1980). The blanks and flans were located in a small depression in a late Hellenistic deposit and are the size of bronze coins issued by Argos in the 3rd and 2nd centuries. This mint debris was interpreted as a dedication in the temple after the minting of the coins on the analogy of the epigraphical evidence for the dedication of retired coin dies in a Delian temple in 166 and on the Athenian Acropolis in 404. But as Camp and Kroll (2001, 158, n. 31) point out, the collection published from the temple at Argos appears to be the sweepings from the floor of the mint (something like the contents of the fire pit at Halieis). They propose that the Argive blanks and flans are better interpreted as evidence for minting inside the temple or were brought there from another location as fill. If the former interpretation holds, the temple at Argos becomes another secure public place for minting offical bronze coins similar to the Northeast Command Post at Halieis. The simplicity of both the Halieis and Argos mints would also suggest that more mints may be located in unexpected secure places if care is taken to look for coin blanks and flans among the metal scraps recovered.[26] Mints might lie behind other examples of flans such as the hoard of twenty-five from Pergamon.[27] Another possible example is the hoard of twenty-three flans found at Laos in South Italy.[28]

Catalog

Details of the find spots are given under the boldface catalog numbers in the context summary at the end this chapter, listed by trench grid and unit number. Those illustrated are on Pls. 22–24 identified by the catalog number. Abbreviations: L. = length (or thickness when the object has been flattened), D. = diameter, g = weight in grams, m = meter.

A. Coin blanks

All the Halieis coin blanks are sections of a forged cylindrical bronze rod cut by chiseling, usually with evidence of preliminary scoring on one or both ends unless stated otherwise (the ends that were cleanly split off by the chisel thus have no evidence of preliminary scoring). The find spots of those found in the same unit are grouped here while those found individually are listed under their catalog number below: **2–24** were originally inventoried with the bronze scrap of HM 666 and **25–27** were originally inventoried with the bronze scrap of HM 837; **29–47** are from TR 135/375 unit 21; **48–50** are from TR 135/375 unit 22; **52–56** are from TR 135/380 unit 2; and **59–62** are from TR 130/375 unit 5.

1 (HN 1962-24) formerly HM 6, TR T, L. 0.009, D. 0.009 m, 2.80 g

2 (HN 1972-29) L. 0.018, D. 0.008 m, 6.75 g, scored in two places, forming three parts each L. 0.005 m, 2.3 g

3 (HN 1972-31) L. 0.007, D. 0.0085 m, 2.64 g

4 (HN 1972-32) L. 0.009, D. 0.009 m, 3.00 g

5 (HN 1972-33) L. 0.007, D. 0.008 m, 2.50 g

6 (HN 1972-34) L. 0.009, D. 0.008 m, 3.70 g, flattened into an oval shape with lines of the anvil.

7 (HN 1972-35) L. 0.011, D. 0.008 m, 3.20 g, scored in four places with both sides of two fully preserved.

8 (HN 1972-36) L. 0.01, D. 0.009 m, 3.19 g, scored in four places.

9 (HN 1972-37) L. 0.012, D. 0.008 m, 3.30 g, scored in four places, one cutting more than half way after which the rod had been bent and snapped off.

10 (HN 1972-38) L. 0.009, D. 0.009 m, 3.10 g

11 (HN 1972-39) L. 0.009, D. 0.008 m, 2.25 g

12 (HN 1972-40) L. 0.010, D. 0.009 m, 3.10 g

13 (HN 1972-41) L. 0.012, D. 0.008 m, 3.05 g, the chisel cut through on one end after scoring, leaving a projecting tongue.

14 (HN 1972-42) L. 0.008, D. 0.008 m, 2.51 g

15 (HN 1972-43) L. 0.009, D. 0.008 m, 2.41 g

---

[26] Was the Northeast Command Post also the place for the production of silver coins at Halieis? Certainly small silver coins like the ones attributed to Tiryns (see Chapter 9) were minted in the same fashion as bronze. See the late 3rd-century hoard reported to contain 120 of these found in the environs of Chalkis in 1913 (Thompson, Mørkholm, and Kraay 1973, 194, no. 194). Camp and Kroll (2001, 159, n. 38) list the known examples and correct the misattribution to Eretria. An additional example is in the University of Illinois Spurlock Museum (1928.16.0004). But if silver coins were minted in the Northeast Command Post, there is no indication as yet. Certainly silver scraps would have been recovered more carefully than bronze at the time of minting, leaving little if any evidence. Probably Athenian silver coins were not produced at the Agora mint (Camp and Kroll, 145).

[27] Official or unofficial, this has been suggested to be the hoard of a thief and no bronze scraps or blanks were reported (Voegtli 1990, 48–51). It was found in the substructure of the theater, perhaps secreted there. But the find spot might easily have been made a secure place for minting if it had enough ventilation. This early 2nd-century hoard contained two double-struck locally minted coins from issues weighing the same as the flans.

[28] Cantilena 1989, reported as cast, but Camp and Kroll (2001, 159) suggest they might have been hammered from blanks.

16 (HN 1972-44) L. 0.008, D. 0.008 m, 3.94 g, the side opposite the scoring has been flattened by the blow, indicating that the rod was warm enough to be malleable when scored.

17 (HN 1972-45) L. 0.0065, D. 0.008 m, 2.61 g

18 (HN 1972-46) L. 0.006, D. 0.008 m, 1.42 g

19 (HN 1972-47) L. 0.006, D. 0.008 m, 1.40 g, flattened into an oval shape.

20 (HN 1972-48) L. 0.006, D. 0.005 m, 1.31 g

21 (HN 1972-49) L. 0.006, D. 0.007 m, 1.00 g, the side opposite the scoring has been flattened by the blow, indicating that the rod was warm enough to be malleable when scored.

22 (HN 1972-51) L. 0.005, D. 0.008 m, 1.10 g

23 (HN 1972-53) L. 0.005, D. 0.007 m, 0.79 g

24 (HN 1972-54) L. 0.006, est. D. 0.008 m, 1.06 g, half of coin blank.

25 (HN 1972-55) L. 0.007, D. 0.006–0.007 m, 2.40 g

26 (HN 1972-56) L. 0.0055, D. 0.008 m, 2.20 g

27 (HN 1972-57) L. 0.007, D. 0.007 m, 2.00 g

28 (HN 1975-16) TR 135/375 unit 20, L. 0.0046, D. 0.013 m, 2.90 g, partially hammered into a flan but discarded before this was completed.

29 (HN 1975-9) L. 0.008, D. 0.009 m, 3.09 g

30 (HN 1975-10) L. 0.006, D. 0.011, 2.75 g, one end is beveled and probably the other end of the original rod from which it was chiseled.

31 (HN 1975-28) L. 0.008, D. 0.009 m, 1.66 g, wedge shaped

32 (HN 1975-29) L. 0.0055, D. 0.009 m, 1.11 g

33 (HN 1975-30) L. 0.006, D. 0.008 m, 1.48 g

34 (HN 1975-31) L. 0.0047, D. 0.011 m, 1.33 g, wedge shaped

35 (HN 1975-38) L. 0.005, D. 0.011 m, 1.67 g, wedge shaped

36 (HN 1975-39) L. 0.005, D. 0.012 m, 1.72 g

37 (HN 1975-40) L. 0.008, D. 0.009 m, 2.91 g

38 (HN 1975-41) L. 0.009, D. 0.010 m, 2.55 g

39 (HN 1975-42) L. 0.004, D. 0.008 m, 0.91 g, wedge shaped

40 (HN 1975-43) L. 0.007, D. 0.008 m, 1.31 g

41 (HN 1975-44) L. 0.007, D. 0.007 m, 1.35 g

42 (HN 1975-45) L. 0.005, D. 0.008, 1.16 g, wedge shaped

43 (HN 1975-46) L. 0.007, D. 0.009, 1.15 g wedge shaped

44 (HN 1975-48) L. 0.005, D. 0.008, 1.05 g

45 (HN 1975-49) L. 0.008, D. 0.008 m, 1.54 g, incompletely forged end of a rod.

46 (HN 1975-50) L. 0.002, est. D. 0.010 m, 0.35 g, ca. half a coin blank.

47 (HN 1975-51) L. 0.003, est. D. 0.009 m, 0.27 g, ca. half a coin blank.

48 (HN 1975-58) L. 0.008, D. 0.007 m, 1.49 g

49 (HN 1975-59) L. 0.003, est. D. 0.010 m, 0.52 g, ca. half a coin blank.

50 (HN 1975-60) L. 0.004, D. 0.010 m, 0.76 g, one end is beveled and probably the other end of the original rod from which it was chiseled.

51 (HN 1975-67) TR 135/375 unit 23, L. 0.005, D. 0.009 m, 1.22 g, very corroded

52 (HN 1975-52) L. 0.005, D. 0.009 m, 2.02 g

53 (HN 1975-53) L. 0.007, D. 0.007 m, 1.11 g, incompletely forged end of a rod.

54 (HN 1975-54) L. 0.004, D. 0.008 m, 0.82 g, one end is beveled and probably the other end of the original rod from which it was chiseled.

55 (HN 1975-55) L. 0.005, D. 0.008 m, 0.74 g, incompletely forged end of a rod.

56 (HN 1975-56) L. 0.002, D. 0.010 m, 0.38 g, ca. half a coin blank.

57 (HN 1975-74) TR 135/380 unit 3, L. 0.003, D. 0.010 m, 0.78 g

58 (HN 1975-57) TR 135/380 unit 4, L. 0.006, D. 0.009 m, 2.83 g

59 (HN 1975-61) L. 0.008, D. 0.009 m, 2.93 g

60 (HN 1975-62) L. 0.010, D. 0.008 m, 2.46 g

61 (HN 1975-63) L. 0.008, D. 0.008 m, 2.38 g

62 (HN 1975-71) L. 0.007, D. 0.010 m, 3.12 g, one end is beveled and probably the other end of the original rod from which it was chiseled.

B. Unstruck flans

All the Halieis unstruck flans are prepared by hammering a coin blank into a flat, thinner, larger diameter, roughly circular in shape, ready for striking with the obverse and reverse dies to make a coin. Flans **64** and **65** (found together) and **66** and **67** (found together) are from TR 135/375 unit 20; **68–75** are from unit 23; **78** and **79** are from TR 135/380 unit 6; **80–82** are from unit 2 (**81** and **82** were found together).

63 (HN 1972-50) extracted from HM 666, L. 0.003, D. 0.0125 m, 0.85 g

64 (HN 1975-5) L. 0.00375, D. 0.014 m, 3.32 g

65 (HN 1975-6) L. 0.004, D. 0.012 m, 2.77 g

66 (HN 1975-7) L. 0.0044, D. 0. 014 m, 3.08 g

67 (HN 1975-8) L. 0.003, D. 0.015 m, 3.05 g

68 (HN 1975-20) L. 0.003, D. 0.015 m, 2.82 g

69 (HN 1975-21) L. 0.006, est. D. 0.015 m, 1.99 g, broken, only about one-third preserved.

70 (HN 1975-23) L. 0.0035, D. 0.014 m, 2.73 g

71 (HN 1975-24) L. 0.00415, D. 0.014 m, 2.73 g

72 (HN 1975-26) L. 0.0044, D. 0.012 m, 2.44 g, incompletely hammered with part of the edge of the coin blank preserved.

73 (HN 1975-27) L. 0.00365, D. 0.011 m, 1.08 g, broken during hammering.

74 (HN 1975-32) L. 0.003, D. 0.015 m, 2.62 g

75 (HN 1975-47) L. 0.002, est. D. 0.010 m, 0.33 g, broken, only about one-third preserved.

76 (HN 1975-68) TR 135/375 unit 23, L. 0.003, D. 0.011 m, 1.24 g, broken into sharp-cornered diamond shape.

77 (HN 1975-65) L. 0.003, D. 0.015 m, 2.87 g

78 (HN 1975-69) L. 0.0037, D. 0.015 m, 3.04 g

79 (HN 1975-70) L. 0.004, D. 0.012 m, 1.29 g

80 (HN 1975-80) L. 0.002, D. 0.012 m, 1.06 g, incompletely hammered with part of the edge of the coin blank preserved.

81 (HN 1975-83) L. 0.003, D. 0.010 m, 0.81 g, half preserved; perhaps the original flan cracked during hammering and subsequent corrosion broke **82** off. The two almost join.

82 (HN 1975-84) L. 0.004, D. 0.019 m, 0.96 g, probably other half of **81**.

C. Crudely struck flan

A flat circle-like punch was used as a reverse, producing a circular, worn wreath-like appearance around two-thirds of the edge. A misstruck wreath like that on the coins of Sikyon can be read but this is probably the effect of corrosion. The surface of the punch had been gouged or chipped before striking, leaving a pattern that with corrosion looks like the remnants of letters but is not. This punch might have been the head of an iron or bronze nail common at Halieis. It was also clearly not the same tool (hammer?) used to create the flans cataloged above. The obverse was created by a striated surface onto which this flan was struck. The striation, combined with corrosion, resembles the feathers of a bird such as the dove on the coins of Sikyon, but since the "feathers" cover the whole surface and are of equal depth throughout (unlike the oval shape of a bird in low relief), this is not a Sikyonian or likely any other officially minted coin. The striated impression might be that of a rough stone such as one of the grindstones/mortars (commonly found at Halieis) whose surface was gouged by repeated rubbing.[29] This was found in Area 6, TR 110/355 unit 18 at 109.55/352.51 +0.24 m in Room 6-77, which is the

entrance to a house opening to Avenue B at the southwest corner of the intersection of Street 4 and Avenue B (see Ault 2005, fig. 3, for the location). Whether this was irregularly produced at the Halieis mint, imported, or made as a forgery in one of the other houses or metal working areas of the site not yet excavated is unknown.[30] I have included this here as a possible struck waste product taken from the mint that might have circulated as a coin. But the only evidence is the object itself and its find spot, which is across the avenue from the entrance to House A, about 18 m southwest of the Northeast Command Post (see Ault 2005, fig. 2).

83 (HN 1976-2) L. 0.004, D. 0.016 m, 2.45 g

Weights of the Blanks, Flans, and Coins from the Mint

The scoring on the blanks suggests that a measured length of bronze rod was used to decide the weight of each coin. Although it is possible that each blank was weighed after it had been chiseled from its rod, the variety of the weights of the blanks and flans and the great variations in the weights of surviving Tirynthian bronze coins do not support this. Instead, blanks of the correct size and presumably with the weight roughly estimated by hand were judged adequate for hammering into flans and then minting. Thus the speed of production was emphasized over the accuracy of the weight of each coin produced.[31] Nevertheless some kind of weight standard, however loose, was employed. This is seen by comparing the weights of the bronze blanks and flans, Table 1, with those of the local Tirynthian coins, Tables 2–5, when both have been plotted on a histogram. The weights of the blanks and flans have a very wide range, confirming that they were rejected from further processing. But they also fall into two groups, one with a peak at 3.1 and the other peaking at 1.1 g.[32]

---

[29] Compare the grind stones from Halieis considered by Runnels (1981, 117–27, 296–97, 302, 310, figs. 22–27).

[30] Possibly this is a crude attempt at counterfeiting, using tools at hand. When newly struck, it could have easily passed as a stamped coin of unfamiliar obverse and reverse types.

[31] Kroll (1993, 1–2) makes similar observations from the Athenian bronzes, citing in his note 2 Roman republican evidence. Camp and Kroll (2001, 158), however, do suggest that the presence of balance weights in the Athenian mint may indicate occasional checking of the weights of the blanks there. No weights were identified from the Northeast Command Post at Halieis. In general, Classical and Hellenistic silver coins were much more

carefully weighed because of the high value of the metal compared with that of bronze.

[32] Another way to interpret Table 1 is that each of the two peaks represents two different denominations of coins. The heavier denomination was intended to weigh about 3.1 to 3.3+ g. The lighter was intended to weigh about half of the heavier denomination, about 1.1 to 1.5+ g. These are close to the histogram weights of the Apollo l. type (Table 3) and those of the H reverse coins (Table 5). These coins, however, likely date earlier (see Chapter 9) than the blanks and flans from the fire pit. In addition the number of blanks and flans whose weights fall between the two peaks argues against this interpretation.

The Mint

Table 1. Frequency of weights (by tenth of a gram) of A. blanks (–) **1–62**, B. flans (+) **63–82**, and C. struck flan (*) **83**

Weight	
3.9	–
3.8	
3.7	–
3.6	
3.5	
3.4	
3.3	–+
3.2	––
3.1	–––––++
3.0	–+
2.9	–––+
2.8	–––++
2.7	++
2.6	–––+
2.5	–––*
2.4	–––+
2.3	––––
2.2	–
2.1	
2.0	––+
1.9	
1.8	
1.7	–––
1.6	
1.5	–––
1.4	–––
1.3	–––+
1.2	–––+
1.1	–––––++
1.0	–+
0.9	–+
0.8	––––+
0.7	–
0.6	
0.5	–
0.4	––
0.3	–+

Table 2. Frequency of weights of Tiryns, Apollo r. coins, (–) **197–294** from excavations and (+) from collections listed in Svoronos 1907

Weight	
2.6	–+
2.5	––
2.4	––+
2.3	––––+
2.2	––––––
2.1	––––––++++
2.0	–––––––––+++
1.9	––––––––––––––++++++
1.8	–––––––––––––++++++++++
1.7	–––––––++++++++++++++
1.6	–––––––––––+++++++++
1.5	––––––––––––––+++++++
1.4	–––––+++++++
1.3	–––+
1.2	
1.1	+
1.0	
0.9	
0.8	
0.7	
0.6	
0.5	–

Table 3. Frequency of weights of Tiryns, Apollo l. coins, (–) **183–96** from excavations and (+) from collections listed in Svoronos 1907

Weight	
3.6	–
3.5	
3.4	
3.3	
3.2	
3.1	
3.0	–+
2.9	–++
2.8	––+
2.7	––––
2.6	–––+
2.5	
2.4	
2.3	+
2.2	
2.1	
2.0	+
1.9	
1.8	+
1.7	–
1.6	
1.5	
1.4	
1.3	–

Table 4. Frequency of weights of Tiryns, Herakles coins, (–) **174–82** from excavations, (+) from collections listed in Svoronos 1907, and overstruck Amphora/T (*) from excavations **305–10**

Weight	
4.9	–
4.8	
4.7	–+
4.6	
4.5	
4.4	
4.3	
4.2	
4.1	–+
4.0	–*
3.9	
3.8	–*
3.7	–***
3.6	––
3.5	+
3.4	
3.3	
3.2	
3.1	
3.0	
2.9	
2.8	
2.7	*
2.6	
2.5	
2.4	–

Table 5. Frequency of weights of Tiryns, Helmeted Head/H in wreath, (–) **296–304**, (+) **295** Helmeted Head/H in incuse with ethnic, and (*) **311–17** Amphora/T tesserae, all from excavations

Weight	
3.1	*
3.0	
2.9	
2.8	
2.7	
2.6	
2.5	
2.4	*
2.3	
2.2	
2.1	
2.0	
1.9	*
1.8	
1.7	*
1.6	*
1.5	–+
1.4	–––––
1.3	–*
1.2	*
1.1	
1.0	–
0.9	
0.8	–

Tables 1–5 have been aligned at 2.6, the highest recorded weight in Table 2, so that the differences between the weights of the different coin types and those of the blanks and flans from the mint are visually apparent even though the five tables are independent of each other.

In Table 1, some blanks and flans fall in the valley between the two peaks of the histogram. This suggests that attributes other than weight alone could result in rejection from further processing (including dropping a correctly sized/weighted piece). The coin blanks and flans as waste from the last minting of coins at Halieis should be compared with the latest coins issued by the polis. Stylistically these are the Tirynthian coins with the Apollo r. type (see Chapter 9).

The weights of the issues of the Apollo r. coins, Table 2, however, form a distinct cluster between the two peaks of the blanks and flans. If account is taken for wear and corrosion of the coins, they were probably intended to weigh roughly 2.2 to 2.4 g. The number of issues of the Apollo r. type, as well as the number of surviving examples, indicates that they were minted over a period of time. This might have introduced a gradual change of weight, probably reducing the weight toward which they were struck over time. Not enough of the individual issues survive nor do the coins change in size or form sufficiently to support this, however.

The Apollo head facing left type (hereafter Apollo l.), however, was clearly struck at a higher weight standard (Table 3), likely 2.9 to 3.1 g, taking account of wear and corrosion. Since style differences suggest a gap in time between these and the Apollo r. issues (see Chapter 9), the change to the Apollo r. type perhaps signals this weight reduction.[33]

The earliest Halieis bronzes stylistically and stratigraphically (see Chapter 9) are those with the Herakles head type (Table 4). These are even heavier than the Apollo l. type. Since some of the Herakles type coins were later overstruck by the Amphora/T issue, these have been included in Table 4 as well.

Only the Herakles type was overstruck with the Amphora/T dies. This, together with stylistic developments, indicates an interval of time between these two and the minting of the earliest Apollo types.[34] The Herakles types (with the Amphora/T coins) were probably struck to be about 4.0 to 4.2 g.

In Table 5 the two H types likely designate half denominations of the local bronze coins of the polis (see Chapter 9). The Amphora/T tesserae, too, may have been intended as half denominations of the Amphora/T type. The poor quality of the dies, the wide range of weights, and the roughly cut tesserae themselves suggest that they were made before the H reverse coins since these were apparently not available to be overstruck like the Herakles types.

No surviving specimen of the small tessera type is overstruck on a previously minted coin. Instead they are all on irregularly cut scraps of bronze as if blanks or flans were too much trouble to create for this small denomination. Clearly the Amphora/T tesserae were not carefully chosen for their approximation to the weight standard intended for them. But the H types were more carefully struck toward a standard, even if the limited number of examples does not lend itself to proof.

These H coins were probably struck to be about 1.5 g or about half of the Apollo l. type (again taking account of the limited number of examples in Table 5). The H coins are definitely not a half denomination of the Apollo r. type (Table 2) and therefore not intended to be minted from the blanks and flans in the lower peak of Table 1.

The weights of the Halieis coins revealed by the histograms can be compared with that of the bronze weight, HM 1186, inscribed *tritaion*, likely meaning one-third, discovered in House B southwest of the open area in front of the mint (Ault 2005, 31, n. 71).[35] The object is doughnut shaped and weighs 218.4 g. If this is multiplied by three in order to calculate the weight unit of which it is one-third, it equals 655.2 g. This is slightly above the weight of an Aeginetic mina of

---

[33] The two Apollo types do not seem to indicate two different denominations but rather a decline in the rough weight standard toward which they were struck over the intervening time.

[34] For the stylistic changes, see Chapter 9. This argument assumes that no Apollo type was ever overstruck with an Amphora/T. The small number of the Herakles or Amphora/T types compared to the Apollo r. examples (and even to the Apollo l.

coins) suggests this suggestion is correct. While it would take only the discovery of one Apollo type overstruck with an Amphora/T to negate this, from the number of Apollo coins found, at least one should have been recovered by now if an Apollo head had ever been overstruck with an Amphora/T.

[35] The full publication will appear in the discussion of writing at Halieis, Jameson n.d., chapter 9.

630 g, the weight standard common in the Peloponnesos.[36] If the weight does indicate a mina of about 660 g (taking account of loss from corrosion and wear), a drachma would be 6.6 g by weight and an obol, one-sixth of that, would be 1.1 g. The Apollo r. coins (Table 2) were then intended to be about two obols in weight each. The Herakles head coins are nearly four obols in weight and Apollo l. type approximates three obols in weight. The H coins were intended to weigh about one obol each (the Amphora/T tesserae are too varied to include here). These, of course, are the weights of the bronze used and not necessarily an indication of the denomination or value of the coin as money. Nor do the weights indicate value in terms of silver. But since the weights of the coins correlate so well with that proposed for HM 1186, weights in units of obols do seem to be intended.

This discussion of the weights of the Halieis coins anticipates the material in Chapter 9. It is placed here because the coin blanks and flans are crucial to the identification of mint. Comparing their histograms of weight frequency with those of the bronze coin issues confirms that the remains from the Northeast Command Post are indeed those of the mint that produced the Apollo r. type Tirynthian coins.

Coins Found in the Mint and Open Area to the Southwest

After the preparation of the blanks and flans, the actual minting of the coins may have taken place inside the Northeast Command Post as well. Some of the coins found there may have been lost during the last minting activity represented by the fire pit. But more likely they were coins minted earlier, rejected, and set aside for recycling. Therefore they were not preserved as carefully as those suitable for circulation.

There were fifteen coins recovered from inside the building. Excluding the six from the fire pit already listed above, these are: Apollo r. **198**, **200**, **221**, **254**, **276**, **282**, **290**, and H in wreath **303** and **304** (details of the find spots are in the context summary below). The trenches of 1972 and 1975 included about 28.5 m square of the area inside the building. All these coins were found within that area except for **200**, which was found in 1962 approximately a meter north of the north scarp of TR 135/375. Excluding **200**, there were 0.491 coins per square meter found inside the mint building area excavated in 1972 and 1975.

New coins may have been lost just outside the mint building when they were removed for circulation. Older coins, in addition to casual losses, were more likely to have been dropped as they were being carried into the mint for recycling. The northwest part of the open area directly southwest of the Northeast Command Post was partially excavated in TRs 130/370, 130/375, 135/370, and 135/375 (see the context summary below for details), with a total area of about 51 m square. Only four coins were found here: Apollo r. **238**, **261**, **266**, and Corinth **123**, a density of about 0.078 coins per square meter excavated.[37]

The southwestern part of this open area where it borders on Houses A and B was also partially excavated.[38] While the entrances of Houses A and B both open onto Avenue B, that of House A is at the corner of Street 4 running northeast to this area. Houses A and B share a common wall except that the northeast corner of House B projects beyond the northwest corner of House A at an obtuse angle to form the southwest corner of the open area. The northeast wall of House A borders the open area (compare Fig. 18 with figs. 2 and 3 of Ault 2005).[39] Eighteen coins were recovered from an excavated area of about 48 m square along the southwestern side of the open space: Apollo r. **214–16**, **220**, **234–37**, **239**, **240**,

---

[36] For a concise presentation of some ancient weight standards, see the *Oxford Classical Dictionary*, 3d ed., s.v. weights. Osborne (1996, 253–55) records fourteen weight standards in use when silver coinage began; local variations probably developed in many poleis. The 25.2 g difference in the Halieis weight from its putative standard suggests that the local variation was slightly heavier. Of course, we only have analogy to the hypothetical Aeginetic weight standard to suggest the local names for weight units at Halieis.

[37] One other Apollo r. **245** was found in 1962 near the drain through the fortification walls at the northeast corner of the building.

[38] The whole open area may have been as large as 13 x 15 m (see above, 69). It was created at the time of the construction of the Northeast Command Post by demolishing the building(s)

already there. The central part of this area has not been excavated and might conceivably contain a small narrow house sharing the northeast wall of House A. But the walls found in both the southwest and northeast parts of this area so far excavated are below the floor levels found at its northeastern end (see above, 102–3) and also below the floors of the Northeast Command Post and House A, supporting the conclusion that this was all open area and not partially filled with a house.

[39] Five trenches overlapped the southwest portion of this open area, creating a series of four triangles with the southeastern two overlapping at one corner. From northwest to southeast, these are: TRs 130/360, 125/360, 125/365, 120/365 and 120/370. All of 1962 Trench T lay to the north and east of these trenches.

253, 255, 259, 279–81 (the last coin double struck), Aigina **117**, and Anastasius **338**.[40] Excluding this last Early Byzantine coin, there were about 0.354 coins per square meter in this excavated part of the open area. Together, the southwestern and northeastern sections of the excavated part comprise about 99 m square with a total of twenty-one Classical/Early Hellenistic coins found, or 0.212 coins per square meter. In addition, **106**, another Aiginetan coin, was found at or near the intersection of Street 4 and Avenue B about five meters southeast on the way to enter this open area.

The quantity of coins recovered both inside and outside the Northeast Command Post is remarkable for Halieis. The best way to document this is to compare the numbers of coins found in the houses.[41] This also reveals the difference between the number of local coins in the mint and its environs in contrast to those from the houses. Both of these comparisons help to confirm the location for the production of the Halieis coins in the Northeast Command Post. The calculation of the number of coins found per square meter of excavated area in the houses, the Northeast Command Post, and the open area is provided for comparison. It should be stressed that the areas were used very differently: the houses are domestic while the Northeast Command Post and the open area are public and defensive.[42] In addition the area excavated in the latter two is much smaller than that of the houses. Nevertheless the comparison is instructive.

House B in which the weight (HM 1186 discussed above) was found forms the southwest corner of the open area where it abuts House A. Ault (2005, 21–22, figs. 2 and 3) describes the house but does not include it in his artifact analysis because the information from the parts excavated in 1962 was not comparable with the data from those excavated

later, and the total area of the house excavated is not provided. Ten coins were probably found in House B:[43] Apollo r. **288** and **289**, H in wreath **302**, Amphora/T **310**, Phokis silver **86**, Aigina **118**, Corinth **129**, Sikyon **140**, Epidauros **156**, and Hermion **170**. Comprising more than half of the coins, the variety of the foreign mints represented in this house is unusual for houses at Halieis although the total number of coins here is not.

A detailed analysis of the artifacts from the other five nearly complete houses at Halieis in Level A is published in Ault 2005. Adjacent to House B, House A forms the southwest boundary of the open area up to its entry off Street 4. This house was the smallest of the excavated Halieis houses, 133 m square, and contained the largest number of coins from any house known from Halieis (Ault 2005, 25 and 31). The twenty-one coins include: Apollo r. **209, 218, 225, 243, 264, 268, 269, 275, 287**; Apollo l. **191, 192**; Herakles **178, 179**; Aigina **99, 103, 108, 114–16**; Hermion **167**; and Troizen **321**.[44] House A contained about 0.158 coins per square meter.

The other houses extend southwest of the Northeast Command Post in Areas 6 and 7 in the following order. House C covers an area of about 208 m square with about 80 percent of that excavated or about 169 m square (Ault 2005, 32, fig. 2). There were only two coins recovered from this house: Apollo r. **206** and **232** (Ault 2005, 100, appendix 2, and 123, table 7), about 0.012 coins per square meter. Either the occupants of this house were more careful not to lose coins than those in the other houses, had fewer to hide, or more coins remain in the unexcavated parts. House D had about 180 of its total of 240 m square excavated or 75 percent of its area (Ault 2005, 39, fig. 2). There were eighteen coins: Apollo r. **197, 210, 224, 230, 231, 247, 249, 257, 262, 278**; Apollo l. **189**; H in wreath **300**; Aigina bronze **97**; Epidauros

---

[40] TR 120/370 produced **220** and **281**, and TR 120/365 contained **117**, while the rest were from units 3–6 of TR 125/365 spread over the trench with the Early Byzantine Anastasius coin coming from unit 6; House E had a Late Roman intrusive coin as well (see below, 112).

[41] This comparison omits a nearly complete house excavated on the west side of the town in 1962 Tr M, Area 4 (see Ault 2005, 69, Jameson 1969, 328, and Young, 1963, 3–5, with a plan). The coins from Area 4 are reported in Chapter 9, but the finds need to be studied to locate them to the rooms either inside or outside the house there.

[42] On the Halieis acropolis, nearly 1500 m square were excavated and forty-three Classical/Early Hellenistic coins were found—about 0.029 per square meter. If this excavated area is reduced by a third to account for the area occupied by the almost sterile

mud-brick fortification walls, there are still only 0.043 coins per square meter (with the coins recovered including two found outside Tower **6**). When the acropolis was occupied by a garrison, public access was likely limited to festivals or sacrifices at the sanctuary. For the acropolis excavations, see Williams n.d.; the acropolis coins are included here in Chapter 9.

[43] Some might have been from small areas overlapping both a room and the outside of the house. But more likely all are from the larger portions of the trenches located inside the house. Details are provided under the catalog numbers of the coins in Chapter 9.

[44] There are four Tirynthian coins, **178, 192, 225**, and **287**, from earlier levels. They are not included with the seventeen coins listed from Level A in the house (Ault 2005, 96–98, appendix 2, and 118, table 4).

154, 155, 157; and Troizen **325, 326**.[45] This is 0.10 coins per square meter.

In House E, 148 of its estimated 203 m square were excavated (Ault 2005, 48, fig. 2), or almost 75 percent of its area. Eight coins were recovered: Apollo r. **203**, Apollo l. **188**, H with ethnic **295**, H in wreath **299**, Amphora/T tesserae **316, 317**, Arkadia **327**, and Arcadius **334** (Ault 2005, 105–8, appendix 2, and 138, table 14).[46] Excluding the last, there were 0.043 coins recovered per square meter here. The reason for the small number of coins here may be the same as that for the even smaller number from House C above. All of House 7 covering about 231 m square was excavated (Ault 2005, 13). Eleven coins were found in the house: Apollo r. **217, 244**; Apollo l. **187**; Amphora/T **307, 308**; Aigina **111**; Hermion **160, 163, 166, 172**; and Thebes silver **89**.[47] This is about 0.052 coins per square meter.

This survey of the coins from the houses emphasizes the greater density of coins found in the Northeast Command Post and open area to its southwest. Clearly more coins were lost in these areas than in the houses even if the latter includes those, like the silver coins, which were more likely consciously hidden inside the house rather than carelessly lost. In addition, the greater density of coins found along the southwest side of the open area compared with that of the coins found just outside the entrance of the Northeast Command Post is remarkable. This difference can be explained by one of the following:[48]

1. A hoard or hoards from inside the upper parts of the walls of House A (see the reconstruction in Ault 2005, fig. 12) spread in the open area as the mud-brick wall of the house collapsed. This is a complicated though not impossible sequence of events, but accounting for the area of the spread is still difficult.

2. Earth swept from inside the mint scattered over the open area (the center of which was never excavated) but not nearby the mint itself, accounting for the smaller number of coins recovered there. Moving this earth to the enclosed southwest corner of the open area would put it out of the way of the more trafficked part near the door of the Northeast Command Post and the other three entrances into the open area (see Figs. 18, 27). Later the earth washed away during annual rains with the heavier debris becoming embedded in the surface of the open area. The absence of small blanks and flans might be accounted for by the lack of sieving in the excavations of these two triangles, but it seems unlikely that not one would be found.

3. There may have been minting in the southwestern part of the open area (with fire pits in the unexcavated central portions). But this would not be as secure as the interior of the Northeast Command Post. And here too, the lack of minting debris argues against this.[49]

4. The open area was used to exchange coins for goods. This accounts for the absence of blanks, flans, and other mint debris. But why would so many coins be lost here? This open area may have been one of the locations at Halieis for tables of money changers/bankers (see Plato *Apology* 17c and Lysias 9.5) where goods could be exchanged for coins, and vice versa. The quantity of coins required may have been such that they were more easily lost than in the houses or even the mint itself.[50] The scarcity of foreign coins in the open area suggests that the foreign exchange may have been located closer to the harbor or agora of the town.[51]

Perhaps after the construction of the Northeast Command Post, the open area in front originally planned for mustering troops also became the site of the local exchange once minting began in the Northeast Command Post. With appropriate caution, this seems to me the best explanation for the unusual quantity of Tirynthian coins found in that part of

---

[45] There are three coins, **157, 224**, and **262**, from earlier levels. They are not included with the coins noted from Level A in the house (Ault 2005, 101–5, appendix 2 with 15 coins, and 130, Table 10 with 14 coins).

[46] The Arcadius coin is a rare intrusion below the surface deposits where Late Roman/Early Byzantine spirally grooved ware is common. Ault (2005, 54, n. 149) mentions the scarcity of sherd evidence for disturbance from the Late Roman to Early Byzantine occupation at Halieis. See the context summary below for spirally grooved sherds in and around the Northeast Command Post. The Anastasius nummus (see above, 111) is another example, as are a few spirally grooved sherds found in the fill of some of the Classical/Early Hellenistic wells. This occupation is discussed in Chapter 7 above.

[47] There are four coins, **89, 111, 307**, and **308**, from levels not included with the seven coins listed from Level A in the house (Ault 2005, 93–94, appendix 1, and 113, table 4).

[48] Or some other explanation might emerge with future excavations in this area, such as a small, narrow house here; see note 38 above.

[49] The only possible evidence for minting debris is **281**, a double struck Apollo r. that may have been intended for recycling.

[50] Similarly, fewer coins on the acropolis or Industrial Terrace would result in fewer lost (see above, note 42).

[51] In any case, these coins were rarer here than the much more plentiful local coinage. Houses A and B certainly had more foreign coins than found here. Perhaps these were less useful than the local coins (and so treated more carelessly). On the other hand, the owners of these houses might have had more financial dealings with other poleis, for which foreign coins were useful.

the open area bordering the walls of Houses A and B. The northeastern part of the open area likely had more traffic than this corner at the southwest. More evidence for the use of the entire open area is likely to be found if the central part is excavated. But the the southwestern part seems appropriate for some kind of financial exchange, based on the concentration of local coins there.[52]

Other Metal Objects from the Mint and Open Area

There is an unusual amount of metal objects from inside and immediately outside the Northeast Command Post, considering the small total area of the excavations there, compared to that recovered from the houses (see Table 6).[53] While the metal analysis for the houses deals primarily with the latest habitation debris, that for the Northeast Command Post probably includes some metal remains from the construction of the building or even earlier (see above, 103).[54] Still there is enough difference between the domestic metal and that from the mint area to indicate that there was more metal found here than in the houses.

While the quantities of metal objects per square meter are different between the houses and the Northeast Command Post area, the object types are similar. Compare those listed in Ault's tables (cited in note 53) with those listed in the context summary below. There is even a bronze rooster in each data set: HM 1256, 9.02 g, House 7; HM 818, 25.02 g, TR 135/373 unit 4 (Pl. 21f). Both collections of metal objects are primarily broken fragments. But there are more complete or nearly complete objects (such as hardware and nails) from the houses than from the area of the Northeast Command Post (Pl. 21g–i). This is also true for the metal objects from the acropolis and Industrial Terrace (see Dengate n.d., chapter 8).

While the metal, especially that from inside the Northeast Command Post, should contain more objects with a clearly identifiable military character, given its proximity to the defenses, this is not the case.[55] If complete objects with metal parts used for the defense of the town had been stored there, they were removed before the town was abandoned. Any broken ones either had already been replaced or repaired or had been removed with the others. If any fragments were lost, they were not identifiable as possible defensive objects when excavated. Unlike the Halieis acropolis, where there were clearly many metal objects of military nature (see Dengate n.d.,

Table 6. Numbers of metal objects

	Excavated area, m²	Iron	Bronze	Lead	Unidentified metals	Total	Number per m²
NECP inside	28.5	20	21	8	0	49	1.719
NECP outside	51	16	6	4	0	26	0.510
House A	133	12	10	1	25+	48+	0.361
House C	208	21	11	3	34+	69+	0.332
House D	180	18	31	5	8+	62+	0.344
House E	148	23	16	6	27?	72?	0.486
House 7	231	43	16	5	26?	90?	0.309

[52] For the evidence of banking in other ancient Greek cities, see Bogaert 1968. In the Athenian Agora, Thompson and Wycherley (1972, 171, n. 12) infer that "tables" of bankers and money changers were located near the northwest corner in a well-defined, compact area.

[53] The metal objects have not been quantified for either House B or the excavated triangular parts at the southeastern open area facing the Northeast Command Post. The data from the other Halieis houses are found in Ault 2005, 25 and 118, table 4 for House A; 32 and 123, table 7 for House C; 39 and 129–30, table 10 for House D; 48 and 137–38, table 14 for House E; and 13, 112–13, table 1 for House 7. Ault's tables contain a category of "unidentified metals" for small fragments, which have been included in the totals. Objects made of two different metals are included with the count of the heavier metal in Table 6.

[54] Table 6 does not include the two cast bronze arrowheads from TR 135/380 Level C units 15 and 16, HM 1498 and HM 1499, deposited before the construction of the Northeast Command Post and therefore irrelevant to the consideration of the mint or any other use of the later building. These are similar to the arrowheads found on the acropolis (Dengate n.d., chapter 8), many of which are related to Deposit IV, the attack and destruction in the early 5th century (see Chapter 9, Table 7), and the arrowhead, HM 543, mentioned above (26, note 24).

[55] The arrowheads, HM 1498 and HM 1499, are in fact the only clearly martial remains identified from the area of the Northeast Command Post. These may indicate this area's earlier strategic importance for defense, perhaps contributing to the later decision to locate the Northeast Command Post here.

chapter 8), the metal objects in the Northeast Command Post (where they can be identified at all) are generally nonmilitary in nature. Like the metal objects from the houses, these could have been lost on the floors or simply left when the structure was abandoned as not worth the effort to remove. As indicated above (102), the bronze scrap from minting was left in place probably with the intention of recycling later. The unusual concentration of other metal scrap objects in the mint area, then, supports the suggestion that the building was used to collect and store metal for recycling as well as its other uses suggested above (67, note 19). These metal fragments might be some of the items traded in the open area outside for coins produced by the mint.

The total weight of iron objects recorded from inside the Northeast Command Post is 529.67 g, bronze (other than the coins, blanks, and flans) is 266.72 g, and lead is 1040.86 g. The open area just outside the building contained 526.04 g of iron, 36.26 g of bronze, and 65.24 g of lead. Using the suggested 660 g mina from the weight HM 1186 found in House B (see above, 109), we can calculate that there was inside the building 80.3 drachmae of iron, 40.4 drachmae of bronze, and 1588.2 drachmae or over 1.5 minas of lead by weight. Just outside the building were 79.8 drachmae of iron, 5.5 drachmae of bronze, and almost 10 drachmae of lead by weight. While this is only the weight of the metal recovered by excavation, it does illustrate, in terms of the local Halieis weight standard, just how much waste metal was found inside and outside the Northeast Command Post. This suggests that there was originally a much larger quantity of metal scrap there when the building was in active use (with useful objects likely removed before abandonment).

Other Remains from the Mint and the Open Area to the Southwest

The materials recorded during the excavations of Trench T in 1962 and the later five gridded trenches have been listed in the context summary appended at the end of this chapter. Ault (2005, 11) used the artifact clusters in the various rooms of the houses to help differentiate their particular

functions. The Northeast Command Post seems to have been built as a single large room. The fragmentary artifacts found inside the building, however, do suggest different activities here. But their identification is complicated by the fact that the building was placed over the foundations of earlier structures, which had been destroyed to their foundations. Consequently, it is probable that some of the artifacts may have come from the earlier structures rather than from the later Northeast Command Post (e.g., HP 2499 a Geometric bowl rim from TR 135/375 unit 20).

The sherds and other artifacts from inside the building are generally similar to those found in the excavations of the houses, acropolis, and Industrial Terrace. The red and yellow plaster fragments (e.g., HV 2 from 1962 TR T) and wall plaster fragments noted in some units of the later trenches indicate that the walls inside the Northeast Command Post were plastered in part, if not completely. The shells inside the building are common in the houses and probably are the waste from food brought in and discarded where eaten. In contrast, the animal bones probably were discarded from more formal meals.[56] The greatest quantity of identified pottery is from vessels used for eating and drinking in both black glaze and plain wares. This is followed by cooking-ware shapes and fabrics. Storage vessels such as amphoras exist but, in comparison with the other sherds from the building, are rare and are more frequently found in the same units as the Late Roman/Early Byzantine spirally grooved body sherds. Since the only evidence for fires is the mint activity itself, and remains of terracotta braziers were not identified, this suggests that the cooking vessels were brought with food already prepared and used with the eating and drinking pottery for dining. Perhaps the small andron noted by Ault (2005, 27–28) for House A was supplemented by the use of the much larger area inside the Northeast Command Post.[57] Banquets, perhaps, are suggested by the presence of red-figure vessels including HP 2645, HP 2974, and HP 2994, and the plaster walls of the building with its stone capitals provide an appropriate setting for formal dining. The lamp fragments suggest use of the building at night. Some religious activity might be indicated by the miniature kotylai, including

---

[56] The faunal remains from the lower town have yet to be analyzed.
[57] Dining at public expense inside the Tholos in the Athenian Agora might be an appropriate parallel (Wycherley 1957, 179–84; Thompson and Wycherley, 1972, 41–46; and Camp 1986, 94–

97). But we know next to nothing about the organization of the Halieis government although HL 73, a lamp base with the graffito *damasion* from the acropolis, is suggestive (see Jameson n.d., chapter 9). See above, 40 and n. 78.

HP 1201, but these are common at Halieis and are present in such small numbers in the Northeast Command Post as to be inconclusive. This is also true of HP 1238 (a phiale), HC 444 (a terracotta figurine head), and HC 480 (a terracotta figurine leg). Perhaps even more striking is the presence of only one terracotta loom weight, HC 400. Groups of these weights were used by Ault (2005, 78–79) to identify areas of the houses used for weaving or loom storage. Consequently, it does not seem that weaving was done inside the Northeast Command Post. Obsidian and flint blades and chips are also common at Halieis and are found here as well (e.g., HS 595 and HS 628). (See Runnels 1982, 365–71, for the use of chipped stone at Halieis.)

The areas just outside the Northeast Command Post to the southwest contained more broken artifacts, probably to be expected in a public open space. They could also be remains swept out from the floor of the building. These artifacts are generally similar to the debris found inside the building except that outside there are more remains of storage vessels (such as HP 1273, a stamped amphora handle), perhaps broken while being carried through the streets. Terracotta loom weights are also infrequent, as might be expected in a public area outside an enclosed house. If the debris here is not sweepings from the Northeast Command Post or another structure as yet unexcavated,[58] then this open area might also have been the site of outdoor dining. Red-figure and black-figure sherds were found here as well as more fragments of eating and drinking vessels than found inside the building. The presence of shells and animal bones support this.[59]

Conclusion

Given the proximity of Houses A and B to the Northeast Command Post and the number of coins in the former with the inscribed weight found in the latter, perhaps the owner/occupants of these houses had some control of access to the Northeast Command Post, collected metal and other goods there to exchange for coins, and were the individuals responsible for minting when new bronze coinage was needed (compare Ault 2005, 31 and n. 71). In addition, they could have been involved with the building's defensive use. Perhaps these duties were inherited along with the houses. While this might be possible, the supposition is based on limited excavation evidence, since houses both to the west and east of the Northeast Command Post have not been excavated.[60] Nor do we have any evidence for how the polis of Halies administered its minting, distribution of coins, recycling of metals, and defense. At the least, the owners of both Houses A and B might have been merchants who may have had access to the Northeast Command Post and played a part in the process of minting, circulating coinage, and recycling of metal. They may even have used the building for dining with their friends or for public events, as well as the defense of this part of the city.

No dies were found in the mint but these were probably considered valuable and were either saved for reuse or, when no longer useful, dedicated in a sanctuary.[61] Nor is there other evidence for tools used in minting: no anvils, punches, or pincers to hold hot metal objects such as those shown in ancient representations of minting (Vermeule 1957). Whatever wooden shelving or other furniture that may have been used for storage were likely removed when the polis was abandoned.[62] The unrecycled mint debris and other small fragments of metal objects are a melancholy testimony to those who left the town, knowing that it would no longer need coins of its own. After this, the mud-brick fortification walls slowly decayed from neglect, and the building became a convenient source of quarried stone to the extent that the superstructure is gone, except for a few blocks remaining at the time of excavation.

The date of the coins and minting debris found on the floor of the mint must be before the abandonment of the fortifications (see above, 83–84). Table 7 in Chapter 9 indicates a date of 300±10 for

---

[58] TR 135/370 has a pattern of walls that can be interpreted as a prothyron for a doorway to a house; see the context summary below and for the type of prothyron at Halieis, see Ault 2005, 59–60. But not enough of the southwest area has been uncovered to confirm or deny this.

[59] Again, indications of religious activity, if the presence of miniature kotylai can be called that, are scarce. Obsidian and flint are also present.

[60] Only the 1962 test TR T indicates walls, probably of houses,

there. There is the elaborate andron of a house just north of House B (Ault 2005, 36 and 69–70).

[61] See Kalligas 1997 for a bronze die from Sounion and references to the dedication of coin dies on the Acropolis at Athens; see also Harris 1995, 119, number 34. For other dies, see Vermeule 1954 and Malkmus 1989–93.

[62] Compare a similar suggestion for the mess building on the Halieis acropolis and rafters from houses (Dengate n.d., chapter 11).

the end of the acropolis and a not too different one for the lower town, although there is some pottery indicating later occupation there. Nevertheless, the last minting of coins for the polis would likely have been when it still expected to exist, if not flourish. Sometime in the last quarter of the fourth century,

perhaps later rather than earlier, the last issues of the Tirynthian coins of Halieis were produced here in the mint. Circumstances did not permit a final recovery of the mint debris from this last production. The building and such fragments not worth carrying away were abandoned.

Context Summary

This summary is based on a preliminary study of the excavation results both from the notebooks written at the trenches and the find notebooks written in the study/laboratory area after the sherds had been washed and the other finds preliminarily cleaned.[63] Where shapes can be distinguished, pottery descriptions have been interpreted to represent an estimate of minimum number of whole pots that the sherds represent, not a complete count of all fragments as the find notebooks record. In contrast the number of body sherds are only counted or estimated. Blanks, flans, and coins in the catalog of both chapters 8 and 9 are given bold face numbers with the name of the mint of the coins except those from Tiryns, and other products of the Halieis mint are identified by type as abbreviated in Tables 2–5 above. Future study of the pottery and stratigraphy for final publication may alter some details, particularly the interpretation of the Levels A, B, etc. But this overall analysis gives a general picture of ancient activities in and around the Northeast Command Post (NECP). Probable dates for the Levels appear below in Chapter 9, Table 7. Halieis inventory numbers are preceded by letters indicating the category of object (HC = Halieis clay, HL = lamp, HM = metal, HN = numismata [coins], HP = pottery, HS = stone, HV = various other materials). The following abbreviations are used here: TR = trench, BF = black figure, BG = black gloss ("glaze"),[64] RF = red figure, CW (cooking ware), PW (plain ware), g = gram, kg = kilogram, m = meter, initials are used for North, South, East and West, and NECP for Northeast Command Post. Spirally grooved = the type pottery for the Late Roman/Early Byzantine occupation at Halieis (see the bath complex in Chapter 7 above and Rudolph 1979). Lead strips in the records have had "or ingots" added following the conclusions of Raubitschek (1998, 155–57) about similar objects from Isthmia. But

until the Halieis metal objects are more completely studied, these may either be "ingots" or "strips" or even some other classification. Because of slightly different readings of the two sets of excavation data and the limitations of that record noted above, the account below cannot be directly equated with the evidence listed in tables 1–19 (Ault 2005, 110–44) of the contents of the five houses he analyzed: Houses 7, A, and C–E, although limited general comparisons can be drawn if the size of the houses and rooms is compared with the size of the trenches inside and outside the Northeast Command Post.

TR T (Tom) 1962, House Pi (NECP) walls, some of the interior including the central column base and NW half of the line of stones inside the NE side of the building, the NE corner area including the outer fortification wall, bastion foundations, drain cover blocks through the fortification wall, and the SE corner of the interior. These excavations are reported in NB 1.1 and 1.2 by Thomas Jacobsen (with Michael Jameson and Michael Cheilik filling in when he was absent, with the pottery notes from John H. Young). The index in NB 1.1, 199, lists the pages of both notebooks recording the excavations under the heading "Building 'Pi.'" Finds clearly from outside the immediate area of the NECP have been excluded. The double elevations are explained in note 12 above and find spots are interpreted from the original trial trench designations for ease of comprehension. The trenches were later refilled with the earth that had been removed from them adding lead tokens stamped with the Greek initials of the American School of Classical Studies at Athens. Some of these were recovered in the parts re-excavated in 1972 and 1975. Pottery from the NECP is described in NB 1.1, 119–22 and 137–38, with almost all thrown except for some BG and profiled pieces which, although initially saved, were not later inventoried. Apparently no TR T sherds from the NECP were described in the 1971 TR T find notebook or kept-

---

[63] In 1975 a separate record of metal fragments not worthy of inventory was recorded in the kept-metal notebook. Earlier similar scraps had either been inventoried or discarded.

[64] BG does not specify a place of manufacture such as Attic,

Argolic, or local. Corinthian fabric can usually be determined but the other wares are hard to distinguish except by the occasional high quality of the Attic similar to that of Attic RF and BF.

sherd notebook and likely all had been discarded to reduce bulk before the finds were transferred to Nauplion. From the description, there was clearly a roof-tile fragment layer with Late Roman spirally grooved sherds concentrated above it.

1 blank, between HS 6 and the 1972 findspot of HM 666, depth ca. 0.40 m below surface of trench (recalculated elevation +0.40 m), Level A?

200 Apollo r., inside the NECP near the center of the NW wall, 0.30 m below surface of trench (recalculated elevation of +0.50 m), above Level A

245 Apollo r., outside NE corner over and E of drain, 0.48 m. below surface of trench (recalculated elevation of +0.32 m), Level A or above Level A

303 H in wreath, on the foundations of the NECP near the threshold block, 0.28 m below the surface of the trench (recalculated elevation of +0.52 m), Level A?

HM 5 iron nail fragments (not weighed), 0.45 m NW of HS 6, depth 0.15 m (recalculated elevation of +0.45 m), Level A?

HM 13 iron nail fragment, Level A?

HS 6 Ionic capital of shelly limestone found by southwest plinth, see above 68, depth 0.42 m (recalculated elevation of +0.38 m), above Level A

HS 10 carved stone molding fragment, about 0.25 m S of central column base at a depth of ca. 0.30 m (recalculated elevation of +0.50 m), above Level A

HV 2 plaster painted fragments, red and yellow, see above 67, depth ca. 0.35 m (recalculated elevation of +0.45 m), Level A?

The excavation methods at Halieis from 1972 on are described by Ault (2005, 5–6). The highest and lowest elevation for each unit is given for the following trenches although most of the excavation of each concentrated between these extremes, which explains the overlapping of elevations between adjacent units. The year of excavation follows the grid number of the trench. Excavation in subsequent years follows the first unit number assigned to that season as units of a given trench were numbered sequentially in order of excavation. Each excavator and find notebook recorder had a slightly different style of writing and describing certain details or not (e.g., shells). In addition, conditions when writing each account, especially the weather — often extremely hot, could affect the detail recorded. Such variations need to be kept in mind when drawing conclusions from the account below. Faunal remains have not yet been identified. Counts of fragments of roof tiles are given and where reported are subdivided by type, L = Laconian and C = Corinthian, and whether pan or cover tile. Tiles were often collected in wooden boxes constructed for later find storage. These containers measured about 1 x 0.25 x 0.1 m for the "small boxes" and held about 0.025 cubic meters. A "large box" was 1 x 0.25 x 0.2 m, holding about 0.05 cubic meters. Plastic storage bags were used to collect smaller tiles, sherds, shells, etc. A full bag approximates about 0.001 cubic meter (if the contents were emptied out and used to fill a cubic meter-sized container). Sometimes a small bag, ca. one-fourth the capacity of the standard bag, was specified in the record.

TR 130/370 1972 directly SW of NECP, 4 x 4 m trench with the 1 m E balk excavated in 1975 for a total area of 20 m square. Two sherds join units 32 and 34.

Unit 1 +0.88–0.67 m, surface, above Level A. BG: 1 skyphos handle; PW: 9 amphora rims, 1 bowl base, ca. 150 body fragments; 25 spirally grooved body fragments. Tile fragments: half large box; piece of floor cement.

Unit 2 +0.68–0.53 m, N half of trench, fill from TR T of 1962, intrusive in Level A. BG: 1 cup rim, 2 body fragments; CW: 3 body fragments; PW: 7 amphora rims, ca. 80 body fragments; 33 spirally grooved body fragments. Tile fragments: half large box.

Unit 3 +0.55–0.44 m, TR T of 1962, intrusive in Level A. Corinthian: 1 body fragment; BG: 1 bowl foot, 1 body fragment; PW: 2 amphora rims, 32 body fragments; 5 spirally grooved body fragments, 1 Late Roman red-ware plate rim. Tile fragments: half small box; one shell.

Unit 4 +0.75–0.60 m, S half of trench above Level A or intrusive in Level A. BG: 1 cup foot, 1 bowl rim, 1 body fragment; CW: 2 body fragments; PW: 2 amphora rims, 1 jug rim, 1 bowl base, half large box body fragments; 41 spirally grooved body fragments. Tile fragments: ca. 30. One modern glass fragment.

Unit 5 +0.62–0.53 m, above Level A or intrusive in Level A. Corinthian: squat jug rim; BG: 1 cup-kantharos rim, 2 cup-skyphos rims, 3 skyphos bases, ca. 20 body fragments; CW: 21 body fragments; PW: 1 large pitcher rim, 7 jug rims, 2 amphora bases, 1 large box body fragments; ca. 40 spirally grooved body fragments. Tile fragments: ca. 800; several red wall plaster fragments; shells.

HP 1247 RF fragment

HP 1263 BG bowl base with rouletting

HM 825 iron strip, 10.51 g

HV 253 conical green glass fragment

Unit 6 +0.55–0.40 m, Level A. Corinthian: ca. 10 kotyle fragments; BG: 1 krater rim, 1 large bowl rim, 1 cup rim, 3 stemless cup rims, 4 cup-skyphos rims, 1 skyphos rim, 1 oinochoe shoulder, 1 bolsal base, 5 body fragments with stamped decoration, ca. 40 body fragments; CW: 6 rims, 2 handles, 30 body fragments; PW: 7 amphora handles, 3 jug rims, 1 jug rim and handle, 1 pitcher handle; 1 spirally grooved body fragment. Tile fragments: ca. 800; ca. 30 red plaster fragments; 23 animal bone and teeth fragments, 38 shells.
HL 187A BG lamp fragment, mid-4th-early 3d
HL 187B BG lamp fragment, mid-4th-early 3d
HM 895 bronze swinging handle, 0.82 g

Unit 7 +0.44–0.29 m, N part of trench, Level A. BG: 1 small bowl fragment; PW: 1 small jug handle, 1 bowl rim, 18 body fragments; 1 spirally grooved body fragment. Tile fragments: 4; 1 animal bone, 1 shell.

Unit 8 +0.31–0.18 m, S three-fourths of trench, Level A, to floor(?), rubble wall foundations appear. Corinthian: 3 kotyle rims; BG: 1 krater(?) rim, a lekythos(?) rim, 4 bowl rims, 1 cup body and handle, 8 skyphoi rims, 1 skyphos rim and handle, 4 stemless cup rims, 1 bolsal rim, 1 stamped plate base, ca. 80 body fragments; CW: 3 lopas rims, ca. 50 body fragments; PW: 2 basin(?) rims with relief. Fragments of pithos with relief. Tile fragments: 15; 11 white plaster fragments; 11 shell fragments.
123 Corinth at 128.05/367.35, +0.17 m
HP 1283 Corinthian lekanis, late 5th
HL 125 Corinthian(?) BG lamp rim, late 5th into 4th
HM 771 iron fragment, 5.52 g
HM 798 bronze punch(?), 6.59 g
HM 799 iron nail fragments, 4.63 g

Unit 9 +0.20–0.12 m, NE corner of trench inside rubble wall foundations, Level A. Corinthian: 6 kotyle body fragments, 1 miniature kotyle; BG: 2 skyphos rims, 5 cup-skyphos rims, 1 bowl rim, ca. 20 body fragments; CW: lopas lid, 3 chytra rims, ca. 50 body fragments; 1 blister-ware body fragment; PW: 1 jug handle, 2 amphora handles, ca. 100 body fragments; pithos base. Tile fragments: half small box; 2 shells; carbonized wood.
266 at 127.53/368.36 Apollo r.
HP 1200 BF cup-skyphos fragment
HP 1212 BG plate, late 4th
HP 1213 BG saltcellar
HP 1223 BG plate, late 4th
HP 1240 BG cup-skyphos rim fragment
HP 1264 Corinthian mortar, mid-5th–mid-4th
HP 1391 Corinthian pyxis lid fragment
HM 770 Iron blade fragments, 250 g

Unit 10 +0.12 to -0.13 m, Level A/B. Corinthian: 1 miniature kotyle; BG: 2 skyphos rims, ca. 20 body

fragments; CW: 11 body fragments; PW: 1 jug handle; 30 body fragments. Tile fragments: 5; 1 obsidian chip.
HM 903 iron fragments, 19.0 g

Unit 11 +0.28–0.11 m, NW corner of trench inside rubble wall foundations, Level A. Corinthian: 1(?) kotyle fragments; BG: 1 bowl rim, 1 cup-skyphos rim, 1 oinochoe(?); CW: 2 body fragments; PW: 12 body fragments; 1 spirally grooved body fragment. Tile fragments: 5; some wall plaster fragments.
HS 403 obsidian blade fragment

Unit 12 +0.17–0.10 m, S central part of trench inside rubble wall foundations to floor? Level A or A/B. Corinthian: 1 amphora(?) rim, 1 kotyle rim, 1 skyphos rim, 1 miniature kotyle rim; BG: 1 krater rim, 1 oinochoe(?) handle, 1 cup foot, 1 bowl rim, 1 skyphos foot, ca. 10 body fragments; CW: 3 lid fragments, ca. 30 body fragments; PW: 1 amphora handle, 1 jug or amphora base, 55 body fragments; coarse-ware pithos rim, body fragments with relief. Tile fragments: half small box; 3 shells, 4 shell fragments.
HP 1390 BG cup-skyphos
HC 461 pyramidal loom weight
HM 848 iron fibula bow, 10.97 g
HM 879 iron rod(?) fragments, 85 g
HM 882 iron fragment, 2.5 g

Unit 13 +0.11 to -0.09 m, NE corner of trench, Level A/B or B. Corinthian: 1 plate rim, 1 small bowl(?) rim; BG: 1 krater rim, 1 kantharos base, 1 small bowl base, 2 cup-skyphos rims, ca. 20 body fragments; CW: 1 chytra rim, 7 body fragments; PW: 1 jug base, 3 bowl rims, ca. 70 body fragments. Tile fragments: 6; 12 shells and 12 shell fragments.
HP 1385 Corinthian Geometric krater rim
HP 1386 Corinthian Geometric kotyle rim

Unit 14 +0.13 to -0.06 m, S central part of trench, Level A/B or B. Corinthian: 1 oinochoe body fragment, 1 large kotyle rim, 3 kotyle bases, 1 small bowl rim, ca. 10 body fragments; BG: 1 krater(?) rim, 1 lekanis rim, 1 skyphos rim, 2 cup-skyphos rims, 1 bolsal base, 4 bowl bases, ca. 60 body fragments; CW: 1 lid knob, ca. 50 body fragments; PW: 1 jug base, ca. 50 body fragments; coarse-ware basin rim. Tile fragments: ca. 20; 4 white floor plaster fragments; 8 shell fragments.
HP 1242 BF rim fragment
HP 1272 BG kylix foot
HL 154 BG lamp rim, late 6th?
HM 850 bronze fragments (not weighed)
HM 888 iron fragment, 5.0 g
HM 924 lead strip or ingot, 16.6 g

Unit 15 -0.10–0.25 m, down to clay floor, Level A/B or B. Corinthian: 2 krater(?) rims, 1 kothon rim, 2

ray-based kotylai fragments, 2 ray-based bowl fragments, ca. 100 body fragments; BG: 4 oinochoe(?) rims, 1 lekanis rim, 1 cup rim, 1 cup foot, 1 skyphos rim, 4 cup-skyphos rims, ca. 30 body fragments; CW: ca. 100 body fragments; PW: 3 amphora handles, 2 hydria rims, 1 jug rim, ca. 50 body fragments; coarse-ware basin rim. Tile fragments: ca. 10; some wood and charcoal, 18 shells, animal bone and teeth fragments.
HP 1245 pithos base
HP 1277 pyxis knob
HP 1387 BF cup rim
HL 140 Argive(?) BG lamp fragments, late 6th?
HM 839 iron fragments, 9.29 g
HS 386 steatite spindle whorl

Unit 16 -0.28–0.42 m, NE corner of trench, Level B/C. Corinthian: 1 jug(?) body fragment, 1 krater(?) rim, 2 kotyle rims, ca. 30 body fragments; BG: 3 oinochoe body fragments, 1 krater(?) rim, 1 bowl(?) rim, 3 cup-skyphos rims, ca. 20 body fragments; CW: 1 chytra rim, ca. 20 body fragments; PW: 1 bowl rim, grooved, 2 jug bases, ca. 30 body fragments. Fragments of charcoal, animal bones, 1 small bag shells.
HP 1994 Corinthian(?) body fragment
HP 2047 Corinthian BF krater(?) fragment

Unit 17 -0.23–0.33 m, S central part of trench, Level B/C. Corinthian: krater rim, pitcher(?) rim, large pyxis(?) body fragment, ca. 80 kotyle fragments; 1 blister-ware base; CW: chytra rim, ca. 25 body fragments. Tile fragments: 4; 23 shells.
HP 1392 Late Geometric Corinthian amphora
    fragment
HP 1393 stemless cup
HL 188 Argive(?) unglazed lamp, late 6th/early
    5th
HC 478 pyramidal loom-weight fragment

Unit 18 -0.36–0.41 m, Level C. Corinthian: 4 krater rim fragments, 4 kotyle rims, ca. 80 body fragments; BG: 2 oinochoe rims, 9 body fragments; PW: 4 jug/pitcher rims, 3 lekanis rims, 1 bowl rim, 1 plate(?) rim, ca. one-fourth small box very worn body fragments. A few fragments of tile/pithos fabric, 15 animal bone fragments, 1 bag of shells, carbonized seeds.
HP 1995 BF body fragments
[HL 202] BG bowl(?) fragment
HM 904 iron slag(?) (not weighed)
HS 626 obsidian flake

Unit 19 -0.37–0.55 m, NE corner of trench, Level C/D, down to pebble area. Corinthian: 2 krater base fragments, 2 kotyle body fragments; BG: 2 pitcher rims, 1 cup-skyphos rim, ca. 70 body fragments; CW: 2 body fragments; PW: basin rim, pitcher rim, ca. 60 body fragments. Carbonized seeds, 4 animal bone fragments, 1 bag shells.

Unit 20 +0.14–0.08 m, SW corner of trench to plaster floor, Level A. PW: 2 body fragments. Tile fragments: 5 pan.

Unit 21 +0.09 to -0.02 m, 2 superimposed plaster floors, Level A/B. White floor plaster, 4 fragments.
HP 1381 Corinthian kotyle rim

Unit 22 -0.04–0.07 m, Level B. Corinthian: 4 kotyle body fragments; CW: 10 body fragments; PW: 12 body fragments; ca. 10 coarse-ware body fragments; 1 pan tile fragment.

Unit 23 -0.47–0.57 m, S central part of trench, Level C/D. Corinthian: fragments of several large kotylai; BG: base and handle of jug, 12 skyphos or bowl rims, ca. 100 body fragments; CW: ca. 25 body fragments; PW: 6 small jug handles, ca. 200 small body fragments. Tile fragments: 19; iron fragments, 1 small bag animal bone fragments, 1 bag shells, seeds, some carbon.
HP 1984 BF bowl rim
HP 1989 coarse-ware storage jar fragment
HM 898 iron fragments, 20.0 g

Unit 24 -0.55–0.62 m, Level C/D. Corinthian: small lekanis(?) fragment; BG: trefoil-mouthed oinochoe rim; PW: 4 jug rims, 1 large bowl rim, ca. 40 body fragments. Tile fragments: 23; 2 fragments of red baked brick. Some animal bone fragments, carbonized seeds, charcoal.
HP 1293 East Greek(?) plate rim fragment
HP 1389 Late Geometric Argive(?) krater rim
HS 625 obsidian bladelet segment

Unit 25 -0.60–0.72 m, NW part of S central trench, Level C/D. Corinthian: small lekanis(?) fragment; BG: 1 jug handle, 1 krater rim, 3 skyphos rims, 1 bowl rim, ca. 80 body fragments; PW: jug rim, 3 jug handles, ca. 90 body fragments. A few animal bone fragments, 1 small bag shells.
HP 2016 handmade, unglazed body fragments
    (Neolithic?)[65]
HS 624 obsidian bladelet segments

---

[65] Or perhaps Bronze Age. See the Halieis acropolis prehistoric pottery in Pullen 2000. But handmade Iron Age pottery was also found there; see Williams 1981, 148, n. 17. The other sherds identified as Neolithic or prehistoric below in units 26, 27, and 29 and TR 130/375, unit 8 may also prove to be Neolithic, Bronze Age, or Iron Age when studied.

Unit 26 -0.70–0.84 m, Level C/D. Corinthian: 9 kotyle bases; BG: 1 oinochoe(?) rim, 2 krater rims; PW: 1 shallow bowl rim, 1 deep bowl rim; coarse-ware fragments that may contain Neolithic(?): 2 pitcher rims, 1 pitcher base, ca. 50 body fragments. Tile fragments: 15; 1 bag shells, animal bones and 1 tooth fragment.

Unit 27 -0.82–1.07 m, half of NW part of S central trench, Level C/D, below sea level. BG: 1 krater rim, 2 skyphos rims, 11 body fragments; PW: 1 pitcher base, ca. 20 body fragments; Neolithic(?): 2 body fragments. One small bag shells, 2 animal bone fragments.
HP 1287 BG amphora(?) base
HS 627 obsidian bladelet segments

Unit 28 -1.05–1.14 m, Level D/E. PW: 9 very worn body fragments. One small bag shells; 2 animal bone fragments.
HS 623 obsidian bladelet segment

Unit 29 -1.12–1.37 m, Level D/E. BG: 1 skyphos handle, 3 body fragments; PW: 6 body fragments. A few shells. One prehistoric(?) pottery fragment with decorative band.
HS 622 obsidian bladelet segment and obsidian flake

Unit 30 1975 +0.92–0.55 m, E balk, surface with fill from TR T 1962, intrusive in Level A. PW: 2 body fragments; 1 spirally grooved body fragment. Tile fragments: 7 L pan.

Unit 31 +0.70–0.27 m, N three-fourths trench = TR T fill, intrusive in Level A. Corinthian: 1 kotyle rim fragment; BG: 1 skyphos rim, 2 body fragments; PW: small jug rim, 12 body fragments; 2 spirally grooved body fragments. Tile fragments: 1 C body, 2 L cover, 50 L pan edge, 155 L pan body.
HP 2579 BG stemless-cup base, mid-4th

Unit 32 +0.79–0.50 m, S one-fourth trench, tile layer, Level A. PW: 1 bowl rim, 1 small dish rim, 1 jug base, 3 body fragments; CW: 1 body fragment; a coarse-ware basin fragment; 1 spirally grooved body fragment. Tile fragments: 1 L pan edge, 17 L pan body.

Unit 33 +0.40–0.07 m, N three-fourths trench, Level A. Tile fragments: ca. 30 L pan, 1 C cover, 1 C pan.

Unit 34 +0.67–0.15 m, S one-fourth trench, Level A. BG: oinochoe fragments, 1 kantharos foot, 3 skyphos bases, 1 stemless cup foot, 3 bolsal fragments, stamped bowl base, small bowl rim, ca. 30 body fragments; CW: lekane rim; PW: 6 jug rims, 1 amphora base, ca. 40 body fragments. Tile fragments: ca. 120 L pan, 5 L cover, 3 C pan; iron lump; shells: 1 cerastoderma, 4 cerithium.
193 Apollo l. at 125.6/369.1, +38 m
Iron lump, 337 g

Unit 35 +0.31–0.15 m, pebble layer, Level A. BG: 2 body fragments; PW: 12 body fragments. Tile fragments: 6 L pan.

TR 130/375 1975 E and N sides of trench are 5 m long with the property line preventing excavation across the SW side of the square. The NE corner of the trench overlaps a triangular area of the NECP of about 4.2 m square including the width of the NECP foundation walls. The rest of the trench is an irregular pentagonal shape of about 11 m square. Sherds join units 2 and 4, units 3 and 6, units 6 and 7, and units 7 and 8.

Unit 1 +0.95–0.55 m, surface and fill in TR T, above and intrusive in Level A. BG: 1 bowl rim, 1 skyphos(?) handle, ca. 10 body fragments; CW: 2 body fragments; PW: 2 amphora rims, ca. 50 body fragments; 5 spirally grooved body fragments. Tile fragments: ca. 100 L pan, 5 L cover, 2 C pan; 4 fragments worked shelly limestone; 2 cerithium shells.
HS 566 grinder fragment

Unit 2 +0.80–0.45 m, S corner of TR, Level A. Tile fragments: 25 L pan.

Unit 3 +0.63–0.35 m, NW corner of TR, Level A. Corinthian: 1 body fragment; BG: 1 skyphos rim; PW: 1 amphora handle, 1 body fragment. Tile fragments: 5 L pan; 1 spondylus shell.

Unit 4 +0.79–0.35 m, SE corner of TR, Level A. Corinthian: 6 body fragments; BG: 1 kantharos rim, 1 skyphos rim, 1 mug rim, 1 cup foot, 1 stamped bowl base, 2 stemless cup feet, 1 lid(?) rim, ca. 20 body fragments; CW: 12 lopas handles, 9 body fragments; PW: 2 amphora handles and foot, 1 jug base, ca. 12 body fragments. Tile fragments: ca. 60 L pan and 1 L cover; 1 cerastoderma shell.
Bronze fragment, 0.21 g

Unit 5 +0.55–0.29 m inside NECP, on or below floor, Level A. Corinthian: 1 miniature kotyle; BG: 2 bowl rims, 7 body fragments; PW: 4 body fragments. Tile fragments: 5 L pan, 1 C pan; 2 cerastoderma and 1 murex shell fragments; flint chips, 1 shelly limestone fragment.
59–62
HL 305 BG lamp fragment, late 5th?
HM 1194, bronze fragments, 2.30 g

Unit 6 +0.35–0.04 m 1 by 2 m test outside SW foundation of NECP, Level A or A/B. Corinthian: 1 kotyle base, 8 body fragments; BG: 1 bowl rim, 5 skyphos rims, 1 mug base, ca. 20 body fragments; CW: 1 lopas rim, 14 body fragments; PW: 1 jug base, 25 body fragments. Tile fragments: 23 L pan; iron

nail fragment; 2 pinna nobilis fragments, 1 cerithium shell; 11 small shelly limestone fragments.
HL 307 BG lamp fragment
Iron nail shaft, 18.23 g

Unit 7 +0.06 to -0.10 m, Level A/B or B. Corinthian: miniature kotyle rim, ca. 10 body fragments, BG: 1 skyphos rim, 1 cup-skyphos rim, 6 body fragments; CW: 3 body fragments; PW: lekane(?) rim, 13 body fragments. Flint chips; 3 cerastoderma shells, 2 cerithium, 3 pinna nobilis, 1 murex fragment.
HM 1193 bronze fibula fragment, 2.84 g
Lead sheet, 8.44 g

Unit 8 -0.06–0.10 m, Level B/C and earlier, pebble layer upper part. Corinthian: krater rim, aryballos rim, 2 kotyle bases, 1 miniature kotyle base, 6 body fragments; BG: trefoil-mouthed oinochoe rim, 1 bowl base, 1 skyphos foot, 11 body fragments; PW: 1 jug rim, 6 body fragments; 1 blister-ware(?) fragment, 2 Neolithic(?) body fragments.

Unit 9 -0.34–0.55 m, Level C pebble layer lower part. Tile fragments: 2 C pan.

Unit 10 1976 +0.344 to -0.42 m, scarp cleaning, few sherds and tiles, Levels A through C. Corinthian: 2 body fragments; 1 blister-ware strap handle; BG: jug shoulder fragment, skyphos handle, stemless cup handle, 11 body fragments; CW: 7 body fragments; PW: ca. 40 body fragments. Tile fragments: 3 L pan; shells: 2 murex, 1 pinna nobilis, 3 cockle fragments.
HM 913 lead strip or ingot, 8.9 g
Lead sheet remains from object having been cut out, 15.9 g

Unit 11 -0.38–0.49 m, cleaning accumulation washed in over the winter and leveling to pebble floor over half of trench, Level C/D. BG: 3 body fragments; PW: 9 body fragments. Tile fragments: 2 L pan; shell fragments: 3 murex, 1 pinna nobilis.

TR 135/370 1972 SW of the NECP, including the beginning of the narrow passage along its NW side with parts of the rooms? bordering the other side of that passage (only in the NW corner of the trench), and over the SW corner of the NECP, a 4 x 5 m trench including the E balk with a total area of 20 m square, most all of which is in the open area SW of the NECP. The wall fragments in the N part of the trench suggest in plan, Fig. 27 below, that this might be a prothyron providing entrance to a house to the NW of the trench, units 6–7, 12–13, and 18 recorded this area (for the Halieis type of prothyron see Ault 2005, 59–60). The dark brown soil without the presence of charcoal or burning suggested to the excavator that the finds from unit 7 might be a kitchen area or now following Ault's

study (2005, 63–65) perhaps part of a kopron. But without more excavation, possible prothyron, kitchen, or kopron remains a conjecture. Whatever these wall fragments formed, they were not enclosed inside a house but were open to the area southwest of the NECP. TR NB 135/370, p. 59: "Since the excavation of trench began as season drawing to a close, we were unable to excavate fully. The small finds and the pottery in particular have not as yet been subjected to final analysis." The find notebook for this trench only records 1972 units 1–2 and 1975 units 22–23. The finds from the other 1972 units may still be awaiting analysis stored in the Porto Kheli apotheke or they may have been lost after the end of the 1972 excavation season. Sherds join units 10 and 11, 22, and 23.

Unit 1 +0.73–0.55 m, 4 x 4 trench surface, above Level A. BG: 1 skyphos rim; PW: 28 body fragments; spirally grooved: 2 rims, 2 body fragments. Tile fragments: 200 L pan, 10 L cover, 3 C body, 1 C cover.
HS 620 grinder(?)

Unit 2 +0.53–0.46 m, TR T fill in NW corner down to plaster paving found in 1962, intrusion in Level A. Corinthian: 1 body fragment; BG: 1 ribbed oinochoe body fragment, 4 body fragments; CW: 6 body fragments; PW: 17 body fragments. Tile fragments: 17.
HC 477 roof tile

Unit 3 +0.60–0.38 m, E side of trench, Level A. Red painted plaster and tile fragments.

Unit 4 +0.53–0.42 m, W side of TR excluding TR T fill in SW corner, Level A.
HP 1273 stamped amphora handle

Unit 5 +0.49–0.25 m, Level A. Four red painted plaster fragments, tile fragments.
261 Apollo r.

Unit 6 +0.32–0.20 m, NE corner, Level A. BG: skyphos rim, ca. 10 body fragments; CW: 4 rims, ca. 100 body fragments.
238 Apollo r.
HP 1301 BG bowl. Early 4th
HP 1410 BG ribbed amphoriskos
HL 152 Attic BG lamp fragment, ca. 480

Unit 7 +0.34–0.31 m, N part of trench, Level A.
HL 161 Argive(?) BG lamp rim, late 5th/early 4th
HL 162 Corinthian(?) lamp fragment, late 5th/
    early 4th

Unit 8 +0.41–0.40 m, fill in TR T in SW corner, intrusion in Level A. PW: 5 body fragments. Four tile fragments.

Unit 9 +0.26–0.16 m, N part of trench, Level A. Four tile fragments.
HP 1302 lekane fragments. Late 5th
HP 1412 BG bolsal
HL 191 BG lamp fragments

Unit 10 +0.30–0.16 m, Level A. A few tile fragments.
HP 1419 (joins with Unit 11) BG cup-kantharos
HS 636 obsidian flake

Unit 11 +0.30–0.17 m, S side TR T fill intrusion in Level A.

Unit 12 +0.10–0.06 m, NW corner of trench, Level A or A/B.
HL 150 Argive(?) BG lamp fragment, late 5th/
    early 4th

Unit 13 +0.11–0.02 m, N central part of trench, Level A or A/B.
HP 1268 BG salt cellar, ca. 480
HL 185 Corinthian BG lamp rim, mid- to late 5th
HM 856 iron nail fragments, 20.45 g

Unit 14 +0.13 to -0.01 m, SW part of trench to clay floor in S central part of trench, Level A or A/B.
HL 163 Attic BG lamp fragment, 350 into early 3d

Unit 15 +0.11–0.03 m, triangle in N central TR Level A or A/B.

Unit 16 +0.04 to -0.03 m, NW corner of trench, Level A/B.

Unit 17 +0.03 to -0.16 m, SW part of trench, to white earth floor, Level A/B or B.
HP 1411 BF cup-skyphos
HM 925 iron lump, 99 g

Unit 18 +0.04 to -0.15 m, NW corner of trench, Level A/B or B.
HP 1421 BG stemless-cup fragment

Unit 19 -0.07–0.16 m, SW part of trench, below white earth floor, Level B.
HP 1413 BF cup-skyphos
HS 633 obsidian bladelet proximal end

Unit 20 -0.19–0.33 m, W half of trench, Level B/C or C.
HP 1422 BF body fragment
HP 1423 Late Geometric krater fragment
HL 192 Corinthian(?) lamp fragment, late 7th to
    mid-6th

Unit 21 -0.29–0.69 m, W half of trench to pebble paving, Level C or C/D.
HP 1303 Corinthian(?) Geometric krater fragment
HP 1304 Geometric krater rim

HP 1305 small Geometric krater rim
HP 1306 Geometric body fragment

Unit 22 1975 +0.72–0.37 m, E balk with SW corner of NECP, above Level A. Corinthian: small jug(?) base; BG: stamped oinochoe body fragment; PW: amphora handle, 32 body fragments; 1 spirally grooved body fragment. Tile fragments: ca. 200 L pan, 3 C pan and 1 C cover.

Unit 23 +0.44–0.18 m, fill in TR T over SW corner of NECP, intrusive in Level A. BG: 1 oinochoe rim, foot, and body fragments, 1 bowl rim, lattice-based skyphos body fragments, 1 bolsal body fragment, 2 cup-skyphos bases; CW: 1 chytra rim; PW: 1 amphora rim, 1 jug rim; 1 spirally grooved body fragment. Tile fragments: ca. 230 L pan and 3 C pan; shells: 2 cerithium, 2 pinna nobilis fragments.
HL 322 BG lamp fragment, mid-4th into early 3d?
Iron nail shaft, 5.94 g

TR 135/375 a 5 by 5 m trench dug in 1972 as a 4 by 4 m with the N and E balks excavated in 1975 and 1976. About 1 m square triangular area of the trench at the SW corner is outside of the NECP foundation walls with the total area of the NECP in the trench of about 24 m square. Sherds join units 6 and 9, 20 and 21, units 23 and 24, and units 20, 22, and 23.

Unit 1 +0.79–0.60 m, surface, above Level A. Spirally grooved body fragments, worn tile fragments, 1 BG body fragment.

Unit 2 +0.67–0.52 m, above Level A. Spirally grooved fragments, large tile fragments, 1 BG rim fragment.
HS 549 whetstone(?)

Unit 3 +0.65–0.58 m, 1962 TR T over SW corner defined, intrusion in Level A. BG: 3 body fragments; one glass fragment; tile fragments.
HS 381 Doric capital of shelly limestone, upper
    portions

Unit 4 +0.60–0.38 m, intrusion in Level A, clearing fill in TR T. 4 BG including lamp spout, amphora handle, and tiles.
HM 818 bronze rooster, 25.02 g, in SW scarp of TR T
    not in fill from 1962 (Pl. 21f)

Unit 5 +0.61–0.40 m, Level A, SE half of the triangle outside NECP. BG: 1 bowl rim, 2 skyphos bases, 6 body fragments; PW: 4 body fragments. Many tile and CW fragments.
HP 1211 BG kantharos, Type D, mid-5th

Unit 6 +0.47–0.31 m, Level A, floor of 1975 fire pit. Corinthian: 1 kotyle base, 1 body fragment; BG: 2

cup-skyphos handles; ca. 30 body fragments; CW: 3 body fragments; PW: 1 krater(?) base, ca 35 body fragments; 1 coarse-ware handle and one shoulder fragment. Tile fragments: ca. 45 pan.
2–24, 63 extracted from HM 666
130 Corinth, at 130.85/373.89, +0.027 m
292 Apollo r. miss struck at 130.69/373.86, +0.34 m
315 Amphora/T tessera extracted from HM 666
HL 117 Argive BG lamp fragments, late 5th
HC 444 terracotta figurine head
HM 661 lead clamp with pottery remaining, 35 g
HM 666 130.6/375.10, +0.36, bronze scrap including needle fragment and nail shaft, 24.18 g after blanks, flans, and amphora/T tessera extracted. Same applies to Unit 9, HM 837 below (Pl. 21a–e).
HS 381 Doric capital of shelly limestone, above 68–69, Fig. 15.

Unit 7 +0.40–0.35 m, Level A, SE half of triangle outside NECP. Corinthian: 1 kotyle(?) body fragment; BG: 1 oinochoe handle, 1 cup rim, 1 cup-skyphos rim, 12 body fragments; CW: 2 body fragments; PW 5 body fragments. One lamp nozzle. Tile fragments: 4 pan.
HM 773 lead strip or ingot, 15.4 g

Unit 8 +0.61–0.28 m, Level A, NW half of triangle outside NECP. Corinthian: 5 body fragments; BG: 1 oinochoe(?) shoulder, 1 bowl rim, 1 skyphos rim, 1 stamped bolsal base, 1 cup-skyphos base, ca. 20 body fragments; CW: 8 body fragments; PW: 1 jug handle, 1 amphora(?) fragment, ca. 25 body fragments. Tile fragments: ca. 20.
HM 823 bronze fragment, 1.6 g

Unit 9 +0.31–0.23 m, Level A, inside NECP SE of rubble wall foundations, lower part of fire pit of 1975. Corinthian: 5 kotylae body fragments; BG: 1 oinochoe foot, 1 skyphos rim, 1 cup-skyphos rim, 1 small bowl base, ca. 15 body fragments; CW: ladle(?) handle, 1 lid knob, 1 lekanis rim, ca. 20 body fragments; PW: jug(?) 7 body fragments, ca. 15 body fragments.
25–27 extracted from HM 837
194 Apollo l. at 130.77/373.94, +0.18
258 Apollo r. at 131.02/372,31, +0.12
304 H in wreath at 130.8/374, +0.14
HL 126 BG lamp rim (joins HL 117, unit 6)
HC 400 terracotta pyramidal loom weight
HC 480 terracotta figurine, leg fragment
HM 837 130.56/373.51, +0.09, bronze scrap, 11.0 g

Unit 10 +0.11–0.08 m, Level A or A/B. Corinthian: 1 miniature kotyle handle, 1 kotyle(?) body fragment; BG: 1 oinochoe(?) body fragment, 1 jug(?) rim, 1 skyphos rim, 1 bowl rim, ca. 20 body fragments; CW: 5 body fragments; PW 1 amphora handle, 1 jug handle, ca. 25 body fragments. Tile fragments: ca. 50.

Unit 11 +0.24–0.14 m, Level A, NW of rubble foundations in the SW corner of NECP. Corinthian: 1 kotyle rim, 1 mug(?) handle; CW: 1 rim fragment, 16 body fragments; PW: 1 amphora rim, 1 basin rim, 35 body fragments. Tile fragments: ca. 40; some wall plaster.
HM 662 lead strip (clamp or ingot), 45.3 g

Unit 12 +0.13 to -0.19 m, Level A/B. Corinthian: 2–3 kotylai; BG: 1 jug rim, 1 bowl rim, 1 Type B skyphos base, 1 cup-skyphos rim, 1 small bowl rim, 3 plate bases, 1 saltcellar(?) base; CW: 1 rim fragment, 7 body fragments; PW: 1 jug(?) base, ca. 150 body fragments. Tile fragments: 24.
198 Apollo r.
290 Apollo r.
HP 1201 miniature kotyle
HP 1238 BG phiale fragment
HM 663 lead drip, 124.9 g
HM 664 iron nail and wood, 47.97 g
HM 665 lead fragments 673.1 g, also in unit 13
HM 667 bronze pin, 6.96 g
HM 668 bronze nail and lead fragment, 14.46 g
HM 774 lead fragments, 6.6 g
HM 775 lead strip or ingot, 9.5 g
HM 781 iron nail with traces of wood, 34.62 g
HM 800 bent iron strip, 8.27 g
HM 801 iron lump, 22.86 g
HM 813 bronze palmette ornament, 28.13 g (Pl. 21g)
HM 816 bronze swinging handle, 23.4 g (Pl. 21i)
HM 819 iron nail, 7.1 g
HM 826 bronze strainer fragments, 8.21 g (Pl. 21h)
HM 838 iron fragment, 21.9 g
HM 840 iron clamp?, 10 g
HM 841 iron strip, 39.65 g
HM 842 iron spike, 92 g
HM 844 iron nail, 7.87 g
HM 846 bronze fragments, mineralized and tiny, less than 0.0002 m maximum dimension, not weighed
HM 865 iron rod, 18.54 g
HM 877 iron nail, 29.19 g
HM 886 iron blade, 31.36 g
HM 889 bronze rod fragment, 6.36 g
HM 919 iron lid with lead ring, 132.0 g
HM 926 iron fragments, 20.0 g
HS 396 grinder

Unit 13 -0.17–0.26 m, Level A/B or B. BG: 1 cup rim, 1 oinochoe(?) neck, 6 body fragments; CW: 2 rim fragments, 13 body fragments; PW: 1 strap handle, 18 body fragments; 1 blister-ware neck fragment. Tile fragments: ca. 10; 3 shells.
HM 665 lead fragments, see unit 12
HM 669 bronze nail fragment, 13.7 g
HM 802 iron fragment, 2.5 g
HM 807 iron strip, 90 g

Unit 14 -0.23–0.48 m, Level B. BG: 1 krater(?) body fragments, 1 cup-skyphos rim; CW: 1 lid fragment, 13 body fragments; PW: 3 body fragments. Tile fragment, 7 shells.

Unit 15 -0.46–0.64 m, Level B/C, pebble layer. Ca. 10 body fragments of CW, PW, coarse ware, and 4 body fragments identified as Corinthian; 4 seashells. HS 628 obsidian bladelet segment

Unit 16 -057–0.73 m, Level C, below pebbles. No finds.

Unit 17 -0.71–0.85 m Level C, rubble and mud. No finds.

Unit 18 -0.83–1.24 m (drill holes -1.28, -1.34) Level C, both test trench and drill holes may have reached bed rock (or a lot of rubble). No finds.

Unit 19 1975 N and E balks of the trench +0.535–0.435 m, surface above Level A, TR T over SW wall of NECP fill removed. BG: 1 skyphos rim; PW: 1 amphora handle, 1 jug(?) handle, 29 body fragments; 3 spirally grooved body fragments. Tile fragments: 61 L pan.

Unit 20 +0.535–0.22 m adding NE corner 1 m triangle not excavated in 1972, Level A. Corinthian: 1 miniature oinochoe; BG: 1 cup-kantharos rim, 1 skyphos rim, 1 bowl rim, 1 bolsal base, ca. 10 body fragments; CW: 12 body fragments; PW: 2 handle fragments, 44 body fragments; 1 blister-ware body fragment. Tile fragments: 58 L pan; some shells, 1 animal bone fragment.
28, 64–67
HP 2499 Geometric bowl rim
HM 1152 bronze fragments, 2.48 g
Bronze sheet fragments, 1.63 g.

Unit 21 +0.29–0.17 m, Level A fire pit and mud brick over SE part of it. BG: 1 stamped knob, 1 body fragment; CW: 1 lopas handle; PW: 2 body fragments.Tile fragments: 3 L pan; shell fragments: 4 murex, 1 cerithium, 1 cerastoderma.
29–47, 68–75
274 Apollo r.
HM 1176 bronze fragments, 33.94 g
HM 1177 iron fragments, 40.96 g
HM 1178 bronze fragments, 56.74 g
HM 1179 iron fragments, 4.88 g
Bronze sheet, drips, and possible handle fragment, 11.91 g
Iron lump, 48.84 g
Iron fragment, flattened, 29.54 g

Unit 22 +0.23–0.02 m Level A lowest part of fire pit. CW: 1 body fragment; PW: 2 body fragments. Shell fragments: 2 murex, 1 cerithium.
48–50
HM 1182 bronze fragments, 13.95 g

Unit 23 +0.27–0.00 m, 1 x 1 m test in fire pit area. Level A or A/B. Corinthian: 1 bowl rim, 1 kotyle base, 10 body fragments; BG: 1 Attic stemless cup(?) body fragment, 15 body fragments; CW: 1 lopas handle, 27 body fragments. Tile fragments: 5 L pan; shell fragments: 7 cerastoderma, 4 cerithium, 26 murex.
51, 76
276 Apollo r.
HM 1191 bronze fragments, 11.2 g
HM 1192 bronze nail, 2.48 g

Unit 24 +0.05 to -0.13 m Level A or A/B. BG: 1 cup rim with carination, 1 skyphos rim, 11 body fragments; CW: 1 lid fragment, 12 body fragments. Tile fragments: 6 L pan.
HS 545 worked shale fragment

TR 135/380 1975 Restricted by property line to a triangular trench with the NW corner a right angle on the grid lines, the W side 5 m long and the N side 3.8 m long with a total area of about 9.65 m square. TR T between 1.5 to 2 m wide divided the trench in half from the NW corner to the SE including the central column base of the NECP. Sherds join units 1, 5, and 6; units 6 and 7; units 7 and 8, and units 8 and 9.

Unit 1 +0.76–0.37 m, surface and fill from TR T, above Level A. BG: 2 body fragments; CW: 1 body fragment; PW: 1 amphora handle and foot fragment, 38 body fragments; 1 spirally grooved body fragment. Tile fragments: 40 L pan, 12 L cover, 3 C pan; 1 cerastoderma shell fragment; flint flakes.

Unit 2 +0.53–0.37 m, Level A, portion SW of TR T, foundations of earlier wall begin to appear. Corinthian: 1 miniature kotyle base; BG: 1 oinochoe(?) neck and shoulder, 1 bowl rim, 1 skyphos(?) handle, 1 cup-skyphos rim, 8 body fragments; CW: 1 body fragment; PW: 10 body fragments. Tile fragments: 7 L pan, 1 L cover; 1 murex shell fragment, flint flakes.
52–56, 80–82
HM 1180 bronze fragments, 2.35 g
HM 1181 bronze fragments, 17.88 g
Bronze scrap, 1.46 g
HS 595 obsidian bladelet segments

Unit 3 +0.39–0.24 m, intrusion in Level A, pit NE of earlier wall. CW: 1 body fragment, PW: 4 body fragments; blister-ware body fragment. Lamp fragments(?). Tile fragments: 2 L pan; 2 murex shell fragments.
58

Unit 4 +0.49–0.22 m, Level A. Corinthian: 1 miniature kotyle handle; BG: 1 body fragment; CW: 1 lopas rim, 6 body fragments; PW: 2 body fragments. Tile fragments: 6 L pan. Flint and obsidian chips.
57
254, 282 Apollo r. both partially struck

Unit 5 +0.48–0.34 m, Level A, NE of TR T, tile layer: more than 300 L pan, 20 L cover, and 2 C pan = 44.8 kg.

Unit 6 +0.39–0.20 m, Level A, clearing to floor of fire pit of TR 135/375. Corinthian: 1 kotylai handle, 6 body fragments; BG: 1 lekythos rim, 1 small bowl rim, 1 cup-kantharos rim, 1 skyphos base with miltos, 13 handle fragments, some from stemless cups(?), ca. 50 body fragments; CW: 1 lopas rim, 1 bowl rim, 1 lid fragment, 7 body fragments; PW: 1 amphora rim, 1 plate base, 39 body fragments; 1 spirally grooved body fragment. Tile fragments: 54 L pan, 4 L cover, 1 C pan = 10.11 kg; murex, cerithium, and helix shells, herbivore tooth and animal bones, flint chips.
77–79
221 Apollo r.
HP 2974 RF krater fragment
HP 2975 BG bowl fragment. Mid-5th.

Unit 7 +0.28 to -0.16 m, Level A or A/B, test trench 1.5 by 1 m, parallel and SW of central column base of NECP. Corinthian: oinochoe(?) body fragments, ribbed mug(?) body fragments, 1 miniature kotyle; BG: krater(?) body fragments, 1 oinochoe neck, 2 bowl rims, 1 lekanis-pyxis rim, 1 lattice-based skyphos body fragment, 1 bolsal body fragment, 1 stemless cup base, 3 cup-skyphos bases; CW: 1 lid fragment, 1 chytra rim, ca. 10 body fragments; PW: 1 amphora rim, 2 jug bases, ca. 90 body fragments; 1 blister-ware oinochoe rim. Tile fragments: 91 L pan, 16 L cover, 1 C pan = 12.8 kg; shell fragments: 11 murex, 3 cerastoderma, 1 pinna nobilis; many limestone chips, flint chip, animal bone fragment.
HP 2645 RF skyphos rim
HL 306 BG lamp fragment

Unit 8 -0.08–0.30 m, Level A/B stone packing of mostly poros with some shelly limestone and conglomerate. BG: 8 body fragments; CW: 3 body fragments; PW: 1 jug(?) handle, 8 body fragments. Tile fragments: 13 L pan, 1 L cover.

Unit 9 -0.22–0.32 m, Level A/B or B, trench stopped arbitrarily. Corinthian: 1 small jug(?) base; BG: krater rim, 1 skyphos rim, 1 cup-skyphos rim, ca. 40 body fragments; CW: 5 body fragments; PW: 1 amphora(?) neck, louterion rim, 5 body fragments. Tile fragments: 5 L pan; shell fragments: 1 cerastoderma, 5 murex, 1 pinna nobilis; bird(?) bone.

Units 10–12 1976 continuing below unit 9, TR notebook record missing with unit 12 mentioned in unit 13, but the TR notebook pages are numbered sequentially without units 10–12 being included, at least one if not more of the missing units would be for scarp cleaning and/or clearing out the silt and accumulation washed into the test TR over the winter between the two summer seasons. Yet the much lower elevation of unit 12 from that of unit 9 suggests about 0.2 m of excavation occurred in at least one unit (or more) as well. The find notebook for this TR provides the records summarized below:

Unit 10 Surface. CW: 1 lopas rim; ca. 10 body fragments of BG and PW; 1 coarse-ware body fragment, 1 cerastoderma shell.

Unit 11 Level A/B or B? Corinthian: 2 kotyle rims; BG: 1 krater handle, 1 oinochoe(?) handle, 1 molded plate(?) rim, 1 cup rim, 1 skyphos rim, 1 mug(?) rim, ca. 45 body fragments; CW: 1 lopas rim, 1 chytra rim; PW: 1 amphora rim, jug rim, 1 handle from krater or bowl, ca. 50 body fragments; 2 blister-ware body fragments. Tile fragments: 70 L pan(?); 1 bronze fragment; 1 flint chip; 1 bag animal bones; 1 bag land and sea shells.
HP 2994 RF closed shape fragment
HC 894 BG roof tile with graffito

Unit 12 Level A/B or B? Corinthian: 1 kotyle handle, 1 jug(?) base, ca. 10 body fragments; BG: krater (?) 5 body fragments, 1 cup rim, 1 large skyphos lower body, 1 Corinthian-type skyphos rim, 1 one-handler rim, 1 bolsal rim,1 cup-skyphos handle, 1 mug(?) base, ca. 50 body fragments; CW: shallow tray with flat rim, 2 chytras rims; PW: 1 lekane rim, ca. 100 body fragments; coarse-ware basin rim. Tile fragments: ca. 50 L pan(?); 1 bag animal bones, 1 bag shells.

Unit 13 -0.569–0.785 m, Level B or B/C, limestone and conglomerate pebbles. Corinthian: 1 pyxis(?) rim, 2 kotyle rims, 1 miniature kotyle rim, ca. 10 body fragments; BG: 1 krater rim, 1 large bowl rim, 1 trefoil-mouthed oinochoe rim, 1 small bowl base, 1 cup rim, 1 Corinthian-type skyphos rim, 1 one-handler rim, 1 stemed dish with concave wall body fragment, ca. 60 body fragments; PW: 1 lid rim, 1 amphora rim, 1 small amphora rim, 3 lekane rims, 1 tub rim. Tile fragments: 14 L pan; 1 bag animal bones, 1 bag cerastoderma and murex shells.

Unit 14 -0.739–0.821 m, Level C. Corinthian: 1 bowl rim, 1 jug(?) neck, 1 kotyle rim, 1 miniature kotyle rim, ca. 40 body fragments; BG: 1 trefoil-mouthed oinochoe rim, 1 jug rim, 1 krater handle, 1 cup rim, 1 skyphos foot, ca. 20 body fragments; CW: 1 griddle rim fragment, 1 lopas handle, 16 body fragments;

PW: 1 amphora handle, 1 lid rim, ca. 40 body fragments; 7 blister-ware body fragments. Tile fragments: one-fourth small box L pan(?); one bag animal bones, one bag cerastoderma and monodonta shells, some hellicella cernuella.

Unit 15 -0.798–1.009 m, Level C. Corinthian: 1 bowl(?) rim, 3 kotyle rims, 2 miniature kotyle rims; BG: 1 krater rim, 1 bowl foot, 1 oinochoe(?) foot, 2 bolsal rims; CW: 1 lopas rim, 1 chytra handle, ca. 20 body fragments; PW: 1 amphora rim, ca. 50 body fragments; 2 blister-ware body fragments. Tile fragments: 1 small box L pan, 10 L pan edges, 1 L pan corner, 2 L cover, 21 C cover; 1 bag animal bones, 1 bag shells.
HP 3016 Corinthian oinochoe(?) fragment
HM 1498 cast bronze arrowhead, 1.4 g
HS 619 spherical grinder

Unit 16 -0.966–1.099 m, Level C. Corinthian: pyxis(?) and lid rim, 2 kotyle rims and 2 torus feet; BG: 1 krater(?) handle, 2 skyphos rims, 1 cup(?) foot, 1 mug rim, 1 plate rim, ca. 50 body fragments; CW: 3 body fragments; PW: 1 small bag body fragments. Tile fragments: 47 L pan, 3 C pan(?); 1 animal tooth, shell fragments: 3 cerithium, 8 murex.
HP 3030 BG open vessel fragment
HM 1499 cast bronze arrowhead, 1.3 g

Unit 17 -1.028–1.192 m, Level C. Corinthian: 1 small bowl(?) rim, 1 skyphos rim, 3 kotyle rims, 1 miniature kotyle base, ca. 10 body fragments; BG: 1 jug rim, 1 lekythos(?) rim, 1 krater rim, 1 bowl rim, 1 cup stem, 3 skyphos rims, ca. 70 body fragments; CW: chytra handle, ca. 10 body fragments; PW: 1 jug rim, 1 bag body fragments; 1 spirally grooved body fragment.[66] Tile fragments: 49 L pan; 4 animal bones; marine shells: cerastoderma, cerethium, monodonta, pinna nobilis; terrestrial: hellicella cernuella.

Unit 18 -1.115–1.208 m, Level C/D. Corinthian: 1 amphora(?) handle, 1 pyxis(?) handle/body fragment, 1 ray-based kotyle, 2 kotyle feet, ca. 10 body fragments; BG: 1 jug(?) rim, 2 bowl rims, 1 phiale(?) rim, 1 cup rim, 1 kantharos rim, 1 skyphos rim, 1 bolsal rim, ca. 30 body fragments; CW: 2 chytra rims, 5 body fragments; PW: 1 amphora/jug handle, 41 body fragments; 1 coarse-ware pithos rim. Terracotta figurine(?) fragment. Tile fragments: 26 L pan; 3 animal bones, 1 cerithium shell.

---

[66] The elevations and the consistency of the other finds suggest that this single sherd was not deposited in antiquity but fell into the trench during excavation or was mixed into the finds during washing or sorting.

– CHAPTER NINE –

The Coins: Provenances

JAMES A. DENGATE

Because the Northeast Command Post was attached to the fortification walls and contained the mint, the evidence for the minting activities at Halieis is included in this volume as Chapter 8. Rather than consider the mint coins in isolation, it seemed most useful to publish the entire collection here so that the local coins could be placed in the context of all other mints represented at the site.

The original plan for the Halieis final publications was to have separate volumes for the upper town and sanctuary of Apollo, followed by a series of volumes for the lower town, including the fortifications, houses, and other finds. The coins from each area were to be published with each separate report. Later, with the discovery of the mint, combining the lower and upper town coins into one volume seemed the simplest way to publish the excavation coins. As originally planned, the first volume of the Halieis excavation series was to be the acropolis and Industrial Terrace, the first areas of the site to be extensively explored. It was to include the history of the polis and of the excavations, written by Michael H. Jameson. The unexpected death of Jameson forced a change in this sequence.[1] It was decided that the fortifications and the houses would become the first two volumes. This meant that the coins would appear before Jameson's history of the site. But any detailed discussion of the Halieis excavation coins is dependent on the history of the polis in which they circulated. While completing this chapter, I realized that I was incorporating many historical issues I had discussed with Jameson. In fact, adding the necessary historical context meant that I was presenting fragments of his views prior to their presentation as a whole in the upper town volume.

Consequently, I am publishing the 262 excavation coins in two parts. The first part, presented here, combines brief identifications and dates with detailed provenances. I decided that further documentation required a full treatment that could not be done without reference to Jameson's historical discussion.[2] Therefore, the second part will contain complete documentation for the identifications and dating in a chapter following the history of the polis (Jameson n.d., chapter 1 and Dengate n.d., chapter 5). Also in the second part, numismatic issues and groups/ hoards of coins will be considered. The circulation of coins in the polis, beyond that discussed already in Chapter 8, will appear in the second part because of its interconnection with the history. This includes, most obviously, the end of the polis at Halieis for which the excavation coins are primary witnesses. While circumstances necessitated this two part publication of the coins, it resolves a problem always inherent in the study of excavation coins—how to publish both their contexts and the scholarly apparatus of their documentation and interpretation.[3] The provenances of the Halieis excavation coins are given a coherent presentation here to be followed by their numismatic and historical significance in the second part.

It is almost a century since coins were first attributed to Halieis. I. N. Svoronos (1907), after cataloging the specimens known at that time and collecting all of the ancient references, suggested this city as the mint for the bronzes with head of Herakles or Apollo on the obverse and a palm tree

---

[1] Jameson had completed drafts of his chapters but they had not yet been incorporated into the volume as a whole.
[2] Because of their quantity, the coins minted at Halieis are treated more fully, with references to the works of Svoronos provided here.

[3] Walker (1997, 17–26) considers general problems with the identification and significance of excavation coins based on those discovered in the Athenian Agora.

on the reverse with the Tirynthian ethnic in part or in full.[4] He reasoned that they were produced by the descendants of the refugees from the destruction of Tiryns who settled at Halieis, according to Herodotus (6.86 and 7.137) and other sources. Svoronos's evidence, in addition to ancient literature, was the "Kranidhi Hoard," the only hoard then known to have contained Tirynthian coins. The hoard is listed in Thompson, Møkholm, and Kraay (1973, 92, no. 87) and will be discussed in detail in the upper town volume.

The 121 Herakles and Apollo head Tirnythian coins from the Halieis excavations clearly confirm Svoronos's identification of the site as the place settled by the expelled Tirythians.[5] These coins are cataloged below followed by 23 examples of other types from the excavations, also clearly minted at Halieis judging from the quantities found and their rarity elsewhere.[6] These 144 examples minted at Halieis and 102 from other mints make a total of 246 coins produced when the Halieis polis existed. Thus, local coins comprise 58.5 percent of the excavation coins and foreign coins comprise 41.5 percent, or almost a 6 to 4 ratio of local to foreign coins. These totals exclude the sixteen coins in the catalog from Roman times and later that were lost at the site long after Halieis had ceased to be a polis (see Chapter 7 above and Rudolph 1979 for the Halieis Late Roman/Early Byzantine occupation).

The Excavation Areas

The coins fall into three groups, according to their find spots: (1) the acropolis and Industrial Terrace; (2) the lower town[7] and other nearby sites excavated on land;[8] and (3) the sanctuary of Apollo, now submerged in the harbor of Porto Kheli, about a half kilometer northeast of the lower town.[9] Because each of these areas was excavated separately and at different times, several systems of location are involved.

The acropolis coins are located by Roman numerals, each representing a layer of habitation debris (Deposits I–VII), and letters, representing an area on the acropolis. To these are added additional numbers and letters representing subdivisions, when these are required. (A detailed deposit list with subdivisions and all inventoried finds listed by deposit and area will appear in the acropolis volume.[10]) Table 7 presents the acropolis chronology, which is based on architectural phases and the deposits of artifacts associated with each phase. The table includes approximate chronological parallels with the lower town.[11] Figure 42 shows the find spots of coins from the western side of the acropolis.[12] Coins from the eastern side may be located using the architectural features in Figure 21.[13]

The Industrial Terrace coins are located by the architectural unit and room letter

---

[4] Svoronos (1907) also attributed some silver issues to Halieis. These will be discussed in the second part of the publication of the excavation coins.

[5] See Jameson et al. 1994, 75, 77, and 83 and Jameson n.d., chapter 1 with the ancient testimonia.

[6] These include the Amphora/T types, **305–17**. One example, which Svoronos (1898, 54 no. 11, 93–97, pl. E' 11) had earlier classified as an Athenian token, was formerly in the Six Collection and is now in the Hague royal coin collection (I am grateful to J. P. Guépin for providing a cast). Svoronos (1926, pl. 102, 2) also published an example that he recorded as from the Athens Collection. Dr. Mando Oikonomidou kindly made an exhaustive search of the Athens numismatic collection and could not find the piece. A close comparison of the two plates reveals a chip in the lower left edge of each example. The apparent difference in the size of the two tokens is owing, no doubt, to the printing of the two plates. Svoronos probably published a photograph of a cast of the Six Collection piece that he had in Athens. The six new examples from the excavations and the seven tesserae of similar types confirm their minting at Halieis, not Athens. All the coin examples are overstruck with the undertype Herakles/Palm of Tiryns (where it can be read). The helmeted head/H coins (Pl. 24), **295–304**, have not previously been published as far as I know. Further details and documentation will appear in the second part of this report.

[7] This has two areas defined by their elevations: the larger area is nearer sea level and the smaller is on the terraces between the

acropolis/Industrial Terrace and lower town, that is the parts excavated as Areas 2 and 3.

[8] These are the Lorenzo kiln (Jameson et al. 1994, 527, site A18) and the Koukouras sanctuary (ibid, 426, site A24 with an additional Roman coin found in the site survey).

[9] The coins from the sanctuary of Apollo will be published in Jameson et al., *The Sanctuary of Apollo,* The Excavations at Ancient Halieis, 4 (Bloomington: Indiana University Press, forthcoming). Treating these coins separately is appropriate because they were found outside the city proper and are also substantially different from the rest of the Halieis excavation coins, essentially constituting a hoard of early Aiginetan silver. See Thompson, Mørkholm, and Kraay (1973, 35, no. 36).

[10] Dengate, n.d. chapter 11.

[11] The lower town levels, in parentheses, indicate a rough chronological relationship with the acropolis deposits. The amount of time between the lower town levels and the deposit dates for the acropolis has not yet been determined and is unlikely to be simultaneous.

[12] This figure was prepared in 1966 by Marian H. McAllister. It locates the acropolis west excavation trenches and identifies the coins by HN numbers, for which see Appendix D.

[13] From north to south these are the altar and monument bases, Building A, Building B (or barracks), with its rooms numbered 1–3 from east to west, the square tower overlapping room 1, and Tower **6** with two access stairways between it and Building B.

Table 7. Acropolis Chronology

DATE/HISTORY	ARCHITECTURE	POTTERY/OTHER FINDS
before ca. 700/650 (lower town [Level E?])		{Deposit I, prehistoric: Pullen 2000 PG and G pots, no architecture}
before ca. 600/590 (lower town Level D)	Phases 1, 2, and 3	
ca. 600/590 (lower town Level C)	Phases 1, 2, and 3 destroyed	Deposit II in pottery
after ca. 590 (lower town Level C)	acropolis unprotected? {first known phase of shrine but no architecture and location unsure}	{Deposit III in pottery Lakonian III, after ca. 580 to end of 5th?}
before ca. 460/50 (lower town Level C)	Phase 4 cellular wall and berm, mud-brick wall under square tower	
ca. 460/50 Athenian attack (lower town Level C)		Deposit IV, graffiti
ca. 420 Athenian garrison	white lime floor (could be earlier)	
Spartan hegemony		
ca. 400±10 (lower town Level B, early)	Phase 5 square tower, shrine relocated, first mess, and terrace wall with fill behind it	Deposit V, four coins of Tiryns: Herakles and Amphora/T
Theban hegemony, post Leuktra		
(lower town Level B, late)	Phase 6 Tower 6, barracks, mess continues	
before ca. 300±10 (lower town Level A)	Phase 7 fortification walls thickened	
ca, 300±10 (lower town Level A)	destruction and abandonment	Deposit VI, coins later than pottery
(lower town Late Roman/ Early Byzantine ca. 4th/5th–early 7th)	Post-destruction, Building A	Deposit VII, spirally grooved sherds

Note: Phases are numbered by each change in the fortifications. Braces { } enclose disturbed phases or deposits for which the evidence was recovered within later deposits. For lower town levels, see Boyd and Rudolph 1978, 334–35; Rudolph 1984, 123–70.

designations.[14] The units (Western, Central, and Eastern) correspond to three discrete architectural complexes on the terrace (Jameson 1969, 322, fig. 4). Rooms within each unit are designated by a letter and the contexts are named alpha for the floor level, beta for the fill above the floor, and gamma for the surface level throughout the Industrial Terrace.

The coins from the lower town were recorded under three different excavation systems, described above, 3.[15] In the exploratory season of 1962 when John H. Young was field director, each trench and excavation record notebook was named. The acropolis was an obvious landmark and became the name for the notebook written by Charles K. Williams, II (now NB 5). The other three trenches were named after trench masters: The northeast side of the lower town excavated by Thomas W. Jacobsen became Trench Tom later abbreviated "T." The northwest side excavated by Michael Cheilik became Trench Mike, later abbreviated "M." The second terrace to the northeast of the acropolis excavated by Michael H. Jameson became Area Karolos or Trench Charles, later abbreviated "C," since Mike had already been used; this trench was again later renamed, first the Dye Works, and second, the Industrial Terrace. In 1962, records were kept by trench name with notebook numbers only being assigned in 1965 when Charles K. Williams, II, was the field director at the same time the coins were recataloged from HM metal objects to HN coins.

The 1965 and 1966 work continued the notebook numbers and concentrated on land purchased in the upper town. In 1967–69 when Thomas W. Jacobsen was field director the land excavations were on the northeast side of the lower town. Trenches were assigned letters of the alphabet from A and the trench notebooks were later numbered starting at 500. In 1970 when Wolf Rudolph began as field director letters continued to be used to name trenches but the notebooks started at 100. Thus the letters C, M, and T were again used to name trenches. Care must be taken to distinguish these later trenches from those of the same letter designation excavated in 1962.[16] Other 1970 trenches used an alphanumeric grid (above, 3).

In 1972, and thereafter, each lower town trench was confined to a five-meter square and named according to the grid numbers of the northeast corner.[17] Thus, each coin has a trench number to locate it within the lower town grid. It also has a unit number that provides the vertical level and the location of the earth cleared in each trench.[18] Although these numbers locate the coins precisely in each excavation trench, the actual locations of the trenches within the site are not clear to those unfamiliar with the Halieis grid system. Therefore, I have added to the catalog entries the excavation areas, using those designated by Rudolph (1979, fig. 1).[19]

On the key plan of the site (Fig. 19) and the actual state plan (Fig. 18) Area 1 includes Tower **10** (East Tower) and the East Gate. Area 2 comprises the excavated part of the chambered curtain or barracks in the southeast wall including Tower **8** and parts of buildings nearby. Area 3 is

---

[14] These locations are taken from a draft prepared by Michael H. Jameson before his death. He had planned to make final adjustments to them before publication; hence, some slight changes may appear in the final publication of the Industrial Terrace (Jameson n.d. chapter 3).

[15] I was unable to see any coins recovered during the excavations in the lower town by the Greek Archaeological Service in 1979 in the small region called the "Ephoreia Field" adjacent to Street 5, see above 4 and Ault 2005, 21, n. 34.

[16] During this evolution, no more land excavations were conducted on the northwest side of the lower town. But the records and artifacts from this area had been consulted throughout this time. Thus, the records of the coins from the 1962 excavation of Trench M had been recorded as from NB 4. Meanwhile others had cited the same notebook as NB 2, thinking of Trench T as NB 1 only (even though two notebooks had been used in 1962) and the second area of the lower town tested in 1962 logically becomes NB 2. In part this is a result of not always having the original records at hand in Porto Kheli during excavations as the finds and records were stored in Nauplion. Later the lower town finds and records were returned to Porto Kheli where they are stored today while those from the upper town and sea are still stored in Nauplion in the Leonardo annex

to the archaeological museum. The Indiana University Archives then became the single place where the records from all areas of the excavations were brought together. Because of the number of citations of Trench M as NB 2 in the records, it seemed better to use that. Trench T then with two notebooks become NB 1.1 and NB 1.2. The NB 4 designation for Trench M is preserved in the records as the number assigned to this area of the site, Area 4. But there are some other early references to NB 4 in the excavation archives in addition to those for the coins that can possibly cause confusion. Fortunately there is normally enough redundancy in the records with the date 1962, or Trench Mike or M to prevent error.

[17] E.g., TR 135/375 (abbreviated by dropping the kilometer numbers from 7,135/16,375). See Fig. 18 and Ault 2005, 5–6. For the elevations see below, Cooper, Appendix C.

[18] See Ault (2005, 5) for the definition of a unit.

[19] In Rudolph 1973 the excavation areas were labeled by the field numbers assigned to the owners of each parcel. Area 1 includes the southern part of Field 27 and Area 7 the northern part of the same field. Area 5 is Field 10 and Area 6 is Field 24. Only Areas 6 and 7 were ultimately purchased and deeded to the Greek state for excavation and to be left as a permanent archaeological zone (as had happened earlier with the acropolis and Industrial Terrace).

the middle wall region around Tower **19**. Area 4 is the only excavation above modern sea level on the western side of the polis, between Streets c and d and Towers **15** and **16**. It includes an almost complete house in Trench M of 1962 reported in Jameson 1963 and Young 1963 (with a plan). Area 5 (Field 10) runs inland along the modern shore between Towers **11** and **15**. This large area was tested by a series of independent trenches in 1972 (Rudolph 1973). Area 6 from the north includes the Northeast Command Post with House B and environs partially excavated as 1962 Trench T, and Field 24 south through Avenue C crossing both Streets 3 and 4. Area 7 includes Tower **9**, the Southeast Gate, House 7 and parts of other houses near the intersection of Avenue C and Street 1.

Thanks to Bradley A. Ault's work, some of the lower town coins can be placed more tangibly within the life of the polis. Ault (2005) describes assemblages of artifacts dating to the final occupation (Levels A and A/B) in five of the most complete houses excavated at Halieis. His analysis helps to recreate the activities within each household and connects the coins to the lives of the inhabitants. If a coin can be associated with a particular room in one of the five houses, I have included this information. In addition, for coins found in Areas 6 or 7 but not clearly from a house, I refer to the appropriate figure in Ault 2005 in order to illustrate the coin find spot.

The levels established for the lower town (Levels A, B, and so forth) are based on the study of the artifacts from the units excavated in the various trenches. Ault presents the data for the identification of levels in the houses he has analyzed.[20] The rest of the lower town coins have been assigned to levels according to descriptions in the trench and find notebooks.[21] Most of the coins are from Level A or A/B, the latest habitation levels, or the surface. In this they correspond to most of the acropolis coins, which are from Deposits VI or VII, and to all of the Industrial Terrace coins.

The following catalog comprises 262 items (in addition to the mint debris in Chapter 8) recorded from 1962 through the 1983 season.[22] Of these 246 likely were deposited at the time of the Halieis polis. The excavations on the acropolis and Industrial Terrace produced 60 Greek coins and tesserae.[23] In addition, 184 Greek coins and tesserae were found in the lower town and 2 in the environs of Halieis.[24] Estimating from the actual state plan of the site (Fig. 18), the area opened by excavations in the lower town roughly approaches about ten times that of the acropolis and Industrial Terrace combined. Clearly there were more coins lost or secreted (and recovered by excavations) on the Acropolis and Industrial Terrace than in the lower town.[25] Consequently the former likely had more coins in circulation than the latter. In addition there were 16 coins minted after the classical/early Hellenistic date of the majority from the time of the polis. Most of these are from the Late Roman/Early Byzantine occupation of the site, see the Roman Bath in Chapter 7 above.

---

[20] See Ault 2005, 82–92, Appendix 1, "Concordance by House of Loci, Rooms, Trenches, and Units Forming Level A–Level A/B Strata," and, 93–108, Appendix 2, "Inventoried Finds from Level A–Level A/B Strata by House and Locus, Houses 7, A, C, D, and E."

[21] I thank Bradley Ault for providing evidence for some of the coins from Areas 6 and 7. I analyzed the rest from the data available to me and am solely responsible for any mistakes. Most of the trenches not included in Ault 2005 Appendices 1 and 2 await detailed study so my interpretation of the level of the coins found there is preliminary.

[22] As mentioned above, the coins from the sanctuary of Apollo are not included here. In addition, some coins found in the environs of Halieis were included in the inventory system, that is, they were assigned HN numbers. But because they were not found as part of the actual Halieis excavation project, they do not appear in the catalog. See Appendix D. Therefore, the sequence of inventory numbers has a few gaps. These include coins from the Franchthi Cave (published in Dengate 1999), Mases, and Fournoi, (Jameson et al. 1994, 469, Mases temple, site C17; 512, Fourni well, site F27; and 426, Metochi, Site A23). The finds from the latter site were published in Rudolph, 1974.

There were no coins excavated from Metochi; Field 29, 1968 Trenches A, C, and D, Jacobsen 1969, 124–29; or the Halieis necropolis. The latter was excavated by Nicholas Verdelis in 1958 and Christina Dengate in 1966 (see C. Dengate 1976) and from 1974 by the Halieis excavation team (see Rafn 1991).

[23] Michael Jameson suggested I study the Halieis excavation coins; his encouragement during this undertaking has been of great help. The coins were described in a preliminary report for a paper of the American School of Classical Studies in Athens in 1966, during which time my work was supported by a Fulbright Fellowship. Additional research in Athens was supported by a Grant-In-Aid from the American Council of Learned Societies. I am grateful to Charles Williams II for a rigorous introduction to field work in classical archaeology during the 1965 and 1966 seasons.

[24] Excluding **330**, the illegible Greek Imperial.

[25] For the figures comparing the acropolis coins with those from the mint area and houses see above 111 and note 42. Areas 1, 6, and 7 were more extensively excavated than the others but even with that in mind coins were more concentrated on the acropolis and Industrial Terrace, except for the immediate area of the mint where the greatest concentration of coins at the site was found.

Catalog of Coin Types with Provenances and Dates

The coins are bronze unless it is stated otherwise. The catalog numbers (**84–345**) continue the sequence of those for the mint (**1–83**) in Chapter 8. In the exploratory season of 1962 the coins were cataloged as HM (Halieis Metal) but, starting in 1965, coins were cataloged as HN (Haleis Numismata = coins) with the excavation year and the number of the coin in the annual sequence. Coins from 1962 and those found later that had already been given an HM number were recataloged in the HN series, except for two HMs, which were never renumbered. See Appendix D for a concordance of HN and HM inventory numbers with their catalog numbers.[26] Find spots are based on the areas of excavation discussed above, with compass directions abbreviated E, N, S, and W. See Fig. 42 for Acropolis W. and Fig. 21 for Acropolis E. Coins found together are listed after the provenance of the first example with reference back to this catalog number for later coins from the same place.[27] Those from the mint area listed in the context summary at the end of chapter 8 are indicated by NECP (for Northeast Command Post) after the trench and unit number. The order of the catalogue follows Head (1911) except that all coins I propose were minted at Halieis are listed under Tiryns. Roman and Byzantine coins follow the Greek in chronological order of the emperors followed by modern coins. Dates are before Christ unless stated otherwise. Plaster casts are currently in my possession and will be deposited in the Indiana University Archives. Tirynthian types are classified according to the system of Svoronos (1907: 5–34) with the number of each issue prefaced by Sv. Other abbreviations: Obv. and Rev. = obverse and reverse; l. or r. = left or right; c. = century; TR = trench; NB = notebook.

MACEDONIA: Philip II, 359–336 or posthumous
Obv. Head of Apollo (or youth) l. wearing a taenia
Rev. Nude horseman (not wearing kausia) r.
84 (HN 1974-8) Area 7, TR 990/350, unit 8, Level A, Room 7-1 or drain through fortifications to east of blocked gate at Tower **9**, Ault 2005, fig. 6.

Alexander III, AR tetradrachm before October 323, mint of Sidon year 10
Obv. Head of Herakles r., wearing a lion skin
Rev. Zeus enthroned l., eagle in outstretched r. hand, scepter in l. hand

85 (HN 1962-1) Industrial Terrace, Western Unit, Room F, alpha context on floor, Jameson n.d., chapter 3.

PHOKIS: Phokian League, AR half-drachma, ca. 478–ca. 460
Obv. Frontal bull's head
Rev. Head of Artemis r.
86 (HN 1975-123) Area 6, TR 130/355, unit 2, above Level A, House B, Room 6-90 or 6-91, Ault 2005, 21, fig. 3.

Mid 4th–346
Obv. Three bulls' heads with fillets arranged in a triangular pattern
Rev. T within laurel wreath likely as a mark of value
87 (HN 1962-7 = HM 114) Area 4, TR M, NB 2, 62, Level A(?), Jameson 1963, 74, Young 1963, 3–5 with plan.

BOIOTIA: Boiotian League, 338–early 3d
Obv. Boiotian shield
Rev. Ornamented trident
88 (HN 1965-30) Industrial Terrace, Central Unit, Room E, beta context, Jameson n.d., chapter 3.

Thebes, AR stater, ca. 400–390
Obv. Boiotian shield
Rev. Amphora with ornamental handles, between them, caduceus
89 (HN 1975-124) Area 7, TR 010/355, unit 7, early Level A/B to C, House 7, Room 7-14, Ault 2005, fig. 6.

EUBOEA: Chalkis, ca. 290 to 273/71
Obv. Bust of Hera, facing wearing diadem with five disks
Rev. Eagle flying r. holding snake with wings clearly on each side of body
90 (HN 1965-33) Acropolis E, Building B, room 1, Deposit VI V 1, Dengate n.d., chapter 11.

ATTICA: Athens, ca. early or mid 330s–322/317
Obv. Head of Athena r. wearing Attic helmet
Rev. Double-bodied owl, facing
91 (HN 1965-5) Acropolis W, Deposit VI/VII A, Dengate n.d., chapter 11.
92 (HN 1965-9) Acropolis W, Deposit VI Y 4, Dengate n.d., chapter 11.

---

[26] The blanks and flans from the mint in Chapter 8 were also recataloged as HN from their earlier HM numbers. All HNs are currently stored in the Leonardo annex of the Nauplion Archaeological Museum. A few objects were identified in the field as coins but, when cleaned and examined, were found not to be. These were either discarded or inventoried as HM, HS (Halieis Stone), or HV (Halieis Varia).

[27] Coins found in the same excavation context but not together are given individual provenances.

Eleusis as Athenian festival coinage, ca. 350s–early
or mid 330s
Obv. Triptolemos holding wheat ears in r. hand,
seated 1. in winged chariot drawn by two snakes
Rev. Piglet standing r. on mystic staff
93 (HN 1965-7) Acropolis W, Deposit VI/VII A.
  Dengate n. d., chapter 11.

AIGINA: AR stater, 480–470 or not much later
Obv. Sea turtle
Rev. Incuse in large skew pattern
94 (HN 1965-25) Acropolis W, Deposit VI Y 3,
  Dengate n.d., chapter 11.

AR obol, 480–457
Obv. Sea turtle
Rev. Incuse in large skew pattern
95 (HN 1974-16) Area 6, TR 110/345, unit 4, above
  Level A(?), Rooms 6-74, 6-75, or 6-76, Ault
  2005, fig. 3.

4th–first half 3d
Obv. A between two dolphins upwards
Rev. Incuse square divided into five compartments
96 (HN 1965-17) Acropolis E, Building B, room 2,
  Deposit VI V 2, Dengate n.d., chapter 11
  with **126**, **142**, and **159**.
97 (HN 1974-7) Area 6, TR 070/325, unit 4, Level
  A, House D, Locus XV, Room 6-35a, Ault
  2005, 90, 104, fig. 17.
98 (HN 1970-15) Area 2, TR H4-4, NB 102, 33,
  Room B spread along wall on floor with
  101, **102**, **110**, **135**, **144**, **168**, **270**, **284**, Level
  A, upper southeast wall with chambered
  curtain and Tower **8**, Fig. 23.
99 (HN 1975-149) Area 6, TR 125/360, unit 11,
  Level A, House A, Locus XVIII, Room 6-
  87, Ault 2005, 98, fig. 11.
100 (HN 1965-1) Between Industrial Terrace and
  Area 2 (upper southeast wall with
  chambered curtain and Tower **8**), inside line
  of fortification walls, surface find, Fig. 19.
101 (HN 1970-12) Area 2, see **98**.
102 (HN 1970-13) Area 2, see **98**.
103 (HN 1975-94) Area 6, TR 120/365, unit 6, Level
  A, House A, Locus VI, Room 6-81c, Ault
  2005, 97, fig. 11.
104 (HN 1966-6) Acropolis W, Deposit VI Y 10,
  Dengate n.d., chapter 11.
105 (HN 1973-1) Acropolis W, Deposit VI Y 11 b,
  Dengate n.d., chapter 11.
106 (HN 1975-120) Area 6, TR 110/360, unit 12,
  Level A(?), Avenue B and Street 4
  intersection (or small part of N corner of
  Room 6-71?), Ault 2005, fig. 3.
107 (HN 1970-3) Area 2, TR H4-4, NB 102, 18,
  Level A, upper southeast wall with
  chambered curtain and Tower **8**, Fig. 23.

108 (HN 1975-151) Area 6, TR 125/360, unit 11,
  Level A, House A, Locus XVIII, Room 6-
  87, Ault 2005, 98, fig. 11.
109 (HN 1970-5) Area 3, TR F5-1, NB 104, 29, Level
  A, middle wall region at Tower **19**, Fig. 31.
110 (HN 1970-14) Area 2, see **98**.
111 (HN 1975-113) Area 7, TR 010/355, unit 6,
  early Level A/B to Level C, House 7, room
  7-14, Ault 2005, fig. 6.
112 (HN 1975-18) Area 6, TR 075/335, unit 9, Level
  A, Room 6-41, also containing fishhook
  hoard, Ault 2005, fig. 5.
113 (HN 1980-1) Area 6, House C, Room 6-62,
  embedded below previously excavated
  floor, Level A or A/B, Ault 2005, fig. 8.
114 (HN 1975-37) Area 6, TR 125/355, unit 6, early
  or mixed Level A/B, House A, Room 6-83,
  Ault 2005, fig. 3.
115 (HN 1975-73) Area 6, TR 125/360, unit 5, Level
  A, House A, Locus XVIII, Room 6-87, Ault
  2005, 98, fig. 11.
116 (HN 1975-99) Area 6, TR 120/365, unit 6, Level
  A/B(?), House A, Locus VI, Room 6-81c,
  Ault 2005, 97, fig. 11.
117 (HN 1975-96) Area 6, TR 120/365, unit 5,
  above Level A(?), in open area SW of
  NECP, at NE of Room 6-82 of House A,
  Ault 2005, fig. 3. See above 110–11, notes
  39 and 40.
118 (HN 1975-118) Area 6, TR 130/360, unit 4,
  above Level A(?), House B, Room 6-91, or 6-
  92, or NW of House A, Ault 2005, 21, fig. 3.

CORINTHIA: Corinth, late 5th to 3d
Obv. Pegasus flying 1. or r.
Rev. Trident
119 (HN 1965-20) Acropolis W, Deposit VI Y 6,
  Dengate n.d., chapter 11.
120 (HN 1966-8) Acropolis W, Deposit VI Y 10,
  Dengate n.d., chapter 11.
121 (HN 1962-10) Industrial Terrace, Central Unit,
  Room K, Jameson n.d., chapter 3.
122 (HN 1965-3) Acropolis W, Deposit VI Y 2,
  Dengate n.d., chapter 11.
123 (HN 1972-15) Area 6, NECP, TR 130/370, unit
  8.
124 (HN 1965-32) Acropolis E, Building B, room 2,
  Deposit VI V 3, Dengate n.d., chapter 11.
125 (HN 1965-31) Acropolis W, Deposit V/VI C,
  Dengate n.d., chapter 11.
126 (HN 1965-16) Acropolis E, with **96**.
127 (HN 1965-38) Acropolis E, altar area, Deposit
  VI Z 14, Dengate n.d., chapter 11.
128 (HN 1965-2) Acropolis W, Deposit VI Y 2,
  Dengate n.d., chapter 11.
129 (HN 1975-111) Area 6, TR 130/355, unit 2,
  above Level A, House B, Room 6-90 or 6-
  91, Ault 2005, 21, fig. 3.

130 (HN 1972-1) Area 6, NECP, TR 135/375, unit 6.
131 (HN 1970-1) Koukouras sanctuary, NB 111, 1, Jameson et al. 1994, 426, site A24.

PHLIASIA: Phlius, 4th
Obv. Bull butting 1.
Rev. Phi in four pellets
132 (HN 1965-19) Industrial Terrace, Central Unit, Room C or D, alpha context, Jameson n.d., chapter 3.
133 (HN 1966-7) Acropolis W, VI Y 10, Dengate n.d., chapter 11.

SIKYONIA: Sikyon, AR triobol, 4th
Obv. Chimaera 1.
Rev. Dove flying 1.
134 (HN 1966-2) Acropolis W, Deposit VI Y 11 a, Dengate n.d., chapter 11.

330 to 290(?)
Obv. Dove flying l. or r.
Rev. Olive wreath in which letter(s), monogram or no legend
135 (HN 1970-7) Area 2, see **98**.
136 (HN 1965-6) Acropolis W, Deposit VI/VII A, Dengate n.d., chapter 11.
137 (HN 1962-5) Acropolis E, altar area, Deposit VI Z 2 a, Dengate n.d., chapter 11.
138 (HN 1965-37) Acropolis E, altar area, Deposit VI Z 14, Dengate n.d., chapter 11.
139 (HN 1965-39) Acropolis E, altar area, Deposit VI Z 14, Dengate n.d., chapter 11.
140 (HN 1975-117) Area 6, TR 130/360, unit 4, above Level A(?), House B, Room 6-91, or 6-92, or NW of House A, Ault 2005, 21, fig. 3.
141 (HN 1965-10) Industrial Terrace, Central Unit, room not identifiable, gamma context, Jameson n.d., chapter 3.
142 (HN 1965-14) Acropolis E, with **96**.
143 (HN 1966-4) Acropolis E, altar area, Deposit VI Z 21, Dengate n.d., chapter 11.
144 (HN 1970-8) Area 2, see **98**.
145 (HN 1962-13) Acropolis E, altar area, Deposit VII N 3, Dengate n.d., chapter 11.

ARGOLID: Argos, AR triobol, mid 4th through 3d
Obv. Forepart of wolf l.
Rev. A in incuse
146 (HN 1970-23) Area 3, TR F5-1, W section, near burials 5 and 7, NB 122, 9–10, in a stone vessel (HS 347), above Level A or Level A, middle wall region at Tower **19**, Fig. 31.
147 (HN 1970-24) Area 3, with **146**.

Kleonai, late 4th century
Obv. Head of Herakles in lion's skin r.
Rev. First four letters of ethnic in parsley wreath

148 (HN 1965-18) Industrial Terrace, Central Unit, Room A, alpha context, Jameson n.d., chapter 3.

Epidauros, ca. 323 to ca. 240
Obv. Head of Apollo laureate 1.
Rev. E in laurel wreath
149 (HN 1962-15) Acropolis E, altar area, Deposit VI Z 6, Dengate n.d., chapter 11.
150 (HN 1965-27) Industrial Terrace, Central Unit, Room L, alpha context, Jameson n.d., chapter 3.
151 (HN 1975-1) Area 6, TR 055/325, unit 26, mixed deposit of Level A/B and Level C, Room 6-22, near the SE wall of House D, Ault 2005, fig. 5.
152 (HN 1975-14) Area 6, TR 075/335, unit 7, Level A, Room 6-41, also containing fishhook hoard, Ault 2005, fig. 5.
153 (HN 1975-15) Area 6, TR 075/335, unit 7, Level A, Room 6-41, also containing fishhook hoard, Ault 2005, fig. 5.
154 (HN 1975-100) Area 6, TR 070/330, unit 10 B, Level A, Locus XVI, House D, Room 6-36 and small area of 6-35b, Ault 2005, 105, fig. 17.
155 (HN 1975-102) Area 6, TR 065/330, unit 29, Level A, Locus XIV, House D, Room 6-35b, Ault 2005, 103, fig. 17.
156 (HN 1975-115) Area 6, TR 130/360, unit 4, above Level A(?), House B, Room 6-91, or 6-92, or NW of House A, Ault 2005, 21, fig. 3.
157 (HN 1975-148) Area 6, TR 070/330, unit 53, early Level A/B and Level C, House D, deep sounding in SE corner of Room 6-35, Ault 2005, fig. 16.
158 (HN 1972-14) Area 5, TR 155/220, unit 8, Level A(?), Rudolph 1973, 162.

Hermion, second quarter of 4th
Obv. Head of Demeter 1.
Rev. EP with torch in grain wreath
159 (HN 1965-15) Acropolis E, with **96**.
160 (HN 1975-134) Area 7, TR 005/355, unit 20, Level A/B, Locus XXIV, House 7, Room 7-16, Ault 2005, 21, 95, fig. 8.
161 (HN 1974-11) Area 6, TR 090/335, unit 4, above Level A or Level A(?), Room 6-52, southeast of House C, Ault 2005, fig. 4.
162 (HN 1975-155) Area 6, TR 075/325, unit 4, above Level A(?), Room 6-37, 6-38, or 6-39, Ault 2005, fig. 5.
163 (HN 1975-97) Area 7, TR 005/360, unit 3, Level A/B, Locus XXV, House 7, Rooms 7-7, 7-16, and 7-17, Ault 2005, 21, 95, fig. 8.
164 (HN 1975-33) Area 6, TR 040/310, unit 3, above Level A or Level A, Street 3 or Room 6-2 or NW corner of Room 6-3, Ault 2005, fig. 5.

165 (HN 1970-4) Area 3, TR F5-1, NB 104, 23, Level A(?), middle wall region at Tower **19**, Fig. 31.

166 (HN 1975-127) Area 7, TR 000/345, unit 2, Level A, Locus I, Avenue C outside House 7, Ault 2005, 93, fig. 8.

167 (HN 1975-88) Area 6, TR 125/360, unit 8, Level A, Locus XV, House A, Room 6-86, Ault 2005, 36, 98, fig. 11.

168 (HN 1970-9) Area 2, see **98**.

169 (HN 1965-36) Acropolis E, outside Tower **6**, Deposit VI N, Dengate n.d., chapter 11.

170 (HN 1962-4) Area 6, TR T, NB 1.1, 145, above Level A, House B, Ault 2005, fig. 3.

171 (HN 1965-34) Acropolis E, outside Tower **6**, Deposit VI N, Dengate n.d., chapter 11.

172 (HN 1975-106) Area 7, TR 000/355, unit 5, Level A/B, Locus III, House 7, Rooms 7-7 and 7-8, Ault 2005, 94, fig. 8.

173 (HN 1965-28) Industrial Terrace, Central Unit, Room H, alpha context, Jameson n.d., chapter 3.

Tiryns, minted at Halieis, late 5th through early 4th
Obv. Head of bearded Herakles r., in lion's skin
Rev. T-I Palm tree in incuse
Sv. no. 5. Contexts establish a date and confirm Svoronos's stylistic placement of this issue first in the bronze series.

174 (HN 1975-89) Area 6, TR 075/335, unit 18, Level A(?), Room 6-41 (also containing fishhook hoard) and parts of Rooms 6-40, 6-42, 6-43, and 6-47, Ault 2005, fig. 4.

175 (HN 1974-12) Area 6, TR 110/345, unit 4, above Level A(?), Rooms 6-72, 6-73, 6-74, and eastern part of 6-75, Ault 2005, fig. 3.

176 (HN 1965-26) Acropolis E, altar area, Deposit V S 12 b, Dengate n.d., chapter 11.

177 (HN 1970-6) Area 3, TR F6-2, NB 122, 6, Level A, middle wall region at Tower **19**, Fig. 31.

178 (HN 1975-17) Area 6, TR 125/355, unit 7, early or mixed Level A/B, House A, Room 6-83, SE half, Ault 2005, fig. 3.

179 (HN 1975-79) Area 6, TR 125/360, unit 7, Level A/B, Locus XVIII, House A, Room 6-87, Ault 2005, 98, fig. 11.

180 (HN 1962-18) Area 4, TR M, NB 2, 132, Level A(?), Jameson 1963, 74, Young 1963, 3–5 with plan.

181 (HN 1975-22) Area 6, TR 125/355, unit 7, early or mixed Level A/B, House A, Room 6-83, SE half, Ault 2005, fig. 3.

182 (HN 1972-18) Area 5, TR 180/130, unit 3, above Level A(?), Rudolph 1973, 162.

During first half of 4th
Obv. Head of Apollo, laureate, l., with long hair
Rev. T-I Palm tree, lyre to l., bunch of grapes r.

Sv. no. 6. Contexts suggest the date and confirm Svoronos's stylistic placement second in the series of bronzes.

183 (HN 1965-13) Acropolis W, Deposit VI Y 6, Dengate n.d., chapter 11.

184 (HN 1966-9) Acropolis E, E of altar, Deposit V/VI E, Dengate n.d., chapter 11.

185 (HN 1965-4) Industrial Terrace, Eastern Unit, Room A, alpha context, Jameson n.d., chapter 3.

186 (HN 1970-16) Area 2, TR H4-4, NB 102, 33, Room B, Level A, upper southeast wall with chambered curtain and tower **8**, Fig. 23.

187 (HN 1974-13) Area 7, TR 000/350, unit 12, Level A, Locus I, Avenue C outside House 7, Ault 2005, 93, fig. 8.

188 (HN 1974-19) Area 6, TR 055/320, unit 14, Level A, Locus IX, House E, Room 6-18, Ault 2005, 56 and 106, fig. 20.

189 (HN 1975-104) Area 6, TR 070/330, unit 17, Level A, Locus XIV, House D, Room 6-35b, Ault 2005, 103, fig. 17.

190 (HN 1974-24) Area 6, TR 090/335, unit 3, Level A/B, Room 6-52, outside of southeast wall of House C, Ault 2005, fig. 4.

191 (HN 1974-3) Area 6, TR 115/360, unit 6, Level A(?), Locus I, House A, Room 6-81, Ault 2005, 96, fig. 11.

192 (HN 1983-1) Area 6, TR 125/360, unit 11, Level A(?) or A/B, House A, Room 6-81c, Ault 2005, fig. 11.

193 (HN 1975-25) Area 6, NECP, TR 130/370, unit 34.

194 (HN 1972-4) Area 6, NECP, TR 135/375, unit 9.

195 (HN 1962-20) Area 6, TR T, NB 1.2, 48, Level A(?), northwest of House B in andron area, Ault 2005, fig. 3.

196 (HN 1972-10) Area 5, TR 145/250, unit 2, above Level A, Rudolph 1973, 159–62.

After ca. 375 through ca. 300
Obv. Head of Apollo, laureate, r., hair rolled
Rev. Palm tree with abbreviated or full ethnic and/or symbols, letters or monogram

Dates of the changes to Apollo r. are suggested by contexts and confirm Svoronos's stylistic placement of these as the latest of the Tirynthian issues. The context evidence does not justify any changes in the Svoronos order of the issues but the full ethnic on **295** suggests that the issues with the complete or almost complete ethnic may be earlier rather than later. In general, Svoronos's ordering of Apollo r. issues is not chronological.

TI on its side to l., lyre to r., Sv. no. 7
197 (HN 1975-121) Area 6, TR 065/325, unit 20, Level A, Locus VIII, House D, Room 6-28, Ault 2005, 102, fig. 17.

198 (HN 1972-6) Area 6, NECP, TR 135/375, unit 12.
199 (HN 1965-11) Acropolis W, Deposit VI Y 1, Dengate n.d., chapter 11.
200 (HN 1962-11) Area 6, NECP, TR T, NB 1.1, 97.

TI on its side to l., A on its side to r., Sv. no. 8
201 (HN 1965-22) Industrial Terrace, Central Unit, Room C or D, alpha context, Jameson n.d., chapter 3.
202 (HN 1962-22) Industrial Terrace, Eastern Unit, room not identifiable, gamma context, Jameson n.d., chapter 3.
203 (HN 1974-25) Area 6, TR 060/320, unit 8, Level A, Locus XIIa, House E, Room 6-20, Ault 2005, 56 and 106, fig. 20.
204 (HN 1966-1) Acropolis E, near square tower, Deposit V/VI D, Dengate n.d., chapter 11.
205 (HN 1970-17) Area 2, TR H4-4, NB 102, 33, Room D, Level A, upper southeast wall with chambered curtain and Tower **8**, Fig. 23.

IT to l., cockle shell to r., Sv. no. 9
206 (HN 1974-6) Area 6, TR 090/340, unit 6, Level A, Locus IX, House C, Room 6-54, Ault 2005, 100, fig. 14.
207 (HN 1972-12) Area 6, TR 150/365, unit 19, Level A(?), ca. 15 m N of NW corner of House B, ca. 15 m NW of NECP and ca. 3 m SW of fortification wall, Ault 2005, fig. 2.
208 (HN 1962-17) Acropolis E, altar area, Deposit VI Z 8 c, Dengate n.d., chapter 11.
209 (HN 1975-152) Area 6, TR 125/360, unit 11, Level A, Locus XVIII, House A, Room 6-87, Ault 2005, 98, fig. 11.
210 (HN 1975-101) Area 6, TR 065/330, unit 29, Level A, Locus XIV, House D, Room 6-35b, Ault 2005, 103, fig. 17.
211 (HN 1975-140) Area 6, TR 055/325, unit 32, Level A/B and C, deep sounding in Street 3 near SE wall of House D, Ault 2005, fig. 5.
212 (HN 1962-3) Acropolis W, Deposit VI D 1, Dengate n.d., chapter 11.
213 (HN 1965-24) Industrial Terrace, Central Unit, Room E, alpha context, Jameson n.d., chapter 3.
214 (HN 1975-130) Area 6, TR 125/365, unit 3, above Level A, directly NE of House A in open area SW of NECP, Ault 2005, fig. 3. See above 110–11, notes 39 and 40.
215 (HN 1975-136) Area 6, TR 125/365, unit 5, above Level A(?). See **214**.
216 (HN 1975-139) Area 6, TR 125/365, unit 5, above Level A(?). See **214**.
217 (HN 1975-135) Area 7, TR 005/355, unit 20, Level A/B, Locus XXIV, House 7, Room 7-16, Ault 2005, 21 and 95, fig 8.
218 (HN 1975-75) Area 6, TR 125/360, unit 7, Level A/B, Locus XVIII, House A, Room 6-87,

Ault 2005, 98, fig. 11.
219 (HN 1970-25) Area 3, TR F6-4, NB 122, 25, above Level A, middle wall region at Tower **19**, Fig. 31.

Sv. no. 7, 8, or 9
220 (HN 1975-87) Area 6, TR 120/370, unit 3, above Level A, in open area SW of NECP, at NE of Room 6-82 of House A, Ault 2005, fig. 3. See above 110–11, notes 39 and 40.
221 (HN 1975-64) Area 6, NECP, TR 135/380, unit 6.
222 (HN 1965-29) Industrial Terrace, Central Unit, Room F, alpha or beta context, Jameson n.d., chapter 3.
223 (HN 1975-156) Area 6, TR 075/325, unit 4, above Level A(?), Room 6-37, 6-38, or 6-39, Ault 2005, fig. 5.
224 (HN 1975-114) Area 6, TR 070/330, unit 21, early Level A/B, House D, Room 6-35, Ault 2005, fig. 16.

I-T, Sv. no. 10.
225 (HN 1975-19) Area 6, TR 125/355, unit 7, early or mixed Level A/B, House A, SE half of Room 6-83, Ault 2005, fig. 3.
226 (HN 1962-6) Acropolis W, Deposit VI Y 14, Dengate n.d., chapter 11.
227 (HN 1975-143) Area 6, TR 070/330, unit 31, early Level A/B(?), deep sounding Room 6-36, Ault 2005, fig. 5.

T-I, Sv. no. 11.
228 (HN 1962-14) Acropolis E, altar area, Deposit VI Z 8 b, Dengate n.d., chapter 11.
229 (HN 1970-18) Area 2, TR H4-4, NB 102, 35, Level A(?), Room D, upper southeast wall with chambered curtain and Tower **8**, Fig. 23.
230 (HN 1975-154) Area 6, TR 065/325, unit 21, Levels A/B or B(?), Locus VIII, House D, Room 6-28, Ault 2005, 42, 102, fig.17.
231 (HN 1975-2) Area 6, TR 070/325, unit 12, Level A, Locus XV, House D, Room 6-35a, Ault 2005, 104, fig. 17.
232 (HN 1975-119) Area 6, TR 090/345, unit 13, Level A, Locus X, House C, Rooms 6-53 and 6-54, Ault 2005, 100 fig. 14.
233 (HN 1974-17) Area 6, TR 105/345, unit 5, above or Level A? Street 4 SW of Avenue B, SE corner of Room 6-74 and SW corners of Rooms 6-76, 6-70, Ault 2005, figs. 3, 4.
234 (HN 1975-129) Area 6, TR 125/365, unit 3, above Level A. See **214**.
235 (HN 1975-137) Area 6, TR 125/365, unit 5, above Level A(?). See **214**.
236 (HN 1975-138) Area 6, TR 125/365, unit 5, above Level A(?). See **214**.

237 (HN 1975-150) Area 6, TR 125/365, unit 6, above Level A(?). See **214**.
238 (HN 1972-20) Area 6, NECP, TR 135/370, unit 6.
239 (HN 1975-128) Area 6, TR 125/365, unit 3, above Level A. See **214**.
240 (HN 1975-146) Area 6, TR 125/365, unit 5, above Level A(?). See **214**.
241 (HN 1976-1) Area 6, TR 100/345, unit 11, Level A, on SE side of Street 4, near doorway to House C, Ault 2005, fig. 4.
242 (HN 1965-23) Industrial Terrace, Central Unit, Room E, alpha context, Jameson n.d., chapter 3.
243 (HN 1975-72) Area 6, TR 125/360, unit 3, Level A/B, Locus XV, House A, Room 6-86, Ault 2005, 98, fig. 11.
244 (HN 1975-157) Area 7, TR 005/355, unit 16, Level A, Locus IV, House 7, Room 7-7, Ault 2005, 94, fig. 8.

Sv. no. 10 or 11
245 (HN 1962-19) Area 6, TR T, NB 1.2, 38, Level A or above Level A. NE of NECP, over and east of drain.
246 (HN 1975-93) Area 6, TR 080/340, unit 9, Level A(?), Room 6-46 or 6-48, Ault 2005, fig. 4.
247 (HN 1975-92) Area 6, TR 070/330, unit 10, Level A, Locus XVI, House D, Room 6-36, Ault 2005, 105, fig. 17.
248 (HN 1962-16) Acropolis E, altar area, Deposit VI Z 8 c, Dengate n.d., chapter 11.
249 (HN 1975-95) Area 6, TR 065/330, unit 29, Level A, Locus XIV, House D, Room 6-35b, Ault 2005, 103, fig. 17.
250 (HN 1975-98) Area 6, TR 070/335, unit 19, Level A(?), Room 6-40 or 6-43 at NW of House D, Ault 2005, fig. 4.
251 (HN 1975-126) Area 6, TR 120/355, unit 9, Level A(?), Avenue B to N of intersection with Street 4, Ault 2005, fig. 3.
252 (HN 1975-103) Area 6, TR 070/330, unit 18, above Level A, Room 6-36 and part of Room 6-35, Ault 2005, fig. 5.
253 (HN 1975-147) Area 6, TR 125/365, unit 5, above Level A(?). See **214**.
254 (HN 1975-78) Area 6, NECP, TR 135/380, unit 4.

T-IP or T-IR, Sv. no. 12
255 (HN 1975-142) Area 6, TR 125/365, unit 5, above Level A(?). See **214**.
256 (HN 1972-25) Area 5, TR 150/205, unit 16, above Level A or Level A(?), Rudolph 1973, 159–62.

257 (HN 1975-153) Area 6, TR 065/325, unit 21, Levels A/B or B? Locus VIII, House D, Room 6-28, Ault 2005, 42, n. 105, 102, fig. 17.
258 (HN 1972-3) Area 6, NECP, TR 135/375, unit 9.
259 (HN 1975-133) Area 6, TR 125/365, unit 3, above Level A(?). See **214**.
260 (HN 1975-141) Area 6, TR 080/335, unit 15, Level A(?), Room 6-45, 6-46, or 6-47, Ault 2005, fig. 4.
261 (HN 1972-19) Area 6, NECP, TR 135/370, unit 5.

TI-RY each on its side, Sv. no. 16
262 (HN 1975-107) Area 6, TR 065/330, unit 35, above Level A, House D, Room 6-35, Ault 2005, fig. 16.
263 (HN 1974-23) Area 6, TR 075/330, unit 8, Level A/B, Room 6-40 near northeast corner of House D, Ault 2005, fig. 5.

TI-RYN each on its side, Sv. no. 18
264 (HN 1975-82) Area 6, TR 125/360, unit 5, Level A, Locus XVIII, House A, Room 6-87, Ault 2005, 98, fig. 11.
265 (HN 1974-18) Area 6, TR 080/340, unit 6, above Level A or Level A, Room 6-46 or 6-48, Ault 2005, fig. 5.
266 (HN 1972-16) Area 6, NECP, TR 130/370, unit 9.
267 (HN 1970-19) Area 1, TR W, NB 119, 25, above Level A or Level A? Near Tower **10**, Fig. 26.

TI-PYN each on its side, Sv. no. 19
268 (HN 1975-76) Area 6, TR 125/360, unit 5, Level A, Locus XVIII, House A, Room 6-87, Ault 2005, 98, fig. 11.
269 (HN 1975-77) Area 6, TR 125/360, unit 6, Level A, Locus XVI, House A, Room 6-88, Ault 2005, 98, fig. 11.

Sv. no. 18 or 19
270 (HN 1970-11) Area 2, see **98**.
271 (HN 1962-2) Area 4, TR M, NB 2, 98, Level A(?), Jameson 1963, 74, Young 1963, 3–5 with plan.

Full ethnic curving on each side of tree trunk, Sv. no. 22
272 (HN 1972-11) Area 5, TR 145/250, unit 7, Level A(?), Rudolph 1973, 159–62.
273 (HN 1972-21) Area 6, TR 040/320, unit 2, above Level A?[28]

---

[28] This trench notebook exists, and is mentioned in Rudolph (1973, 163), but the grids of the trench place only its NW corner in Field 24 = Area 6. So this might be a surveying error as it was the first and only trench in the southern part of the field in 1972. If this is so, it should be one of the trenches dug nearby in Area 6: TR 040/315 Rooms 6-1, 6-2, 6-3, or 6-4; TR 045/320 Rooms 6-5, 6-6, 6-7, or 6-8, and Street 3; TR 040/310 Rooms 6-2 or 6-3 and Avenue C, or some other combination of grid numbers near 040/320 at the southern end of the field owned by the excavations. See Ault 2005, fig. 5.

Issues not listed in Sv.
274 (HN 1975-36) Area 6, NECP, TR 135/375, unit 21.
275 (HN 1975-91) Area 6, TR 120/365, unit 3,
       above Level A, Locus VI, House A, Room
       6-81, fig. 11.
276 (HN 1975-66) Area 6, NECP, TR 135/375, unit
       23.
277 (HN 1975-13) Area 6, TR 075/335, unit 7, Level
       A, Room 6-41, also containing fishhook
       hoard, Ault 2005, fig. 5.

Letters/symbols illegible or anepigraphic, Sv. no. 23
278 (HN 1975-116) Area 6, TR 070/330, unit 20,
       Level A, Locus XVI, House D, Room 6-36,
       Ault 2005, 105, fig. 17.
279 (HN 1975-131) Area 6. See **214**.
280 (HN 1975-132) Area 6. See **215**.
281 (HN 1975-90) Area 6, TR 120/370, unit 2,
       above Level A, in open area southwest of
       NECP, at northeast of Room 6-82 of House
       A, Ault 2005, fig. 3. See above 110–11,
       notes 39 and 40.
282 (HN 1975-81) Area 6, NECP, TR 135/380, unit 4.
283 (HN 1965-35) Acropolis E, outside Tower **6**,
       Deposit VI N, Dengate n.d., chapter 11.
284 (HN 1970-10) Area 2, see **98**.
285 (HN 1970-21) Area 1, TR W, NB 119, 29, above
       or Level A? Near Tower **10**, Fig. 26.
286 (HN 1975-11) Area 6, TR 075/335, unit 7, Level
       A, Room 6-41, also containing fishhook
       hoard, Ault 2005, 24, fig. 5.
287 (HN 1975-34) Area 6, TR 125/355, unit 7, early
       or mixed Level A/B, House A, Room 6-83,
       Ault 2005, fig. 3.
288 (HN 1975-112) Area 6, TR 130/355, unit 1,
       above Level A, House B, Room 6-90 or 6-
       91, Ault 2005, fig. 3.
289 (HN 1975-158) Area 6, TR 130/355, unit 4,
       above Level A(?), House B, Room 6-90 or
       6-91, Ault 2005, fig. 3.
290 (HN 1972-7) Area 6, NECP, TR 135/375, unit
       12.
291 (HN 1972-17) Area 5, TR 165/210, unit 20,
       Level A(?), Rudolph 1973, 162.
292 (HN 1972-2) Area 6, NECP, TR 135/375, unit 6.
293 (HN 1972-13) Area 5, TR 155/220, unit 22,
       Level A(?), Rudolph 1973, 162.
294 (HN 1967-1) Lorenzo kiln, Jacobsen 1968, 145,
       Jameson 1969, 341–42, Jameson et al. 1994,
       527, site A18.

During first half of 4th as half denomination of **183–
96** (see 108–9).
Obv. Head of bearded male r. in crested Corinthian
helmet
Rev. H with incurving verticals as mark of value in
incuse square around which the full ethnic
295 (HN 1974-21) Area 6, TR 065/320, unit 5, Level
       A, Locus XXI, House E, Room 6-25 and 6-
       23, Ault 2005, 56 and 108, fig. 20; Pl. 24.

Obv. Same
Rev. H in laurel wreath
296 (HN 1965-21) Acropolis W, Deposit VI Y 9,
       Dengate n.d., chapter 11; Pl. 24.
297 (HN 1970-20) Area 1, TR R and TR P balk, NB
       103, 27, above Level A, near Tower **10**, Fig.
       26.
298 (HN 1970-22) Area 1, TR P, NB 106, 34, Level A
       (?), near Tower **10**, Fig. 26.
299 (HN 1974-9) Area 6, TR 055/320, unit 11, Level
       A, Locus VI, House E, Room 6-19, Ault
       2005, 56, 105, fig. 2.
300 (HN 1975-85) Area 6, TR 070/330, unit 9, Level
       A abandonment(?), Locus XVI, House D,
       Rooms 6-36 and part of 6-35b, Ault 2005,
       105, fig. 17.
301 (HN 1975-35) Area 6, TR 075/335, unit 10,
       Level A(?), Room 6-41, also containing
       fishhook hoard, and parts of Rooms 6-40,
       6-42, 6-43, 6-47.
302 (HN 1975-125) Area 6, TR 130/355, unit 4,
       above Level A(?), House B, Rooms 6-90,
       6-91, Ault 2005, 21, fig. 3.
303 (HN 1962-8) Area 6, NECP, TR T, NB 1.1, 73.
304 (HN 1972-5) Area 6, NECP, TR 135/375, unit 9.

Minted at Halieis[29] but probably not in the name of
the Tirynthians since all examples are overstruck
(where the undertype when legible is clearly
Herakles/Palm of Sv. no. 6, **174–82** above). Dated
just after the Herakles/Palm by context to late 5th
through early 4th.
Obv. Amphora, die crudely cut and poorly struck
Rev. Object shaped like a T but probably intended
to be read as a palm tree, anchor, double ax, or Ionic
column with volutes; the die is so crudely cut and
poorly struck that all of these or some other
identification are possible.[30]
305 (HN 1962-9) Acropolis E, south of Building B,
       Deposit VI I 1, Dengate n.d., chapter 11.

---

[29] See note 6 above.
[30] Possibly T as mark of value, not an abbreviation for Tiryns
because this overstriking was done on coins already marked
with T-I to identify the ethnic. Yet even this is not sure. Perhaps
the change from the obverse type of Herakles was the significant
factor. Sparta also had connections to Herakles since both its
kings traced their ancestry back to this hero. But the T would be
read as the initial of Tiryns whether it was a mark of value or
not. A wily politician, however, might have convinced an anti-
Tirynthian faction to accept T as a mark of value as a compromise
to satisfy the Tirynthian group. But this seems overly
complicated and the variety of the forms of the T suggests a
letter was not intended.

306 (HN 1966-5) Acropolis E, altar area, Deposit V
  S 14 d, Dengate n.d., chapter 11.
307 (HN 1975-108) Area 7, TR 010/355, unit 7,
  early Level A/B to Level C, House 7,
  Room 7-14, Ault 2005, fig. 6.
308 (HN 1975-109) Area 7, TR 010/355, unit 7,
  early Level A/B to Level C, House 7,
  Room 7-14, Ault 2005, fig. 6.
309 (HN 1974-4) Area 6, TR 110/345, unit 4, above
  Level A, Room 6-76 or small part of Room
  6-74 or 6-75, Ault 2005, fig. 3.
310 (HN 1975-144) Area 6, TR 125/350, unit 1,
  above Level A, Avenue A entrance of
  House B and part of Room 6-89.

Tesserae minted at Halieis likely as a half
denomination of **305–10**, struck on roughly
rectangular piece cut from thick bronze strip or sheet
and dated the same as the Amphora/T issue. The
random weights and dimensions of these tesserae
confirm that they were not manufactured to be used
as weights on a balance. (See above, 108–9.)
Obv. Same but with even less care at die cutting and
striking
Rev. Same but with even less care at die cutting and
striking
311 (HN 1962-23) Acropolis E, south of Building B,
  Deposit VI I 1, Dengate n.d., chapter 11.
312 (HN 1965-40) Acropolis W, Deposit IV/V B 1,
  Dengate n.d., chapter 11.
313 (HN 1971-3) Acropolis W, Deposit V B,
  Dengate n.d., chapter 11.
314 (HN 1972-52) Area 5, TR 145/235, unit 21,
  Level A(?), Rudolph 1973, 161.
315 (HN 1972-30) Area 6, NECP, TR 135/375, unit
  6.
316 (HM 1202) Area 6, TR 060/320, unit 21e, Level
  A/B, Locus XX, House E, Room 6-24, Ault
  2005, 56, 107, fig. 8.
317 (HM 1203) Area 6, TR 060/320, unit 21e, Level
  A/B, Locus XX, House E, Room 6-24, Ault
  2005, 56, 107, fig. 8.

Troizen, 4th through 3d
Obv. Head of Athena
Rev. Trident
318 (HN 1965-12) Acropolis W, Deposit VI/VII A,
  Dengate n.d., chapter 11.
319 (HN 1972-24) Area 5, TR 150/205, unit 14,
  Level A(?), Rudolph 1973, 159–62.
320 (HN 1974-14) Area 6, TR 120/350, unit 5,
  above Level A(?), Avenue B outside of
  House A or Room 6-79 or NW corner of
  Room 6-78, Ault 2005, fig. 3.
321 (HN 1975-86) Area 6, TR 120/365, unit 3, Level
  A, Locus VI, House A, Room 6-81, Ault
  2005, 31, 97, fig. 11.
322 (HN 1975-3) Area 6, TR 075/335, unit 7, Level

A, Room 6-41, also containing fishhook
  hoard, Ault 2005, 24, fig. 5.
323 (HN 1975-4) Area 6, TR 075/335, unit 7, Level
  A, Room 6-41, also containing fishhook
  hoard, Ault 2005, 24, fig. 5.
324 (HN 1975-12) Area 6, TR 075/335, unit 7, Level
  A, Room 6-41, also containing fishhook
  hoard, Ault 2005, fig. 5.
325 (HN 1975-105) Area 6, TR 065/330, unit 29,
  Level A, Locus XIV, House D, Room 6-35b,
  Ault 2005, 103, fig. 17.
326 (HN 1974-10) Area 6, TR 060/325, unit 19,
  Level A, Locus II, House D, Room 6-26
  kopron, Ault 2005, 46 and 101, fig. 17.

ARKADIA: Arkadian League, ca. 363–ca. 280
Obv. Head of young Pan, l. with goat horns
Rev. Monogram of Arkadia, below syrinx
327 (HN 1974-15) Area 6, TR 055/320, unit 11,
  Level A, Locus VI, House E, Room 6-19,
  Ault 2005, 56 and 105, fig. 20.

TROAS: Abydos, AR fraction, ca. 320 to ca. 280 or
later
Obv. Head of Apollo r.
Rev. Eagle standing l., ABY to r.
328 (HN 1974-5) Area 6, TR 085/335, unit 19, Level
  A (or earlier when well was filled?), well
  in Room 6-46, Ault 2005, fig. 4.

IONIA: Miletus, mid to late 4th
Obv. Head of Apollo, laureate, r.
Rev. Lion walking r., looking back; above eight rayed
star
329 (HN 1965-8) Acropolis W, Deposit VI Y 1,
  Dengate n.d., chapter 11.

ROMAN PERIOD
Greek Imperial, 1st to 3d CE
Obv. Bust r. with illegible letters around
Rev. Traces of figure or figures
330 (HN 1974-22) Area 6, TR 050/320, unit 3,
  above Level A, Rooms 6-19 or 6-20 or
  Street 3, Ault 2005, fig. 5.

Antoninianus of Aurelianus, 270–275 CE
Obv. Radiate bust of emperor r.
Rev. Figure standing l. receiving something from a
figure off flan
331 (HN 1972-9) Area 5, TR 165/250, unit 4, above
  Level A or intrusion in Level A? Rudolph
  1973, 161.

Antoninianus of Marcus Aurelius Numerianus, mint
of Ticinum, 283-284 CE
Obv. Radiate bust of emperor r.
Rev. Providentia standing l., holding ears of corn and
cornucopiae, at foot, modius

332 (HN 1970-2) Koukouras sanctuary, NB 111, 12,
          Jameson et al. 1994, 426, site A24.

Constantius II, AE 3, 351–361 CE
Obv. Bust of emperor r.
Rev. Virtus spearing fallen horseman
333 (HN 1968-1) Sea, submerged remains of the
          fortification walls, between Towers **13**
          and **14**, Fig. 36, NB 504, 71, Jacobsen
          1969, 125.

Arcadius, mint of Heraclea, AE 4, 383 CE
Obv. Bust of emperor r.
Rev. VOT V in wreath, below SMHB
334 (HN 1975-110) Area 6, TR 055/315, unit 11,
          collapse debris to Level A, Locus IX,
          House E, Room 6-18, Ault 2005, 54, n. 149,
          and 106, fig. 20.

Arcadius, Honorius, or Theodosius II, AE 4, 395–408
CE
Obv. Bust of emperor r.
Rev. Cross
335 (HN 1962-12) Area 4, TR M, NB 2, 66, above
          Level A(?), Jameson 1963, 74, Young 1963,
          3–5.

Unidentified Late Roman AE 4, ca. mid 4th through
early 5th CE
Obv. Traces of bust of emperor r.
Rev. Traces of Nike and letters around
336 (HN 1972-22) Area 5, TR 185/150, unit 13,
          above Level A or intrusion into Level A?
          Rudolph 1973, 159–62.

BYZANTINE PERIOD
Anastasius, mint of Constantinople, follis, 491–518
CE
Obv. Bust of emperor r.
Rev. M with * to l. and r., cross above, CON in exurge
337 (HN 1975-122) Area 6, TR 045/320, unit 1,
          plow soil above Level A, Rooms 6-5, 6-6, 6-
          7, 6-8, or Street 3, Ault 2005, fig. 5.

Nummus
Obv. Bust of emperor r.
Rev. monogram of Anastasius
338 (HN 1975-145) Area 6, TR 125/365, unit 6,
          above Level A(?). See **214**.

Phokas, mint of Kyzikos, half follis, 605-606 CE
Obv. Bust of emperor facing, letters preserved but
illegible
Rev. XX, IIII to r., cross above, KYZB in exurge
339 (HN 1971-2) Lower town surface find on
          beach, N7815/E16,300, NB 743, 6, above
          Level A, NB 743, 6.

VENETIAN PERIOD
Venice, anonymous colonial issue of the Islands and
the Levant decreed after 1686
Obv. Lion of St. Mark, *S·MARCVS·VE*, *II* in exurge
Rev. CO[R]FV, CEFAL, ZANTE
340 (HN 1974-20) Area 6, TR 110/360, unit 6,
          above Level A or intrusive in Level A?
          Intersection of Avenue B and Street 4 and
          the N corner of Room 6-71.

MODERN GREEK STATE
King George I of Greece 1878, 10 lepta
341 (HN 1973-2) Lower town surface find?

2 lepta
342 (HN 1972-8) Area 5, TR 165/250, unit 2, above
          Level A, Rudolph 1973, 161.

1 leptona
343 (HN 1970-43) Area 1, TR R, NB 103, 2, above
          Level A(?), near Tower **10**, Fig. 26.
344 (HN 1972-23) Area 7, TR 990/360, unit 1, over
          surface of Tower **9**, above Level A(?).

Aluminum alloy 10 lepta, details on rev. and obv.
illegible
345 (HN 1962-21) Industrial Terrace, Central Unit,
          Room I, gamma context, Jameson n.d.,
          chapter 3.

– APPENDIX A –

Halieis Select Bibliography with Annotations

JAMES A. DENGATE

CHRISTINA DENGATE

A. Preliminary Reports (in chronological order by journal)

Archaiologikon Deltion

Jameson, M. H. 1963 [1965]. "Excavations at Porto-Cheli." 18.2:73–74.

Jameson, M. H., and C. K. Williams II. 1966 [1968]. "Halieis." 21.2:148–51.

Williams, C. K. II. 1967. "Halieis." 22.2:195–96.

Jacobsen, T. W. 1968. "Halieis (Porto-Cheli)." 23.2:144–48.

———. 1969 [1970]. "Excavations at Porto Cheli." 24.2:124–29.

Jameson, M. H. 1971 [1974]. "Excavations at Porto Cheli." 26.2:114–19.

———. 1972 [1976]. "Excavations at Porto Cheli. Excavations at Halieis, Final Report." 27.2:233–36.

———. 1973–1974 [1979]. "Excavations at Halieis (Porto Cheli) 1973." 29.2:261–64.

Rudolph, W. W. 1973 [1977]. "Excavations in Halieis (Porto Cheli)." 28.2:159–63.

———. 1973–1974 [1979]. "Final Report, 1974." 29.2:265–68.

———. 1975 [1983]. "Final Report: Halieis." 30.2:64–73.

———. 1976 [1984]. "Halieis Excavations." 31.2:72–74.

American School of Classical Studies [W. W. Rudolph]. 1979 [1987]. "Excavations in the Necropolis of Halieis." 34.2:128–29.

Expedition

Young, J. H. 1963. "A Migrant City in the Peloponnesus." 5.3:2–11.

Dublin, S. 1969. "A Greek Acropolis and Its Goddess." 11.2:26–29.

Hesperia

Jameson, M. H. 1969. "Excavations at Porto Cheli and Vicinity, Preliminary Report, I: Halieis, 1962–1968." 38:311–42.

Boyd, T. D., and W. W. Rudolph. 1978. "Excavations at Porto Cheli and Vicinity, Preliminary Report IV: The Lower Town of Halieis, 1970–1977." 47:333–55.

Rudolph, W. W. 1979. "Excavations at Porto Cheli and Vicinity, Preliminary Report V: The Early Byzantine Remains." 48:294–324.

———. 1984. "Excavations at Porto Cheli and Vicinity, Preliminary Report VI: Halieis, the Stratigraphy of the Streets in the Northeast Quarter of the Lower Town." 53:123–70.

Jameson, M. H. 1972a. "The City-State of Halieis." *Ekistics* 33:92–94.

———. 1972b. "Halieis at Porto Cheli in the Argolid." *International Journal of Nautical Archaeology and Underwater Exploration* 1:195–96.

———. 1973. "Halieis at Porto Cheli." *Colston Papers, Being the Proceedings of the Twentythird Symposium of the Colston Research Society Held in the University of Bristol, April 4th to April 8th, 1971* 23:219–29. London: Butterworths Scientific Publications.

———. 1974. "The Excavation of a Drowned Greek Temple." *Scientific American* 231.4:110–19. Reprinted in *Avenues to Antiquity. Readings from* Scientific American, ed. B. M. Fagan, 289–98. San Francisco: W. H. Freeman and Co., 1976.

———. 1982. "The Submerged Sanctuary of Apollo at Halieis in the Argolid of Greece." *National Geographic Society Research Reports* 14:363–67.

Dengate, J. A. 1975. "Material Excavated from the Undersea Sanctuary of Apollo at Halieis, Greece." *The American Philosophical Society. Year Book 1975*:528–29.

B. Summaries of Preliminary Reports (in chronological order by journal)

Bulletin de correspondance hellénique

Daux, G. 1960. "Chronique des fouilles, 1959." 84:688.
———. 1963. "Chronique des fouilles, 1962." 87:756–59.
———. 1966. "Chronique des fouilles, 1965." 90:786–91.
———. 1967. "Chronique des fouilles, 1966." 91:659–61.
———. 1968. "Chronique des fouilles, 1967." 92:799–807.
Michaud, J.-P. 1970. "Chronique des fouilles en 1968 et 1969." 94:969–73.
———. 1971. "Chronique des fouilles, 1970." 95:875–78.
———. 1972. "Chronique des fouilles, 1971." 96:651–52.
———. 1973. "Chronique des fouilles, 1972." 97:305–6.
———. 1974. "Chronique des fouilles, 1973." 98:610.
Aupert, P. 1975. "Chronique des fouilles, 1974." 99:618.
———. 1976. "Chronique des fouilles, 1975." 100:610–15.
Touchais, G. 1977. "Chronique des fouilles, 1976." 101:554–55.
———. 1980. "Chronique des fouilles, 1979." 104:603–5.

Archaeological Reports

Megaw, A. H. S. 1963. "Archaeology in Greece, 1962–63." 9:16–17.
———. 1966. "Archaeology in Greece, 1965–66." 12:8.
———. 1967. "Archaeology in Greece, 1966–67." 13:10.
———. 1968. "Archaeology in Greece, 1967–68." 14:9–10.
Fraser, P. M. 1969. "Archaeology in Greece, 1968–69." 15:14.
———. 1971. "Archaeology in Greece, 1970–71." 17:11–12.
Catling, H. W. 1972. "Archaeology in Greece, 1971–72." 18:9–10.
———. 1973. "Archaeology in Greece, 1972–73." 19:15–16.
———. 1974. "Archaeology in Greece, 1973–74." 20:11–13.
———. 1975. "Archaeology in Greece, 1974–75." 21:10–11.
———. 1976. "Archaeology in Greece, 1975–76." 22:12–13.
———. 1978. "Archaeology in Greece, 1976–77." 24:28.
———. 1980. "Archaeology in Greece, 1979–80." 26:31.
———. 1982. "Archaeology in Greece, 1981–82." 28:23.

American Journal of Archaeology

Ervin, M. 1967. "News Letter from Greece." 71:299.
———. 1968. "News Letter from Greece." 72:270.
———. 1969. "News Letter from Greece." 73:347.
Caskey, M. E. 1971. "News Letter from Greece." 75:301–2.

C. Studies and Interpretations of Excavation Finds and Architecture

Acheson, P. E. 1997. "Does the 'Economic Explanation' Work? Settlement, Agriculture and Erosion in the Territory of Halieis in the Late Classical-Early Hellenistic Period." *Journal of Mediterranean Archaeology* 10.2:165–90. (Uses Halieis to challenge the conclusions of the Stanford site survey.)

Ault, B. A. 1995. "Koprones and Oil Presses: Domestic Installations Related to Agricultural Productivity and Processing at Classical Halieis." In *Structure rurales et sociétés antiques*. Actes du colloque de Corfou (14–16 Mai 1992), ed. P. N. Doukellis and L. G. Mendoni, 197–201. Centre de recherches d'histoire ancienne 26. Annales littéraires de l'Université de Besançon 508. Paris: Les Belles Lettres. (Discusses olive presses and refuse/compost pits in houses at Halieis as evidence for the integration of domestic and agricultural production.)

———.1999. "Koprones and Oil Presses at Halieis: Interaction of Town and Country and the Integration of Domestic and Regional Economies." *Hesperia* 68:549–73.

———. 2000. "Living in the Classical Polis: The Greek House as Microcosm." *Classical World* 93:483–96. (Uses houses at Halieis to support view that Greek household organization reflected social organization.)

Bergquist, B. 1990a. "Primary or Secondary Temple Function: The Case of Halieis." *Opuscula Atheniensia* 18:23–37. Skrifter utgivna av Svenska Institutet i Athen, series in quarto 39. Stockholm: Paul Åströms Förlag. (Reinterprets the temple of Apollo as a dining establishment, with the southern half of the building used as a temple only after the partial destruction of the structure after the mid-5th century.)

———. 1990b. "Primary or Secondary Temple Function: The Case of Halieis [extended abstract]." In *Celebrations of Death and Divinity in the Bronze Age Argolid. Proceedings of the Sixth International Symposium at the Swedish Institute at Athens, 11–13 June, 1988*, ed. R. Hägg and G. C. Nordquist, 225–

28. Skrifter utgivna av Svenska Institutet i Athen, series in quarto, 40. Stockholm: Paul Åströms Förlag. (A condensed version of Bergquist 1990a with the addition of the discussion following her paper, 227–28.)

Boyd, T. D. 1981. "Halieis: A Fourth Planned City in Classical Greece." *Town Planning Review* 52:143–56.

Cooper, N. K. 1989. *The Development of Roof Revetment in the Peloponnese*. Studies in Mediterranean Archaeology and Literature. Pocket book 88. Jonsered: Paul Åströms Förlag. (Places the temple of Apollo tiles among early Corinthian tile systems.)

———. 1990. "Archaic Architectural Terracottas from Halieis and Bassai." In *Proceedings of the First International Conference on Archaic Greek Architectural Terracottas, December 2–4, 1988*, ed. N. A. Winter. *Hesperia* 59:65–93. (Halieis: 65–82, 93; Cooper rejects calling Apollo temple roof "Corinthian," instead naming it "Halieis-style.")

Dengate, C. F. 1976 [1980]. "A Group of Graves Excavated at Halieis." *Archaiologikon Deltion* 31.1:274–324.

Foxhall, L. 1993. "Oil Extraction in Classical Greece." In *La production du vin et de l'huile en Méditerranée*, ed. M.-C. Amouretti and J.-P. Brun. Bulletin de correspondance hellénique supplément 26:183–200. (Argues that the press on the Industrial Terrace and the presses in the Lower Town were not used to produce olive oil, 185–87.)

Frost, F. J. 1985. "The 'Harbour' at Halieis." *Harbour Archaeology. Proceedings of the First International Workshop on Ancient Mediterranean Harbours, Caesarea Maritima, 24–28.6.83 = British Archaeological Reports International Series* 257:63–66.

Jameson, M. H. 1974. "A Treasury of Athena in the Argolid (*IG* IV, 554)." In *Phoros. Tribute to Benjamin Dean Meritt*, ed. D. W. Bradeen and M. F. McGregor, 67–75. Locust Valley, N.Y.: J. J. Augustin. (Suggests that the Halieis acropolis sanctuary was the findspot of *IG* IV, 554; publishes HM 556, three iron keys that identify the sanctuary of Apollo.)

———. 2001a. "A Hero Cult at Halieis." In *ΙΘΑΚΗ. Festschrift für Jörg Schäfer zum 75. Geburtstag am 25. April 2001*, ed. S. Böhm and K.-V. von Eickstedt, 197–202. Würzburg: Ergon Verlag.

———. 2001b. "Oil Presses of the Late Classical/Hellenistic Period." In *Techniques et sociétés en +Méditerranée. Hommage à Marie-Claire Amouretti*, ed. J.-P. Brun and P. Jockey, 281–99. Paris: Maison méditerranéenne des sciences de l'homme : Maisonneuve et Larose. (Discusses evidence that the press on the Industrial Terrace was for the production of olive oil.)

Jameson, M. H. and T. D. Boyd. 1981. "Urban and Rural Land Division in Ancient Greece." *Hesperia* 50:327–42. (Compares the town plan of Halieis to other planned Greek cities.)

Pimpl, H. 1997. *Perirrhanteria und Louteria. Entwicklung und Verwendung grosser Marmor- und Kalksteinbecken auf figürlichem und säulenartigem Untersatz in Griechenland*. Wissenschaftliche Schriftenreihe Archäologie 3. Berlin: Verlag Koster. (Catalog includes fragments of basins and stands from Halieis, 211–12, pl. 4.)

Pullen, D. 2000. "The Prehistoric Remains of the Acropolis at Halieis: A Final Report." *Hesperia* 69:133–87.

Rafn, B. 1984. "The Ritual Use of Pottery in the Nekropolis at Halieis." In *Ancient Greek and Related Pottery. Proceedings of the International Vase Symposium in Amsterdam, 12–15 April 1984*, ed. H. A. G. Brijder, 305–8. Studies in Ancient Civilization. Allard Pierson Series 5. Amsterdam: Allard Pierson Museum.

———. 1991a. "Archaic and Classical Graves at Halieis: A Summary. Recent Danish Research in Classical Archaeology." *Acta Hyperborea* 3:57–71.

———. 1991b. "Two Laconian Black-Glazed Droop Cups from Halieis." In *Stips Votiva. Papers Presented to C. M. Stibbe*, ed. M. Gnade, 163–69. Amsterdam: Allard Pierson Museum.

Romano, D. G. 1983. "The Ancient Stadium: Athletes and Arete." *The Ancient World* 7:9–16. (Halieis: 11–13 and figs. 1, 15.)

———. 1985. "The Panathenaic Stadium and Theater of Lykourgos: A Re-examination of the Facilities on the Pnyx Hill." *American Journal of Archaeology* 89:441–54. (Halieis stadium with plan, Ill. 5, 447, discussed 446–47 and 449.)

———. 1993. *Athletics and Mathematics in Archaic Corinth. The Origins of the Greek Stadion*. Memoirs of the American Philosophical Society Held at Philadelphia for Promoting Useful Knowledge 206. (Discussion of Halieis stadium with plan, 34–37.)

Rudolph, W. W. 1976. "HP 2310: A Lakonian Kylix from Halieis." *Hesperia* 45:240–52.

———. 1991. "Eine orientalisierende Pyxis aus Halieis." In *Stips Votiva. Papers Presented to C. M. Stibbe*, ed. M. Gnade, 177–83. Amsterdam: Allard Pierson Museum.

Runnels, C. 1982. "Flaked-stone Artifacts in Greece during the Historical Period." *Journal of Field Archaeology* 9:363–73. (Artifacts from Halieis discussed, 365–69, 371.)

———. 1988. "Early Bronze-age Stone Mortars from the Southern Argolid." *Hesperia* 57:257–72. (HS 337, mortar fragment, cataloged, 260, no. 5, fig. 3; see also 265, n. 8.)

Wickander, C. Review of N. K. Cooper, *The Development of Roof Revetment in the Peloponnese* and J. Heiden, *Korinthische Dachziegel. Opuscula Atheniensia* 19: 188–90. (Notes that Cooper's treatment of the terracotta roof as a whole is rare; some discussion of the temple of Apollo roof system.)

D. Theses

Ault, B. A. 1994. *Classical Houses and Households: An Architectural and Artifactual Case Study from Halieis, Greece*. Ph.D. diss., Indiana University. Ann Arbor: University Microfilms International. Order No. DA9518532. *Dissertation Abstracts International* 56.2 (1995): 606-A.

Cooper, N. K. 1977. *Three Roofs from the Sanctuary of Apollo, Halieis*. M.A. thesis, University of Minnesota.

———. 1983. *The Development of Roof Revetment in the Peloponnese*. Ph.D. diss., University of Minnesota. Ann Arbor: University Microfilms International. Order No. 83-29506. *Dissertation Abstracts International* 44.9 (1984): 2809-A.

Dengate, C. F. 1988. *The Sanctuaries of Apollo in the Peloponnesos*. Ph.D. diss., University of Chicago. Available from the University of Chicago. *Dissertation Abstracts International* 49.4 (1988): 858-A. (Halieis: 40, 44, 49, 55, 93, 95, 98, 164, 199, 204, 231–39.)

McAllister, M. H. 1973. *The Fortifications of Ancient Halieis*. Ph.D. diss., Bryn Mawr College. Ann Arbor: University Microfilms International. Order No. 76-13, 775. *Dissertation Abstracts International* 36.12 (1976): 8143-A.

McClellan, M. C. 1984. *Core-Formed Glass from Dated Contexts*. Ph.D. diss., University of Pennsylvania. Ann Arbor: University Microfilms International. Order No. DA8505107. *Dissertation Abstracts International* 46.1 (1985): 186-A. (Includes glass from Halieis.)

Romano, D. G. 1981. *The Stadia of the Peloponnesos*. Ph.D. diss., University of Pennsylvania. Ann Arbor: University Microfilms International. Order No. 81-17843. *Dissertation Abstracts International* 42.3 (1981): 1269-A. (Discusses the stadion in the sanctuary of Apollo.)

Runnels, C. N. 1981. *A Diachronic Study and Economic Analysis of Millstones from the Argolid, Greece*. Ph.D. diss., Indiana University. Ann Arbor: University Microfilms International. Order No. 81-19022. *Dissertation Abstracts International* 42.3 (1981): 1225-A. (Halieis: 117–27, 296–97, 302, 310, figs. 22–27.)

Rupp, D. W. 1974. *Greek Altars of the Northeastern Peloponnese c. 750/725 B.C. to c. 300/275 B.C.* Ph.D. diss., Bryn Mawr College. Ann Arbor: University Microfilms International. Order No. 75-13940. *Dissertation Abstracts International* 36.1 (1975): 465-A. (Halieis: 259–72, 302, 305–6, 363–66.)

Skon-Jedele, N. J. 1994. *"Aigyptiaka": A Catalogue of Egyptian and Egyptianizing Objects Excavated from Greek Archaeological Sites, ca. 1100–525 B.C., with Historical Commentary*. Ph.D. diss., University of Pennsylvania. Ann Arbor: University Microfilms International. Order No. DA9427615. *Dissertation Abstracts International* 55.5 (1994): 1356-A. (Includes HP 2309, a faience aryballos grave offering.)

E. Summaries, Citations, and/or Illustrations of Excavation Finds and Architecture (in addition to those included in preliminary reports)

Alcock, S., J. Cherry, and J. Davis. 1994. "Intensive Survey, Agricultural Practice and the Classical Landscape of Greece." In *Classical Greece: Ancient Histories and Modern Archaeologies*, ed. I. Morris, 137–70. New Directions in Archaeology. Cambridge: Cambridge University Press. (Mentions the relationship between the refuse pits [koprones] found at Halieis and artifact scatters found by surveys, 169–70.)

Amyx, D. A. 1988. *Corinthian Vase-Painting of the Archaic Period*. California Studies in the History of Art 25. Berkeley: University of California Press. (Mentions the Corinthian aryballos with female plastic head [HP 2295] from the necropolis, 444.)

Anderson-Stovanovitch, V. 1997. Review of Bowkett 1995. *Journal of Hellenic Studies* 117:244–45. (Criticizes Bowkett for supporting the dye-works interpretation when both the Halieis Industrial Terrace excavation [as discussed by Ault and Jameson] and her own work at the Rachi Settlement, Isthmia, have established "dye works" there as olive presses.)

Ault, B. A. 1999. "Die klassische *Aule*. Höfe und Freiraum." In *Geschichte des Wohnens*, vol. 1, *5000 v. Chr.–500 n. Chr. Vorgeschichte Frühgeschichte Antike*, ed. Wolfram Hoepfner, 537–44. Stuttgart: Deutsche Verlags-Anstalt. (Halieis houses with courtyards typical of ancient Mediterranean domestic architecture.)

Ault, B. A. and L. C. Nevett. 1999. "Digging Houses: Archaeologies of Classical and Hellenistic Greek Domestic Assemblages." In *The Archaeology of Household Activities*, ed. P. M. Allison, 43–56. London: Routledge. (Discussion of three Halieis houses with artifact counts.)

Barakari-Gleni, K. 1984 [1990]. "Anaskafe Taphon sto Argos." *Archaiologikon Deltion* 39, A:171–204. (Compares a convex pyxis, a bronze pomegranate pin, and iron sandal soles to similar objects found at the Halieis necropolis, 179 n. 14, 199 n. 93, 200 n. 101.)

Bergquist, B. 1990. "The Archaic Temenos in Western Greece. A Survey and Two Inquiries." In *Le sanctuaire Grec*, ed. A. Schachter. Fondation Hardt.

Entretiens sur l'antiquité classique 37:109–58. Geneva: Fondation Hardt. (Mentions possible canopy over sanctuary of Apollo altar, 142.)

Billot, M.-F. 1990. "Terres cuites architecturales d'Argos et d'Épidaure. Notes de typologie et d'histoire." In *Proceedings of the First International Conference on Archaic Greek Architectural Terracottas, December 2–4, 1988*, ed. N. A. Winter. *Hesperia* 59:95–139. (Halieis: 116–17, 138.)

Birge, D. E. 1992. "The Sacred Square." In *Excavations at Nemea. Topographical and Architectural Studies: The Sacred Square, the Xenon, and the Bath*, ed. S. G. Miller, 1–98. Berkeley: University of California Press. (Describes the similarities between the sanctuary of Apollo altar at Halieis and the altar of Zeus at Nemea, 31 and n. 95.)

Bökönyi, S. 1993. "The Sacrificial Remains from the Votive Deposit in F11." In *Fourth Century B.C. Magna Graecia: A Case Study*, ed. M Gualtieri, 125–27. Jonsered: Paul Åströms Förlag. (Bones of at least twelve caprovines sacrificed at Halieis sanctuary of Apollo, primarily from right side, 127.)

Bowkett, L. C. 1995. *The Hellenistic Dye-Works*. Well-Built Mycenae 36. The Helleno-British Excavations within the Citadel at Mycenae, 1959–1969, ed. W. D. Taylour, E. B. French, K. A. Wardle. Oxford: Oxbow Books. (Mentions the "dye-works" at Halieis.)

Boyd, T. D. 1988. "Urban Planning." In *Civilization of the Ancient Mediterranean: Greece and Rome*, ed. M. Grant and R. Kitzinger, 3.1691–1700. New York: Charles Scribner's Sons. (Reconstructed orthogonal plan of Halieis, 1695, fig. 2.)

Brandt, H. 1992. "IG IV 554: aus Argos oder Halieis?" *Chiron* 22:83–90. (Argues that the inscription mentioning a treasury of Athena is Argive.)

Brijder, H. A. G. 1983. *Siana Cups 1 and Komast Cups*. Studies in Ancient Civilization. Allard Pierson Series 4. Amsterdam: Allard Pierson Museum. (Cites a Type A komast cup [K 109] and a Type C komast cup [K 149] from the necropolis, 89, 92.)

Cartledge, P. 1998. *The Cambridge Illustrated History of Ancient Greece*. Cambridge: Cambridge University Press. (Illustration of fishhook hoard from Halieis, 27.)

Catling, R. W. V. 1992. "A Votive Deposit of Seventh-century Pottery. In *Philolakon: Lakonian Studies in Honour of Hector Catling*, ed. J. Sanders, 57–75. London: The British School at Athens. (Mentions two Laconian mugs found at Halieis, 64 and n. 13.)

Christien, J. 1992. "De Sparte à la côte est." In *Polydipsion Argos: Argos de la fin des palais mycéniens à la constitution de l'État classique*, ed. M. Piérart. Bulletin de correspondance hellénique supplément 22:157–71. Athens: École française d'Athènes. (Mentions Spartan presence at Halieis, 158.)

Delivorrias, A., ed. 1987. *Greece and the Sea: Catalogue of the Exhibition in Honour of Amsterdam Cultural Capital of Europe 1987*. Amsterdam: De Nieuwe Kerk and Athens: Andromeda Books. (Refers to HP 2310, the Boreas Painter cup [illustrated], 182, no. 82.)

Demand, N. H. 1990. *Urban Relocation in Archaic and Classical Greece. Flight and Consolidation*. Oklahoma Series in Classical Culture. Norman: University of Oklahoma Press. (Cites and accepts conclusions of excavation reports, 60, 179, n. 5, 192, n. 8, 199, n. 104.)

Faustoferri, A. "Tentativo d'interpretazione dei soggetti raffigurati all'interno delle coppe laconiche del VI sec. a.c." *Studi sulla ceramica laconica: Atti del seminario Perugia, 23–24 Febbraio 1981. Archaeologia Perusina* 3:119–147. (Reference to HP 2310, the Boreas Painter cup, 123.)

Foley, A. 1988. *The Argolid 800–600 B.C.: An Archaeological Survey. Together with an Index of Sites from the Neolithic to the Roman Period*. Studies in Mediterranean Archaeology 80. Göteborg: Paul Åströms Förlag.(Brief description of the sanctuary of Apollo, the acropolis sanctuary, and the "sanctuary of Demeter" east of the acropolis, 149.)

Fortunelli, F. and G. Manca di Mores. 1986. "Il pittore dei Boreade." *Studi sulla ceramica laconica: Atti del seminario Perugia, 23–24 Febbraio 1981. Archaeologia Perusina* 3:21–26. (Reference to HP 2310, the Boreas Painter cup, 21, 23.)

Fusaro, D. and F. Pompili. 1986. "Gruppe di forme." *Studi sulla ceramica laconica. Atti del seminario Perugia, 23–24 Febbraio 1981. Archaeologia Perusina* 3:11–18. (Reference to HP 2310, the Boreas Painter cup, 13.)

Garlan, Y. 1974. *Recherches de poliorcétique grecque*. Bibliothèque des Écoles françaises d'Athènes et de Rome 253. (Halieis 91, 149, 341, 388, 391.)

Gill, D. 1997. "The Coinage of Methana." In *A Rough and Rocky Place: The Landscape and Settlement History of the Methana Peninsula, Greece*, ed. C. Mee and H. Forbes, 278-81. Liverpool Monographs in Archaeology and Oriental Studies. Liverpool: Liverpool University Press. (Mentions similarity of Methana coins to those of Halieis, 279.)

Granjean, C. 1990. "Le monnayage d'argent et de bronze d'Hermioné, Argolide." *Revue Numismatique*, 3d. ser., 32:289–55. (Includes excavation coins in her catalog, HN 1965-15, 1970-4, 1974-11, 1975-33, 97, 127, 134, and 155, dating them after 360 or 352–346 through the third quarter of the 4th century.)

Grant, M. 1990. *The Visible Past. Greek and Roman History from Archaeology, 1960–1990*. New York: Charles Scribner's Sons. (General summary emphasizes underwater excavation, does not mention grid plan or survey, 23–27. Other brief references to Halieis: 12, 81, 182, and 197.)

Hall, J. M. 1995. "Approaches to Ethnicity in the Early Iron Age of Greece." In *Time, Tradition and Society: Bridging the "Great Divide,"* ed. N. Spencer, 6–27. Theoretical Archaeology Group (TAG). London and

New York: Routledge. 6–27. (Notes that a 7th-century cremation burial at Halieis is unusual for the Argolid, 11.)

Hammond, N. G. L. 1982. "The Peloponnese." In *The Cambridge Ancient History*, vol. 2, part 3, *The Expansion of the Greek World, Eighth to Sixth Centuries B.C.*, ed. J. Boardman and N. G. L. Hammond, 321–59. 2d ed. Cambridge: Cambridge University Press. (Mentions Halieis as an example of a non-Dorian small town defended by a mud-brick citadel, 326; notes presence of Laconian pottery and possible Laconian architectural influence, 338.)

Hoepfner, W. and E.-L. Schwandner. 1986. *Haus und Stadt im klassischen Griechenland*. Wohnen in der klassischen Polis 1. Deutsches Archäologisches Institut Architecturreferat. Munich: Deutscher Kunstverlag. (Halieis accepted as the first archaic gridded city in Greece, 2; the only parallel for a house type in a north-south oriented planned city is the dwelling house in Area 7 of Halieis and uniform type dwellings at Halieis are still not detectable from the excavations to date, 279, n. 120.)

———. 1994. *Haus und Stadt im klassischen Griechenland*. Wohnen in der klassischen Polis 1. Deutsches Archäologisches Institut Architecturreferat. Munich: Deutscher Kunstverlag. (Updated references, 11 and n. 16, 337–38, and n. 252.)

Jameson, M. H. 1976. "Halieis." In *The Princeton Encyclopedia of Classical Sites*, ed. R. Stillwell, W. A. MacDonald, and M. H. McAllister, 375. Princeton: Princeton University Press.

———. 1990a. "Domestic Space and the Greek City-State." In *Domestic Architecture and the Use of Space: An Interdisciplinary, Cross-cultural Approach*, ed. S. Kent, 92–113. New Directions in Archaeology. Cambridge: Cambridge University Press. (Halieis, 102, 110, nn. 7 and 10, 111, nn. 11 and 17, 94, fig. 7.2, 111, fig. 7.15.)

———. 1990b. "Private Space and the Greek City." In *The Greek City from Homer to Alexander*, ed. O. Murray and S. Price, 171–95. Oxford: Clarendon Press. (Halieis 177, 180, 184, 185, 189, and 193.)

———.1995. "Halieis." *Enciclopedia dell'Arte Antica*. 2d supplement, 1971–1994, vol. 3, 21–23.

Jeffery, L. H. 1990. *The Local Scripts of Archaic Greece*, With corrections and supplement by Alan W. Johnston. New York: Oxford University Press. (Includes in the catalog of the eastern Argolid HP 208 [SOS amphora], HC 99 [tile fragment], HS 22 + 33 [marble perirrhanterion fragments], and HM 556 [iron keys from temple of Apollo], 445–46.)

Johnston, A. W. 1978. "The 'SOS' Amphora." *Annual of the British School at Athens* 73:103–41. (Mentions HP 403: 123, 125, and HP 298: 471, 536, 111; discusses HP 298 and 471 graffiti, 131–32.)

———. 1979. *Trademarks on Greek Vases*. Warminster, England: Aris and Phillips. (Says that his Type 11c, no. 1, is also found on the base of "a fluted glaze bowl from Halieis"; does not give HP number, 242.)

Kalpaxis, A. E. 1976. *Frükarchaische Baukunst in Griechenland und Kleinasien*. Athens. (Brief description of the temple of Apollo, emphasizing its unusual proportions and room divisions, 28, 119, figs. 5, 77.)

Kardulias, P. N., and C. Runnels. 1995. "The Lithic Artifacts: Flaked Stone and Other Nonflaked Lithics." In *The Prehistoric and Early Iron Age Pottery and the Lithic Artifacts*, ed. C. Runnels, D. J. Pullen, and S. Langdon, vol. 1 of *Artifact and Assemblage: The Finds from a Regional Survey of the Southern Argolid, Greece*. Stanford: Stanford University Press. (Saddle querns, hopper mills, and press beds at Halieis, 116, 122, 129.)

Kelly, N. 1995. "The Archaic Temple of Apollo at Bassai: Correspondences to the Classical Temple." *Hesperia* 64:227–77. (Refers to temple foundations in sanctuary of Apollo, 237, n. 21, temple of Apollo interior columns, 247, nn. 27–29, length of ancient foot used at sanctuary of Apollo, 249, n. 31, sanctuary of Apollo roof tiles, 262, n. 63 and 267, n. 71.)

Koster, H. 1976. "The Thousand Year Road." *Expedition* 19.1:19–28. (Illustrates HM 568 [bronze goat protome], 27, fig. 11, and HM 579 [bronze socket with ram protome], 26–27, fig. 10, both from the temple of Apollo.)

Lambrinoudakis, V. and G. Gruben. 1987. "Das neuentdeckte Heiligtum von Iria auf Naxos." *Archäologischer Anzeiger*: 569–621. (Compares the column bases of a temple at Iria to those at Halieis temple of Apollo, Artemis Orthia, Dreros, etc., 603 and n. 39.)

Lang, F. 1996. *Archaische Siedlungen in Griechenland: Struktur und Entwicklung*. Berlin: Akademie Verlag. (Includes an entry for Halieis in her site register, 176 and fig. 35, as well as brief mentions throughout the text [from index: 22, 27, 31, 33, 58, 61, 67, 70, 72, 77, 86, 113, 142].)

Langdon, S. 1995. "The Pottery of the Early Iron Age and Geometric Periods." In *The Prehistoric and Early Iron Age Pottery and the Lithic Artifacts*, ed. C. Runnels, D. J. Pullen, and S. Langdon, vol. 1 of *Artifact and Assemblage: The Finds from a Regional Survey of the Southern Argolid, Greece*, 57–73. Stanford: Stanford University Press. (Discusses pottery trade between Tiryns and Asine, and Halieis, 57, 68, 72–73.)

Lawrence, A. W. 1979. *Greek Aims in Fortification*. Oxford: Clarendon Press. (Brief mention of Halieis fortifications, 34, 158, 203, 377, 379, 380.)

Leekley, D. and R. Noyes. 1976. *Archaeological Excavations in Southern Greece*. Park Ridge, N.J.: Noyes Press. (Brief description of work at Halieis acropolis and sanctuary of Apollo up to 1975, 69.)

Mallwitz, A. 1981. "Kritisches zur architektur Griechenlands im 8. und 7. jahrhundert." *Archäologischer Anzeiger*: 599–642. (Lists the temple of Apollo among early Greek temples, 621.)

Mazarakis Ainian, A. J. 1985. "Contribution à l'étude de l'architecture religieuse grecque des âges obscurs." *L'Antiquité Classique* 54:5–48. (Gives brief description of the temple of Apollo and says that it is unique, 42–43.)

———. 1987. "Geometric Eretria." *Antike Kunst* 30:3–24. (Lists the temple of Apollo among early temples with posts along the inner face of the walls, 17–18, n. 64.)

———. 1988. "Early Greek Temples: Their Origin and Function." In *Early Greek Cult Practice: Proceedings of the Fifth International Symposium at the Swedish Institute at Athens, 26–29 June, 1986*, ed. R. Hägg, N. Marinatos, and G. C. Nordquist, 105–19. Skrifter utgivna av Svenska Institutet i Athen, series in quarto, 38. Stockholm: Paul Åströms Förlag. (Interprets the temple of Apollo as combining three functions: housing the cult image and serving as a treasury and as a dining hall, 117, fig. 19, n. 43, 118 and n. 47.)

———. 1997. *From Rulers' Dwellings to Temples: Architecture, Religion and Society in Early Iron Age Greece (1100–700)*. Jonsered: Paul Åströms Förlag. (Describes the sanctuary of Apollo, 162–64, figs. 243, 244; at 391 suggests that a room in the temple of Apollo might have served as a hestiatorion.)

Nafissi, M. 1986. "Distribuzione della ceramica laconica." *Studi sulla ceramica laconica: Atti del seminario Perugia, 23–24 Febbraio 1981. Archaeologia Perusina* 3:149–72. (Reference to HP 2310, the Boreas Painter cup, 150.)

Nevett, L. C. 1995a. "Gender Relations in the Classical Greek Household: The Archaeological Evidence." *Annual of the British School at Athens* 90: 363–81. (Halieis House C, 370, fig. 4; brief discussion of Halieis housing, 374f. and n. 47.)

———.1995b. "The Organization of Space in Classical and Hellenistic Houses from Mainland Greece and the Western Colonies." In *Time, Tradition and Society: Bridging the "Great Divide,"* ed. N. Spencer, 89–108. (Brief discussion of Halieis houses, 95, with illus. of Halieis House C, 97, fig. 6.6.)

———. 1999. *House and Society in the Ancient Greek World*. Cambridge: Cambridge University Press. (Mention of Halieis as example of planned city, 99.)

Nicholls, R. V. 1995. "The Stele Goddess Workshop." *Hesperia* 64:405–92. (Includes HP 254, an Attic figurine lekythos from the acropolis, in his series of knucklebone players, 431, n. 123.)

Owens, E. J. 1991. *The City in the Greek and Roman World*. New York: Routledge. (Short description of Halieis town plan, 67, 71, fig.19.)

Petruso, K. M. 2003. "The Halieis Excavation." In *Master Seafarers: The Phoenicians and the Greeks*, ed. M. Moity, M. Rudel, and A.-X. Wurst, 79–81. London: Periplus. (Color area photograph of sanctuary of Apollo and temple keys.)

Pfaff, C. A. 1990. "Three-peaked Antefixes from the Argive Heraion." In *Proceedings of the First International Conference on Archaic Greek Architectural Terracottas, December 2–4, 1988*, ed. N. A. Winter. *Hesperia* 59:149-56. (Halieis: 149–54, discusses dating of horned roofs.)

Reese, D. S. 1985. "Appendix VIII B. The Kition Ostrich Eggshells." In *Excavations at Kition V, part 2*, ed. V. Karageorghes, 371–82. Nicosia: Department of Antiquities. (Mentions fragments of ostrich eggshell, HV 240 and HV 304, found in the temple of Apollo, 374.)

———. 1989. "Faunal Remains from the Altar of Aphrodite Ourania, Athens." *Hesperia* 58:63–70. (Lists a number of sanctuaries where astragali have been found, including the temple of Apollo, 64, n. 6, cf. HV 212–14 and 217–18.)

———. 1994. "Recent Work in Greek Zooarchaeology." In *Beyond the Site: Regional Studies in the Aegean Area*, ed. P. N. Kardulias, 193–221. Landham, Md.: University Press of America. (Brief description of bone and shells from sanctuary of Apollo and acropolis.)

———. 2000. "Worked Astragali." In *Kommos*, vol. 4, *The Greek Sanctuary, Part 1*, ed. J. W. Shaw and M. C. Shaw, 400. (Mentions astragali found at sanctuary of Apollo, most in temple of Apollo cella.)

Roebuck, M. C. 1990. "Archaic Architectural Terracottas from Corinth." In *Proceedings of the First International Conference on Archaic Greek Architectural Terracottas, December 2–4, 1988*, ed. N. A. Winter. *Hesperia* 59:47–63. (Halieis cited for comparanda, 50.)

Rose, M. J. 2000. "The Fish Remains." In *Kommos*, vol. 4, *The Greek Sanctuary, Part 1*, ed. J. W. Shaw and M. C. Shaw, 530. (Describes two fish bones found at sanctuary of Apollo.)

Schallin, A.-L. 1997. "Urban Centers in Greek Islands." In *Acta Hyperborea*. Danish Studies in Classical Archaeology 7, ed. Helle Damgaard Andersen et al., 17–44. (Urbanization in Late Geometric to Archaic periods of southern Argolid results in two poleis: Hermione and Halieis, 30.)

Schattner, T. G. 1990. *Griechische Hausmodelle. Untersuchungen zur frühgriechischen Architektur.* Mitteilungen des Deutschen Archäologischen Instituts Athenische Abteilung 15. (Includes Halieis Apollo temple in his list of buildings with antae, 111.)

Schaus, G. P. 1985. *The Extramural Sanctuary of Demeter and Persephone at Cyrene, Libya, II, The East Greek, Island, and Laconian Pottery*. University of Pennsylvania Museum Monograph 56. (Mentions two rim fragments of Laconian kraters from Halieis, 25, n. 104, and a mug [now at the American School], 45, n. 192.)

Schoder, R. V. 1974. *Ancient Greece from the Air*. London: Thames and Hudson. (Aerial photographs of the acropolis, Industrial Terrace, and the Northeast Quarter with a brief description, 87–89.)

Schwandner, E.-L. 1985. *Der ältere Porostemple der Aphaia auf Aegina*. Denkmäler antiker Architektur 16.

Deutsches Archäologisches Institut. Berlin: Walter de Gruyter. (Dates the Halieis temple of Apollo roof-tile system ca. 600, 127 and nn. 236 and 239 where a date at the beginning of the 6th century is considered more precise. Calls the system "Hörnerdach" or "horned roof.")

Small, A. M., et al. 1994. "A Pit Group of c. 80–70 BC." *Papers of the British School at Rome* 62:197–265. (Identifies his pit as a kopron based on those at Halieis, 201, n. 5.)

Snodgrass, A. 1986. "The Historical Significance of Fortification in Archaic Greece." In *La fortification dans l'histoire du monde grec*. Actes du colloque international. La fortification et sa place dans l'histoire politique, culturelle et sociale du monde grec, Valbonne, Décembre 1982, ed. P. Leriche and H. Tréziny, 125–131. Colloques internationaux du centre national de la recherche scientifique. Paris: ´Editions du centre national de la recherche scientifique. (Mentions Halieis in a summary of archaic defensive walling, 131.)

———. 1994. "Response: The Archaeological Aspect." In *Classical Greece: Ancient Histories and Modern Archaeologies*, ed. I. Morris, 197–200. New Directions in Archaeology. Cambridge: Cambridge University Press. (Discusses the relationship between the refuse pits at Halieis and artifact scatters, 199–200.)

Sparkes, B. A., and L. Talcott. 1970. *Black and Plain Pottery of the 6th, 5th and 4th Centuries B. C.* The Athenian Agora 12. Princeton: American School of Classical Studies at Athens. (Mentions as comparanda HP 62 [strainer], 376 ; HP 113 [Corinthian mushroom jug], 365; HP 117 [Attic black-glazed chous], 63.)

Stibbe, C. M. 1975. "Sparta und Tarent." *Mededeelingen van het Nederlands Instituut te Rome* 37:27–46. (Reference to HP 380, Laconian stemless cup, 34.)

———. 1989. *Laconian Mixing Bowls: A History of the Krater Lakonikos from the Seventh to the Fifth Century B.C. Laconian Black-Glazed Pottery, Part 1.* Allard Pierson Series. Scripta Minora 2. (Reference to HP 3085, black-glazed krater, 113, and to HP 2310, the Boreas Painter cup, 143.)

———. 1991. "Bellerophon and the Chimaira on a Lakonian Cup by the Boreads Painter: Greek Vases in the J. P. Getty Museum." *The J. Paul Getty Museum Journal* 5:5–12. (Refers to HP 2310, the Boreas Painter cup, 10–11 and nn. 35–36.)

——— 1994. *Laconian Drinking Vessels and Other Open Shapes*, Part 2 of *Laconian Black-Glazed Pottery* Allard Pierson Series—Scripta Minora 4. Amsterdam: Allard Pierson Museum. (Includes discussion of some Halieis shapes: cylindrical mugs, 40, 42; one-handled mugs, 46; small goblets, 50, 51; and small cups with low bases, 58.)

Thompson, M., O. Mørkholm, and C. M. Kraay. 1973. *An Inventory of Greek Coin Hoards*. New York: The American Numismatic Society. (Sanctuary of Apollo hoard, 35, no. 36; Kranidhi hoard, 92, no. 87.)

Torrence, R. 1991. "The Chipped Stone." In *Landscape Archaeology as Long-Term History. Northern Keos in the Cycladic Islands from Earliest Settlement until Modern Times*, ed. J. Cherry, J. Davis, and E. Mantzourani, 173–98. Monumenta Archaeologica 16. (Mentions post-prehistoric use of chipped stone at Halieis, 178–82, 193.)

Warren, J. A. 1983. "The Autonomous Bronze Coinage of Sicyon (Part 1)." *Numismatic Chronicle* 143:23–56. (Concludes that most of the Sicyon bronze coins from Halieis belong to her Group V, ca. 330–ca. 290[?], 48.)

———. 1985. "The Autonomous Bronze Coinage of Sicyon (Part 3)." *Numismatic Chronicle* 145:45–66. (Gives reasons for association with Group V, 59.)

Wikander, Ö. 1990. "Archaic Roof Tiles: The First Generation." In *Proceedings of the First International Conference on Archaic Greek Architectural Terracottas, December 2–4, 1988*, ed. N. A. Winter. *Hesperia* 59:285–90. (Halieis, 288.)

———. 1992. "Archaic Roof-Tiles: The First (?) Generation." *Opuscula Atheniensia* 19:151-61. (Locates "horned roofs = Argive system" within a scheme of early roof tile development, 160, fig. 5.)

Williams, C. K. 1981. "A Survey of Pottery from Corinth from 730 to 600 B.C." *Annuario* 59:139–55. (Mentions HP 209, 253, 428, 430, 431, and 525, corded handles, 148, n. 17.)

Winter, F. E. 1971. *Greek Fortifications*. Toronto: University of Toronto Press. (Suggests that round towers at Halieis may have had wooden superstructures, 77, n. 21.)

———. 1986. "A Summary of Recent Work on Greek Fortifications in Greece and Asia Minor. In *La fortification dans l'histoire du monde grec*. Actes du colloque international. La fortification et sa place dans l'histoire politique, culturelle et sociale du monde grec, Valbonne, Décembre 1982, ed. P. Leriche and H. Tréziny, 23–29. Colloques internationaux du centre national de la recherche scientifique. Paris: Éditions du centre national de la recherche scientifique. (Brief mention of harbor defenses at Halieis, 26–27.)

Winter, N. A. 1990. "Defining Regional Styles in Archaic Greek Architectural Terracottas." In *Proceedings of the First International Conference on Archaic Greek Architectural Terracottas, December 2–4, 1988*, ed. N. A. Winter. *Hesperia* 59:13–32. (Halieis: 23–25, accepts suggestion of Cooper 1977 of an Argolid-Aiginetan regional system while disagreeing with Cooper 1983 that this style is a part of the Corinthian system. [See above, section D.])

———. 1993. *Greek Architectural Terracottas from the Prehistoric to the End of the Archaic Period*. Oxford Monographs on Classical Archaeology. Oxford: Clarendon Press. (Halieis: places the "first temple of Apollo" in an Argive regional system, 149, and the "second temple of Apollo" within a possible Arcadian system, 134.)

F. Pre-excavations (of 1958) and Ancient Documentation

Baladié, R. 1978. *Strabon. Géographie, vol. 5, book 8.* Collection des Universités de France. Publiée sous le patronage de l'Association Guillaume Budé. Paris: Société d'édition "Les Belles Lettres." (Brief mention of excavation to explain Strabo's description of "fishermen called 'Halieis' who live on the coast of Hermione," 267.)

Barrett, W. S. 1954. "Bacchylides, Asine and Apollo Pythaieus." *Hermes* 82:421–44.

Bölte, F. 1912. "Halieis." *Paulys Realencyclopädie der classischen Altertumswissenschaft* 7:2246–52. (This includes testimonia and travelers' references.)

Dillon, M. 1997. *Pilgrims and Pilgrimage in Ancient Greece.* London: Routledge. (Discusses establishment of Asklepios cult at Halieis and Sikyon, 199.)

Frickenhaus, A., and W. Müller. 1911. "Aus der Argolis, Bericht über eine Reise von Herbst 1901." *Mitteilungen des (kaiserlich) deutschen archäologischen Instituts, Athenische Abteilung* 36:21–38. (Description of Halieis fortifications, 38.)

IG 4^2 1.42; 121; 122. (Epidaurian cure inscriptions mentioning people of Halieis.)

IG 1^3 75. (Athenian copy of treaty between Halieis and Athens.)

Jameson, V. B. and M. H. Jameson. 1950. "An Archaeological and Topographical Survey of the Hermionid." Papers of the American School of Classical Studies at Athens. (Unpublished; available at ASCSA.)

Musti, D., and M. Torelli. 1986. *Pausania. Guida della Grecia. Libro 2. La Corinzia e l'Argolide.* Milan: Fondazione Lorenzo Valla. (Following Herodotus, they state that Halieis was founded by the Tirynthians after the battle of Plataea; they suggest that the city may have been abandoned because of the great earthquake ca. 250 described by Strabo, 333.)

Papachatzes, N. D. 1976. *Pausaniou Ellados Periegesis. Biblio 2 kai 3. Korinthiaka kai Lakonika.* Athens: Ekdotike Athenon, A.E. (Halieis: 278–79, plus color plans of Halieis, 277, fig. 310; Porto Kheli area with ancient and modern sea levels, 279, fig. 309, with graves, ancient roads, city walls; but a tower [windmill foundation?] is located on summit between acropolis and graves, and the acropolis sanctuary, 279, is identified as dedicated either to Hera or Demeter.)

Paraskevopoulos, G. 1896. *Taxeidia ana ten Ellada.* 2d ed. Athens. (Robbing of ancient graves at Bouzeïka mentioned, 41; not cited in Bölte 1912.)

Philadelpheus, A. 1909. "Ai en Ermionidi Anaskaphai." *Praktika tes en Athenais Archaiologikes Etaireias tou etous 1909*:172–84. (Discusses Halieis walls including those undersea and excavates graves at Bouzeïka, 183.)

Svoronos, J. N. 1907. "'Halieis Hoi ek Tirynthoi' kai ta Nomismata Auton." *Journal International d'Archéologie Numismatique* 10:5–34.

G. Hermionid (and Nearby) Regional Reports Relevant to Halieis

Ekroth, G. 1996. "The Berbati-Limnes Archaeological Survey: The Late Geometric and Archaic Periods." In *The Berbati-Limnes Archaeological Survey, 1988–1990,* ed. B. Wells and C. Runnels, 179–227. Skrifter utgivna av Svenska Institutet i Athen, series in quarto, 44. Stockholm: Paul Åströms Förlag. (Stone tools found at Iron Age sites such as Halieis, 219.)

Frost, F. J. 1977. "Phourkari. A Villa Complex in the Argolid (Greece)." *International Journal of Nautical Archaeology and Underwater Exploration* 6:233–38. (Plan and dating evidence for a parallel to the Halieis harbor villa and bath complex.)

Gerin, D., A. Kyrou, and P. Requier. 1988. "Une trouvaille de quatre fractions d'argent à Porto Heli." *Schweizer Münzblätter* 38:4–8. (Four silver coins [2 Sikyon, 1 Epidauros, 1 Aegina] of late 5th-century burial date, found at Ververonda.)

Harper, D. B. 1976. "Just add water . . ." *Expedition* 19.1:40–49. (Includes Porto Kheli area water sources and Halieis wells.)

Jameson, M. H. 1976a. "A Greek Countryside: Reports from the Argolid Exploration Project." *Expedition* 19.1:2–4.

———. 1976b. "The Southern Argolid: The Setting for Historical and Cultural Studies." In *Regional Variation in Modern Greece and Cyprus: Toward a Perspective on the Ethnography,* ed. M. Dimen and E. Friedl. Annals of the New York Academy of Sciences 268:74–91. (Brief discussion of Halieis, 84–86.)

Jameson, M. H., C. N. Runnels, and T. H. van Andel. 1994. *A Greek Countryside. The Southern Argolid from Prehistory to the Present Day.* Stanford: Stanford University Press. (See index for numerous references to Halieis.)

McAllister, M. H. 1969. "A Temple at Hermione." *Hesperia* 38:169–85. (Historical note on the area by M. H. Jameson, 184–85.)

Penttinen, A. 1996. "The Berbati-Limnes Survey: The Classical and Hellenistic Periods." In *The Berbati-Limnes Archaeological Survey, 1988–1990,* ed. B. Wells and C. Runnels, 229–83. Skrifter utgivna av Svenska Institutet i Athen, series in quarto, 44. Stockholm: Paul Åströms Förlag. (Skyphoi of the Attic compound type are popular drinking vessels at Late Classical sites and are compared to examples at Halieis and vicinity, 273; globular pithoi are common at later sites such as Metochi, near Halieis, 275.)

Pharaklas, N. 1973. *Ermionis - Aliás*. Ancient Greek Cities 19. Athens: Athens Center of Ekistics.

Pope, K. O., and T. H. van Andel. 1984. "Late Quatenary Alluviation and Soil Formation in the Southern Argolid: Its History, Causes and Archaeological Implications." *Journal of Archaeological Science* 11:281–306. (Discusses dates of various alluvial fills in Porto Kheli area.)

Rudolph, W. W. 1974. "Excavations at Porto Cheli and Vicinity, Preliminary Report, III: Excavations at Metochi 1970." *Hesperia* 43:105–31.

Runnels, C., D. J. Pullen, and S. Langdon, eds. 1995. *The Prehistoric and Early Iron Age Pottery and the Lithic Artifacts*, vol. 1 of *Artifact and Assemblage: The Finds from a Regional Survey of the Southern Argolid, Greece*. Stanford: Stanford University Press. (See index under "Halieis.")

Sutton, S. B., ed. 2000. *Contingent Countryside: Settlement, Economy, and Land Use in the Southern Argolid since 1700*. Stanford: Stanford University Press. (See index, "Portokheli," for references to post-classical developments around the site of ancient Halieis.)

van Andel, T. H., and N. Lianos. 1983. "Prehistoric and Historic Shorelines of the Southern Argolid Peninsula: A Subbottom Profiler Study." *International Journal of Nautical Archaeology and Underwater Exploration* 12:303–24. (Considers sedimentation and sea-level rise in Porto Kheli harbor.)

van Andel, T. H., and C. Runnels. 1987. *Beyond the Acropolis: A Rural Greek Past*. Stanford: Stanford University Press. (Halieis is frequently cited; see index, with useful correlation to survey data; no mention of Middle Helladic through Protogeometric material from Fourni Well and Halieis in distribution maps and text.)

Verdeles, N., M. Jameson, and I. Papachristodoulos. 1975. "Archaikai Epigraphai ex Tirynthos." *Archaiologike Ephemeris* 150–205. (Archaeological evidence for Tirynthian presence at Halieis found in coinage and use of Argive alphabet, 191.)

H. Abstracts of Papers Presented at the Annual Meetings of the Archaeological Institute of America

American Journal of Archaeology

Ault, B. A. 1987. "The Spatial Distribution of Cooking Pottery at Ancient Halieis." 91:272–73.

———. 1993. "Koprones and Oil Presses: Domestic Installations Related to Agricultural Productivity and Processing at Classical Halieis." 97:324–25.

———. 1994. "Type-houses, House Types, and *Isonomia* in Classical Greece." 98:314–15.

Ault, B. A. and L. C. Nevett. 1982. "An Orthogonally Planned Town at Iliokastro in Southern Greece." 86:256.

———. 1996. "Digging Houses: Archaeologies of Classical Greek and Hellenistic Domestic Assemblages." 100:349–50.

Dengate, J. A. 1972. "Excavations at Porto Cheli, 1971." 76:208.

———. 1984. "Spear- and Arrow-heads from Halieis." 88:242.

Frost, F. J. 1984. "The 'Harbor' at Halieis." 88:244.

Jacobsen, T. W. 1968. "Investigations at Porto Cheli—Halieis, 1967." 72:167.

Jameson, M. H. 1967. "Halieis: Excavations at Porto Cheli." 71:190.

———. 1969. "Halieis—Porto Cheli, 1968." 73:238.

———. 1971. "Excavations at Porto Cheli." 75:204.

Langdon, S. 1989. "The Geometric Period in the Southern Argolid." 93:277.

Matson, F. R. 1968. "The Shoreline Excavation of a Kiln in Greece." 72:168.

Munn, M. H. 1985. "A Late Classical Rural Settlement Phenomenon in the Southern Argolid, Greece." 89:343.

Munn, M. L. Z. 1985. "A Late Roman Kiln Site in the Hermionid, Greece." 89:342–43.

Pope, K. O., and T. H. van Andel. 1982. "Landscape Evolution and Land Use in the Southern Argolid, Greece." 86:281.

Pullen, D. J. 1981. "Progress Report on the Ceramic Vessel Volume Study at Halieis, Greece." 85:212–13.

Rudolph, W. W. 1973b. "Summer Season 1972 in Halieis, Argolid." 77:225.

———. 1987. "Pottery and Context at Halieis." 91:272–73.

AIA Summaries

Boyd, T. D. 1978. "Indiana University Excavations at Halieis, Greece, 1978." *Archaeological Institute of America, Abstracts of the Papers, Eightieth General Meeting, Vancouver, B.C., December 28–30, 1978* 3:19. New York: A.I.A.

Cooper, N. K. 1977. "Two Roof Tile Systems from Halieis." *Archaeological Institute of America, Abstracts of the Papers, Seventy-ninth General Meeting, Atlanta, GA, December 28–30, 1977* 2:22. New York: A.I.A.

Dengate, J. A. 1974. "The Archaic Doric Temple at Mases." *Archaeological Institute of America, Summaries of the Papers Presented, Seventy-sixth General Meeting, Chicago, IL, December 28–30, 1974*:22. New York: A.I.A.

———. 1975. "The Mint of Ancient Halieis." *Archaeological Institute of America, Summaries of the Papers Presented, Seventy-seventh General Meeting, Washington, D.C., December 28–30, 1975*:4. New York: A.I.A.

Frost, F. J. 1974. "Phourkari: A Villa Complex in the Argolid." *Archaeological Institute of America, Summaries of the Papers Presented, Seventy-sixth General Meeting, Chicago, IL, December 28–30, 1974*:24–25. New York: A.I.A.

Rudolph, W. W. 1974. "Excavations in Halieis: 1974." *Archaeological Institute of America, Summaries of the Papers Presented, Seventy-Sixth General Meeting, Chicago, IL, December 28–30, 1974*:21. New York: A.I.A.

———. 1975. "Excavations in Halieis 1975." *Archaeological Institute of America, Summaries of the Papers Presented, Seventy-seventh General Meeting, Washington, D.C., December 28–30, 1975*:3. New York: A.I.A.

Runnels, C. N. 1978. "Evidence for Flaked Stone Tools in Iron Age Greece." *Archaeological Institute of America, Abstracts of the Papers, Eightieth General Meeting, Vancouver B.C., December 28–30, 1978* 3:48. New York: A.I.A.

– APPENDIX B –

List of Excavation Notebooks and Supervisors

The excavation trenches cited in this volume, their supervisors, and the field notebooks in which their findings were recorded may be grouped by area as follows (for a plan locating the numbered areas, see Boyd and Rudolph 1978, 336, fig. 1):

Industrial Terrace, Michael H. Jameson, NB 3 (1962), NB 8 (1965)
Trench 910/150, Marian H. McAllister (1972)

Section H4 (Upper Southeast Wall), Area 2, trenches 1–3, 5, and 7, Thomas N. Hitzl, NB 112 (1970)

Southeast Gate, Area 7
Trench 985/355, Mariana Siderides (1976)
Trench 990/350, Geoffrey Danielson (1974), Elizabeth Siderides (1976)
Trenches 990/355, 990/360, Stockton Garver (1972)
Trenches 995/355, 995/360, Karl Petruso (1974)
Trench 995/365, Tracy Cullen (1975), Elizabeth Crosthwaite (1976)

Section I5 (Lower Southeast Wall), Area 1, trench 1, Thomas N. Hitzl, NB 105 (1970)
Section J5 (East Gate), Area 1, trenches 1 and 2, Merle K. Langdon, NB 103 (1970)
Section J5 (East Tower), Area 1, trenches B and E, Peter B. Smith, NB 511 (1968)
Trenches H, O (OA, OB, OC), Ortolf von Harl, NB 104 (1970)
Trenches F, L, P, T, and U, Philip Betancourt, NB 106, 107, 118 (1970)
Trenches G, K, N, and S, Stephen Diamant, NB 101, 102 (1970)

Trenches J, M, Thomas N. Hitzl, NB 105 (1970)

Trench W, Fred Winter, NB 119, 120 (1970)

Section J5 (Field 29), east of Area 1, trenches A, C, D, Peter B. Smith, NB 511 (1968)

Northeast Command Post, northern part of Area 6
Trench T, Thomas W. Jacobsen, 1962, NB 1.1 and 1.2
Trench 130/370, Terri Tinker (1972), Christina Dengate (1975)
Trench 130/375, Christina Dengate (1975), Barbara A. Goldhor (1976)
Trench 135/370, Arcadia Kocybala (1972)
Trench 135/375, Terri Tinker, Gregory Elftman (1972), James A. Dengate (1975)
Trench 135/380, James A. Dengate (1975), Heidi L. Wood (1976)

Area 5 (Field 10)
Trench 145/235, David Rupp (1972)
Trenches 165/210, 165/215, John Humphrey (1972)

Sections J5, J6 (Middle Wall), Area 3, Ortolf von Harl (1970)

Trench M, Area 4, Michael Chelik (1962), NB 2

Submerged remains of lower town
NB 15 (1965), Frank Frost, David Owen
NB 504 (1968), Michael H. Jameson
NB 750 (1973), Stephen Hallin, Ralph Mason, Cynthia Patterson, Geoffrey Robinson

– APPENDIX C –

Halieis Engineering Survey Elevations

FREDERICK A. COOPER

Beginning in June 1970, horizontal and vertical controls were laid across the archaeological areas of the greater site of ancient Halieis, which extend from the nekropolis at the southeast to the underwater sanctuary some 1500 m at the northeast. The acropolis and lower town create a spread of approximately 1000 m east to west. The coordinate system and datum is that of the Hellenic Army Geodetic Survey, HAGS (formerly GYS). Numerous Permanent Bench Marks (PBM) and Temporary Bench Marks (TBM) were established over the site using the elevation of 51.35 m Mean Sea Level (MSL, see below) on the acropolis monument (no. 20, N 6,957.22 S 16,058.83) but shown as 51.95 (unadjusted) on the HAGS 1:5,000 topographic map (Spetsai area [1965], sheet 7319,7). The corrected elevation of 51.35 was obtained by trigonometric leveling in 1967 and 1968. The datum is that of Mean Sea Level of Corinth (Poseidonia), of which the value was 1.30600 m in 1962. Usually, an elevation for a MSL datum is taken from numerous (hourly) readings over a period of time (5 years or longer) to obtain the average height of sea level as reduced by least squares adjustment. In other words, 0.00000 m MSL Corinth is a computed value, not a permanent marker. In the following text, MSL refers to the Greek datum at Corinth (Poseidonia). At some point in time, probably in 1984, HAGS converted all Mean Sea Level values at stations around Greece to MSL Kavala. This elevation, or the conversion value, has not been obtained. It is likely that HAGS has yielded

the Greek coordinate system and MSL datum to the Universal Transverse Mercator system (UTM) and the WGS-84 ellipsoid datum (HAE) available by the Global Positioning System (GPS). Conversion of the Greek geodetic survey to UTM is a straightforward process.

In any event, on the day in June 1970 of differential leveling from the acropolis monument (51.35 m MSL) to sea level the altitude was –0.968 m MSL. At later times sea level elevations were –1.03 m, –1.04 m, –1.12 m. The difference in sea levels comes from the action of currents more than it does from effects of a tidal range. Comparable readings were taken at the Franchthi Cave where the variation was found to be greater, ±0.20 m, but had a comparable average of –1.1 m MSL (Jacobsen and Farrand 1987, 17). Thirteen turns each way by differential leveling from the HAGS acropolis monument, no. 20 (51.35 m.) to a Permanent Bench Mark set on the East Tower (+ 2.529 m MSL) produced a closure of 0.003 m. An elevation of –0.668 on a steel pipe in a concrete monument served as the PBM for excavations at the undersea sanctuary. Equalizing the lengths of plus and minus sights more or less cancelled errors due to curvature of the earth. When an elevation is cited, it is understood, unless stated otherwise, that it is on Greek datum MSL Corinth. Plus values may or may not have a leading + but minus values always have a leading – and the day-by-day altitude of the water surface in Porto Kheli Bay was approximately –1.0 m.

Halieis Coins, Blanks, Flans: Concordance of HN and HM Numbers with Catalog Numbers

HN 1962-1 (HM 15)	85	HN 1965-17	96
2 (HM 109)	271	18	148
3 (HM 110)	212	19	132
4 (HM 111)	170	20	119
5 (HM 112)	137	21	296
6 (HM 113)	226	22	201
7 (HM 114)	87	23	242
8 (HM 115)	303	24	213
9 (HM 116)	305	25	94
10 (HM 117)	121	26	176
11 (HM 118)	200	27	150
12 (HM 119)	335	28	173
13 (HM 174)	145	29	222
14 (HM 175)	228	30	88
15 (HM 176)	149	31	125
16 (HM 177)	248	32	124
17 (HM 178)	208	33	90
18 (HM 179)	180	34	171
19 (HM 180)	245	35	283
20 (HM 197)	195	36	169
21 (HM 196)	345	37	138
22 (HM 181)	202	38	127
23 (HM 59)	311	39	139
24 (HM 6)	1	40 (HM 312)	312
HN 1965-1	100	HN 1966-1	204
2	128	2	134
3	122	3	not a coin
4	185	4	143
5	91	5	306
6	136	6	104
7	93	7	133
8	329	8	120
9	92	9	184
10	141	HN 1967-1	294
11	199	HN 1968-1	333
12	318	HN 1970-1	131
13	183	2	332
14	142	3	107
15	159	4	165
16	126	5	109

HN 1970-6	**177**	HN 1972-29 (HM 666)	**2**
7	**135**	30 (HM 666)	**315**
8	**144**	31 (HM 666)	**3**
9	**168**	32 (HM 666)	**4**
10	**284**	33 (HM 666)	**5**
11	**270**	34 (HM 666)	**6**
12	**101**	35 (HM 666)	**7**
13	**102**	36 (HM 666)	**8**
14	**110**	37 (HM 666)	**9**
15	**98**	38 (HM 666)	**10**
16	**186**	39 (HM 666)	**11**
17	**205**	40 (HM 666)	**12**
18	**229**	41 (HM 666)	**13**
19	**267**	42 (HM 666)	**14**
20	**297**	43 (HM 666)	**15**
21	**285**	44 (HM 666)	**16**
22	**298**	45 (HM 666)	**17**
23	**146**	46 (HM 666)	**18**
24	**147**	47 (HM 666)	**19**
25	**219**	48 (HM 666)	**20**
26–42[1]		49 (HM 666)	**21**
43	**343**	50 (HM 666)	**63**
HN 1971-1[2]		51 (HM 666)	**22**
2	**339**	52 (HM 805)	**314**
3 (HM 580)	**313**	53 (HM 666)	**23**
HN 1972-1	**130**	54 (HM 666)	**24**
2	**292**	55 (HM 837)	**25**
3	**258**	56 (HM 837)	**26**
4	**194**	57 (HM 837)	**27**
5	**304**	58–62[4]	
6	**198**	HN 1973-1	**105**
7	**290**	2	**341**
8	**342**	3 (FV 348)[5]	
9	**331**	HN 1974-1 (FV 398)[6]	
10	**196**	2 (FV 391)[7]	
11	**272**	3	**191**
12	**207**	4	**309**
13	**293**	5	**328**
14	**158**	6	**206**
15	**123**	7	**97**
16	**266**	8	**84**
17	**291**	9	**299**
18	**182**	10	**326**
19	**261**	11	**161**
20	**238**	12	**175**
21	**273**	13	**187**
22	**336**	14	**320**
23	**344**	15	**327**
24	**319**	16	**95**
25	**256**	17	**233**
26–28[3]		18	**265**

[1] Aigina AR to be published in *The Sanctuary of Apollo. Excavations at Ancient Halieis 4*. Bloomington: Indiana University Press, forthcoming.

[2] Aigina AR. See note 1 above.

[3] East Argolid survey, site C17. See Jameson et al. 1994, 469; the "local informant" donated the coins to the excavation and survey project.

[4] East Argolid survey, site F27. See Jameson et al. 1994, 512. This is a record number only; the coins were not included among the excavation and survey project finds although plaster casts were made.

[5] From the Franchthi Cave. See Dengate 1999, 112, no. 11.

[6] Ibid., 113, no. 15.

[7] Ibid., 113, no. 14.

HN 1974-19	188	HN 1975-52	52
20	340	53	53
21	295	54	54
22	330	55	55
23	263	56	56
24	190	57	58
25	203	58	48
HN 1975-1	151	59	49
2	231	60	50
3	322	61	59
4	323	62	60
5	64	63	61
6	65	64	221
7	66	65	77
8	67	66	276
9	29	67	51
10	30	68	76
11	286	69	78
12	324	70	79
13	277	71	62
14	152	72	243
15	153	73	115
16	28	74	57
17	178	75	218
18	112	76	268
19	225	77	269
20	68	78	254
21	69	79	179
22	181	80	80
23	70	81	282
24	71	82	264
25	193	83	81
26	72	84	82
27	73	85	300
28	31	86	321
29	32	87	220
30	33	88	167
31	34	89	174
32	74	90	281
33	164	91	275
34	287	92	247
35	301	93	246
36	274	94	103
37	114	95	249
38	35	96	117
39	36	97	163
40	37	98	250
41	38	99	116
42	39	100	154
43	40	101	210
44	41	102	155
45	42	103	252
46	43	104	189
47	75	105	325
48	44	106	172
49	45	107	262
50	46	108	307
51	47	109	308

HN 1975-110	**334**		HM 1202 (1975)	**316**
111	**129**		HM 1203 (1975)	**317**
112	**288**			
113	**111**		HM 6 (HN 1962-24)	**1**
114	**224**		HM 15 (HN 1962-1)	**85**
115	**156**		HM 59 (HN 1962-23)	**311**
116	**278**		HM 109 (HN 1962-2)	**271**
117	**140**		HM 110 (HN 1962-3)	**212**
118	**118**		HM 111 (HN 1962-4)	**170**
119	**232**		HM 112 (HN 1962-5)	**137**
120	**106**		HM 113 (HN 1962-6)	**226**
121	**197**		HM 114 (HN 1962-7)	**87**
122	**337**		HM 115 (HN 1962-8)	**303**
123	**86**		HM 116 (HN 1962-9)	**305**
124	**89**		HM 117 (HN 1962-10)	**121**
125	**302**			
126	**251**			
127	**166**		HM 118 (HN 1962-11)	**200**
128	**239**		HM 119 (HN 1962-12)	**331**
129	**234**		HM 174 (HN 1962-13)	**145**
130	**214**		HM 175 (HN 1962-14)	**228**
131	**279**		HM 176 (HN 1962-15)	**149**
132	**280**		HM 177 (HN 1962-16)	**248**
133	**259**		HM 178 (HN 1962-17)	**208**
134	**160**		HM 179 (HN 1962-18)	**180**
135	**217**		HM 180 (HN 1962-19)	**245**
136	**215**		HM 181 (HN 1962-22)	**202**
137	**235**		HM 196 (HN 1962-21)	**345**
138	**236**		HM 197 (HN 1962-20)	**195**
139	**216**		HM 312 (HN 1965-40)	**312**
140	**211**		HM 580 (HN 1971-3)	**313**
141	**260**		HM 666 (HN 1972-29)	**2**
142	**255**		HM 666 (HN 1972-30)	**315**
143	**227**		HM 666 (HN 1972-31–49)	**3–21**
144	**310**		HM 666 (HN 1972-50)	**63**
145	**338**		HM 666 (HN 1972-51)	**22**
146	**240**		HM 666 (HN 1972-53)	**23**
147	**253**		HM 666 (HN 1972-54)	**24**
148	**157**		HM 805 (HN 1972-52)	**314**
149	**99**		HM 837 (HN 1972-55)	**25**
150	**237**		HM 837 (HN 1972-56)	**26**
151	**108**		HM 837 (HN 1972-57)	**27**
152	**209**		HM 1202 (1975)	**316**
153	**257**		HM 1203 (1975)	**317**
154	**230**			
155	**162**			
156	**223**			
157	**244**			
158	**289**			
HN 1976-1	**241**			
2	**83**			
3 (FV 523)[8]				
4 (FV 524)[9]				
HN 1980-1	**113**			
HN 1983-1	**192**			

---

[8] From the Franchthi Cave. See Dengate 1999, 113, no. 13.   [9] Ibid., no. 12.

Citation List

Adam, J.-P. 1982. *L'architecture militaire grecque*. Paris: Picard.

———. 1992. "Approche et défense des portes dans le monde hellénisé." In *Fortificationes antiquae*, ed. S. Van de Maele and J. M. Fossey, 5–43. Amsterdam: J. C. Gieben.

Aeneas Tacticus. W. A. Oldfather, trans. 1923. Loeb Classical Library. New York: G. P. Putnam's Sons.

Apollodoros of Damascus. See Wescher 1867.

Aravantinos, V., A. Konecny, and R. T. Marchese. 2003. "Plataiai in Boiotia: A Preliminary Report of the 1996–2001 Campaigns." *Hesperia* 72:281–320.

Archontidou-Argyri, A., A. Simossi, and J.-Y. Empereur. 1989. "The Underwater Excavation at the Ancient Port of Thasos, Greece." *International Journal of Underwater Archaeology* 18.1:51–59.

Arvanitopoulos, A. S. 1928. *Graptai Stelai Demetriados-Pagason*. Athens.

Ault, B. A. 1999. "Koprones and Oil Presses at Halieis." *Hesperia* 68:549–73.

———. 2005. *The Houses: The Organization and Use of Domestic Space*. The Excavations at Ancient Halieis 2. Bloomington: Indiana University Press.

Bérard, V. 1892. "Tégée et la Tégéatide." *Bulletin de correspondance hellénique* 16:529–49.

Bernard, P. 1985. *Les monnaies hors des trésor*. Fouilles d'Aï Khanoum 4. Mémoires de la delegation archéologique française en Afghanistan 28. Paris: Boccard.

Bessac, J.-C. 1986. "Approche des problèmes posés par la construction des remparts grec en pierre." In Leriche and Tréziny 1986, 273–82.

Blackman, D. J. 1982. "Ancient Harbours in the Mediterranean." *International Journal of Nautical Archaeology and Underwater Exploration* 11:79–104, 183–211.

Blouet, A. 1833. *Expédition scientifique de la Morée* II, Paris.

Bogaert, R. 1968. *Banques et banquiers dans les cités grecques*, Leiden: A. W. Sijthoff.

Boyd, T. D. and M. H. Jameson. 1981. "Urban and Rural Land Division in Ancient Greece." *Hesperia* 50:327–42.

Boyd, T. D., and W. W. Rudolph. 1978. "Excavations at Porto Cheli and Vicinity, Preliminary Report IV: The Lower Town of Halieis, 1970–1977." *Hesperia* 47:333–55.

Cahill, N. 2002. *Household and City Organization at Olynthus*. New Haven: Yale University Press.

Camp, J. M. II. 1986. *The Athenian Agora: Excavations in the Heart of Classical Athens*. London and New York: Thames and Hudson.

Camp, J. M. II, and J. H. Kroll. 2001. "The Agora Mint and Athenian Bronze Coinage." *Hesperia* 70:127–62.

Cantilena, R. 1989. "Rinvenimento di un'officina monetale a Laos." In *Laos I: Scavi a Marcellina 1973–1985*, ed. E. Greco, S. Luppino, and A. Schnapp, 25–37 and 87–88. Taranto: Istituto per la Storia e l'Archeologia della Magna Grecia.

Carpenter, R., and A. Bon, with A. W. Parsons. 1936. *The Defenses of Acrocorinth and the Lower Town*. Corinth. Results of Excavations Conducted by the American School of Classical Studies at Athens 3.2. Cambridge: Harvard University Press.

Charitonidis, S., and R. Ginouvès. 1955. "Bain romain de Zevgolatio près de Corinthe." *Bulletin de correspondance hellénique* 79:102–20.

Consolaki, H., and T. Hackens. 1980. "Un atelier monétaire dans un temple argien?" In *Études Argiennes*. Bulletin de correspondance hellénique, supplément 6, 279–94. Paris: École française d'Athènes.

Conze, A. 1913. *Altertümer von Pergamon* I, ii, *Die Stadt*, Berlin.

Cooper, F. A. 1987. "The Engineering Survey." In T. W. Jacobsen and W. R. Farrand, *Franchthi Cave and Paralia. Maps, Plans, and Sections*. Excavations at Franchthi Cave, Greece, Fascicle 1: 10–14. Bloomington: Indiana University Press.

Cooper, N. K. 1989. *The Development of Roof Revetment in the Peloponnesos*. Studies in Mediterranean Archaeology and Literature, Pocket book 88. Jonsered: Paul Åströms Förlag.

Coulton, J. J. 1996. "Euboean Phylla and Greek Barracks." In *Minotaur and Centaur: Studies in the Archaeology of Crete and Euboea Presented to Mervyn Popham*, ed. D. Evely, I. S. Lemos, and S. Sherratt. British Archaeological Reports, International Series 638:161–65.

———. 2002. *The Fort at Phylla, Vrachos*. Annual of the British School at Athens Supplement 33.

Dengate, C. F. 1976 [1980]. "A Group of Graves Excavated at Halieis." *Archaiologikon Deltion* 31.1:274–324.

Dengate, C., J. A. Dengate, M. H. Jameson, J. H. Leslie, D. Reese, and C. K. Williams II. n.d. *The Acropolis. The Excavations at Ancient Halieis 3.* Bloomington: Indiana University Press, forthcoming.

Dengate, J. 1975. "The Mint of Ancient Halieis." *Archaeological Institute of America, Summaries of the Papers Presented, Seventy-seventh General Meeting, Washington, D.C., December 28–30, 1975:4.* New York: A.I.A.

———. 1999. "Document 2: Post-Neolithic Franchthi." In K. D. Vitelli, *Franchthi Neolithic Pottery*, vol. 2, *The Later Neolithic Ceramic Phases 3 to 5*, 111–23, 328–29. Excavations at Franchthi Cave, Greece, Fascicle 10. Bloomington: Indiana University Press.

———. n.d. "The Coins: Interpretation" chapter 5, "Metal and Miscellaneous Finds" chapter 8, "Acropolis Deposits" chapter 11. In Dengate, C. et al. n.d.

Ervin, M. 1967. "News Letter from Greece." *American Journal of Archeology* 71:293–306.

Forsell, R. 1996. "The Roman Period." In *The Berbati-Limnes Archaeological Survey 1988–1990*, ed. B. Wells and C. Runnels, 285-343. Skrifter utgivna Svenska Institutet i Athen, series in quarto, 44. Stockholm: Paul Åströms Förlag.

Frickenhaus, A., and W. Müller. 1911. "Aus der Argolis." *Mitteilungen des deutschen archäologischen Instituts, Athenische Abteilung* 36:21–38.

Frost, F. J. 1977. "Phourkari. A Villa Complex in the Argolid (Greece)." *International Journal of Nautical Archaeology and Underwater Exploration* 5:233–38.

———. 1985. "The 'Harbour' at Halieis." In *Harbour Archaeology. Proceedings of the First International Workshop on Ancient Mediterranean Harbours, Caesarea Maritima 24–28.6.83*, ed. A. Raban, 63–66. British Archaeological Reports International Series 257.

Frödin, O., and A. W. Persson. 1938. *Asine. Results of the Swedish Excavations 1922–1930.* Stockholm: Generalstabens Litografiska Anstalts Förlag.

Garlan, Y. 1966. "Contribution à une étude stratigraphique de l'enceinte thasienne." *Bulletin de correspondance hellénique* 90:586–652.

———. 1974. *Recherches de poliorcétique grecque.* Paris: École française d'Athènes.

Georgiades, A. S. 1907. *Les ports de la Grèce dans l'antiquité qui subsistent encore aujourd'hui.* Athens.

Ginouvès, R. 1962. *Balaneutikè.* Bibliothèque des Écoles Françaises d'Athènes et Rome 200. Paris.

———. 1955. "Sur un aspect de l'évolution des bains en grèce vers le IVe siècle de notre ére." *Bulletin de correspondance hellénique* 79:133–52.

Goette, H. R. 1999. In D. Blackman, "Archaeology in Greece, 1998–99." *Archaeological Reports for 1998–1999*:19–20.

Goldman, H. 1940. "The Acropolis of Halae." *Hesperia* 9:381–514.

Golenko, K. 1975. "Nordliches Schwarzmeergebiet." *Chiron* 5: 497–633.

Hackens, T. 1975. "Terminologies et techniques de fabrication." In *Numismatique antique: Problèmes et méthodes: Actes du colloque organisé à Nancy du 27 septembre au 2 octobre 1971 par l'Université de Nancy II et l'Université Catholique de Louvain*, ed. J.-M. Dentzer, Ph. Gauthier, and T. Hackens, 3–21. Études d'archéologie classique 4. Annales de l'est, mémoire 44. Nancy-Louvain: Éditions Peeters.

Harris, D. 1995. *The Treasures of the Parthenon and Erechtheion.* Oxford Monographs on Classical Archaeology. Oxford: Clarendon Press.

Harrison, C. M. 1999. "Triremes at Rest: On the Beach or in the Water?" *Journal of Hellenic Studies* 119:168–71.

Head, B. V. 1911. *Historia Numorum*, 2nd ed. Oxford: Clarendon Press. Reprint 1963. London: Spink and Son.

Hill, B. H. 1966. *The Temple of Zeus at Nemea.* Princeton: The American School of Classical Studies at Athens.

Hill, G. F. 1922. "Ancient Methods of Coining." *Numismatic Chronicle*, ser. 5, 2:1–42.

Höghammar, K. 1984. "The Dating of the Roman Bath at Asine in Argolis." *Opuscula Atheniensia* 15:79–106.

Howgego, C. 1995. *Ancient History from Coins.* Approaching the Ancient World, ed. Richard Stoneman. London: Routledge.

Jacobsen, T. W. 1968. "Halieis (Porto-Cheli)." *Archaiologikon Deltion* 23.2:144–48.

———. 1969 [1970]. "Excavations at Porto Cheli." *Archaiologikon Deltion* 24.2:124–29.

Jameson, M. H. 1963 [1965]. "Excavations at Porto-Cheli." *Archaiologikon Deltion* 18.2:73–74.

———. 1969 [1970]. "Excavations at Porto Cheli and Vicinity, Preliminary Report I: Halieis 1962–1968." *Hesperia* 38:311–42.

———. 1972 [1976]. "Excavations at Porto Cheli. Excavations at Halieis, Final Report." *Archaiologikon Deltion* 27.2:233–36.

———. 1973. "Halieis at Porto Cheli." *Colston Papers, Being the Proceedings of the Twentythird Symposium of the Colston Research Society Held in the University of Bristol, April 4th to April 8th, 1971* 23:219–29. London: Butterworths Scientific Publications.

———. 1973–1974 [1979]. "Excavations at Halieis (Porto Cheli) 1973." *Archaiologikon Deltion* 29.2:261–64.

———. 1974. "A Treasury of Athena in the Argolid (*IG* IV, 554)." In *Phoros. Tribute to Benjamin Dean Meritt*, ed. D. W. Bradeen and M. F. McGregor, 67–75. Locust Valley, N.Y.: J. J. Augustin.

———. 2004. "Mapping Greek Cults." *Chora und Polis*, ed. Frank Kolb, 147–83. Schriften des Historischen Kollegs, Kolloquien 54. Munich: Oldenbourg Verlag.

———. n.d. "History" chapter 1, "The Industrial Terrace" chapter 3, "Writing" chapter 9. In Dengate, C. et al. n.d.

Jameson, M. H., and T. D. Boyd. 1981. "Urban and Rural Land Division in Ancient Greece." *Hesperia* 50:327–42.

M. H. Jameson, C. N. Runnels, and T. H. van Andel, with M. H. Munn. 1994. *A Greek Countryside: The Southern Argolid from Prehistory to the Present Day.* Stanford: Stanford University Press.

Jameson, V. B., and M. H. Jameson. 1950. "An Archaeological and Topographical Survey of the Hermionid." Papers of the American School of Classical Studies at Athens. (Unpublished, available at ASCSA.)

Jerkich, L. n.d. "Some Corinthian Tiles Excavated at Halieis in 1974." (Unpublished paper, Indiana University.)

Judeich, W. 1905. *Handbuch der Klassischen Altertums-Wissenschaft* III 2²: *Topographie von Athen.* Munich: C. H. Beck.

Kalligas, P. G. 1997. "A Bronze Die from Sounion." In *Numismatic Archaeology, Archaeological Numismatics: Proceedings of the International Conference held to honour Dr. Mando Oeconomides in Athens 1995,* ed. K. A. Sheedy and C. Papageorgiadou-Baris, 141–47. The Australian Archaeological Institute at Athens. Oxbow Monograph 75. Oxford: Oxbow Books.

Kostsyushko-Valyuzhinich, D. N. 1914. "Zamiatki, o tekhnike monetnago dela v Khersonese Tavricheskom." *Numizmaticheskii Sbornik.* (Moscow Numismatic Society) 3:162–70. (Abstract in Golenko 1975, 575, no. 286.)

Kraynak, L. H. 1984. *Hostelries of Ancient Greece.* Ph.D. diss., University of California, Berkeley. Ann Arbor: University Microfilms International. Pub. No. AAT 8427018. *Dissertation Abstracts International* 45.9 (1985): 2907.

Krischen, F. 1922. *Milet,* III, ii, *Die Befestigung von Herakleia am Latmos,* Berlin/Leipzig.

———. 1938. *Die griechische Stadt.* Berlin: Verlag gebr. Mann.

Kroll, J. H., with A. S. Walker. 1993. *The Greek Coins.* The Athenian Agora 26. Princeton: The American School of Classical Studies at Athens.

Lawn, B. 1975. "University of Pennsylvania Carbon Dates, XVIII." *Radio-Carbon* 17:196–215.

Lawrence, A. W. 1979. *Greek Aims in Fortification.* Oxford: Clarendon Press.

Lazarides, D. 1975. "Amphipolis." *Athens Annals of Archaeology:* 63–71.

Lehmann-Hartleben, K. 1923. "Die antiken Hafenlagen des Mittelmeeres." *Klio* 14:65–74.

Lerat, L., and F. Chamoux.1947–1948. "Voyage en Locride occidentale." *Bulletin de correspondance hellénique* 71–72:47–80.

Leriche, P., and H. Tréziny, eds. 1986. *La fortification dans l'histoire du monde grec, Actes du Colloque International, la fortification et sa place dans l'histoire politique, culturelle et sociale du monde grec, Valbonne, Décembre 1982.* Éditions du Centre National de la Recherche Scientifique. Paris.

Maier, F. G. 1959. *Griechische Mauerbauinschriften.* vol. 1. Heidelberg: Quelle und Meyer.

Malkmus, W. 1989–93. "Addenda to Vermeule's Catalog of Ancient Coin Dies." *Journal for the Society of Ancient Numismatics,* 17.4:80–85; 18.1:16–22; 18.2:40–49; 18.3:72–77; 18.4:96–105.

Martin, R. 1947–1948. "Gortys." *Bulletin de correspondance hellénique* 71–72:81–147.

———. 1965. *Manuel d'architecture grecque,* I, *Matériaux et techniques,* Paris: Éditions A. et J. Picard.

McAllister, M. H. 1969. "A Temple at Hermione." *Hesperia* 38:169–85.

McNicoll, A. 1986. "Developments in Techniques of Siegecraft and Fortifications in the Greek World ca. 400–100 B.C." In Leriche and Tréziny 1986: 305–13.

McNicoll, A. W., and N. P. Milner. 1997. *Hellenistic Fortifications from the Aegean to the Euphrates.* Oxford: Clarendon Press.

Milner, N. P. 1997. "Conclusions and Recent Developments." In McNicoll and Milner 1997: 207–23.

Mee, C., and H. Forbes. 1997. *A Rough and Rocky Place. The Landscape and Settlement History of the Methana Peninsula, Greece.* Liverpool Monographs in Archaeology and Oriental Studies. Liverpool: Liverpool University Press.

Morrison, J. S., and R. T. Williams. 1968. *Greek Oared Ships 900–322 B.C.* London: Cambridge University Press.

Munn, M. L. Z. 1985. "A Late Roman Kiln Site in the Hermionid, Greece." *American Journal of Archaeology* 89:342–43.

Mussche, H. F. 1961. "La forteresse maritime de Thorikos." *Bulletin de correspondance hellénique* 85:176–205.

Mylonas, G. E. 1975. *To Dytikon Nekrotapheion tes Eleusinos.* vol. 2. Athens.

Nicholls, R. V. 1958–1959. "Old Smyrna: The Iron Age Fortifications and Associated Remains on the City Perimeter." *Annual of the British School at Athens* 53–54:35–137.

Nikolaou, I., and O. Mørkholm. 1976. *Paphos I. A Ptolemaic Coin Hoard.* Nicosia.

Nikolaou, K. 1972a. "Decouvert d'un Hôtel des Monnaies de l'époque ptolemaique à Paphos (Cypre)." *Bulletin de la Société française de numismatique* 27:310–15.

———. 1972b. "Discovery of a Ptolemaic Mint at Nea Paphos." In *Praktika tou protou diethnous Kyprologikou synedriou, Leukosia, 14–19 Apriliou 1969. I. Archaion tmima,* ed. V. Karageorghis and A. Christodoulos. Nicosia.

Noack, F. 1907. "Die Mauern Athens, Ausgrabungen und Untersuchungen." *Mitteilungen des deutschen archäologischen Instituts, Athenische Abteilung* 32:123–60.

Ober, J. 1987. "Early Artillery Towers: Messenia, Boiotia, Attica, Megarid." *American Journal of Archaeology* 91:569–604.

Oikonomidou, M. 1993. "Ena nomismatokopeio stin archaia Pella." In *Archaia Makedonia: Pempto Diethnes Symposio,* 2:1143–54. Thessaloniki.

Orlandos, A. K. 1958. *Ta ylika domes ton archaion Ellenon kai oi tropoi epharmoges auton.* II, Bibilotheke tes en Athenais Archaiologikes Etaireias 37. Athens. Trans. V. Hadjimichali. 1966–68. *Les materiaux de construction et la technique architectural des anciens grecs,* I–II, Paris.

Osborne, R. 1996. *Greece in the Making, 1200–479 BC.* London: Routledge.

Palladio, A. 1997. *The Four Books on Architecture.* Trans. R. Tavernor and R. Schofield. Cambridge: The MIT Press.

Paris, J. 1915. "Contributions à l'étude des ports antiques du monde grec." *Bulletin de correspondance hellénique* 39:5–16.

Payne, H. G. G. 1932. "Archaeology in Greece." *Journal of Hellenic Studies* 52:236–55.

Penttinen, A. 1996. "Excavations on the Acropolis of Asine in 1990." *Opuscula Atheniensia* 21:149–66.

Philadelpheus, A. 1909. "Ai en Ermionidi anaskaphai." *Praktika tes en Athenais Archaiologikes Etaireias tou etous 1909*: 172–84.

Pickard, J. 1891. "A Topographical Study of Eretria." *American Journal of Archaeology,* ser. 1, 7:371–89.

Pouilloux, J. 1954. *La forteresse de Rhamnonte.* Paris: E. de Boccard.

Powell, B. 1904. "Oeniadae: History and Topography." *American Journal of Archaeology,* ser. 2, 8:137–201.

Pullen, D. 2000. "The Prehistoric Remains of the Acropolis at Halieis: A Final Report." *Hesperia* 69:133–87.

Rafn, B. 1991. "Archaic and Classical Graves at Halieis: A Summary." In *Recent Danish Research in Classical Archaeology,* ed. T. Fischer-Hansen et al., 57–71. Acta Hyperborea: Danish Studies in Classical Archaeology 3. Copenhagen: Museum Tusculanum Press.

Raubitschek, I. K. 1998. *The Metal Objects (1952–1989).* Isthmia. Excavations by the University of Chicago 7. Princeton: The American School of Classical Studies at Athens.

Robinson, D. M. 1941. *Metal and Minor Miscellaneous Finds.* Excavations at Olynthus 10. The Johns Hopkins University Studies in Archaeology 31. Baltimore: The Johns Hopkins Press.

———. 1952. *Terracottas, Lamps and Coins Found in 1934 and 1938.* Excavations at Olynthus 14. The Johns Hopkins University Studies in Archaeology 19. Baltimore: The Johns Hopkins Press.

Robinson, D. M., and J. W. Graham. 1938. *The Hellenic House.* Excavations at Olynthus 8. The Johns Hopkins University Studies in Archaeology 25. Baltimore: The Johns Hopkins Press.

Rochas d'Aiglun, E.-A. A. 1881. *Principes de la fortification antique.* Paris.

Rudolph, W. W. 1973 [1977]. "Excavations in Halieis (Porto Cheli)." *Archaiologikon Deltion* 28.2:159–63.

———. 1973–1974 [1979]. "Excavations at Halieis (Porto Cheli) 1973." *Archaiologikon Deltion* 29.2:261–64.

———. 1974. "Excavations at Porto Cheli and Vicinity, Preliminary Report, III: Excavations at Metochi 1970." *Hesperia* 43: 105–31.

———. 1979. "Excavations at Porto Cheli and Vicinity, Preliminary Report V: The Early Byzantine Remains." *Hesperia* 48:294–324.

———. 1984. "Excavations at Porto Cheli and Vicinity, Preliminary Report VI: Halieis, the Stratigraphy of the Streets in the Northeast Quarter of the Lower Town." *Hesperia* 53:123–70.

———. 1991. "Eine orientalisierende Pyxis aus Halieis." In *Stips Votiva. Papers Presented to C. M. Stibbe,* ed. M. Gnade, 177–83. Amsterdam: Allard Pierson Museum.

Runnels, C. N. 1981. *A Diachronic Study and Economic Analysis of Millstones from the Argolid, Greece.* Ph.D. diss., Indiana University. Ann Arbor: University Microfilms International. Order No. 81-19022. *Dissertation Abstracts International* 42.3 (1981): 1225-A.

———. 1982. "Flaked-stone Artifacts in Greece during the Historical Period." *Journal of Field Archaeology* 9:363–73.

Rusch, S. 1997. *Poliorcetic Assault in the Peloponnesian War.* Ph.D. diss., University of Pennsylvania. Ann Arbor: University Microfilms International. Pub. No. AAT 9727289. *Dissertation Abstracts International* 58.3 (1997): 1031.

Sanders, G. D. R. 1999. "A Late Roman Bath at Corinth: Excavations in the Panayia Field, 1995–1996." *Hesperia* 68:441–80.

Schoder, R. V. 1974. *Ancient Greece from the Air.* London: Thames and Hudson.

Scranton, R. L. 1938. "The Fortifications of Athens in the Peloponnesian War." *American Journal of Archaeology* 42:525–36.

Shoe, L. T. 1936. *Profiles of Greek Mouldings.* Cambridge: Harvard University Press.

Snodgrass, A. M. 1964. *Early Greek Armour and Weapons.* Edinburgh: University Press.

———. 1986. "The Historical Significance of Fortification in Archaic Greece." In Leriche and Tréziny 1986: 125–31.

Sparkes, B. A., and L. Talcott. 1970. *Black and Plain Pottery of the 6th, 5th, and 4th Centuries B.C.* The Athenian Agora 12. Princeton: The American School of Classical Studies at Athens.

Stählin, F., E. Meyer, and A. Heidner. 1934. *Demetrias und Pagasai. Beschreibung der Reste und Stadtgeschichte.* Berlin/Leipzig.

Stillwell, A. N. 1948. *The Potters' Quarter.* Corinth. Results of Excavations Conducted by the American School of Classical Studies at Athens 15.1. Princeton: ASCSA.

Sulimirski, T. 1954. "Scythian Antiquities in Western Asia." *Artibus Asiae* 17:282–318.

Svoronos, I. N. 1898. "Peri ton eisitarion ton archaion." *Journal international d'archéologie numismatique* 1:37–120.

———. 1907. "Ermionidos Alieis oi ex Tirinthos kai ta nomismata auton." *Journal international d'archéologie numismatique* 10:5–34.

———. 1926. *Les monnaies d'Athènes.* Completed by B. Pick, English trans. L. W. Higgie, reprint 1975, *Corpus of the Ancient Coins of Athens.* Chicago: Ares.

Thompson, H. A. 1937. "Buildings on the West Side of the Agora." *Hesperia* 6:1–226.

Thompson, H. A., and R. E. Wycherly. 1972. *The Agora of Athens: The History, Shape and Uses of an Ancient City Center.* The Athenian Agora 14. Princeton: The American School of Classical Studies at Athens.

Thompson, M., O. Møkholm, and C. M. Kraay, eds. 1973. *An Inventory of Greek Coin Hoards,* International Numismatic Commission. New York: The American Numismatic Society.

Tomlinson, R. A. 1961. "*Emplekton* Masonry and 'Greek Structura.'" *Journal of Hellenic Studies* 81:133–40.

Tréziny, H. 1986. "Les techniques grecques de fortifications et leur diffusion à la périptérie du monde grec d'occident." In Leriche and Tréziny 1986:185–200.

Van Andel, T. and N. Lianos. 1983. "Prehistoric and Historic Shorelines of the Argolid Peninsula, Greece." *International Journal for Nautical Archaeology and Underwater Exploration* 24:303–24.

Velenis, G. 1996. "Nomismatokopeio stin archaia agora tis Thessalonikis." In *Charaktir: Aphieroma sti Manto Oikonomidou,* 49–60. Athens.

Vermeule, C. C. 1954. *Some Notes on Ancient Dies and Coining Methods.* Reprinted from *Numismatic Circular,* 1953–54. London: Spink and Son.

———. 1957. "Minting Greek and Roman Coins." *Archaeology* 10:100–107.

Voegtli, H. 1990. "Zwei Münzeunde aus Pergamon." *Schweizerische Numismatische Rundschau* 69:41–63.

Von Gerkan, A. 1935. *Milet,* II, iii, *Die Stadtmauern.* Berlin.

Wace, A. J. B. 1905–1906. "Excavations at Sparta, 1906: The City Wall." *Annual of the British School at Athens* 12:284–94.

———. 1906–1907. "Excavations at Sparta, 1907: The City Wall." *Annual of the British School at Athens* 13:5–16.

Wace, A. J. B., and F. W. Hasluck. 1908–1909. "East-Central Laconia." *Annual of the British School at Athens* 15:158–76.

Walker, A. S. 1997. "Excavation Coins: The Use and Misuse of Numismatic Evidence in Archaeology." In *Numismatic Archaeology, Archaeological Numismatics: Proceedings of the International Conference held to honour Dr. Mando Oeconomides in Athens 1995,* ed. K. A. Sheedy and C. Papageorgiadou-Baris, 17–26. The Australian Archaeological Institute at Athens. Oxbow Monograph 75. Oxford: Oxbow Books.

Welter, G. 1938. "Aeginetica I–XII." *Archäologische Anzeiger* 53:8–15.

Wescher, C. 1867. *Poliorcétique des Grecs.* Paris: Imprimerie impériale.

Williams, C. K. II. n.d. "The Architecture." In Dengate et al. n.d., chap. 2.

Williams, C. K. II. 1981. "A Survey of Pottery from Corinth from 730 to 600 B.C." *Annuario* 59:139–55.

Winter, F. E. 1971. *Greek Fortifications.* Phoenix Supplement 9. Toronto: University of Toronto Press.

———. 1986. "A Summary of Recent Work on Greek Fortifications in Greece and Asia Minor." Leriche and Tréziny 1986, 23–29.

———. 1991. "The Chronology of the Ancient Defenses of Acrocorinth: A Reconsideration." *American Journal of Archaeology* 95:109–21.

Wrede, W. 1924–1925. "Phyle." *Mitteilungen des deutschen archäologischen Instituts, Athenische Abteilung* 49/50:153–224.

———. 1933. *Attische Mauern.* Athens: Deutsches Archäologisches Institut.

Wycherley, R. E. 1957. *Literary and Epigraphical Testimonia.* The Athenian Agora 3. Princeton: The American School of Classical Studies at Athens.

———. 1978. *The Stones of Athens.* Princeton: Princeton University Press.

Young, J. H. 1963. "A Migrant City in the Peloponnesus." *Expedition* 5.3:2–11.

Zangger, E. 1994. "The Island of Asine: A Palaeogeographic Reconstruction." *Opuscula Atheniensia* 20:221–39.

Index

Marian H. McAllister holds a doctorate in Classical archaeology
from Bryn Mawr College and a master's degree in architecture
from Columbia University. Her field experience was gained at the
Agora Excavations in Athens and as field architect for the British
excavations at Mycenae, as well as later at Halieis. She has had
articles published in *Hesperia* and the Annual of the British School
in Athens and was assistant editor and contributor for the *Princeton
Encyclopedia of Classical Sites.* At the time of her retirement she
had completed twenty-five years as Editor of Publications for the
American School of Classical Studies at Athens.

Figures

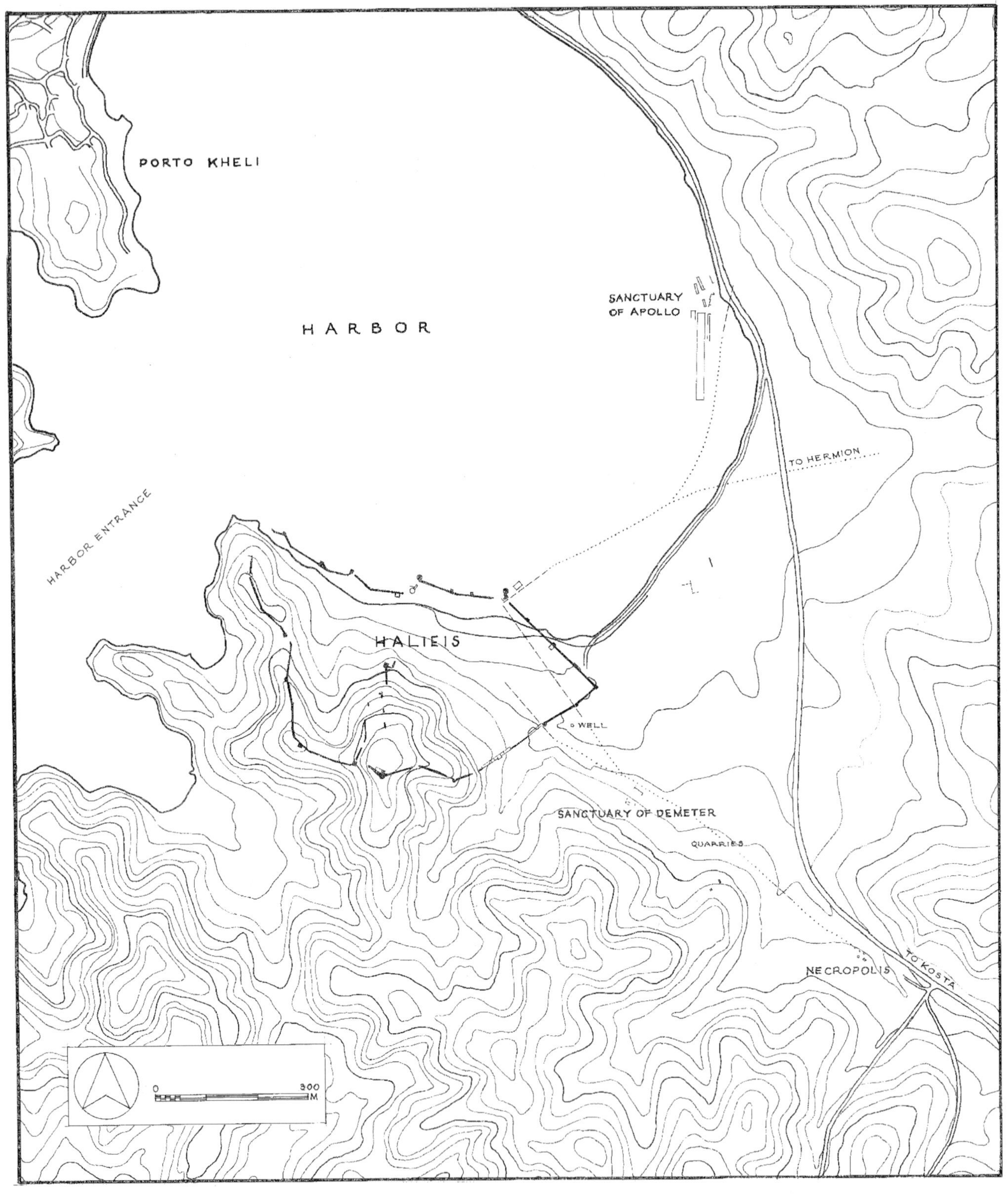

Fig. 17. Site of ancient Halieis and vicinity

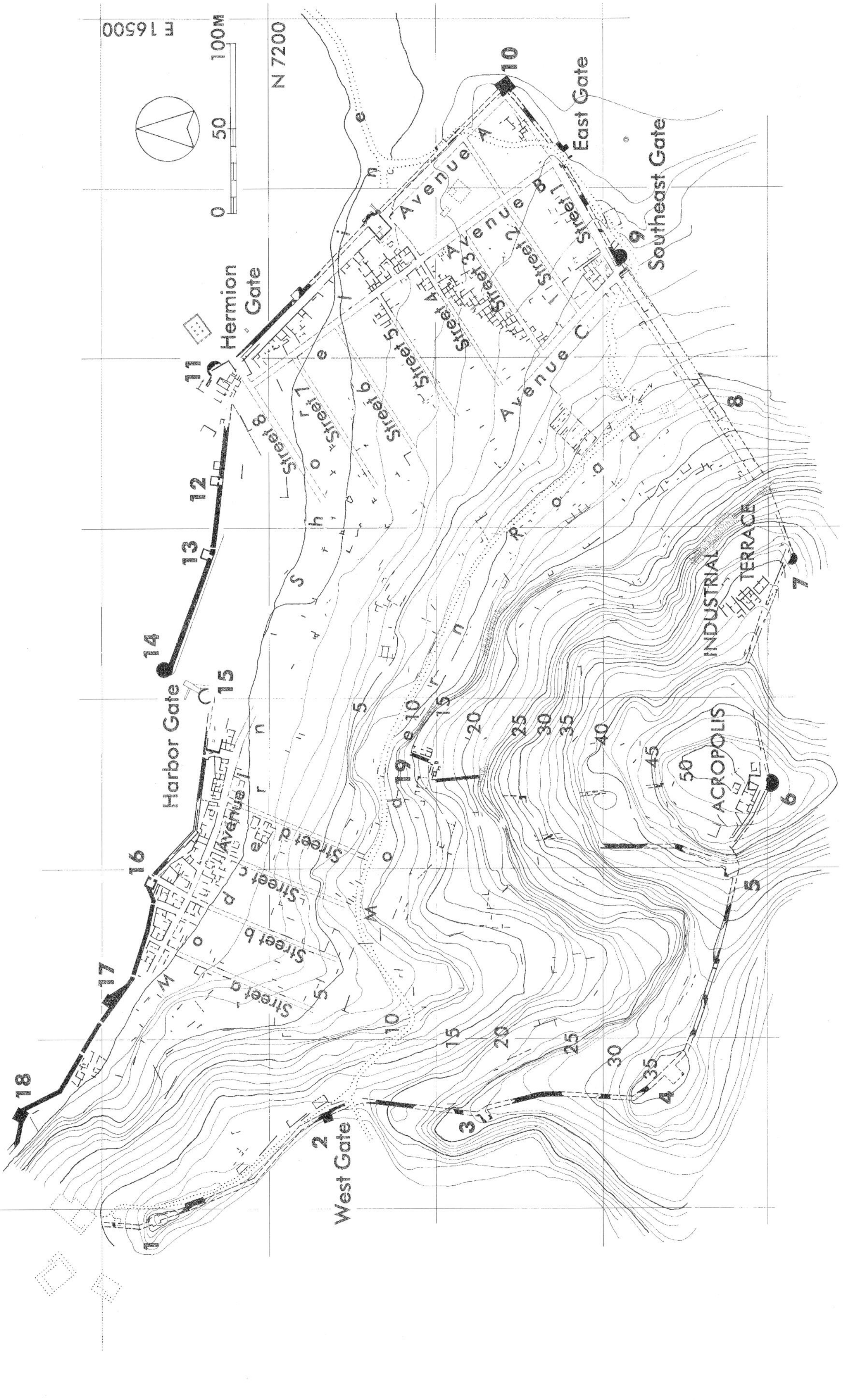

Fig. 18. General site survey plan

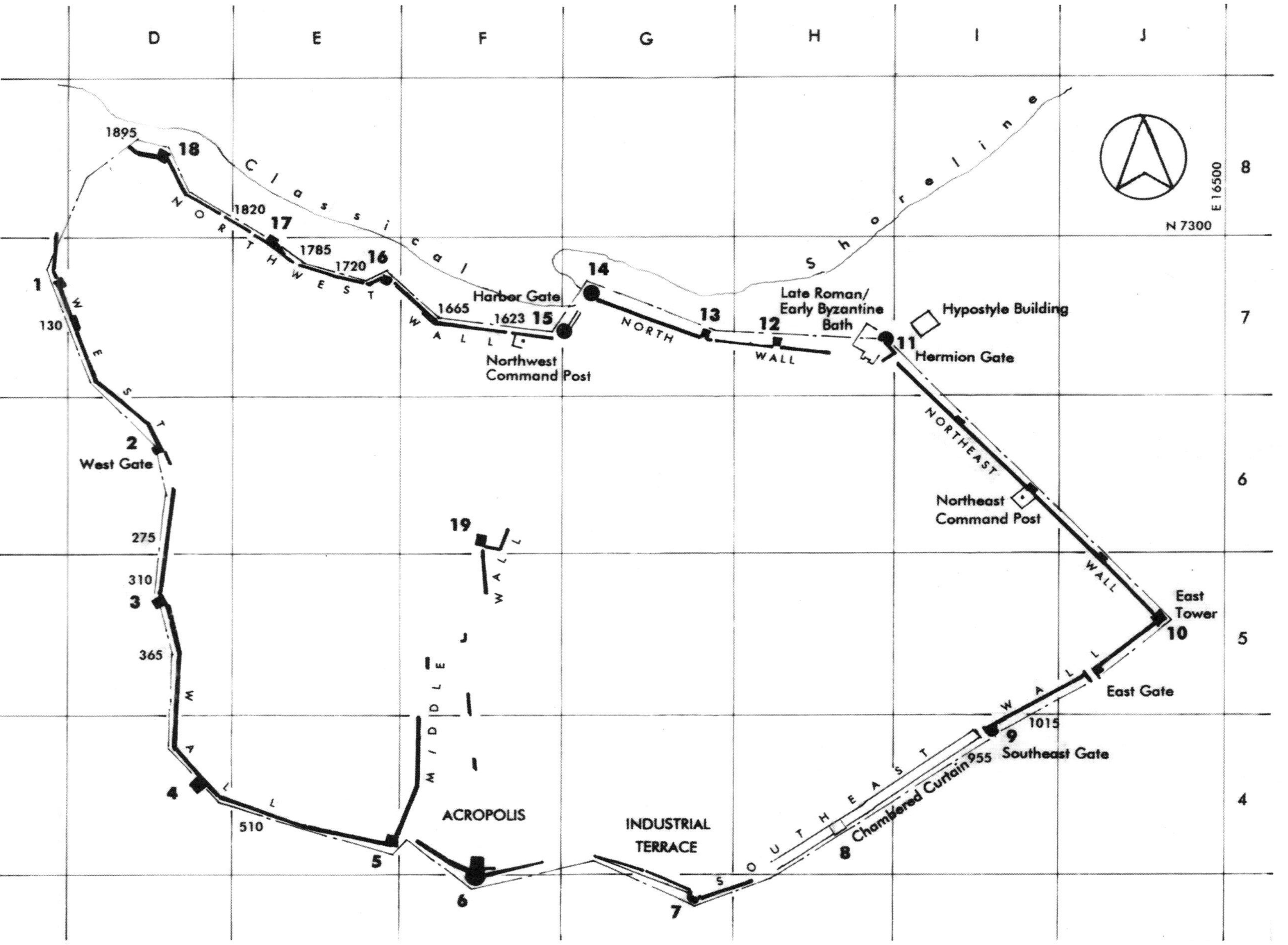

Fig. 19. Key plan showing towers, gates, and sections of curtain wall with running measure line enclosing the circuit; principal structures associated with the fortifications; 100-meter-square excavation sections (1970)

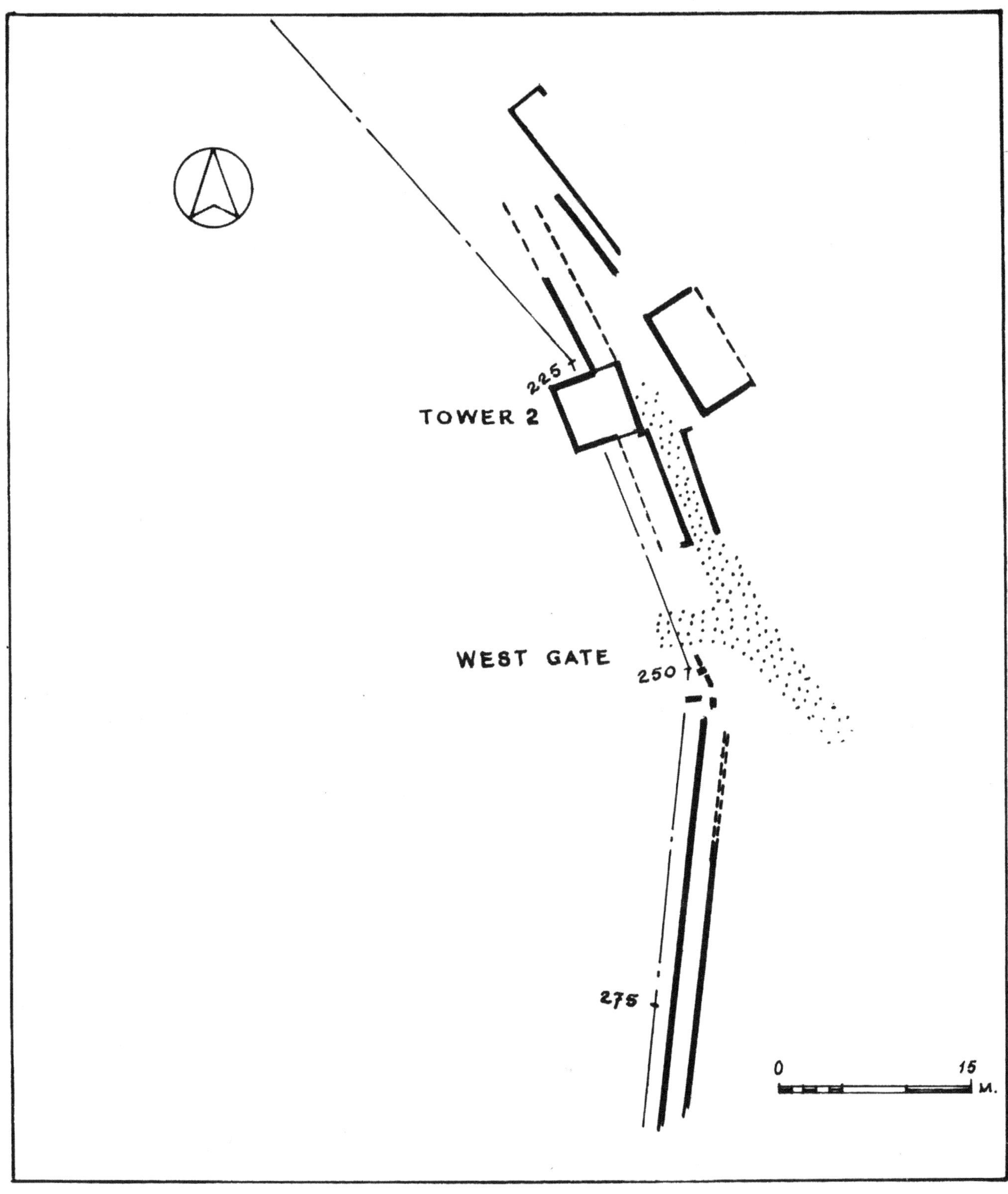

Fig. 20. West Gate and Tower 2

Fig. 21. Acropolis: Tower 6

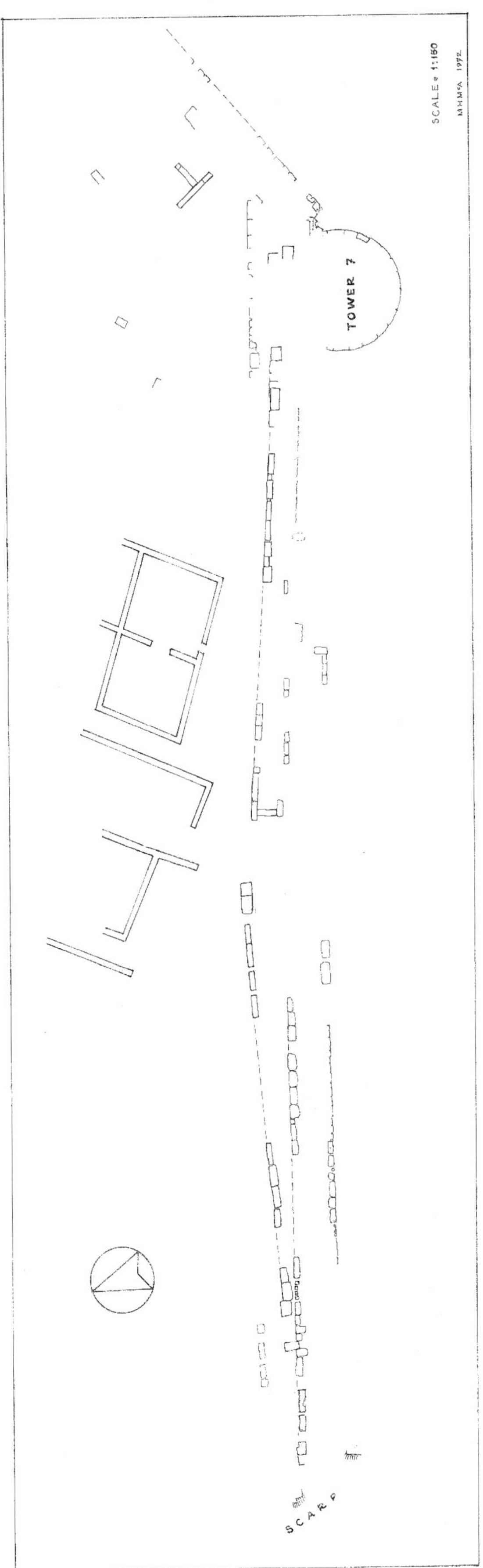

Fig. 22. Industrial Terrace: Tower 7

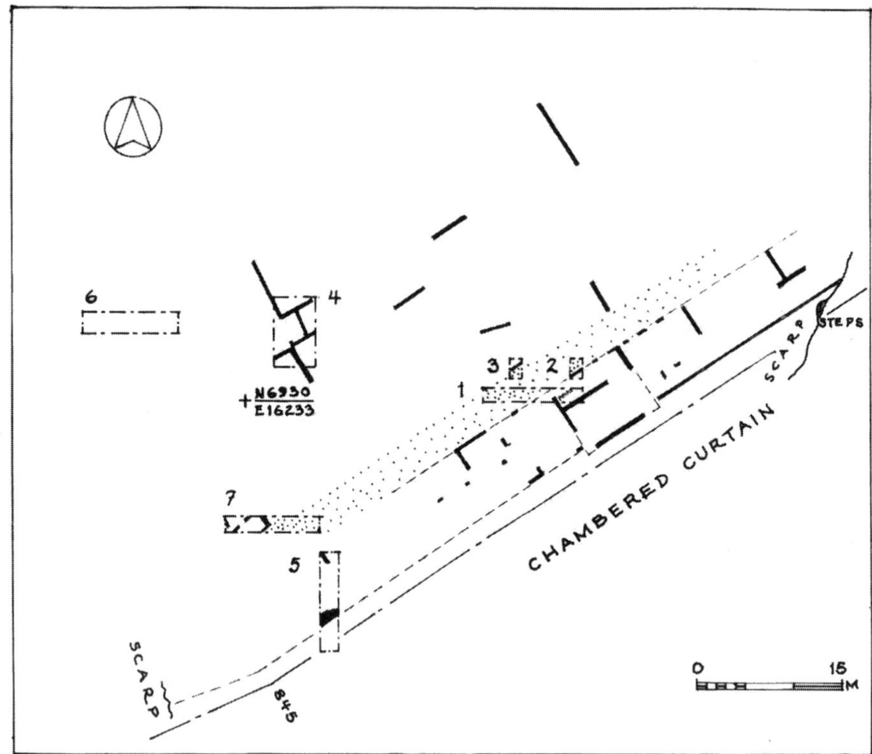

Fig. 23. *Upper Southeast Wall: Chambered Curtain and Tower 8*

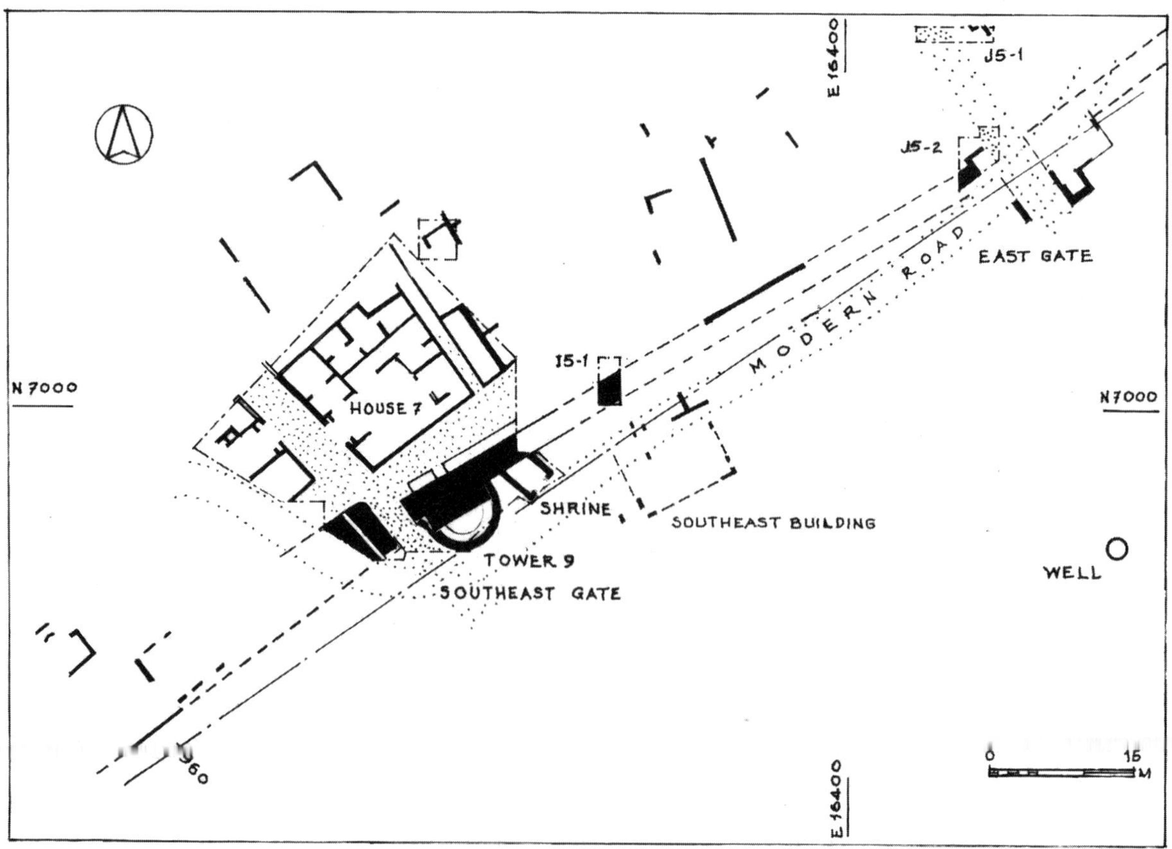

Fig. 24. *Lower Southeast Wall: Tower 9 and East Gate*

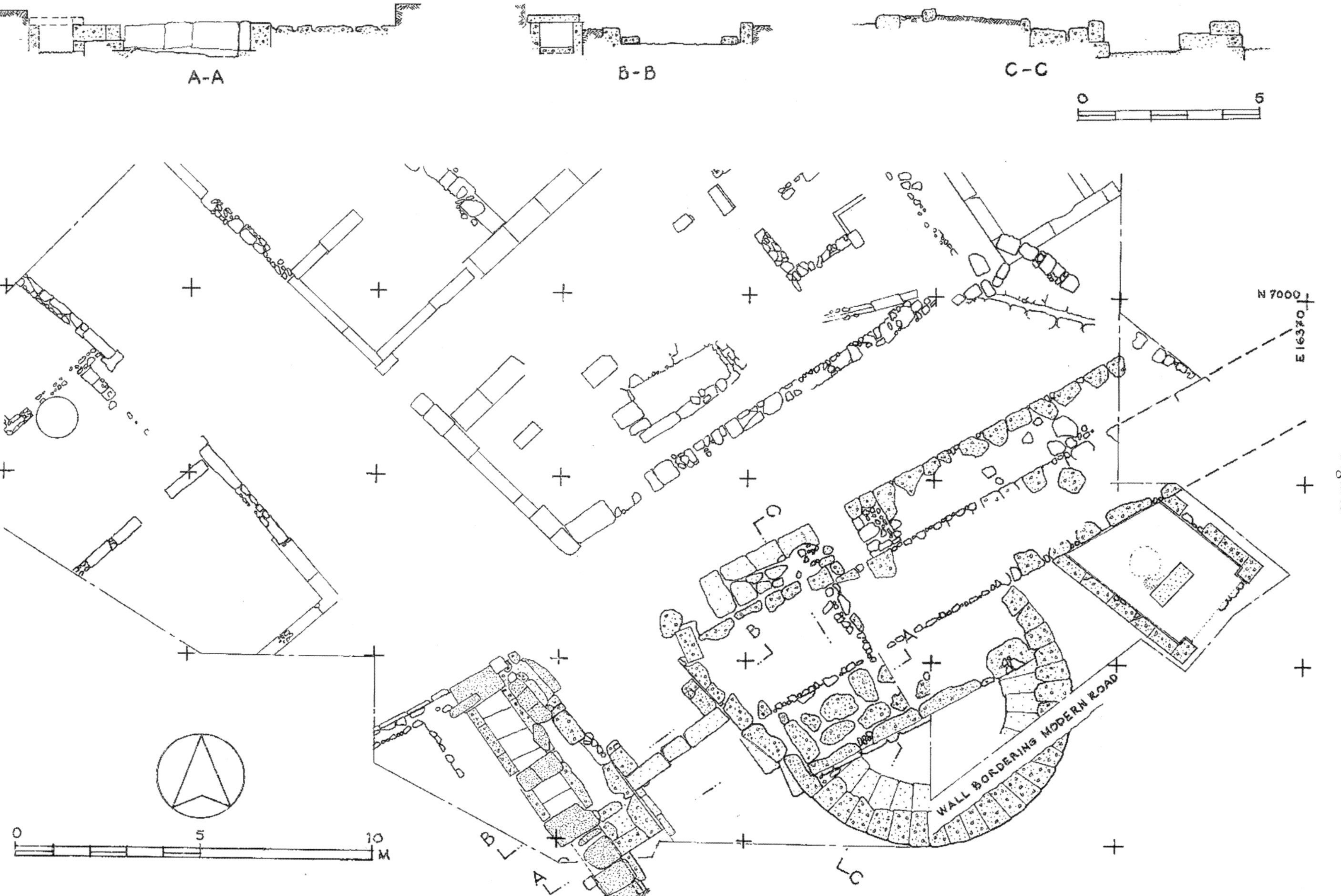

Fig. 25. Southeast Gate area and Tower 9. 1. Sections. 2. Plan

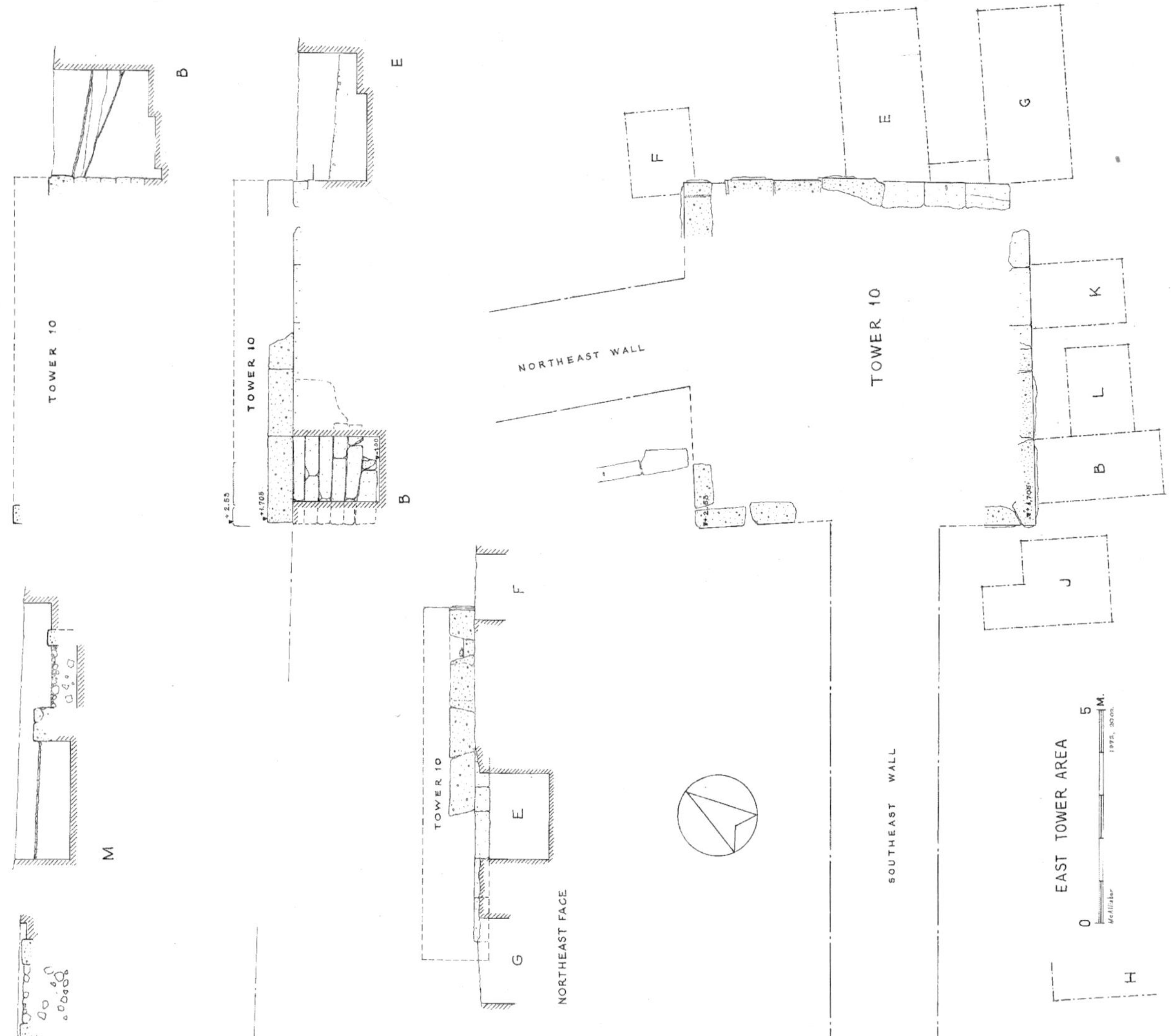

Fig. 26. East Tower area and Tower 10

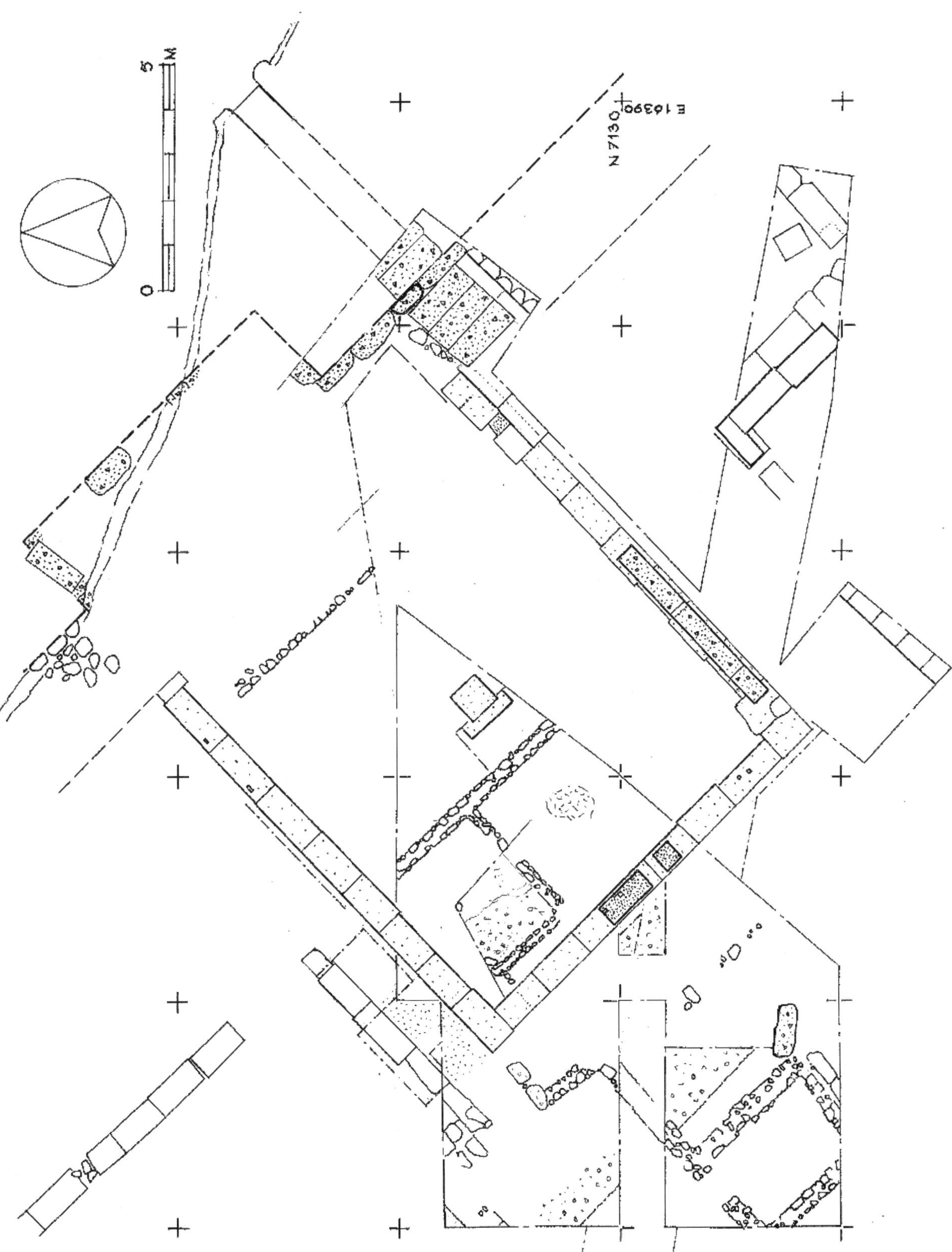

Fig. 27. Northeast Command Post

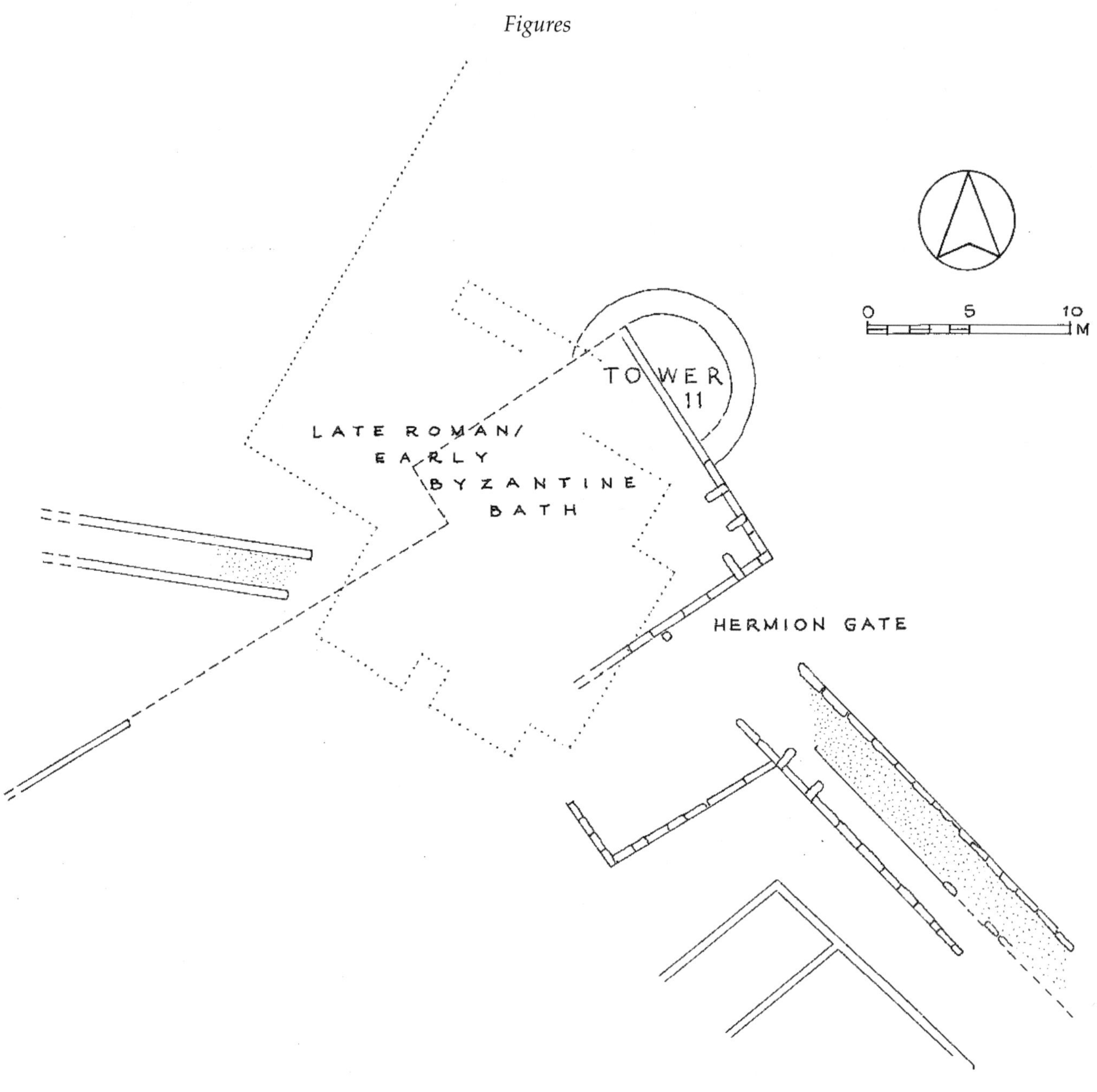

*Fig. 28. Tower **11** and Hermion Gate*

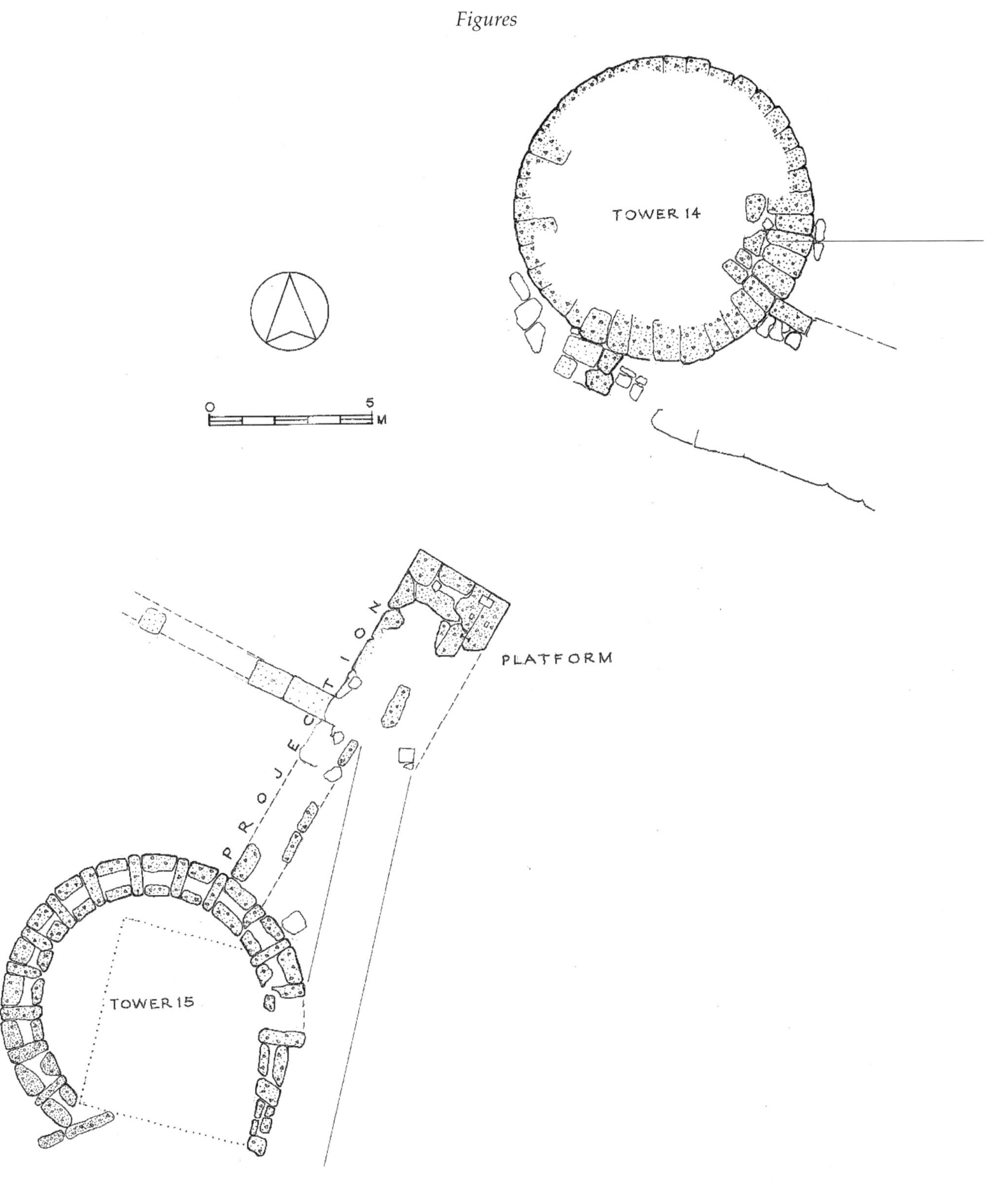

*Fig. 29. Towers **14** and **15** and Harbor Gate*

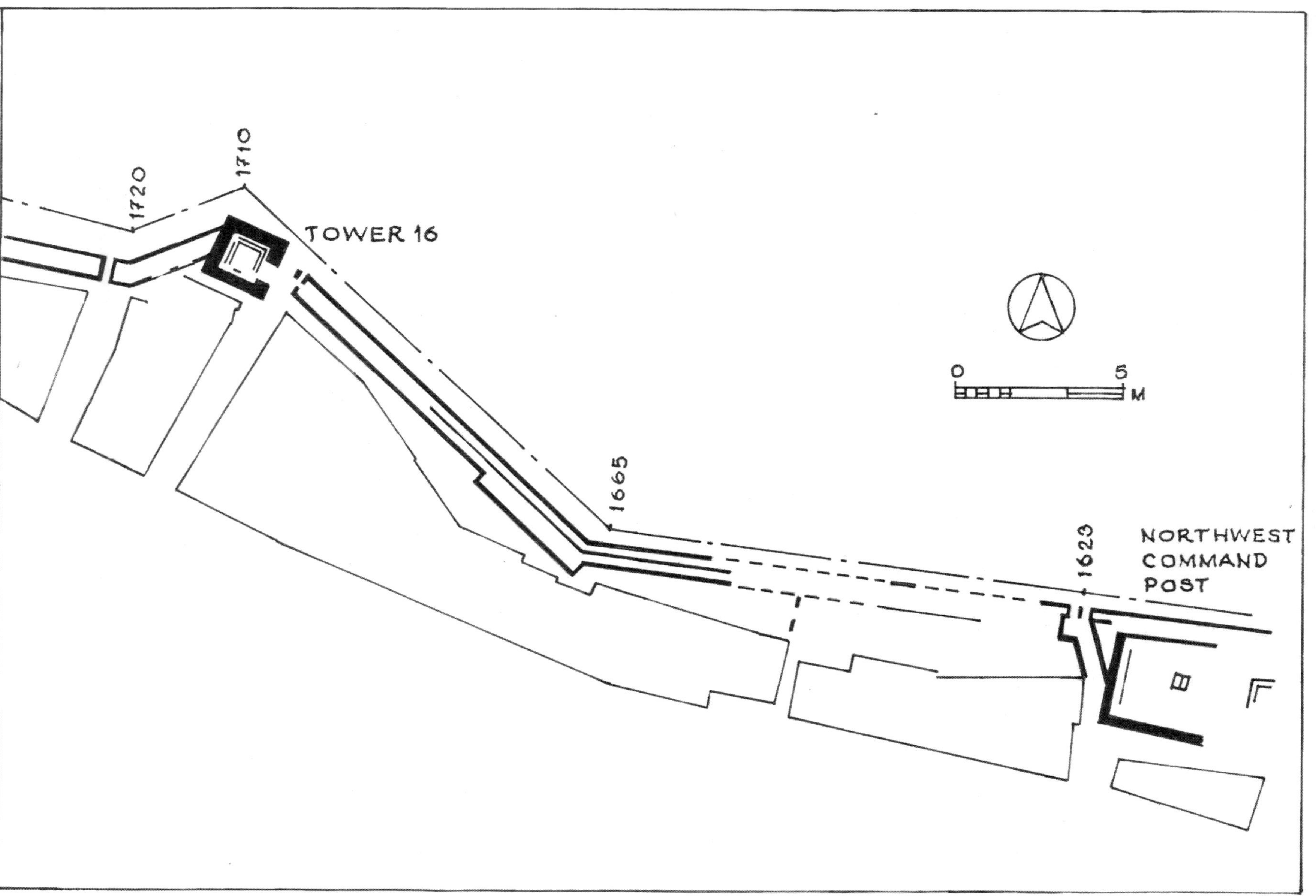

Fig. 30. Northwest Wall: Towers 15, 16, and Northwest Command Post

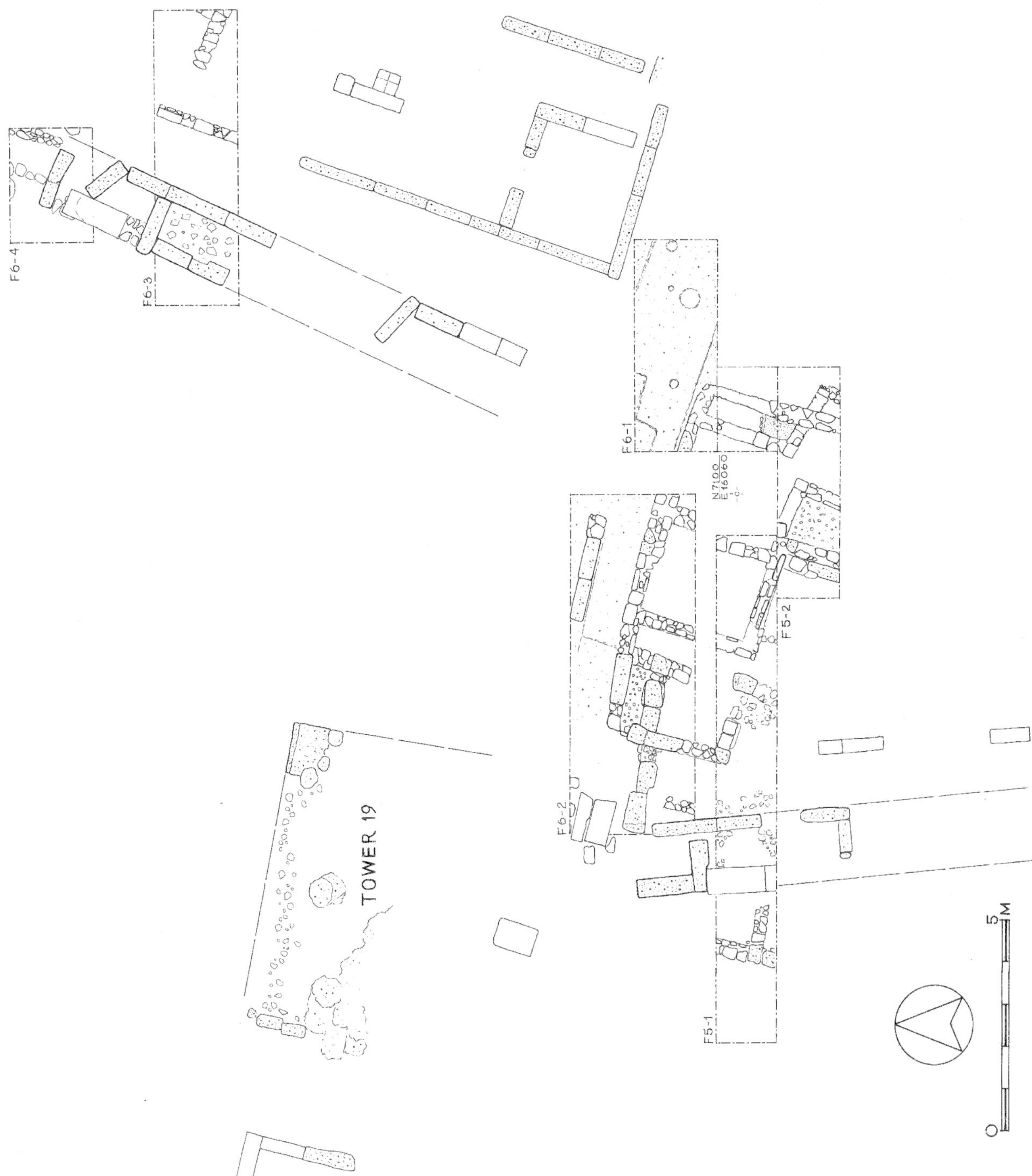

Fig. 31. Middle Wall: Tower 19

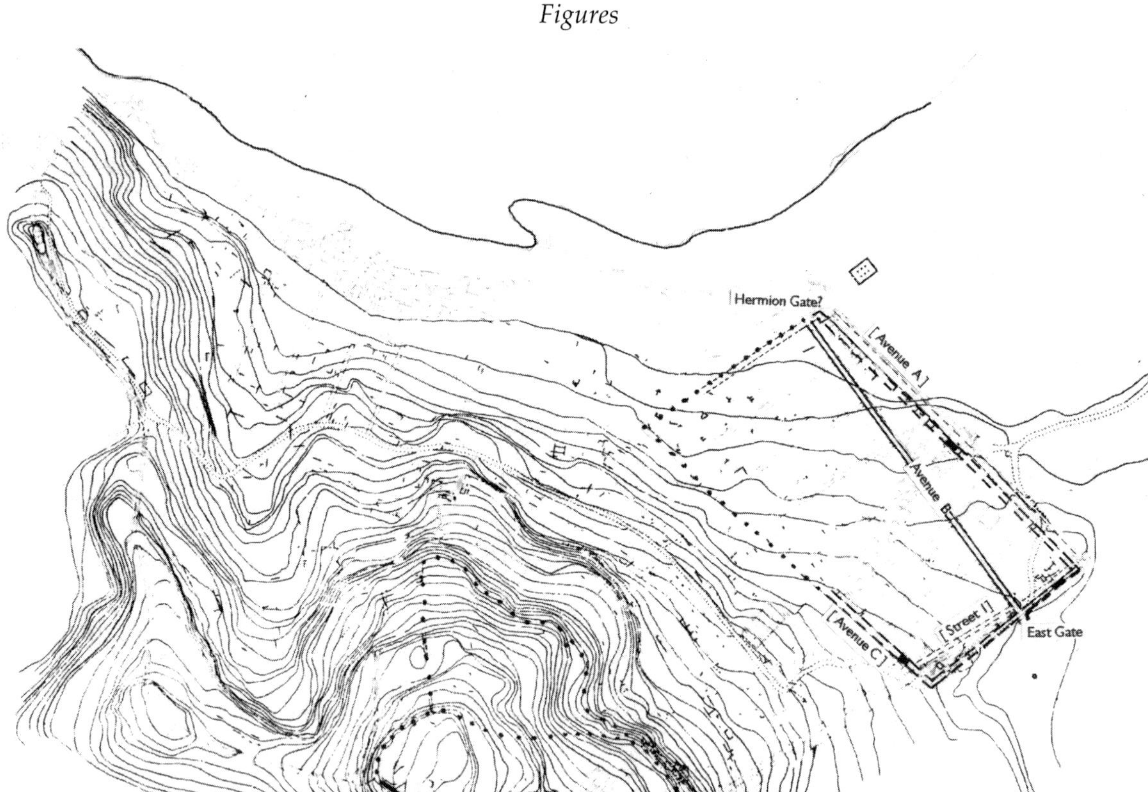

Fig. 32. Development stage 1: Archaic

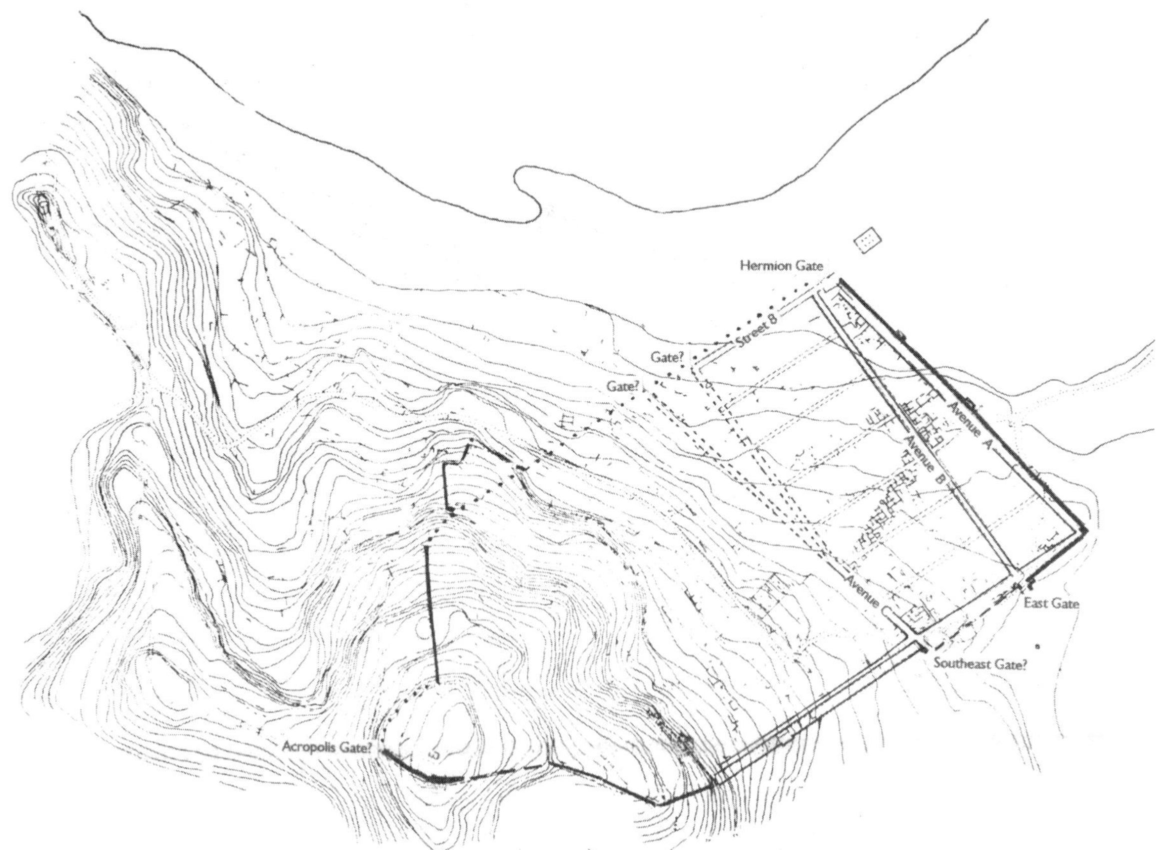

Fig. 33. Development stage 2: Combined circuits

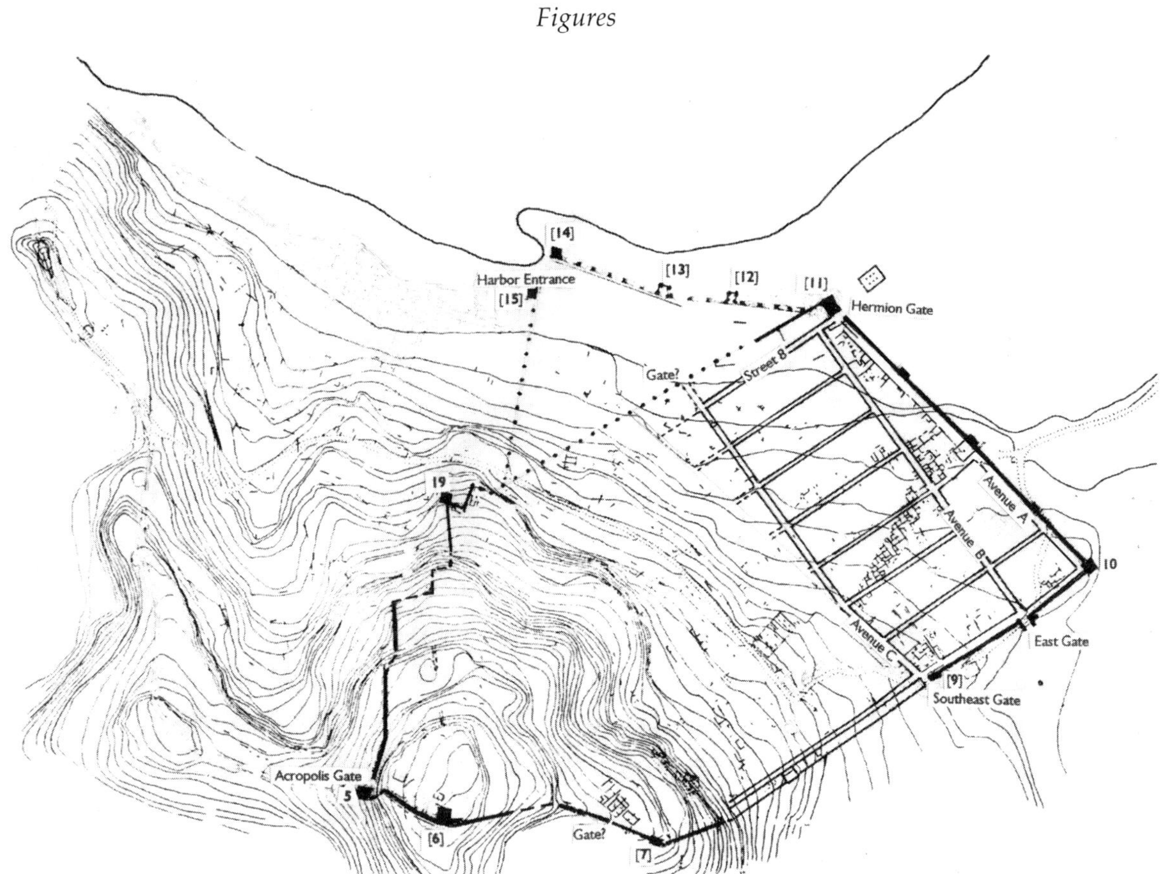

Fig. 34. *Development stage 3: Square-tower program*

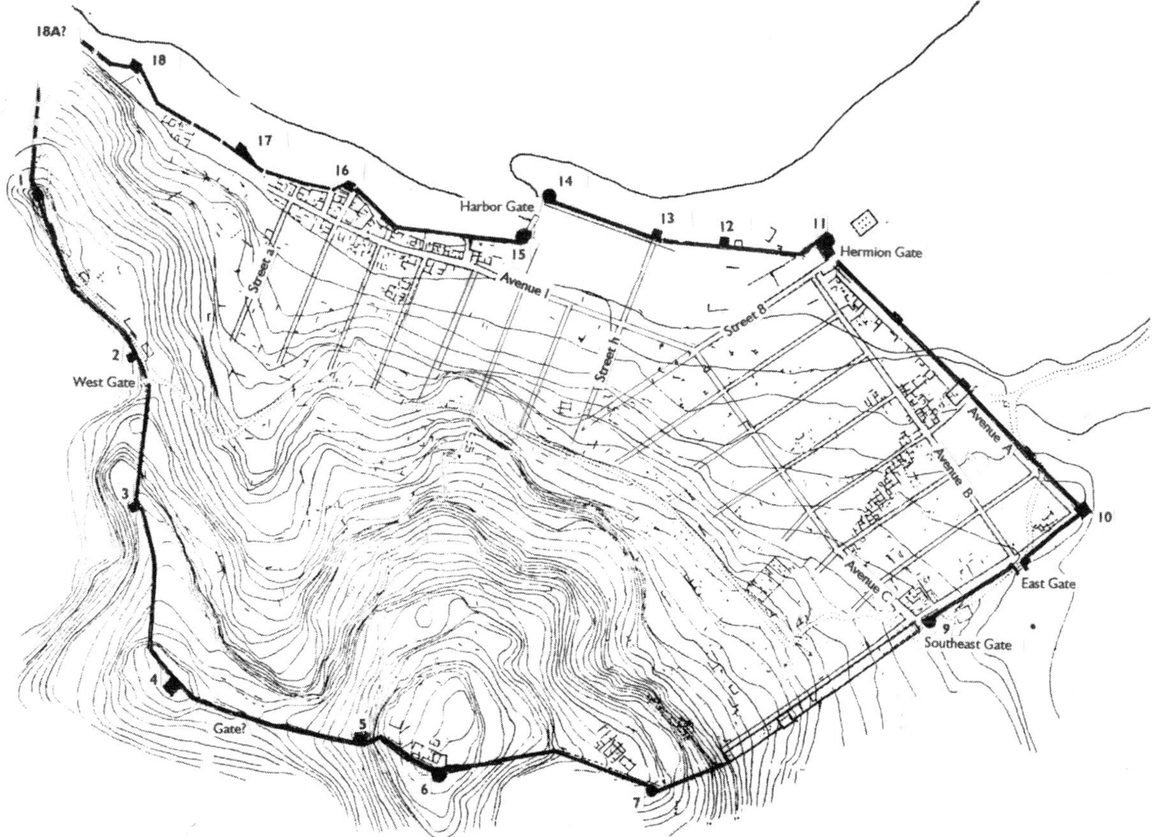

Fig. 35. *Development stage 4: Western defenses*

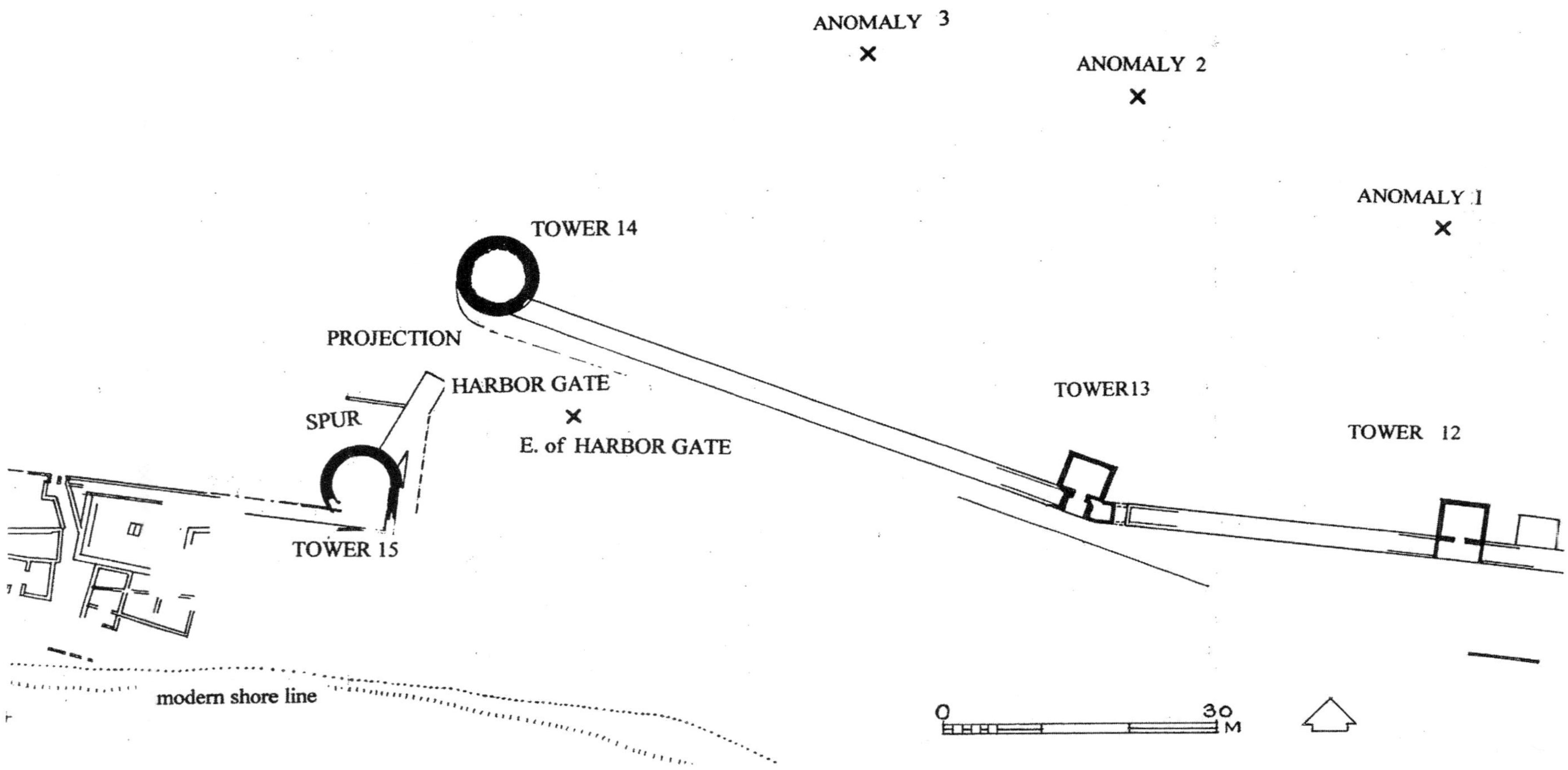

Fig. 36. Anomalies and East of Harbor Gate

Tower **15**	Spur 3 courses	Projection 2 courses	Entrance	White Poros Wall	Tower **14** 3 Courses	E. of Harbor Gate	Anomaly 1	Stadion Supports	N. Starting Line	Temple of Apollo	LR Post
2.50										2.64 C. threshold 2.84 A. column bases	2.80
									3.00		I post 3.20
		3.00		3.15	3.00	3.12 seabed LR		3.46			
	3.25 poros	3.40	3.20 LR pottery		3.20						
	3.60 poros		3.60		3.60	3.82 gravel + BG	(3.60 seabed) sterile gray clay	(3.76)			
	4.00 rubble		4.10 tiles end 4.20 gravel + BG | 4.40 sterile clay			|	|				
						4.72 pebbles white clay	4.75–4.95 rubble organic matter LR pottery				
						|	5.00 BG jug/chytra				
						5.67 I post 6.42	5.30 sterile gray clay to at least 5.75				

Fig. 37. Elevations of the submerged remains in meters below sea level

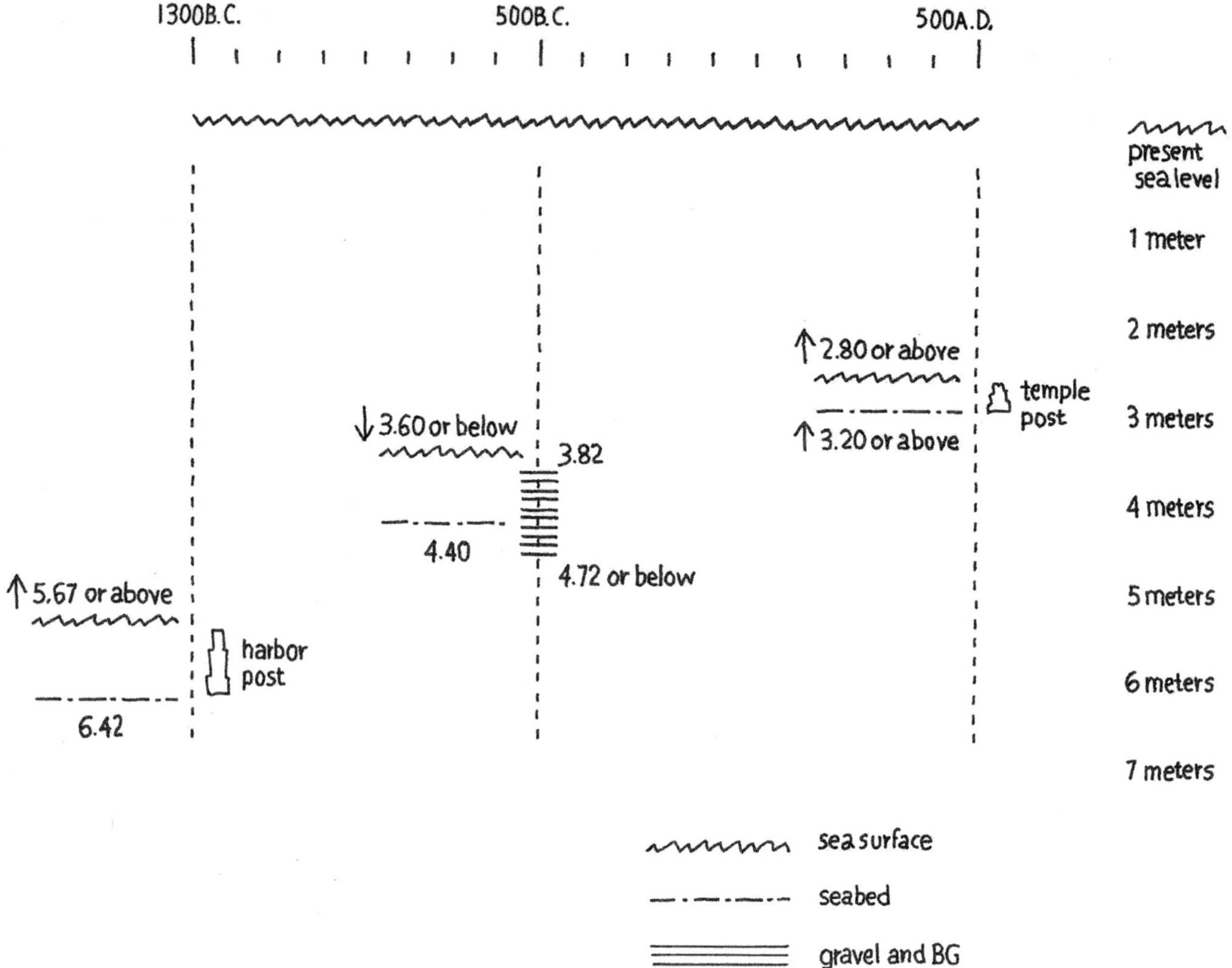

Fig. 38. Evidence for the chronology of sea level and seabed

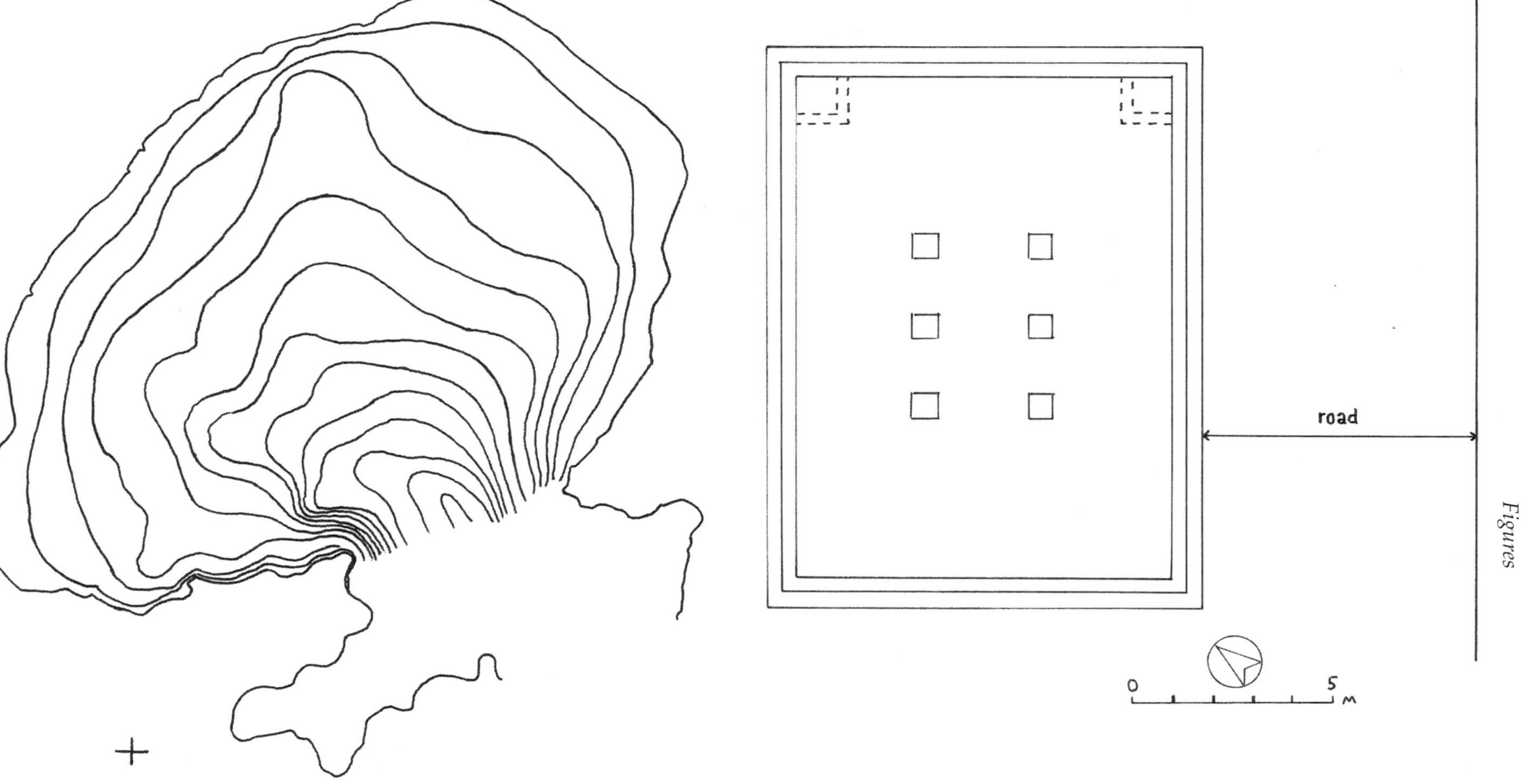

Fig. 39. Fathometer survey, Porto Kheli Harbor, contours at one-meter intervals   *Fig. 40. Hypostyle building*

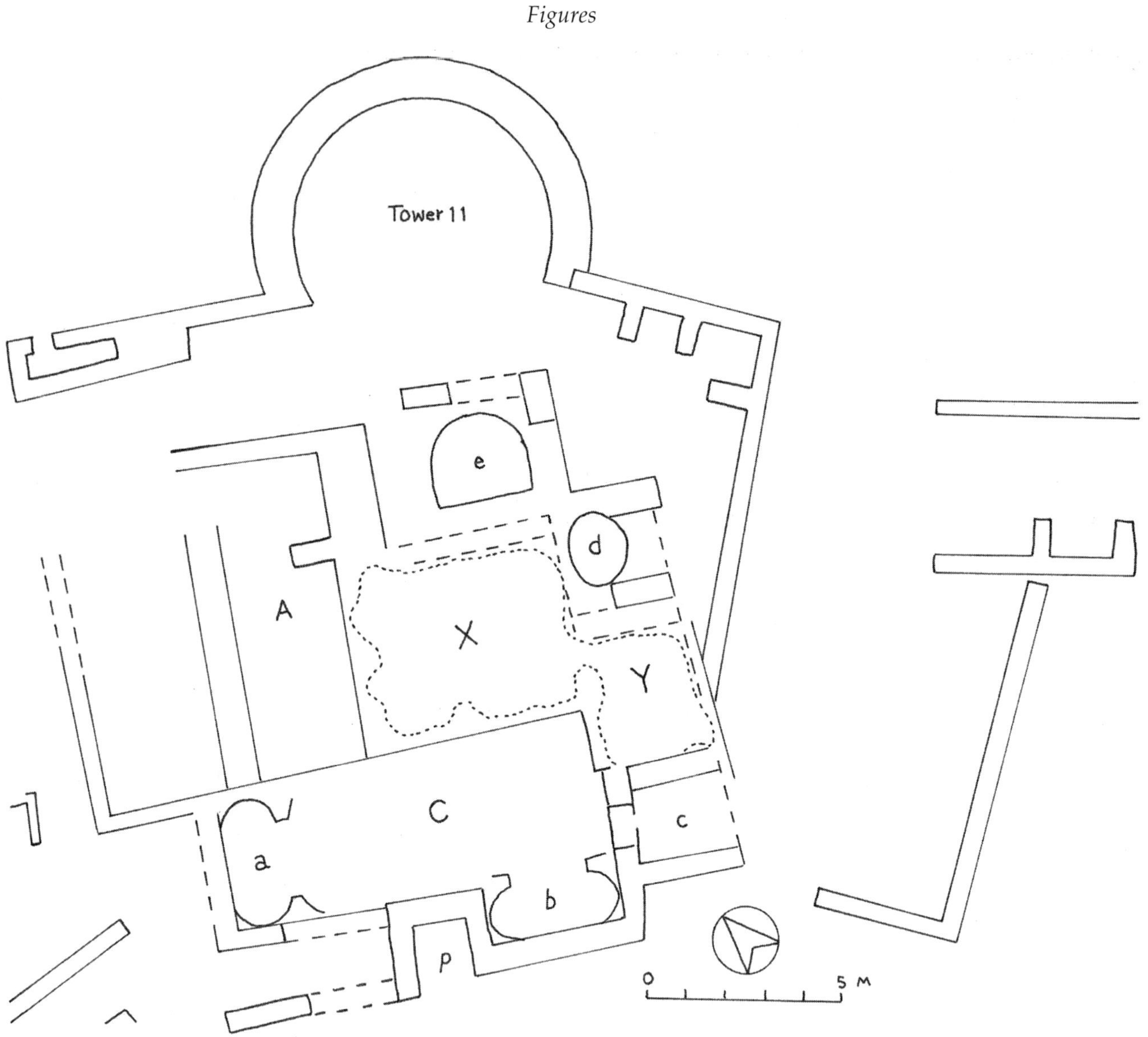

Fig. 41. Bath

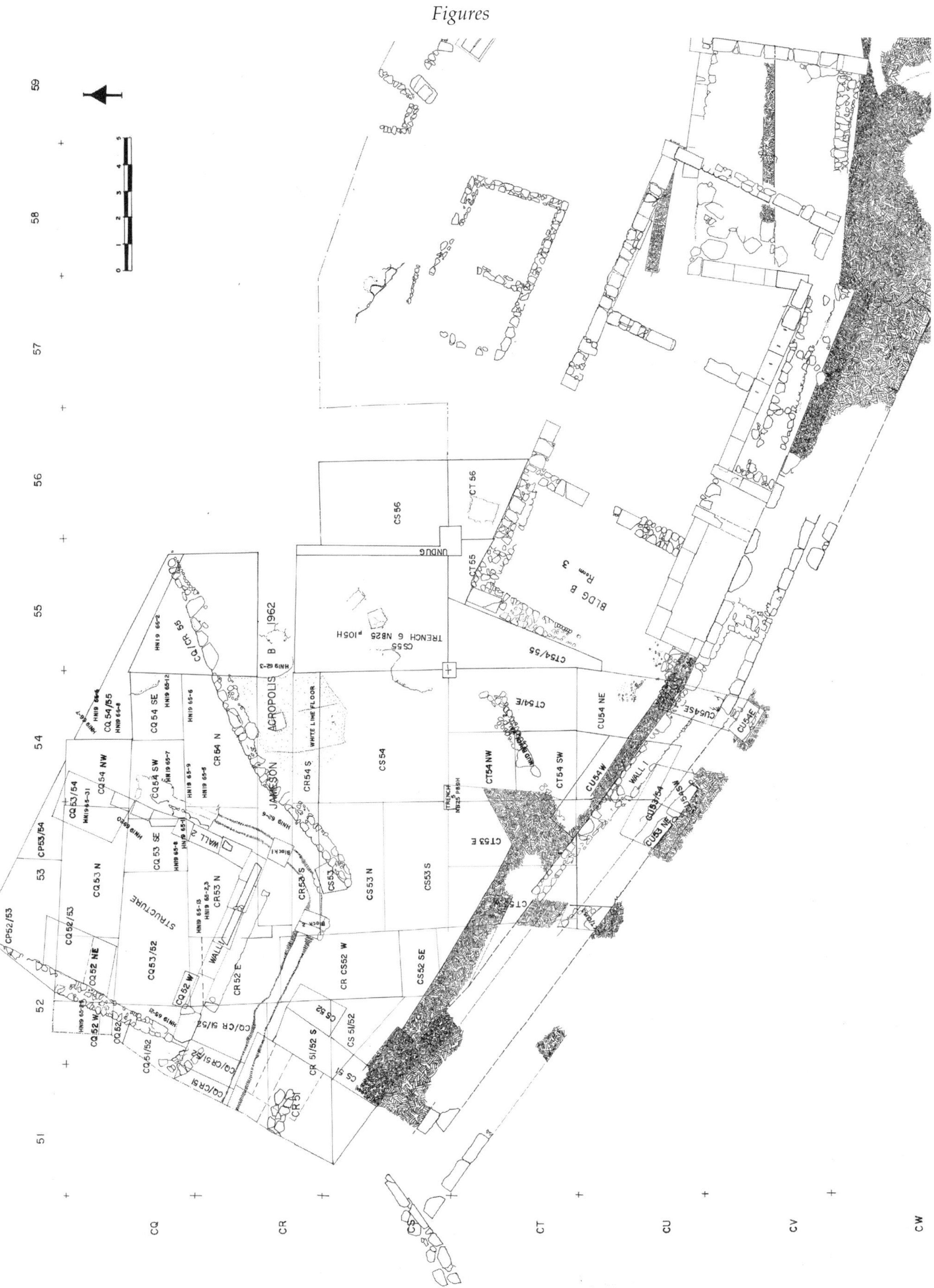

Fig. 42. Acropolis west with trenches and coin locations

Plates

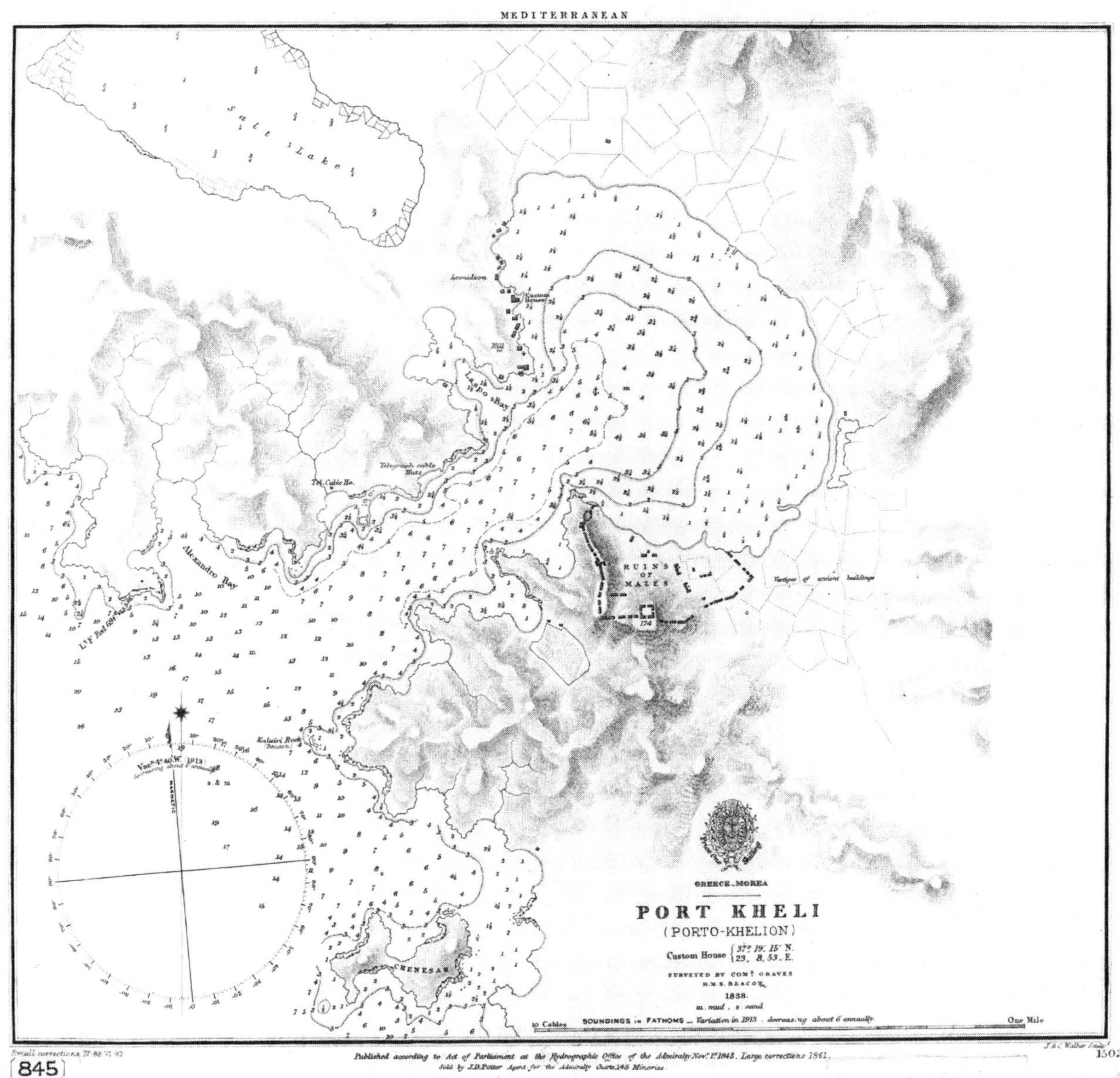

Pl. 1. British Admiralty Chart

*Pl. 2a. West Wall, northernmost stretch near Tower **1** (removed 1971)*

*Pl. 2b. Tower **2**, east side, with offset inner wythe of curtain*

*Pl. 2c. Building opposite Tower **2**, from south*

Pl. 2d. West Wall at Meter 275: conglomerate plinths of inner wythe, from south

Pl. 3a. West Wall at Meter 310: inside face of outer wythe

*Pl. 3b. Tower **3**, north corner, at junction with curtain*

*Pl. 3c. Tower **3**, west corner*

*Pl. 4a. Outer end of harbor entrance channel from Tower **4***

*Pl. 4b. Tower **4**, south corner (curtain at crest of hill to right)*

*Pl. 4c. West Wall between Towers **4** and **5**, outer face*

*Pl. 5a. Acropolis, Phase **5** tower: orthostates and stackwork*

*Pl. 5b. Acropolis, Tower **6**: stepped base and filler blocks*

*Pl. 5c. Acropolis, Tower **6**: courses of mud brick and junction with curtain to east*

Pl. 6a. Industrial Terrace: poros plinths at angle of curtain, conglomerate stretchers to east

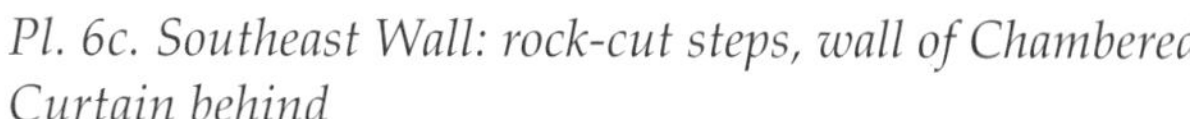

Pl. 6b. Tower 7

Pl. 6c. Southeast Wall: rock-cut steps, wall of Chambered Curtain behind

Pl. 7a. Southeast Gate area from balloon

*Pl. 7b. Tower **9**: poros and conglomerate pie-slice blocks around predecessor*

*Pl. 8a. Southeast Gate: predecessor to Tower **9**, outer face*

Pl. 8b. Southeast Gate: junction with curtain to northeast, blocks of predecessor below

*Pl. 8c. Tower **9**, detail of southwest side*

Pl. 9b. Southeast Gate: northeast pivot block

Pl. 9d. Curved orthostate near Meter 955

Pl. 9a. Southeast Gate: barrier and southwest pivot block

Pl. 9c. Steps at corner of Southeast Gate roadway and Street 1

Pl. 10a. Drain at Southeast Gate, looking outward

Pl. 10b. Drain at Southeast Gate, looking inward: Avenue C between houses in background

Pl. 10c. Drain at Southeast Gate: cuttings in floor for bars at inner end

*Pl. 11a. Shrine, Tower **9** at upper left*

Pl. 11b. Southeast Building: boss on east corner block

Pl. 11c. East Gate from south

Pl. 12a. East Tower Area: foundation for curtain

*Pl. 12b. Tower **10**, from east*

*Pl. 12c. Tower **10**, southeast side: south corner in foreground, poros plinths at top*

*Pl. 13b. Tower **10**, Trench B: deep foundation at south corner*

*Pl. 13d. Tower **10**, drafted north corner from above*

*Pl. 13a. Tower **10**, northeast side: drafted margins, stackwork at right*

*Pl. 13c. Tower **10**, drill marks on inside of west corner block*

Pl. 14b. Northeast Command Post: east corner and drain cover slabs

Pl. 14a. Northeast Command Post: south corner and entrance

Pl. 15a. Ionic capital HS 6 of shelly limestone

Pl. 15b. Northeast Wall, center bastion: late repair

Pl. 15c. Northeast Wall, northwest of center bastion: late repair

Pl. 16a. Middle Wall: western trace, northwest of acropolis

Pl. 16b. Middle Wall: upper end of middle terrace, from east

Pl. 16c. Middle Wall: south end of middle terrace, from north

Pl. 17b. Tower tile

Pl. 17a. Middle Wall: north end of middle terrace, from north

Pl. 17c. Middle Wall: lower terrace, from southeast

Pl. 18a. Main scarp from north

Pl. 18b. Main scarp from northeast

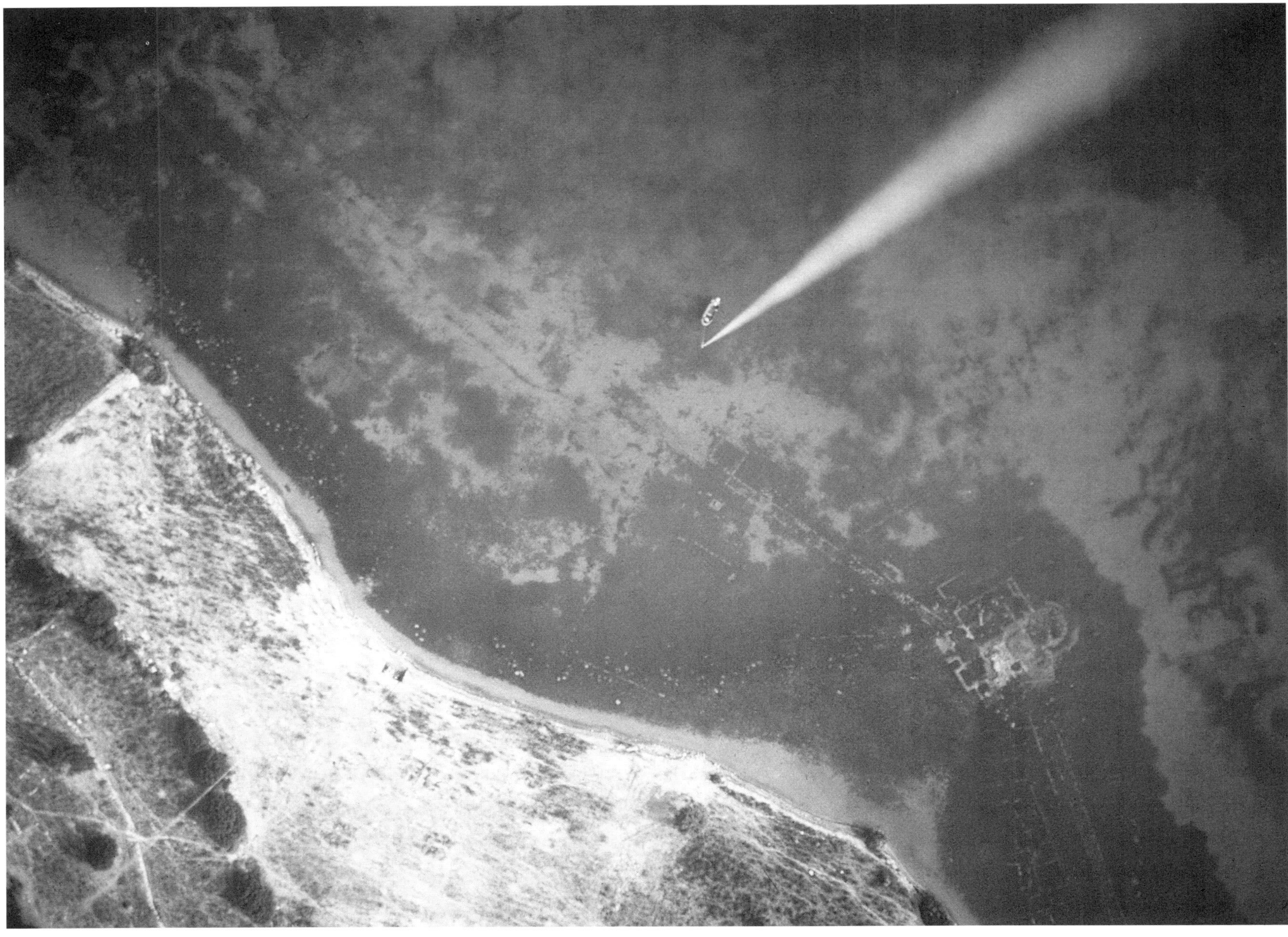

Pl. 19. Submerged remains of fortifications, Hermion Gate, bath, hypostyle building, and Towers **12–15**

a. fire pit, opposite threshold block

b. fire pit, mud brick in situ

c. fire pit, mud brick removed

Pl. 20. Northeast Command Post, 1975 TR 135/375

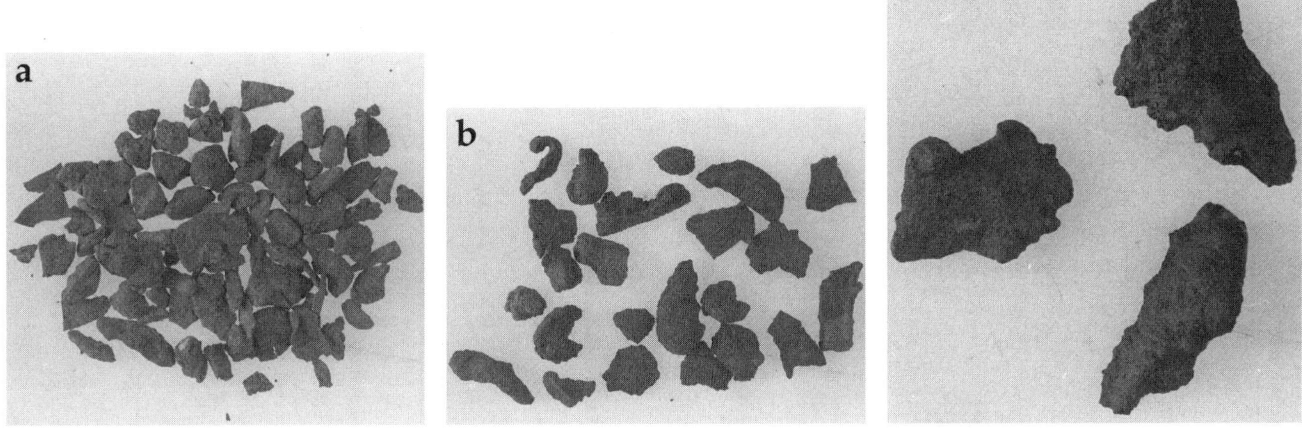

Pl. 21 a–c. HM 666, bronze scraps, small to large

Pl. 21. d, e. HM 837, bronze scraps, small and large; f. TR 135/375, unit 4, HM 818, rooster

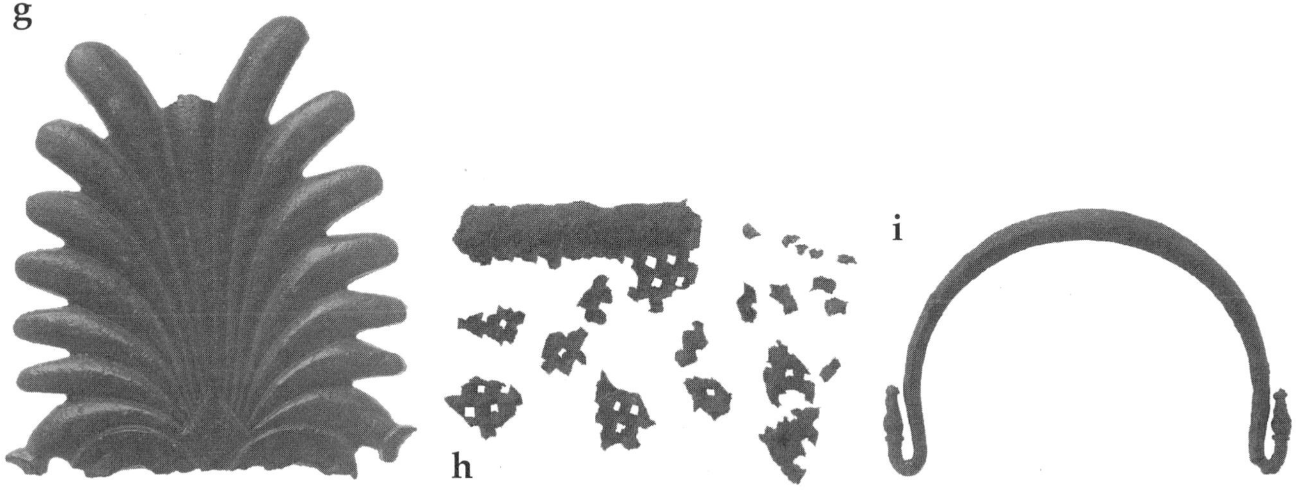

Pl. 21. TR 135/375, unit 12: g. HM 813, bronze palmette; h. HM 826, bronze strainer; i. HM 816, bronze handle

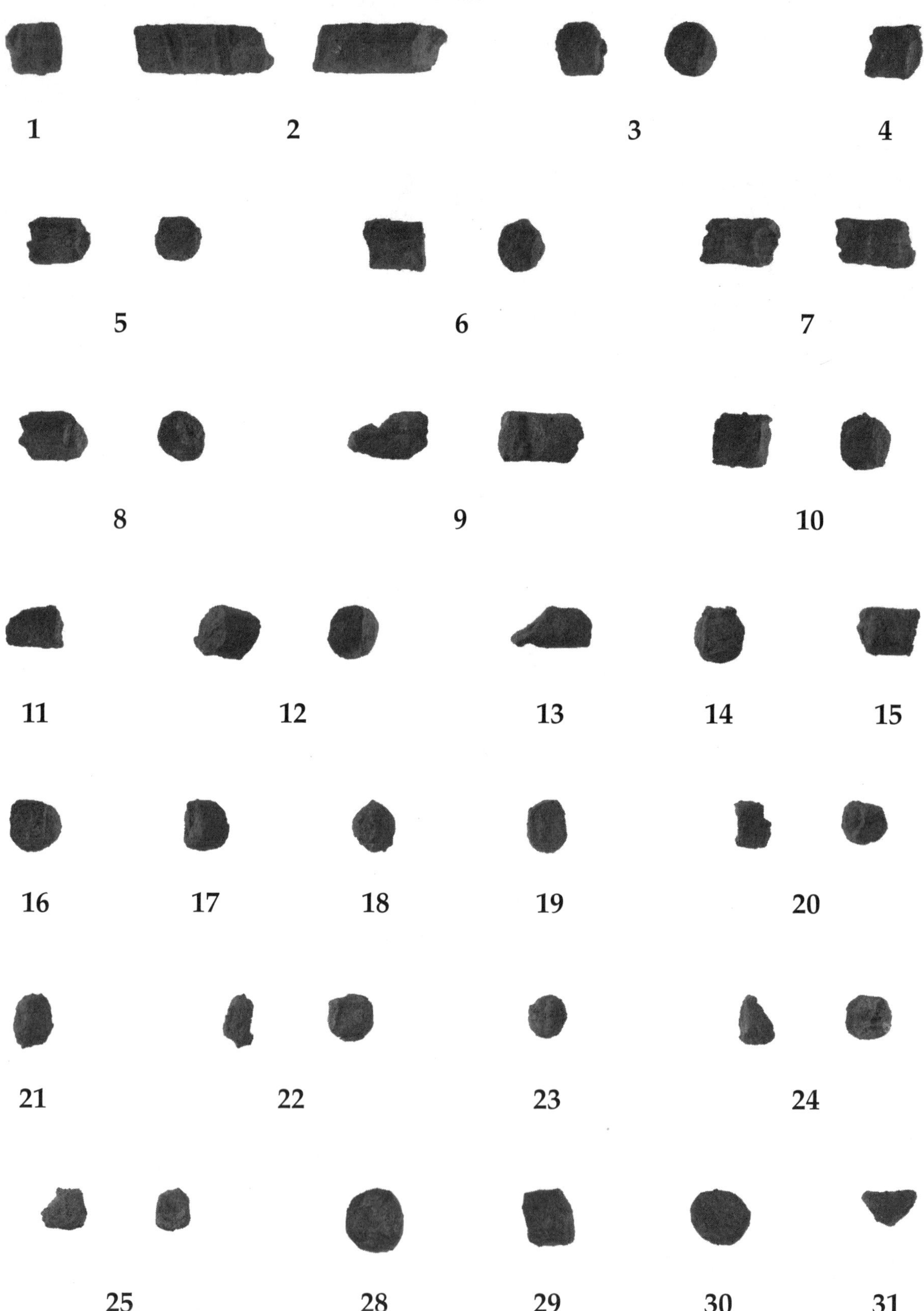

1 2 3 4

5 6 7

8 9 10

11 12 13 14 15

16 17 18 19 20

21 22 23 24

25 28 29 30 31

Pl. 22. Coin blanks. Scale 1:1

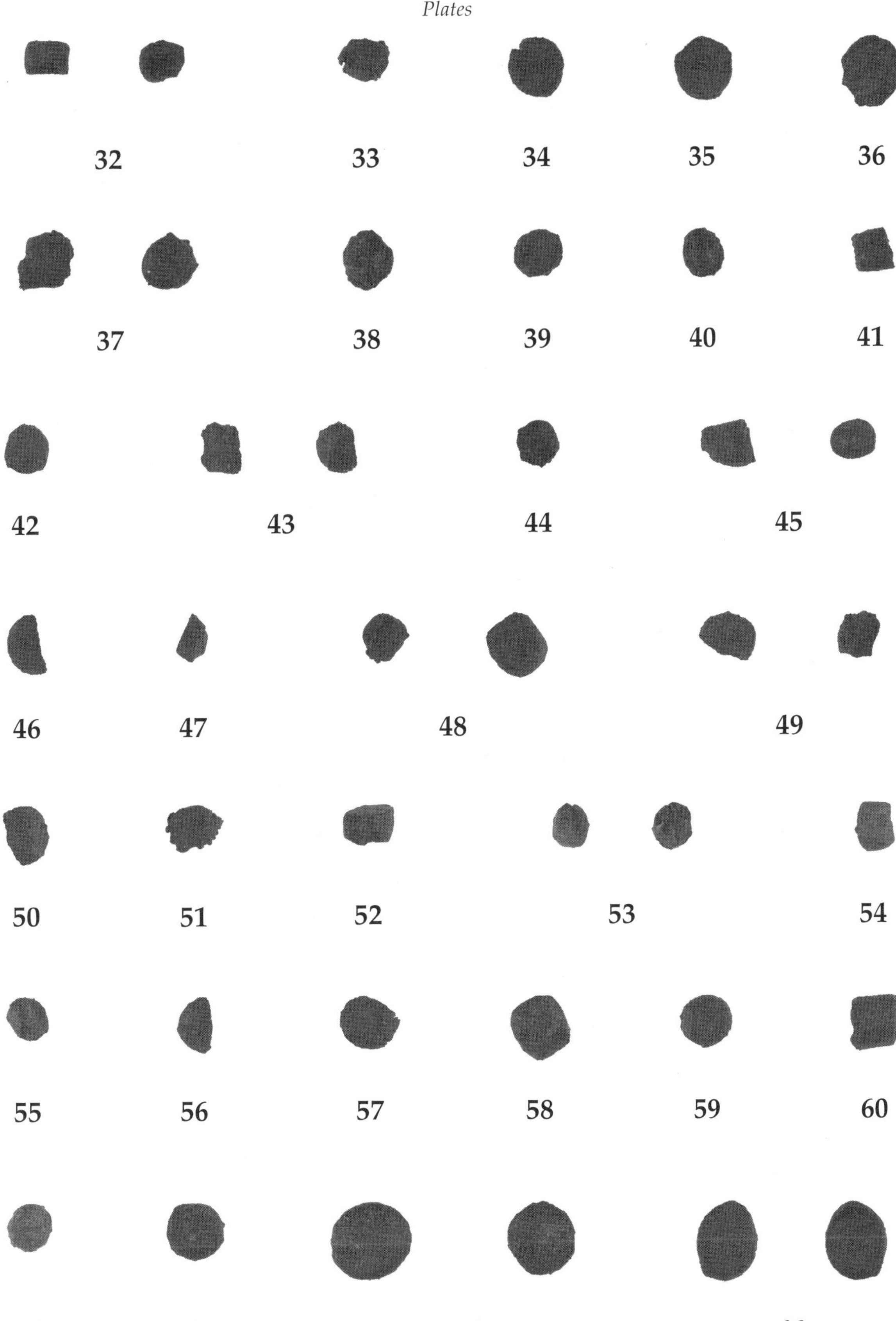

Pl. 23. Coin blanks and unstruck flans. Scale 1:1

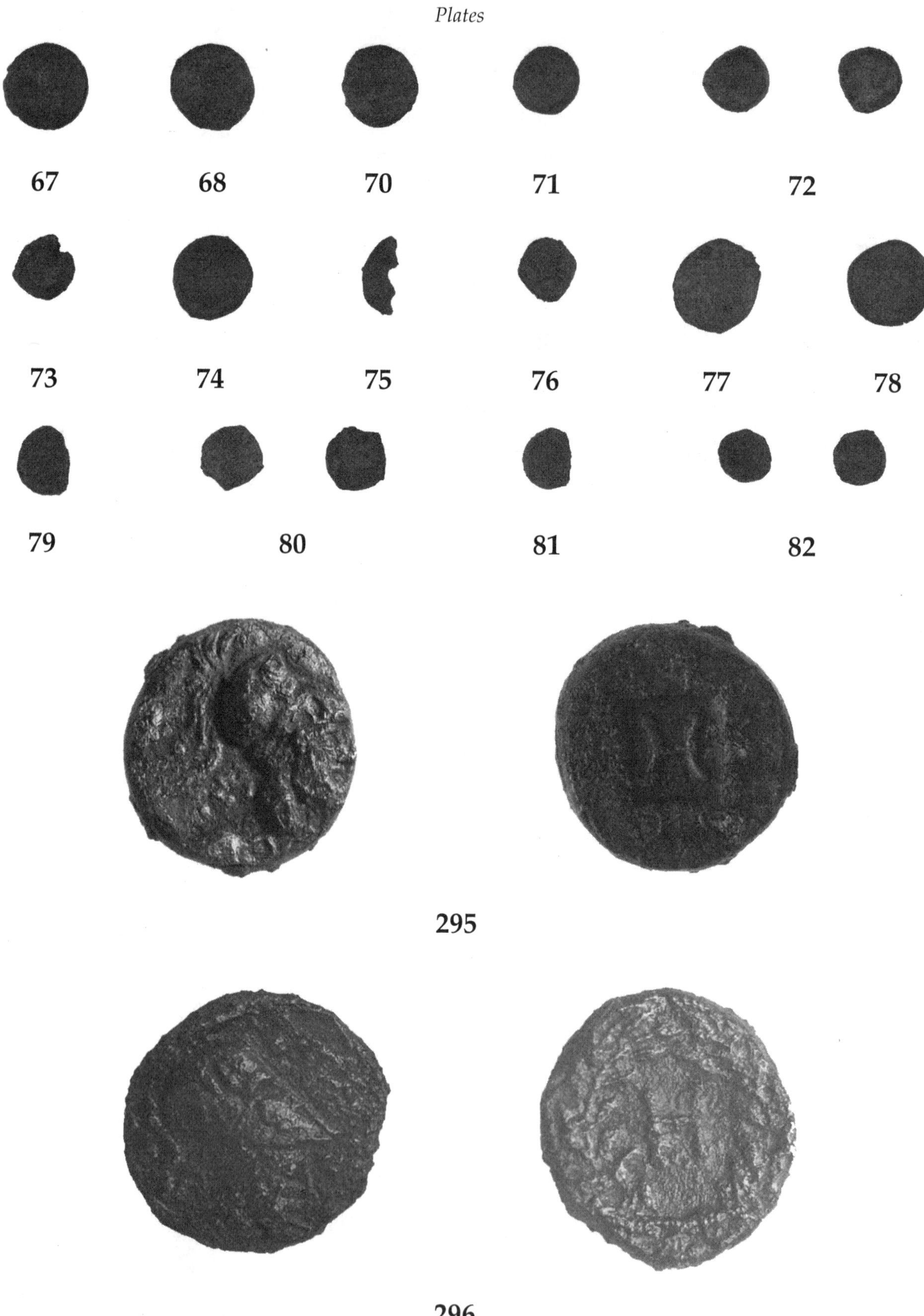

*Pl. 24. Unstruck flans (scale 1:1) and **295**, **296** (scale 1:4)*